Intergenerational Trauma in Refugee Communities

This volume explores intergenerational trauma among refugee communities displaced throughout the world.

Considering patterns and findings across disciplines, cultural contexts, and methodologies, the volume addresses the way trauma is passed on generationally among populations characterized by a large exodus from various regions, and communities in which intergenerational trauma can be observed among second-generation youth. Drawing on studies of displaced communities worldwide, this comprehensive and interdisciplinary analysis examines the effects of transgenerational trauma. It explores definitions and concepts of intergenerational trauma, comparing and contrasting perspectives across generations, and the mechanisms at work in its transmission.

The volume is well suited for scholars across social sciences with interests in memory studies, political violence, and refugee and diaspora studies.

Laura Kromják is Assistant Professor in the Department of Global and Development Studies, Institute of Political and International Studies, ELTE Faculty of Social Sciences in Budapest, Hungary. She teaches migration, international development and European Union related subjects, and her regional focus is the Western Balkans. Her interests include trauma research, memory politics and reconciliation in post-conflict societies. Her work also focuses on post-war family dynamics, especially the challenges facing elderly population both in Bosnia and Herzegovina and its diaspora.

Ajlina Karamehić-Muratović is Associate Professor in the Department of Sociology and Anthropology at St. Louis University in St. Louis, Missouri, USA, where she teaches health-related and research methodology courses. Her interdisciplinary research is health- and community-focused, with an emphasis on issues facing refugees and immigrants. Her research interests also include mental health beliefs and stigma among Arab youth in the Middle East.

Memory Studies: Global Constellations
www.routledge.com/sociology/series/ASHSER1411
Series editor: Henri Lustiger-Thaler
Ramapo College of New Jersey, USA and Ecole des Hautes Etudes en Sciences Sociales, France

The 'past in the present' has returned in the early twenty-first century with a vengeance, and with it the expansion of categories of experience. These experiences have largely been lost in the advance of rationalist and constructivist understandings of subjectivity and their collective representations. The cultural stakes around forgetting, 'useful forgetting' and remembering, locally, regionally, nationally and globally have risen exponentially. It is therefore not unusual that 'migrant memories'; micro-histories; personal and individual memories in their interwoven relation to cultural, political and social narratives; the mnemonic past and present of emotions, embodiment and ritual; and finally, the mnemonic spatiality of geography and territories are receiving more pronounced hearings.

This transpires as the social sciences themselves are consciously globalizing their knowledge bases. In addition to the above, the reconstructive logic of memory in the juggernaut of galloping informationalization is rendering it more and more publicly accessible, and therefore part of a new global public constellation around the coding of meaning and experience. Memory studies as an academic field of social and cultural inquiry emerges at a time when global public debate – buttressed by the fragmentation of national narratives – has accelerated. Societies today, in late globalized conditions, are pregnant with newly unmediated and unfrozen memories once sequestered in wide collective representations. We welcome manuscripts that examine and analyze these profound cultural traces.

Titles in this series

28. Intergenerational Trauma in Refugee Communities
Edited by Laura Kromják and Ajlina Karamehić-Muratović

29. Forgetting Polish Violence Against the Jews
The Great Whitewash
Tomasz Żukowski

30. Memory Institutions and Sámi Heritage
Decolonisation, Restitution, and Repatriation in Sápmi
Edited by Trude Fonneland and Rossella Ragazzi

Intergenerational Trauma in Refugee Communities

Edited by Laura Kromják
and Ajlina Karamehić-Muratović

LONDON AND NEW YORK

First published 2025
by Routledge
4 Park Square, Milton Park, Abingdon, Oxon OX14 4RN

and by Routledge
605 Third Avenue, New York, NY 10158

Routledge is an imprint of the Taylor & Francis Group, an informa business

© 2025 selection and editorial matter, Laura Kromják and Ajlina Karamehić-Muratović; individual chapters, the contributors

The right of Laura Kromják and Ajlina Karamehić-Muratović to be identified as the authors of the editorial material, and of the authors for their individual chapters, has been asserted in accordance with sections 77 and 78 of the Copyright, Designs and Patents Act 1988.

All rights reserved. No part of this book may be reprinted or reproduced or utilised in any form or by any electronic, mechanical, or other means, now known or hereafter invented, including photocopying and recording, or in any information storage or retrieval system, without permission in writing from the publishers.

Trademark notice: Product or corporate names may be trademarks or registered trademarks, and are used only for identification and explanation without intent to infringe.

British Library Cataloguing-in-Publication Data
A catalogue record for this book is available from the British Library

ISBN: 978-1-032-47378-9 (hbk)
ISBN: 978-1-032-47377-2 (pbk)
ISBN: 978-1-003-38582-0 (ebk)

DOI: 10.4324/9781003385820

Typeset in Times New Roman
by Apex CoVantage, LLC

Contents

List of Tables	viii
List of Figures	ix
List of Contributors	x
Acknowledgments	xv

Introduction   1
LAURA KROMJÁK AND AJLINA KARAMEHIĆ-MURATOVIĆ

1 **Returning to the Roots: Transgenerational Trauma, Diaspora Community, and the Armenian Pilgrimage to the Lost Homeland**   11
KONRAD SIEKIERSKI

2 **Refugee Literary Space: Silences, Intergenerational Trauma, and Resilience**   24
SHAHAB NADIMI

3 **Intergenerational Transmission of Traumatic Experiences among Palestinian Refugees**   40
FAYEZ MAHAMID AND DANA BDIER

4 **Holocaust Survivors, Siberians, Refugees, Veterans – Memory and Choice of Jewish Returnees from the USSR to Poland (1945–2024)**   53
LIDIA ZESSIN-JUREK

5 **In the Aftermath of Silence: An Intergenerational Burden of Recognition in Postgeneration Holodomor Survivor Literature**   71
ELISE WESTIN

6 "La Sobrevivencia y La Resistencia" (Survival and
   Resilience): The Experience of Intergenerational Trauma
   Transmission in Nicaraguan American Families   84
   RICARDO PHIPPS AND JANETHE PEÑA

7 Intergenerational Trauma among Refugees in Africa and the
   African Diaspora   98
   MARIO J. AZEVEDO AND TIFFANY D. CAESAR

8 Marginalization as Traumatization: Developmentally Based
   Trauma Framework for Intergenerational Transmission of
   Trauma in Somali Refugees   124
   MUNA SALEH AND HYOJIN IM

9 The Long Shadow of the Eritrean Independence Struggle:
   Transgenerational Transmission of Trauma across Diaspora
   Generations   146
   NICOLE HIRT

10 The Elephant in the Room: Experiences of Intergenerational
   Trauma in Second-Generation Bosnian Americans   160
   AJLINA KARAMEHIĆ-MURATOVIĆ AND LAURA KROMJÁK

11 German Perversions of Mental Health Care: Male Afghan
   Refugees, Deportation, and Carceral Systems during NATO's
   War in Afghanistan   184
   PANIZ MUSAWI NATANZI

12 History, Trauma, and Identity: The Legacy of the Korean
   War for Korean Americans   199
   RAMSAY LIEM

13 The Psychological Well-Being of Children in North Korean
   Defector Families: The Impact of Intergenerational Trauma   215
   SANG HUI CHU

14 Learning Refugee Trauma and Politics through Community
   Arts Organizing   233
   PHI HONG SU

15 **The Unheard and Unseen Perspectives on Intergenerational Trauma**   246
NORA PARR, WENDY SIMS-SCHOUTEN, JENNY PHILLIMORE,
HEATHER FLOWE, SARAH ROCKOWITZ, LAURA STEVENS,
TAMIRACE FAKHOURY, AND RANA DAJANI

Index   *266*

Tables

8.1	Taxonomy of Severe Stressors	131
13.1	The Number of North Korean Defectors Entering South Korea Annually	216
13.2	Current Statistics on North Korean Defector Students by School Type	222

Figures

3.1 First generation of Palestinian refugees during Nakba 41
3.2 Early refugee camp in the mid-1950s 42
3.3 Hope for the future in a drawing of a child from Jabalina refugee camp in Gaza Strip 45

Contributors

Mario J. Azevedo is a Mozambican epidemiologist, historian, professor, and novelist. He is currently the chair of the History Department at Jackson State University, Mississippi, USA. His research interests include tropical diseases, infectious diseases in the developing world, history of Africa, American history, African American history, colonialism and the spread of diseases in Africa, francophone equatorial Africa, southern Africa, human security in Sub-Saharan Africa, diabetes and obesity in Mississippi, malaria and HIV in Africa, and trypanosomiasis.

Dana Bdier is Assistant Professor of clinical psychology in the Department of Psychology and Counseling at An-Najah National University, Nablus, Palestine. Her research focuses on mental health, political trauma, and gender-based violence, particularly within the Palestinian context. Dr. Bdier has led several studies investigating the mental health status of various Palestinian populations, including children, adolescents, women, and health care providers.

Tiffany D. Caesar is an Africana Studies scholar, public historian, and healer. She is Assistant Professor of Africana Studies at San Francisco State University, California, USA. Her research includes healing modalities in Africa and the African Diaspora, in addition to the preservation of Black women's histories. She calls herself a "Black Woman's Archivist" due to her ongoing research on the preservation of transnational Black women. Dr. Caesar is a cultural heritage ambassador for the Nelson Mandela Museum in Mthatha, South Africa.

Rana Dajani is a Richard Von Weizsacker fellow at the Robert Bosch Academy, Germany, and a professor of molecular biology at the Hashemite University in Jordan. Her area of expertise is epigenetics and biomarkers of trauma among refugees. Through her leadership, she has introduced national and regional stem cell laws and presided over numerous scientific boards and United Nations councils, most recently as the President of the Society for the Advancement of Science and Technology in the Arab World. She is the founder of *We Love Reading*, a grassroots initiative to create changemakers in underserved communities by fostering a lifelong love of reading.

Tamirace Fakhoury is an incoming faculty at the Fletcher School of Law and Diplomacy at Tufts University, Massachusetts, USA, and a visiting professor at Sciences Po, Paris. Her research areas include power-sharing and ethno-sectarian conflicts, migration and refugee governance, and the European Union's conflict resolution and migration policy in the Mediterranean. She is a co-investigator on the Rights for Time Research Network where she leads the research stream on policy and time in Lebanon.

Heather Flowe is Professor of Psychology at the University of Birmingham, UK. She studies memory within legal contexts. Her research spans topics such as trauma, eyewitness identification, and witness testimony in sexual assault and other atrocities.

Nicole Hirt is a political scientist associated with the GIGA German Institute for Global and Area Studies, Institute for African Affairs in Hamburg, Germany. Her regional focus is the Horn of Africa, specifically Eritrea and its diaspora. Her current research interests include transnational diaspora policies, the persistence of authoritarian rule, transgenerational transmission of trauma, and memory studies.

Phi Hong Su is Assistant Professor of Sociology at Williams College, Massachusetts, USA. She is interested in people on the move and the attitudes and convictions they carry with them across borders. Her first book, *The Border Within: Vietnamese Migrants Transforming Ethnic Nationalism in Berlin* (Stanford University Press, 2022), offers the clearest expression of this interest.

Sang Hui Chu is Professor in the Department of Nursing, Mo-Im Kim Nursing Research Institute at the Yonsei University College of Nursing, Seoul, South Korea. She has been actively researching the mental health of North Korean defectors and is author of *Current State and Future Challenges of Nursing in North Korea* (Ajou Institute of Korean Unification and Health Care, 2019), and contributor to *Preparing a Health Community on the Korean Peninsula* (Seoul: ParkYeongsa, 2018/2021) and *The Future of Unified Health Care* (Seoul: ParkYeongsa, 2023).

Hyojin Im is Associate Professor at the Virginia Commonwealth University School of Social Work, Virginia, USA. Dr. Im's research focuses on exploring how structural violence impacts mental health experiences and coping mechanisms among marginalized refugee communities, accounting for intersecting marginalities faced by structurally vulnerable groups. With extensive experience working with culturally diverse, trauma-impacted migrant communities, she has collaborated with various refugee-serving organizations such as UNHCR, IOM, and the Center for Victims of Torture, both in the United States and globally.

Ramsay Liem is Professor Emeritus of Psychology, Boston College, affiliated faculty in the Center for Human Rights and International Justice (CHRIJ). He is a co-founder of the Ignacio Martín-Baró Initiative for Wellbeing and Human

Rights and the Asian American Resource Workshop, Boston. He has conducted oral histories with Korean American survivors of the Korean War and directed a multimedia project, *Still Present Pasts: Korean Americans and the "Forgotten War,"* based on this research. He is currently collaborating on a memoir of an early Korean American ex-patriot who played a leading role in the overseas Korean movement for independence, democracy, and reunification.

Fayez Mahamid is Associate Professor in clinical mental health counseling. He is currently lecturing at An-Najah National University, Nablus, Palestine, in undergraduate and graduate mental health programs. Dr. Mahamid supervised several projects in the fields of mental health, group therapy, trauma intervention, and psychosocial rehabilitation in Palestine. His research employs mixed-methods research designs to address dimensions of well-being in war-affected populations, therapeutic intervention, trauma intervention, mental health, internet addiction, clinical supervision, and school counseling.

Paniz Musawi Natanzi is a political theorist and Postdoctoral Associate at the Duke University Middle East Studies Center (DUMESC) and Duke University Islamic Studies Center (DISC) in Durham, NC, USA, during 2023–2024. In her research, Musawi Natanzi is committed to developing anti-colonial political theorization focusing on visual arts and poetry, war, race and labor, men and masculinities, refugees and migration, governmentality, carceral systems, neoliberal capitalism, imperialism, and political geography.

Shahab Nadimi is a Ph.D. candidate in Transnational and Comparative Literatures program at the University of Alberta, Canada. His research interests lie at the intersection of world literature, refugee studies, biopolitics, neoliberalism, and trauma. Shahab's recent publications include "Precarious Refugee: Disturbing Neoliberal Rationality in Rawi Hage's *Cockroach*" (2024) in *Comparative Literature and Culture* and "A Repressed Desire Named Revolution: Social Anomalies and Anxieties in Coetzee's *Waiting for The Barbarians*" (2018) in *Cogent Arts & Humanities*.

Nora Parr is Research Fellow at the University of Birmingham, UK. She is a co-investigator on the Rights for Time Research Network where she also leads the Palestine Case Study with the Palestine Trauma Center. She is also a fellow at the Center for Lebanese Studies. She is co-editor of the journal *Middle Eastern Literatures* and author of *Novel Palestine: Nation through the Works of Ibrahim Nasrallah* (University of California Press, 2023). Her work challenges existing frameworks of trauma theory through work on Palestinian literature and culture.

Janethe Peña is the founder and executive director of DC Doors, Inc., a non-profit organization that empowers and educates individuals to break the cycles of poverty and homelessness. She obtained her M.A. in Counseling from Trinity Washington University, USA, and is a member of the American Counseling Association.

Jenny Phillimore is Chair of Migration and Superdiversity at the University of Birmingham, UK, Fellow of the Academy of Social Sciences, and Leverhulme Major Fellow. She researches refugee integration and has advised governments on every continent on integration strategies and indicators. She leads the SEREDA program, researches civil society and superdiversity, and leads the NODE UK/Japan network on diversity and migration.

Ricardo Phipps is Clinical Associate Professor at the College of William and Mary in Williamsburg, VA, USA. He is a clinical mental health counselor and counselor educator and completed his Ph.D. in Counselor Education and Supervision at the University of Mississippi. Ricardo pursues a scholarly focus on multicultural counseling issues. Most recently, he published "When Truth Hurts: Reactions to the Piloted AP African American Studies Program" (2023) in the *Journal of Academic Freedom*.

Sarah Rockowitz is a doctoral student in the School of Psychology at the University of Birmingham, UK. Her research focuses on sexual and gender-based violence in Kenya, including service provision and barriers to care. She also studies perpetration against forced migrants across the migration pathway.

Muna Saleh, MSW, is a Ph.D. student at the Virginia Commonwealth University School of Social Work, Virginia, USA. Saleh's research interests include the collective health care utilization of refugees, with an emphasis on contextual factors influencing health service access. Saleh is a recipient of the Robert Woods Johnson Foundation's Health Policy Research Scholar grant.

Konrad Siekierski is Lecturer in the Department of Armenian Studies at the Pázmány Péter Catholic University in Budapest, Hungary. He is a co-editor of *Armenia: A Modern Culture from an Anthropological Perspective* (2014), *Armenians in Post-Socialist Europe* (2016), and a special issue of *Entangled Religions* journal on "Religion and Pandemic: Shifts of Interpretations, Popular Lore, and Practices" (2022). He is currently working on research projects: "Lost-but-Found: Armenian Capital Ani at Contested Crossroads" and "Gospel Books as Home Saints: Between Vernacular Christianity and Armenian National Heritage."

Wendy Sims-Schouten is Deputy Director of Arts and Sciences and Associate Professor in Interdisciplinary Psychology at University College London. She is a Chartered Member of the British Psychological Society, and Principal Fellow of the Higher Education Academy. Wendy has an interest in historic and contemporary practices around mental health, well-being, resilience, and safeguarding of marginalized groups in national and international contexts. Wendy is Chair of the Editorial Board for *Children & Society* journal, Co-Editor of the *Psychology Teaching Review* journal, and member of the Editorial Committee for the *Journal of Critical Realism*.

Laura Stevens is a Ph.D. student in the Applied Memory Lab, at the University of Birmingham, UK. Additionally, she is Research Fellow on the Rights for

Time Research Network working alongside the Wangu Kanja Foundation. Her research interests include the use of innovative investigative interviewing techniques to collect memory evidence from vulnerable groups, including survivors of sexual- and gender-based violence. Laura is currently the Student President of the Society for Applied Research in Memory and Cognition.

Elise Westin completed her Ph.D. at the University of Adelaide, Australia, with a dissertation on the representation of victims in Holodomor discourse and how they have both shaped and been shaped by cultural memory and trauma. She has presented her research at a wide range of international conferences and currently teaches at the University of Adelaide, Australia. Elise is a third-generation survivor of the Ukrainian Holodomor.

Lidia Zessin-Jurek is a postdoctoral researcher and Poland expert in the ERC-Project *Unlikely Refuge? Refugees and Citizens in East-Central Europe in the Twentieth Century* (Czech Academy of Sciences, 2019–2025). She works at the European Holocaust Research Infrastructure (EHRI) and as Independent Expert for the European Commission (Holocaust Remembrance, Research, and Education). Beyond academic writing, she publishes in Polish national and international media on refugee movements (on the Polish border with Belarus and Ukraine), memory, and European integration.

Acknowledgments

Numerous individuals have played a role, either directly or indirectly, in creating and shaping this book. Their contributions include written feedback, discussions, time involvement, inspiration, and facilitation efforts over the years. We thank our colleagues in the Institute of Political and International Studies at Eötvös Loránd University, Hungary, and in the Department of Sociology and Anthropology at St. Louis University, USA, and the College of Communication and Media Sciences at Zayed University, UAE, for their advice and feedback on various parts of this volume.

We thank our contributors for their outstanding contributions to this book:

Konrad Siekierski (Chapter 1), Shahab Nadimi (Chapter 2), Fayez Mahamid and Dana Bdier (Chapter 3), Lidia Zessin-Jurek (Chapter 4), Elise Westin (Chapter 5), Ricardo Phipps and Janethe Peña (Chapter 6), Mario J. Azevedo and Tiffany D. Caesar (Chapter 7), Muna Saleh and Hyojin Im (Chapter 8), Nicole Hirt (Chapter 9), Paniz Musawi Natanzi (Chapter 11), Ramsay Liem (Chapter 12), Sang Hui Chu (Chapter 13), Phi Hong Su (Chapter 14), Nora Parr, Wendy Sims-Schouten, Jenny Phillimore, Heather Flowe, Sarah Rockowitz, Laura Stevens, Tamirace Fakhoury, and Rana Dajani (Chapter 15). This book would most certainly not have been actualized were it not for our contributors' expertise, hard work, and patience throughout its production. It has been a pleasure for us to collaborate with you on this book.

We also thank the external reviewers and individuals who provided various other editorial assistance along the way: Adna-Karamehić-Oates, Benjamin Moore, David Borgmeyer, Patrick McCarthy, Rashmi Lee George, Mandana Hendessi, Narae Kim, Joshua R. Snyder, Keith Doubt, Karolina Lendák-Kabók, Yuval Benziman, Dijana Mujkanovic, Mohammed Abu-Nimer, Ilham Nasser, Pramod K. Nayar, Melissa Chiovenda, Nerkez Opacin, Moin Syed, Kathryn Stam, Alfred Sebit Lokuji, Lawrence Meda, Terri L. Weaver, Liza Schuster, Khadija Abbasi, and Alessandro Monsutti. None of them share any responsibility for any errors, factual or otherwise.

Special thanks to Anna Sebestyén, Ons Chaabene, Lorenna Navarro, and Anna Brjezovskaia, aspiring young professionals and teaching assistants at the Institute of Political and International Studies at Eötvös Loránd University. We thank you for your time and diligence in assisting us on the editing process.

We further wish to express our gratitude to the EuMePo Jean Monnet Network and our colleague Ildikó Barna at Eötvös Loránd University, Budapest, Hungary, who opened up an entire panel on "Intergenerational Trauma after Violence" during Europe Canada Network's EuMePo closing conference in Budapest. We thank two of our contributors, namely, Lidia Zessin-Jurek and Rana Dajani, for joining a most productive discussion on this volume and your chapters, respectively. Special thanks to our colleague Christina Griessler from Andrássy University in Budapest, who closely followed the evolution of this edited volume and generously shared her ideas for the volume.

We are also in gratitude to the Institute for the Study of Genocide that assisted in disseminating our call for chapters.

Special thanks and acknowledgment to our respective families for their patience and support through the many stages of this book.

Thank you, Routledge, for your support through this book process and for all the hard work your staff has put into this book. Following our first book, *Remembrance and Forgiveness: Global and Interdisciplinary Perspectives on Genocide and Mass Violence*, we are grateful for the completion of this second volume, confident that it will not be our last collaboration. For any unintentional omission and recognition of contributors, we offer our apologies.

Editing this second book together has been both an odyssey of personal growth and a destination at new professional horizons yet to explore together. This volume stands as a testament to the achievements of true and continuing friendship.

Introduction

Laura Kromják and Ajlina Karamehić-Muratović

Throughout human history, individuals have experienced forced migration, fleeing their countries because of fear of persecution based on identity, beliefs, and affiliations, or because of conflict and violence. According to the UNHCR, more than 117 million individuals have been forcibly displaced worldwide because of persecution, conflict, violence, or human rights violations. Today, there are 37.6 million refugees globally, 41% of whom are estimated to be children below 18 years of age (*Refugee Statistics*, 2024). It is expected that the global refugee crisis will increase in the coming years, with over 2.4 million refugees seeking resettlement in 2024, a 20% increase compared to 2023 (UNHCR, 2023). Furthermore, it is well documented that being a refugee is associated with a myriad of mental health challenges, many of which begin before migration and accumulate as individuals relocate and resettle. With an increasing focus in recent years on the enduring impact of refugees' mental health struggles arising from exposure to war and violence even long after resettlement, there is increasing evidence indicating that the mental health challenges faced by the first generation can affect their families and subsequent generations, including their second-generation children.

In reflecting on the Holocaust families, including survivors and their children, Krell (1979) writes: "It appears that the effects of the Holocaust experience are transmitted by survivor-parents to the children, and that the treatment of such children for related or unrelated psychological problems requires an acute awareness of the unique problems of these families" (p. 560). Following earlier descriptions of the Holocaust syndrome by Niederland (1961) and Rakoff et al. (1966), Krell's (1979) reflections are one of several similar post-Holocaust explorations of intergenerational effects of trauma on second-generation children. In a later pathbreaking study on the adult offspring of Holocaust survivors, Yehuda et al. (1998; 2001) identified an association between parental PTSD and offspring PTSD. An ever-expanding field of inquiry heralded by the enduring legacy of the Holocaust, studies on trauma transmission are now informed by findings available from such studies on intergenerational effects as in families of war veterans (Dekel & Goldblatt, 2008; Castro-Vale et al., 2019), war prisoners (Zerach & Solomon, 2016; Costa et al., 2018), survivors of systemic oppression and racial trauma (Bombay et al., 2014; Hankerson et al., 2022), and witnesses and second generation following 9/11 attacks (Yehuda et al., 2005; Brown, 2020). Arguably, intergenerational

DOI: 10.4324/9781003385820-1

transmission of trauma has gained importance and has renewed significance among second-generation children born to refugee parents who experienced war-related trauma, violence, and PTSD.

Over the last decade, significant progress has been made in the study of intergenerational trauma among refugee populations. While the effects of exposure to trauma to armed conflicts and forced displacement were the focus of early research on refugees' mental health, in recent years, attention has shifted to include distress related to resettlement (Miller & Rasmussen, 2017). A meta-analysis by Sangalang and Vang (2017) and Flanagan et al. (2020) sought to explore mechanisms of trauma transmission between refugee parents and their children born post-resettlement. In a systemic review of 20 publications and a diverse body of research with narratives of adult offspring, Sangalang and Vang (2017) concluded that parenting style and family dynamics are important factors in how trauma is transmitted in refugee families. Based on the analysis of eight studies, Flanagan et al. (2020) posit that parental trauma exposure and its aftermath have a detrimental effect on children, potentially through mechanisms involving insecure attachment and dysfunctional familial interactions. Recent studies on refugee children have likewise shown evidence of a higher prevalence of adverse psychological effects among children of parents with PTSD, highlighting the increased risk of negative psychological repercussions (Back Nielsen et al., 2019; Thorup Dalgaard et al., 2020; Kelstrup & Carlsson, 2022). Furthermore, a cohort study by Bryant et al. (2018) revealed that the trauma exposure and post-migration stresses of refugee parents are linked to increased symptoms of PTSD, which culminate in behavioral and psychological maladaptation in their offspring.

Intergenerational trauma is thus the phenomenon where trauma endured in one generation influences the health and well-being of successive generations, including their children. Categorically, (epi)genetics, prenatal exposure, environmental stressors, and parenting style have been identified as factors that influence intergenerational transmission within families (Goodman et al., 2020). In reviewing the origin of studies of intergenerational trauma effects, Yehuda and Lehrner (2018) suggest that "While some aspects of intergenerational trauma effects remain contested, discussions about whether there are clinically observable intergenerational effects in offspring have become less contentious in the last several years, with the increasing recognition of the universality of this phenomenon" (p. 244). They point out that more recent discussions on the topic have shifted focus to looking at the impact of historical events such as colonization, slavery, and displacement trauma among cultures and communities that experienced war, violence, ethnic cleansing, and genocide. Though Yehuda and Lehrner (2018) primarily explore the epigenetic mechanisms of trauma transmission, it is noteworthy that

> [t]he intense focus on intergenerational effects in these different groups suggests that this topic has broad resonance and global applicability and provides a mandate for increased attention to this area, including prospective, longitudinal studies that can be designed in the future to determine the mechanisms underlying this phenomenon.
>
> (p. 244)

Trauma research is just beginning to explore expressions of generational aspects of trauma transmission. "The study of PTSD could benefit from the wider lens of an intergenerational perspective," says APA Div. 56 (Trauma Psychology) President Diane Castillo, "while the study of intergenerational trauma could learn from the systematic work that's been done on PTSD" (as cited in DeAngelis, 2019, para.5). Through a rich and heterogenic corpus of case studies, Danieli's 1998 edited book *The International Handbook of Multigenerational Legacies of Trauma* pioneered in evidencing an observed presence as well as substantial indications of intergenerational trauma in multiple communities globally. Spearheading multidisciplinary research on the long-term effects of trauma among vulnerable populations, Danieli (1998) also "emphasi[zed] to policymakers that the consequences of decisions that are frequently made with largely short-term considerations in mind cannot only be lifelong but also multigenerational" (p. xvi). It remains imperative for refugees to achieve long-term reconnections to all aspects of a dignified life pre- and post-resettlement.

Our first edited volume *Remembrance and Forgiveness: Global and Interdisciplinary Perspectives on Genocide and Mass Violence* (2020) explored the expanding toolkit used by post-genocidal societies to address past violence as well as ongoing griefs, and alluded to far-reaching problems affecting future generations. As Tatz (2020), the author of one of the volume chapters, aptly illustrates:

> One of the many legacies of the genocidal eras, youth suicide is the starkest, the most poignant. Aboriginal suicide is not about mental illness, clinical depression, depletion of brain hormones, or chemical imbalances in brain. It is about immense sadness, about grief. Even if they [the Aboriginal youth] do not quite know the exquisite details, they have absorbed, or rather osmosed, the immensity of lost connections.
>
> (p. 14)

Furthermore, in the context of East Nusa Tenggara Province, Indonesia, Kolimon (2020), another contributor to the book, remarked as to the legacy of the 1965 anti-communist violence: ". . .due to the repression and marginalization of local culture by the official religion and the state, local capacity for reconciliation can no longer function optimally for the restoration of community. Family relationships have been broken, relationships destroyed, and grandchildren inherit these tensions and suspicions without knowing what really occurred in the past" (p. 59). This volume takes up the investigation from such inquiries into the legacies of massive collective trauma among vulnerable communities and does so in the context of a select (ex)refugee population and from a global and interdisciplinary perspective.

To that end, the goal of the present volume is to explore intergenerational/generational trauma, or ways in which trauma experienced by one generation affects the well-being of future generations, specifically among refugee communities displaced throughout the world. The book focuses on the legacy of trauma and how historical, cultural, and economic trauma affect survivors' future generations. While trauma research literature documents single-episode effects of trauma, the long-term and intergenerational effects of traumatic experiences across refugee communities and cultural contexts is still a gap in the literature. This book further includes patterns and findings across disciplines, cultural contexts, and methodologies addressing how transmission of trauma occurs in specific refugee communities. Specific questions that the book seeks to answer include how the study of generational transmission of trauma can contribute to a more integrated understanding of refugee experience both on a personal and collective level? What locally culturally sensitive approaches can be identified in the prevention and intervention of transgenerational traumatic stress transmission in refugee communities? To what extent and how can attempts made by the descendants of refugees at (re) addressing their inherited trauma contribute to repairing interpersonal and intercommunal bonds?

For this volume, academic experts from around the world discuss the definitions and concepts of intergenerational trauma and provide taken altogether the epistemological commonalities and/or discrepancies between context-specific perspectives of trauma across the generations. Providing pertinent findings from a multidisciplinary scholarship, the chapters examine the main operative methods, manifestations, and representations of intergenerational trauma among former and new refugee groups such as Armenians, Bosnian Americans, Nicaraguans, Somalis, Koreans, and Vietnamese in the United States, Ukrainian Holodomor refugees in Australia, Kurdish, Lebanese, and Iranian refugees from the MENA region, Palestinian Nakba refugees, Polish Jewish refugee survivors in the USSR, African refugees in Eastern and Southern Africa, diaspora Eritreans, Afghans in Germany, and North Korean refugees in South Korea. On their terms, the chapters offer the reader a multidimensional introduction to the complexities of transgenerational transmission of trauma in the defined context and eventually aid them to arrive at a more comprehensive understanding of the concepts.

In Chapter 1, Konrad Siekierski examines Armenian "roots pilgrimage" to *Yergir*, the ancestral location in what is today Turkey. The chapter first overviews the pilgrims' sending community, the Armenian diaspora in the United States, and its ways of remembering the genocide and demanding its recognition. It then illustrates how visiting *Yergir* enables Armenians to connect with their relatives who perished or were displaced during the genocide, fostering a sense of community among the pilgrims and strengthening their commitment to Armenian heritage.

Chapter 2, by Shahab Nadimi, examines three refugee literary works from the Middle East – Azareen Van Der Vliet Oloomi's *Call Me Zebra* (2018), Rawi Hage's *Cockroach* (2008), and Ava Homa's *Daughters of Smoke and Fire* (2020) – to show how narratives can serve as mechanisms of working through trauma and support resilience and resistance. The primary aim of the chapter is to contend that within the literary sphere of refugees, there is a dynamic negotiation between textual narratives and historical traumas, in turn cultivating shared experiences and themes.

Chapter 3, written by Fayez Mahamid and Dana Bdier, focuses on Palestine and explores intergenerational transmission of trauma across four generations of Palestinian Nakba refugees. This chapter goes beyond trauma on an individual level and generational distinctions within a single family, and looks at collective trauma, comprised of unconscious connection between members of the larger group, such as is the case among Palestinians. It further explores mental health challenges prevalent among Palestinian refugees in refugee camps and coping strategies, such as education and hope.

In Chapter 4, Lidia Zessin-Jurek delves into the influences that molded the memory perspectives of Polish Jewish refugees during wartime, specifically those who endured in the USSR and, contrary to those who sought refuge elsewhere, resettled in Poland after the war. It considers the extent to which refugees who experienced displacement as children and youth opted to align themselves with collective trauma in their adulthood. Through interviews, the chapter employs a deconstructive trauma research approach and highlights how trauma is navigated depending on the survivors' causality and identity.

Chapter 5, authored by Elise Westin, highlights the intergenerational transmission of trauma within the Ukrainian–Australian community. It considers this trauma through the lens of postcolonial and post-genocidal frameworks, focusing on the challenges of recognition faced by the descendants of Holodomor survivors. It explores the lingering effects of trauma, which burdens the postgenerations and hinders them from overcoming the painful past.

Chapter 6, contributed by Ricardo Phipps and Janethe Peña, examines the intergenerational trauma experiences of Nicaraguan American families who migrated to the United States during and after the 1979 Sandinista Revolution. Despite the United States government's failure to acknowledge the mass exodus of Nicaraguans from their homeland as a refugee crisis, first- and second-generation Nicaraguans in the United States grappled with adverse experiences they left behind in their homeland. The chapter also addresses intergenerational post-traumatic growth among Nicaraguan Americans, highlighting how surviving a revolutionary war prompted Nicaraguan Americans to work hard in pursuit of the "American dream."

Chapter 7, by Mario J. Azevedo and Tiffany D. Caesar, focuses on intergenerational trauma among refugees in Africa and draws parallels between them and other African diaspora communities such as African Americans. The chapter is informed by onsite studies, both qualitative and quantitative, ethnographies, and primary sources sampled by authors and others. The chapter elaborates on recommendations for future research directions and the collection of precise data to effectively portray and subsequently enhance the psychosomatic challenges faced by African individuals.

In Chapter 8, Muna Saleh and Hyojin Im explore the link between marginalization and trauma proliferation among Somali refugees resettled in the United States. Using the Developmental-Based Trauma Framework (DBTF), the chapter advocates for consideration of system-level traumas occurring in resettlement contexts and highlights the impact of marginalization on family functioning and the potential intergenerational transmission of trauma.

In Chapter 9, Nicole Hirt shifts our attention to Eritrea and explores the experiences of transgenerational transmission of trauma among younger diaspora generations and the newly arrived refugees from Eritrea. Using post-memory as a theoretical framework, the chapter explicates how events of the past, real or imagined, influence identity formation and social agency of diaspora-born generations and refugees. The chapter draws from participant observation spanning the diaspora and Eritrea since the 1980s, as well as interviews conducted with Eritrean diaspora members.

Chapter 10, authored by Ajlina Karamehić-Muratović and Laura Kromják, considers the case of Bosnian Americans who resettled in the United States following the conflict in the early to mid-1990s in Bosnia and Herzegovina. It reviews the literature spanning almost the last three decades to evidence how post-traumatic stress reactions endure among Bosnian refugees resettled in the United States who now largely identify as Bosnian Americans. Using oral histories and interviews with Bosnian American youth residing in St. Louis, Missouri, the chapter presents how experiences of war and trauma inherited from their parents have affected the second-generation Bosnian Americans.

Chapter 11, authored by Paniz Musawi Natanzi, considers the experiences of Afghanis who migrated to Germany following the German-funded projects, particularly the Mental Health and Psychosocial Support (MHPS) initiative, which offered precarious and short-term vocational opportunities to Afghani men in Germany. The chapter posits how Germany's mental health policies, implemented in the military–civil infrastructure that German institutions and organizations constructed in Afghanistan during NATO's (North Atlantic Treaty Organization) war from 2001 to 2021, aimed to humanize deportations and promote "return" among Afghan refugees who applied for asylum in Germany.

Chapter 12, by Ramsay Liem, examines the legacies and memories carried by Korean War civilian survivors living in the United States, stemming from the Korean War that took the lives of 3 million civilians due largely to United States scorched earth bombing. Drawing from an oral history project conducted some two decades ago, the chapter considers how these legacies and memories have permeated the lives of second-generation Korean Americans.

In Chapter 13, Sang Hui Chu, explores the psychological well-being of children in North Korean defectors (NKDs) families, or among individuals who fled North Korea and resettled in South Korea. The well-being of children is examined from the perspective of parent–child interaction, with additional attention devoted to mothers' traumatic experiences on their children's mental health. The chapter underscores the challenges of reaching conclusions regarding the intergenerational transmission of trauma among NKDs.

Chapter 14, contributed by Phi Hong Su, redirects attention toward Vietnamese Americans. Drawing from participant observation and interviews with organizers of the Vietnamese International Film Festival (ViFF) in California's Little Saigon following a documentary screening scrutinizing the first-generation anti-communists, the chapter continues to analyze how children of refugees inherit the legacies of war outside of the family setting and through community arts organizing.

In Chapter 15, Nora Parr, Wendy Sims-Schouten, Jenny Phillimore, Heather Flowe, Sarah Rockowitz, Laura Stevens, Tamirace Fakhoury, and Rana Dajani present five short introductions to five vignettes on intergenerational trauma in refugee communities from the diverse fields of epigenetics, literary analysis, psychology, politics, and social policy. Drawing on experiences from several regions of the world, the authors advocate for considering temporality when thinking about intergenerational harm.

This volume provides perspectives to encourage interdisciplinary and internationally oriented thinking, learning, and research. Because of its multi- and interdisciplinary focus and global perspectives, the text will be useful as a supplement for a variety of academic contexts. It can furthermore serve as a valuable reference for mental health practitioners and social scientists studying trauma, helping them reflect on definitional gaps and inconsistencies among concepts such as intergenerational trauma, historical and cultural traumas, generational transmission, refugees and forced migration, remembrance and reconciliation, families, and communities.

The international framework for refugee protection encompasses all efforts to foster an environment that upholds human dignity; it aims to prevent and alleviate the aftereffects of specific patterns of abuses and massive social trauma such as genocide and mass atrocities, and thus restoring dignified conditions of life through rehabilitation, mental health, social care, and economic integration, among other issues. Yet, it is only recently that a critical aspect of refugees' long-term social reconnection, the intergenerational transmission of trauma has been catapulted by global refugee crises into social discourse and awareness. The recent tragic occurrences in Ukraine and Palestine serve as poignant reminders that anyone, at any point in time, can be forced to migrate and become a refugee, leading to years of mental health struggles for both the first and second generations. According to UNHCR Operational Data Portal, to date, 6,579,700 Ukrainian refugees have been recorded globally, and 1.1 million of them registered only in Germany.[1] About 5.9 million Palestine refugees remain under UNRWA's mandate, and, as of July 31, 2024, up to 1.9 million people (or nine in ten people) across the Gaza Strip are internally displaced. Around 75% of Gaza's total population has been displaced due to the ongoing conflict.[2] Furthermore, of the 16.7 million Syrian people in need, 5.5 million are displaced, including over 2 million who live in last resort sites.[3] In recent years, 2,857,528 Venezuelans have fled their country to seek refuge in Colombia, initiating the largest forced displacement crisis ever in Latin America.[4] Since the start of the conflict in Sudan in mid-April of 2023, the total newly arrived Sudanese refugees, asylum seekers, and returnees amounts at 2,123,175.[5] The humanitarian situation specifically but by no means limited to these regions remains dire as refugee populations are in need of protection and support, in line with international standards. Importantly, children are dramatically overrepresented among the world's refugees, and UNICEF keeps underscoring the special vulnerabilities of young refugees.[6] To that end, the appropriate treatment of human experience that has been traumatically overwhelming for one generation and increasingly may fall as disruptive heritage onto next generations highlights the need to fully comprehend new conceptual views and experiences of trauma, specific relational issues, the contextual modes of transmission, the limits of coping with traumatic memories, the possibilities of resilience and reconciliation, and reparatory practices and preventive considerations.

Being a refugee is inextricably bound up with enduring massive multiple trauma both pre- and post-migration, along with feelings of rejection and helplessness, dehumanization and shame, and loss of dignity and agency in the process of displacement and resettlement. This volume reminds us that the refugee experience can also build resilience and be a process of new possibilities and a hopeful future. As testimonies and vignettes of the forthcoming pages illustrate, the deepest point of the trauma transmission process is reached when emotional and ontological truth is integrated into the stories of successive generations, honoring the memories and the strength of both forbearers and their progeny.

Notes

1 It is noted that for statistical purposes, UNHCR uses the term refugees generically, referring to all individuals having left Ukraine due to the war. For further information, see "UNHCR Operational Data Portal" (July 15, 2024). Retrieved May 29, 2024, from https://data.unhcr.org/en/situations/ukraine
2 For further information, see "UNRWA Situation Report # 125 on the situation in the Gaza Strip and the West Bank, including East Jerusalem" (July 31, 2024). Retrieved July 31, 2024, from https://www.unrwa.org/resources/reports/unrwa-situation-report-125-situation-gaza-strip-and-west-bank-including-east-Jerusalem
3 For further information, see "UNHCR Operational Data Portal" (April 10, 2024). Retrieved May 29, 2024, from https://data.unhcr.org/en/country/syr
4 For further information, see "UNHCR Operational Data Portal" (January 31, 2024). Retrieved May 29, 2024, from https://data.unhcr.org/en/country/col
5 For further information, see "UNHCR Operational Data Portal" (July 29, 2024). Retrieved July 30, 2024, from https://data.unhcr.org/en/situations/sudansituation
6 For further information, see "UNICEF: Child Displacement" (June 2024). Retrieved July 31, 2024, from https://data.unicef.org/topic/child-migration-and-displacement/displacement/

References

Back Nielsen, M., Carlsson, J., Køster Rimvall, M., Petersen, J.H., & Norredam, M. (2019). Risk of childhood psychiatric disorders in children of refugee parents with post-traumatic stress disorder: A nationwide, register-based, cohort study. *Lancet Public Health*, *4*(7), e353–e359. https://doi.org/10.1016/s2468-2667(19)30077-5

Bombay, A., Matheson, K., & Anisman, H. (2014). The intergenerational effects of Indian residential schools: Implications for the concept of historical trauma. *Transcultural Psychiatry*, *51*(3), 320–338.

Brown, R. (2020). The intergenerational impact of terror: Did the 9/11 tragedy impact the initial human capital of the next generation? *Demography*, *57*(4), 1459–1481. https://doi.org/10.1007/s13524-020-00876-6.

Bryant, R.A., Edwards, B., Creamer, M., O'Donnell, M., Forbes, D., Felmingham, K.L., Silove, D., Steel, Z., Nickerson, A., McFarlane, A.C., Van Hooff, M., & Hadzi-Pavlovic, D. (2018). The effect of post-traumatic stress disorder on refugees' parenting and their children's mental health: A cohort study. *Lancet Public Health*, *3*(5), e249–e258. https://doi.org/10.1016/S2468-2667(18)30051-3

Castro-Vale, I., Severo, M., & Carvalho, D. (2019). Intergenerational transmission of war-related trauma assessed 40 years after exposure. *Annals of General Psychiatry*, *18*(14), 1–10. https://doi.org/10.1186/s12991-019-0238-2

Costa, D.L., Yetter, N., & DeSomer, H. (2018). Intergenerational transmission of paternal trauma among US civil war ex-POWs. *Proceedings of the National Academy of Sciences (PNAS)*, *115*(44), 11215–11220. https://doi.org/10.1073/pnas.1803630115

Danieli, Y. (1998). Preface. In Danieli, Y. (Ed.), *International Handbook of Multigenerational Legacies of Trauma* (pp. xv–xvi). New York: Springer.

DeAngelis, T. (2019). The legacy of trauma. *ICMGLT*. Retrieved May 29, 2024, from https://icmglt.org/the-legacy-of-trauma/

Dekel, R., & Goldblatt, H. (2008). Is there intergenerational transmission of trauma? The case of combat veterans' children. *American Journal of Orthopsychiatry*, *78*(3), 281–289. https://doi.org/10.1037/a0013955

Flanagan, N., Travers, A., Vallières, F., Hansen, M., Halpin, R., Sheaf, G., Rottmann, N., & Johnsen, A.T. (2020). Crossing borders: A systematic review identifying potential mechanisms of intergenerational trauma transmission in asylum-seeking and refugee families. *European Journal of Psychotraumatology*, *11*(1), 1790283. https://doi.org/10.1080/20008198.2020.1790283

Goodman, S.H., Simon, H.F.M., Shamblaw, A.L., & Kim, C.Y. (2020). Parenting as a mediator of associations between depression in mothers and children's functioning: A systematic review and meta-analysis. *Clinical Child and Family Psychology Review*, *23*(4), 427–460. https://doi.org/10.1007/s10567-020-00322-4

Hankerson, S.H., Moise, N., Wilson, D., Waller, B.Y., Arnold, K.T., Duarte, C., Lugo-Candelas, C., Weissman, M.M., Wainberg, M., Yehuda, R., & Shim, R. (2022). The intergenerational impact of structural racism and cumulative trauma on depression. *American Journal of Psychiatry*, *179*(6), 434–440. https://doi.org/10.1176/appi.ajp.21101000.

Karamehić-Muratović, A., & Kromják, L. (Eds.) (2020). *Remembrance and Forgiveness: Global and Interdisciplinary Perspectives on Genocide and Mass Violence*. London, New York: Routledge.

Kelstrup, L, & Carlsson, J. (2022). Trauma-affected refugees and their non-exposed children: A review of risk and protective factors for trauma transmission. *Psychiatry Research*, *317*(7), 114604. https://doi.org/10.1016/j.psychres.2022.114604

Kolimon, M. (2020). Commemoration and healing: Finding a balance between state and local mechanisms for dealing with the historical wounds of the 1965 anti-communist violence in East Nusa Tenggara Province, Indonesia. In Karamehić-Muratović, K., & Kromják, L. (Eds.), *Remembrance and Forgiveness: Global and Interdisciplinary Perspectives on Genocide and Mass Violence* (pp. 47–62). London, New York: Routledge.

Krell, R. (1979). Holocaust families: The survivors and their children. *Comprehensive Psychiatry*, *20*(6), 560–568. https://doi.org/10.1016/s0010-440x(79)80008-5

Miller, K.E., & Rasmussen, A. (2017). The mental health of civilians displaced by armed conflict: An ecological model of refugee distress. *Epidemiology and Psychiatric Sciences*, *26*(2), 129–138. https://doi.org/10.1017/s2045796016000172

Niederland, W. G. (1961). The problem of the survivor. *Journal of the Hillside Hospital*, *10*, 233–247.

Rakoff, V, Sigal, J.J., & Epstein, N. (1966). Children and families of concentration camp survivors. *Canada's Mental Health*, *14*, 24–26.

Sangalang, C. C., & Vang, C. (2017). Intergenerational trauma in refugee families: A systematic review. *Journal of Immigrant and Minority Health*, *19*(3), 745–754. https://doi.org/10.1007/s10903-016-0499-7

Tatz, C. (2020). Aboriginal history: Amnesia and absolution. In Karamehic-Muratovic, K., & Kromják, L. (Eds.), *Remembrance and Forgiveness: Global and Interdisciplinary Perspectives on Genocide and Mass Violence* (pp. 7–19). London, New York: Routledge.

Thorup Dalgaard, N., Høgh Thøgersen, M., & Riber, K. (2020). Transgenerational trauma transmission in refugee families: The role of traumatic suffering, attachment representations, and parental caregiving. In De Haene, L., & Rousseau, C. (Eds.), *Working with*

Refugee Families Trauma and Exile in Family Relationships (pp. 36–49). Cambridge: Cambridge University Press. https://doi.org/10.1017/9781108602105.004

The UN Refugee Agency. (n.d.). *Refugee Statistics: USA for UNHCR.* Retrieved May 30, 2024, from www.unrefugees.org/refugee-facts/statistics/

UNHCR Operational Data Portal. (n.d.). Retrieved July 31, 2024, from https://data.unhcr.org/

UNHCR US. (June 26, 2023). *UNHCR: Global Refugee Resettlement Needs Grow in 2024* [Press release]. Retrieved May 29, 2024, from www.unhcr.org/us/news/press-releases/unhcr-global-refugee-resettlement-needs-grow-2024

UNICEF (June 2024). *Child Displacement.* Retrieved July 31, 2024, from https://data.unicef.org/topic/child-migration-and-displacement/displacement/

UNRWA (July 31, 2024). *Situation Report #125 on the Situation in the Gaza Strip and the West Bank, Including East Jerusalem.* Retrieved July 31, 2024, from https://www.unrwa.org/resources/reports/unrwa-situation-report-125-situation-gaza-strip-and-west-bank-including-east-Jerusalem

Yehuda, R., Engel, S.M., Brand, S.R., Seckl, J., Marcus, S.M., & Berkowitz, G.S. (2005). Transgenerational effects of posttraumatic stress disorder in babies of mothers exposed to the World Trade Center attacks during pregnancy. *Journal of Clinical Endocrinology & Metabolism, 90*(7), 4115–4118. https://doi.org/10.1210/jc.2005-0550.

Yehuda, R., Halligan, S.L., & Bierer, L.M. (2001). Relationship of parental trauma exposure and PTSD to PTSD, depressive and anxiety disorders in offspring. *Journal of Psychiatric Research, 35*(5), 261–270. https://doi.org/10.1016/s0022–3956(01)00032–2

Yehuda, R., & Lehrner, A. (2018). Intergenerational transmission of trauma effects: Putative role of epigenetic mechanisms. *World Psychiatry: Official journal of the World Psychiatric Association (WPA), 17*(3), 243–257. https://doi.org/10.1002/wps.20568

Yehuda, R., Schmeidler, J., Giller, E.L., Jr., Siever, L.J., & Binden-Brynes, K. (1998). Relationship between post-traumtic stress disorder characteristics of Holocaust survivors and their adult offspring. *American Journal of Psychiatry, 155*(9), 841–843. https://doi.org/10.1176/ajp.155.6.841

Zerach, G., & Solomon, Z. (2016). Indirect exposure to captivity details is not related to posttraumatic stress symptoms among the spouses and offspring of former prisoners of war. *Journal of Traumatic Stress, 29*(6), 530–536. https://doi.org/10.1002/jts.22140

1 Returning to the Roots

Transgenerational Trauma, Diaspora Community, and the Armenian Pilgrimage to the Lost Homeland

Konrad Siekierski

Homage:

I've come to pay tribute to you and honor you.
I've come to fulfill a dream and pay my respects to you.
You are my ancestors, my roots, my source of strength and survival.
I've come to search for any linkage between today as I look at the vast beauty of the land you called home and that doomed day when you were torn from your peaceful life and killed or put on that death march.
I've come to touch your earth, smell your village air, see your mountains and valleys and feel your presence.
. . .
I feel your presence, my ancestors, my roots, my source of strength and survival.
I have made the journey and I have found you.
Because your presence is within me – now and forever.

(Sarkisian, 2000)[1]

This chapter explores "roots pilgrimage" (Gitlitz & Davidson, 2006) to *Yergir*, Armenians' lost homeland in today's Turkey,[2] as a strategy of dealing with the transgenerational trauma in the American Armenian diaspora community.[3] It follows the descendants of the Armenian Genocide survivors who address their "root shock" – a "traumatic stress reaction to the destruction of [their] emotional ecosystem" (Thompson Fullilove, 2004, p. 11) – by visiting places where their parents, grandparents, or other family members lived until the early 20th century. In these places, roots pilgrims try to find homes for their "exiled memories" (Tošić & Palmberger, 2016, p. 5) when they look at the landscapes, touch the walls of ruined houses, light candles and pray in abandoned churches, drink water from ancient wells, and taste the local dishes, which the survivors used to make in the diaspora. In line with this volume's focus on the communal aspect of trauma, I first offer a brief overview of the pilgrims' sending community, the Armenian diaspora in the United States, and its ways of remembering the genocide and demanding its recognition. Second, against this background, I demonstrate how the experience of visiting *Yergir* allows Armenians to connect with their relatives who were either

DOI: 10.4324/9781003385820-2

killed or displaced during the genocide, creates a sense of community among the pilgrims, and strengthens their commitment to things Armenian.

Historical Background

At the beginning of the 20th century, the bulk of the worldwide Armenian population were citizens of the Ottoman Empire, forming, alongside Greeks, the largest non-Muslim community in the country.[4] However, in the second decade of the century, the increasingly toxic mixture of conflicting Armenian and Turkish nationalisms, the dilapidated condition of the Ottoman state, and the *longue durée* resentments over religious (Muslim versus Christian) differences and economic inequalities proved fatal for the Armenians. From 1915 to the early 1920s, the massacres, deportations, and death marches ordered and orchestrated by Turkish authorities destroyed the world of their Armenian subjects.

These events, called by the survivors *Aghet* (Catastrophe) or *Mets Yeghern* (the Great Crime), have later become internationally known (and denied by Turkey, the successor state of the Ottoman Empire) as the Armenian Genocide.[5] The genocide was a disaster of a magnitude that redrew the Armenian geography and profoundly influenced the historical consciousness of Armenians. It has become *the* reference point on the Armenian scale of time, dividing history into two distinct periods of before and after the Catastrophe happened. Furthermore, it has become "the key uniting force of Armenian nationhood" (Garbis, 2007, p. 17). The duty to remember this tragedy and demand its recognition[6] has kept the Armenian refugee communities together wherever they ended up scattered, from Soviet and post-Soviet Armenia and other parts of the former USSR to the Middle East, Europe, and both Americas.

Transgenerational Trauma in the American Armenian Diaspora

Many Armenian Genocide victims sought refuge in the United States where, over the time, they created a dense network of compatriotic unions, parishes (of Armenian Apostolic, Catholic, and Protestant churches), schools, benevolent organizations, sports clubs, and other community institutions working toward the preservation of ties among refugees and the memory of the "old land," including its customs, cuisine, dialects, dances, and music (Alajaji, 2015; Bertram, 2017).[7]

The US and other countries' condemnation of the Holocaust after World War II set a precedent for Armenians' struggle to publicly recognize their Catastrophe. The symbolic turning point was the 50th anniversary of the Armenian Genocide in 1965, after which the increasingly resourceful and well-established Armenian diaspora in the United States has become one of the leading forces in worldwide Armenian anti-denialist and commemorative activities. From the 1970s onward, these activities have additionally been fueled by a growing trend to "cultivate and cuddle 'ethnic identities' and 'roots'" (van den Berghe, 1981, p. 4) in the American society – the phenomenon that developed in response to an earlier "injustice [of] displacement and dispossession" (Hirsch & Miller, 2011, p. 7) experienced by different segments of this society. Consequently, Armenians found themselves among African Americans raising the question of their enslavement and racial discrimination (Eyerman, 2001, 2004; Haley, 1994), Native Americans speaking of their extermination and deprivation of fundamental rights (Churchill, 2004; Brunner, 2012), and other groups with similarly difficult histories. At the turn of the 21st century,

> with the third generation of post-genocide descendants at the helm, and the means and mechanisms of globalization revolutionizing activism, Armenian diasporic efforts . . . have focused on education, raising awareness, combating denialism, political lobbying, and working toward the official recognition of the genocide.
>
> (Kasbarian, 2018, p. 126)

These efforts culminated in and around 2015, the centennial anniversary of the Great Crime, with nationwide awareness campaigns, publications, cultural events, and mass demonstrations, including a march of 100,000 people in Los Angeles, a city with the largest Armenian population in the United States.

This way, the genocide survivors' "exiled memories" (Tošić & Palmberger, 2016, p. 5) of personal suffering and loss have been exiled not only in the sense that they belonged to displaced people but also in the sense that they outlived the survivors and – in the forms of individual "postmemory" (Hirsch, 2008, 2012) and the "collective memory" (Halbwachs, 1992; Irwin-Zarecka, 2008) – found refuge in the hearts and minds of the next generations. The descendants' postmemory – "the relationship [to] traumatic experiences that preceded [their] births but that were nevertheless transmitted to them so deeply as to seem to constitute memories in their own right" (Hirsch, 2008, p. 103) – was formed through family stories as well as a non-verbal "language of the family – . . . in the sounds of nightmares, the idioms of sighs and illness, of tears and acute aches" (Hoffman, 2004, pp. 9–10). Such a postmemory in the American Armenian diaspora is described by Flora Keshgegian (2006, p. 101), herself an offspring of the genocide survivors, when she writes:

> Even though I have not experienced the terror and trauma of genocide, my life often feels shaped by it. I learned my family's lessons well and took on their charge: Never forget our suffering. Never forget . . . how much we have lost. Remember that we are not at home.

In turn, the collective memory – "a set of ideas, images, feelings about the past . . . best located not in the minds of individuals, but in the resources they share" (Irwin-Zarecka, 2008, p. 4) – of the refugees and their descendants has been shaped by communal forms of commemoration, including religious services, monuments to the victims,[8] literary production, and public statements by Armenian organizations and political parties.

Personal postmemory and collective memory resources have encouraged some descendants of the genocide survivors to visit their lost homeland. The following part of this chapter examines what such an experience entails, why many Armenian travelers to *Yergir* understand their journeys as pilgrimage, and how this pilgrimage creates and strengthens their relationship with one's ancestors, fellow pilgrims, and the wider Armenian community.

Transgenerational Trauma and the Armenian Pilgrimage to the Roots

For several decades after the Armenian Genocide, it was unthinkable for most survivors and their descendants to pay a visit to their lost homeland. This situation gradually began to change from the late 1960s onward. In the peak period starting in the early 1990s and lasting until mid-2010s, organized groups from the United States and individual American Armenians headed in a considerable number to both national cultural landmarks and their native towns and villages in today's Turkey.[9]

Many Armenians who visited *Yergir* framed their experience as pilgrimage (Aroyan, 2013; Corrigan, 2014; Der Yeghiayan, 1989; 2008; Nersoyan, 1990). Likewise, the descendants of the genocide survivors with whom I spoke about their journeys often used this term. For example, according to Armen Aroyan, the most experienced guide to *Yergir* and pilgrimage leader, "It is a pilgrimage because we go to the roots itself, because it is a sort of healing the wound, which was open, by walking the paths of our ancestors. It is a fulfilment of a life-long dream" (Siekierski, personal interview with Armen Aroyan, Los Angeles, 2013). Garbis Der Yeghiayan, another frequent visitor to *Yergir* and pilgrimage leader, echoes Armen:

> To visit Western Armenia is not tourism, because for tourism you go to a foreign land. In a pilgrimage, you go to your own land. It is an appointment with your roots. [And] my roots are deeply grounded in Western Armenia and Cilicia.
> (Siekierski, personal interview with Garbis Der Yeghiayan, Glendale, 2013)[10]

Taking seriously the words of Armen, Garbis, and other Armenians, where "roots" and "pilgrimage" recur and sound particularly strong, I propose that the concept of *roots pilgrimage* best captures their experience of going to the lost homeland. First introduced in the context of Jewish visits to post-Holocaust Poland, it describes the people who

> hope that by walking the walk, tasting the taste, and gossiping with people – or the descendants of the people – whom their ancestors left behind, . . . will come to understand themselves better. The roots pilgrim is a double person. . . . One persona physically travels the world as it is today, as it evolved from the reality of the ancestors' world. The other persona walks in the mythic, remembered world, the world as it must have been the day his or her ancestors left. . . . Roots pilgrims are seekers. Unlike other pilgrims, their

principal goal is not renewed faith or access to miraculous intervention by the divine, but an intensified sense of self, of connectedness to past personal history.

(Gitlitz & Davidson, 2006, p. 213)

This search for and the feeling of the "intensified sense of self" and "connectedness to past personal history" is clearly expressed in Zarouhi Sarkisian's poem quoted in the opening of this chapter. She writes that her ancestors are her roots and the "source of strength and survival" (Sarkisian, 2000, line 3), that she found their presence in *Yergir* and that this way she fulfilled her dream. In other words, she – like Armen, Garbis and other pilgrims – addressed her inherited "root shock" (Thompson Fullilove's, 2004, p. 11) by touching the ground on which her father used to step and drinking from a well from which her mother used to take water. She knew these places through "subtle pedagogies of layered storying" she heard at home, but such knowledge was incomplete, and she felt the need to experience them also "through the senses, through the body" (Somerville, 2013, p. 19).

Likewise, other pilgrims try to get as close as possible to the places where their ancestors used to dwell before the genocide, the places which now stand as "unintentional monuments" (Riegl, 1996, p. 72) to the lost homeland. Thus, they swim in artificial lakes that today cover ancient Armenian villages, collect stones and dust from ruins of Armenian churches, monasteries, and schools, or stay overnight in houses belonging in the past to their families – the latter being the ultimate experience for roots pilgrims. This way, they establish personal connections not only with places belonging to another time before the genocide but also with people who used to and ought to live there. This sensual interaction with the remnants of the destroyed "emotional ecosystem" (Thompson Fullilove, 2004, p. 11) allows pilgrims to connect with their victimized ancestors and relatives, "meet" them there, feel their presence, and better understand them and their suffering. A moving passage penned by Karanian (2015, p. 9) illustrates this effect:

Zara was Mayrig's [grandma's] hometown. . . . I wish I could be a bird, she would tell my Mom. . . . I wish I could be a bird for just one day, so I could fly over my home in Zara and see it just one more time.

And so I travelled to Zara.

. . . Mayrig had left Zara 99 years ago, and until my visit, no one from her family had ever returned.

After 99 years, I imagined that Mayrig's wish had come true. I imagined that she had seen her hometown one last time, through her grandchild's eyes.

And after a lifetime of having only heard about Mayrig, I imagined that I had finally seen her, too.

(Karanian, 2015, p. 9)

However, pilgrims experience the "intensified sense of . . . connectedness to past personal history" (Gitlitz & Davidson, 2006, p. 213) not only through their physical interaction with unintentional monuments and fading traces of *Yergir*.

This experience is also facilitated by the fact that they often travel in groups of like-minded compatriots with whom they share strains of the journey,[11] the most visceral feelings and emotions of immense joy or deep sorrow, and the moments of cathartic release from the burden of grief and trauma.

For many pilgrims, standing in the place where their ancestors and relatives used to live and sharing stories about them with other pilgrims, who in turn tell their stories in their roots places, is a confession-like therapeutic experience. As Sarah, who traveled to *Yergir* with Armen Aroyan, described it during our conversation,

> As we started the trip, Armen said: "You can share." He encouraged that. . . . Each place we went, we told our stories. Some people prepared statements and read them out. Others just told what they knew. . . . It made us cry at each stop, but it was good because it allowed us to make it out and share with each other. . . . I think it makes the experience much more personal. It had more impact on us.
> (Siekierski, personal interview with Sarah, Fresno, 2013)

Varjabedian (2009), who was the first to study Armenian visits to *Yergir*, also describes this kind of support that pilgrims offer one another. Consider the following scene he witnessed:

> David and his mother . . . are visiting the village of Hüsenig . . . where his maternal grandfather had lived as a child. . . . And she breaks down and cries. At that exact moment, one of the pilgrims starts praying the Lord's Prayer in Armenian, sealing the sacredness of the moment.
> (Varjabedian, 2009, p. 515)[12]

The scene described by Varjabedian points also to the importance of religious rituals in Armenian pilgrims' experience. While some of these rituals, such as silent prayers or lighting candles in ruined Armenian churches and monasteries, have an individual and intimate character, other practices obtain affective power from their collective character. Singing in one voice a religious hymn, such as *Hayr Mer* (Lord's Prayer) or *Ter Voghormya* (Lord, Have Mercy), in a place that used to host a congregation of Armenian Christians before the genocide creates a powerful sense of community between the participants. In Sarah's words:

> In Msho Surb Karapet monastery,[13] we would sing a hymn from the liturgy. We did it also in Akhtamar and in every other church that was not converted into a mosque. We said *Hayr Mer* [Lord's Prayer] and then we would sing a *sharakan* [Armenian Christian chant]. Most of our group members were from the Armenian Church, so they all knew those songs from Sunday school.
> (Siekierski, personal interview with Sarah, Fresno, 2013)

Such acts create a sense of belonging to the group and a larger Armenian community not only because pilgrims engage in rituals that are familiar and meaningful to them and represent the culture and values they share and cherish. They also unite those who enact them because they are "a cultural and political statement" (Fröhlig, 2013, p. 74) and "a form of resistance" (Diler, 2014). By the very fact of coming to their ancestral villages and ancient monasteries, pilgrims deny the history that denied them the right to exist. They do not only perform traditional Armenian rituals in places that used to be Armenian, but they also act as if they were the hosts there and – if only for a while – reclaim these places and give them back to those who lost them many years before. Thus, somewhat like Jewish participants of the March of Living to the former Nazi death camp of Auschwitz, they are making a statement: "We are here, You did not succeed" (Gitlitz & Davidson, 2006, p. 177). However, unlike their Jewish counterparts, Armenian pilgrims need to face the Turkish state narrative that negates the Catastrophe. The lack of any monuments acknowledging their tragedy, the neglect or purposeful destruction of tangible Armenian heritage, and the unapologetic or indifferent stance of many current inhabitants of the former Armenian lands only add to pilgrims' bewilderment as they ask themselves: "Do they have a right to be hostile towards us? What reason do they have to be hostile?" (Aghjayan, 2012, para.6). Other pilgrims are dismayed when they realize that many local people approach them only to ask about maps to legendary treasures they believe to be hidden under Armenian churches and houses or at their cemeteries.[14] Some, however, feel relieved when they experience signs of recognition and regret or simply when they start to see in Kurds and Turks not a faceless enemy but people whose everyday joys and concerns do not differ much from their own.

Like participants of reunions of dispersed Anglo-Indians studied by Andrews (2012), roots pilgrims to *Yergir*, "enter a different social space and after the experience return to their former lives . . . renewed, and perhaps transformed, in their sense of being part of a larger body of culturally similar people" (Andrews, 2012, p. 160). Based on this shared experience of a "different social space" created in the process of discovering the lost homeland and finding home for one's "exiled memories" (Tošić & Palmberger, 2016, p. 5), they also keep in touch, meet with each other, or travel to *Yergir* together again. Armen Aroyan even organized four one-week-long reunions for pilgrims who went with him to the lost homeland. These gatherings took the form of biannual Armenian Cultural Legacy Cruises and Armenian Pilgrimage Reunions along the different parts of North America's coast – from Panama and the Caribbean Islands in the south (the first cruise in 1995), to Alaska in the north (the fourth cruise in 2001). The cruises attracted some 70–100 participants each. In addition to typical activities on cruise ships, they included lectures by leading Armenian historians, watching the *Return to Roots* film documenting past pilgrimages to *Yergir*, and other Armenian cultural events.

Visiting *Yergir* can also lead to a personal transformation that orients pilgrims toward the Armenian culture and the wider Armenian community. As Armen summarized this change, "they become closer to their roots, they become better people and better Armenians" (Siekierski, personal interview with Armen Aroyan, Los Angeles, 2013). Armen's own story confirms his words: after traveling to his ancestral village in historic Armenia, he then spent 25 years guiding his compatriots to the native places of their ancestors. Immediately after retirement, he founded Armen Aroyan Foundation and Library-Museum, devoted to "keeping the memory of our rich legacy alive and propagating it for future generations" (Armen Aroyan Foundation, 2019). Likewise, Garbis Der Yeghiayan, who not only organized and led several group pilgrimages to *Yergir* but also served for many years in different Armenian educational institutions in California, explained during our conversation:

> I feel a huge spiritual void if I don't visit my ancestors' home every summer . . . That gives me more momentum, more inspiration. . . . I am revived and rejuvenated to continue serving a new generation when I am back.

He also reflected on the impact of visiting the lost homeland on American Armenian youth: "We had young people who never spoke a word in Armenian, never learnt about Armenian history, but when they returned from our pilgrimage, they became 110 per cent Armenian" (Siekierski, personal interview with Garbis Der Yeghiayan, Glendale, 2013). This observation is further confirmed by the example of Miriam, a pilgrim in her 20s, whom I met during the Armenian language course she attended after visiting *Yergir*. As she told me, "The vow is to keep our culture alive. And going to Western Armenia . . . is one part of it. Learning the language and staying engaged, however I can, are other parts" (Siekierski, personal interview with Miriam, Venice, 2017).

Armen, Garbis, and many other pilgrims published books and articles, gave lectures and presentations, and contributed in other ways to the shared resources of Armenian collective memory of the lost homeland. I met Garbis for the first time when he talked about his latest visit to *Yergir* in a large community hall in Los Angeles. The hall was packed with people who reacted emotionally to his words and pictures, especially when they could identify their native places they had never seen before. Finally, emotions took over Garbis too – he finished his speech in a trembling voice, tears in his eyes. Such meetings, both in large halls and in dining rooms of Armenian houses, bring together the descendants of genocide survivors and, in Armen's words, "establish bridges between generations like 200 years" (Siekierski, personal interview with Armen Aroyan, Los Angeles, 2013).

Conclusion

Roots pilgrimage is a "memory on foot," as Bertram (2014, p. 3) aptly calls it. Pilgrims to *Yergir* touch the walls of stone houses and climb steep hills or smell fragrant fruits and gaze at fertile fields to connect with their relatives who fell victim to the Armenian Genocide, find home to the "exiled memories" (Tošić & Palmberger, 2016, p. 5) they inherited from the survivors, and reclaim, even if only symbolically and for a short while, their lost "emotional ecosystem" (Thompson Fullilove, 2004, p. 11). It is an often once-in-a-lifetime and life-changing personal experience that stirs visceral emotions and touches the deepest part of one's heart. However, there is also a crucial communal aspect to "roots pilgrimage" (Gitlitz &

Davidson, 2006). First, there is the community of experience formed by pilgrims who travel together through the lost homeland of ancestors and support each other with their stories, gestures, and participation in collective rituals. Second, visiting *Yergir* often results in pilgrims' deeper engagement in the present-day Armenian diasporic and transnational community. Finally, roots pilgrimage also impacts those Armenians who have not visited the lost homeland of ancestors themselves. They attend pilgrims' lectures, watch their videos, or read their books and articles, thus coming closer to their *Yergir*. They also receive from pilgrims the soil and stones from their native places, and they put these "relics" in their homes or on the graves of the survivors. By these means, they pay their respect to the victims and renew their commitment to "remember and demand."

Due to various social and political reasons, including an ongoing official Turkish denial of the genocide, Armenian roots pilgrimage has never become a mass phenomenon comparable in its scope and scale to Jewish pilgrimage to post-Holocaust Poland (Gitlitz & Davidson, 2006; cf. Kelner, 2010; Lehrer, 2013) and other countries. Consequently, it has remained an experience of only a few Armenians whose roots stretch back to *Yergir*. Nevertheless, its significant impact on pilgrims and its resonance in wider Armenian community means that roots pilgrimage is an important social mechanism of addressing, expressing, and dealing with trauma inherited by American Armenian descendants of genocide survivors and refugees from the Ottoman Empire.

However, larger questions loom behind the issues I discussed here. As the Armenian Genocide survivors are now gone and their children have already entered the final part of their lives, will next generations of Armenians yearn for the lost homeland and visit *Yergir* to face the traumatic past? If so, will they still search for roots places where their ancestors used to live, or will they rather frequent the few landmarks turned into symbols of the lost homeland? How would the Turkish recognition of the genocide impact the Armenian grief and pain currently exacerbated by the denial? Ultimately, how can Armenians deal, at both individual and communal levels, with the paradox of transgenerational trauma, when "letting go of the sense of injury and loss seems like betraying the original trauma and all that was suffered as a result of it [, whereas] holding on the injury gives the trauma an ongoing power?" (Keshgegian, 2006, p. 102). By asking these questions, this chapter invites more research on the legacy and transmission of trauma within and beyond the post-genocide Armenian transnational community.

Notes

1 The author and editors are grateful to Zarouhi Sarkisian for the permission to publish fragments of her poem titled "Homage" (2000) as a part of this chapter. "Homage" was written in the memory of her parents Ardash and Nvart (Der Stepanian) Sarkisian.
2 The word *Yergir* has different meanings in the Armenian language, including the earth, the world, country, province, and soil. However, after the Armenian Genocide, it has also started to denote one particular place: Armenians' lost homeland in Turkey. The phrase "Western Armenia" (Arm. *Arevmetyan Hayastan*), which is often used instead of *Yergir*, points to a recurring sociopolitical division of territories considered by Armenians as

their homeland between the Roman Empire/Byzantium/the Ottoman Empire/Turkey (Western Armenia), on the one hand, and Persia/the Russian Empire/the USSR (Eastern Armenia), on the other hand.

Parts of modern Turkey, which were home to the Armenian population prior to the genocide, but which were located outside of Western Armenia, include Cilicia (the former Armenian principality and kingdom existing during 11th–14th centuries in today's southern Turkey), the regions of Caesarea (Kayseri) and Yozgat in central Turkey, and cities and towns in all remaining parts of the country, including Constantinople (Istanbul), Smyrna (Izmir), Ankara, Kütahya, Ordu, and many others.. Consequently, these places are also remembered by Armenians as the *Yergir* of their ancestors.

3 While this chapter focuses on American Armenians, the descendants of the genocide survivors from other countries, such as Canada, France, the United Kingdom, and Armenia, also undertake similar journeys. I conducted interviews with children and grandchildren of the genocide survivors from different parts of the United States, chiefly from California, between 2013 and 2018 for my doctoral research project, *A Vow to Go: Religion, Reunion, and Roots in Armenian Pilgrimage*. This project was supported by the Calouste Gulbenkian Foundation (2016–2019) and the London Arts and Humanities Partnership (2017–2021). Other works on Armenian journeys to the lost homeland include Bertram (2014, 2018, 2022), Korkmaz (2021), Manoogian & Bakalian (2017), Turan Hoffman (2014), Turan & Bakalian (2015), and Varjabedian (2009).

4 According to the state census of 1914, they numbered over a million, whereas in 1912 the Armenian Apostolic Church counted over 2 million of its faithful in the Ottoman Empire (Bijak & Lubman, 2016, p. 30).

5 An abundant English-language scholarly literature on the Armenian Genocide is available, from pioneering works by Richard Hovannisian (1986, 1992) to more recent publications by Armenian, Turkish, and other authors, including Taner Akçam (2004, 2007), Peter Balakian (2004), Vahakn N. Dadrian (2003), and Ronald Grigor Suny (2015). The estimations of the genocide's casualties range from less than 1 million to 1.5 million dead, the latter being the widespread figure in Armenian national symbolism and popular discourse (Bijak & Lubman, 2016, pp. 30–34). Beyond this, the numbers reported by the US Department of State ("Approximate," 1922) include around 800,000 refugees and 100,000 "remnants of the sword," the latter being primarily children and young women, who were "converted and absorbed in Muslim households" (Sarafian, 2001, p. 211). At the same time, Armenian property was destroyed, looted, or confiscated and redistributed.

6 The centennial anniversary of the Armenian Genocide was commemorated worldwide in 2015 under the slogan "We Remember and Demand."

7 Between 1915 and the 1920s, around 100,000 Armenians from the Ottoman Empire fled to the United States. Later, immigration restrictions introduced by the US government curbed this flow, but many genocide survivors still managed to reach the country, for example, via Mexico.

8 According to the Armenian Genocide Memorials Database, there are at least 75 such monuments in the United States, mainly in the form of *khachkars* – Armenian cross-stones ("Armenian National Institute," n.d.).

9 This period was characterized by the growing popularity of Turkey as a tourist destination, a relatively peaceful situation in eastern regions of the country (otherwise often shattered by Turkish–Kurdish conflict), and – especially in the first and early second decade of the 21st century – moments of goodwill gestures in political relations between Armenia and Turkey.

It is difficult to estimate how many Armenians from the United States and other countries have traveled to Turkey in search of the villages and towns of their ancestors and to visit Armenian landmarks such as the Holy Cross Cathedral on Akhtamar Island, the medieval Armenian capital of Ani, or the city of Van. Of two pilgrimage organizers and

group leaders I spoke with, Armen Aroyan took with him during 1991–2015 around a hundred groups with almost 1,500 participants in total. Garbis Ter-Yeghiayan organized nine pilgrimage tours for some 300–400 people in a similar period.
10 Except for two group leaders – Armen Aroyan and Garbis Ter-Yeghiayan – I use pseudonyms when quoting the interviews.
11 For example, a typical two-week-long itinerary of Armen Aroyan's pilgrimages included some 4,000-km-long ride on a minibus through central and eastern Turkey, in addition to flights between the United States and Turkey, and internal flights from Istanbul to Adana, Van, or other locations.
12 Varjabedian (2009, p. 511) also underlines the feeling of gratitude the group members have toward their peers. In his words, "pilgrims always thank the members of the group for being present and helping them out."
13 Msho Surb Karapet, or St. Karapet of Moush Monastery, used to be a major pilgrimage site for Armenian Christians prior to the genocide.
14 On the widespread phenomenon of hunting for "Armenia gold" in Turkey, see, for example: von Bieberstein (2017), Korkmaz (2021), and Varjabedian (2009, pp. 536–541).

References

Aghjayan, S. (2012, June 22). Home at Last: An AYFer Visits Historic Armenia. *The Armenian Weekly*. Retrieved February 12, 2023, from https://armenianweekly.com/2012/06/22/home-at-last-an-ayfer-visits-historic-armenia/

Akçam, T. (2004). *From Empire to Republic: Turkish Nationalism and the Armenian Genocide*. London: Zed Books.

Akçam, T. (2007). *A Shameful Act: The Armenian Genocide and the Question of Turkish Responsibility*. New York, NY: Holt Paperbacks.

Alajaji, S. (2015). *Music and the Armenian Diaspora: Searching for Home in Exile*. Bloomington, IN: Indiana University Press.

Andrews, R. (2012). Anglo-Indian Reunions: Secular Pilgrimage? *South Asian Diaspora*, 4(2), 159–173. https://doi.org/10.1080/19438192.2012.675723

Approximate. (1922, November). *Approximate Number of Armenians in the World. The US Department of State*. Retrieved November 14, 2020, from https://upload.wikimedia.org/wikipedia/commons/6/66/US_State_Department_document_on_Armenian_Refugess_in_1921.jpg

Armen Aroyan Foundation. (2019). *About Armen*. Retrieved May 3, 2022, from www.armenaroyanfoundation.org/about

Armenian National Institute. (n.d.). *Armenian Genocide Memorials – United States*. Retrieved May 3, 2022, from www.armenian-genocide.org/current_category.75/memorials_list.html

Aroyan, A. (2013). *The Pilgrim Speaks: An Armenian Discovery of Ancestral Roots*. (Unpublished Book). [On file with the author of this chapter].

Balakian, P. (2004). *The Burning Tigris: The Armenian Genocide and America's Response*. New York, NY: Perennial.

Bertram, C. (2014). *Journeys of the Descendants of Trauma: An Armenian Search for the Houses and Villages of a Lost Ottoman Past*. (Unpublished Paper Presented at the Conference 'Trauma & History,' University of Texas at Austin, 20–21.03.2014).

Bertram, C. (2017). Armenians in America: The Role and Realm of Music in Coming to Terms with Home and Homeland. *Journal of the Society for Armenian Studies*, 26, 135–149.

Bertram, C. (2018). Dinner in the Homeland: Memory, Food and the Armenian Diaspora. In S. Marshall (Ed.), *Memory, Migration, and Travel* (pp. 189–212). New York, NY: Routledge.

Bertram, C. (2022). *A House in the Homeland: Armenian Pilgrimages to Places of Ancestral Memory*. Redwood City, CA: Stanford University Press.

Bijak, J., & Lubman, S. (2016). The Disputed Numbers: In Search of the Demographic Basis for Studies of Armenian Population Losses, 1915–1923. In A. Demirdjian (Ed.), *The Armenian Genocide Legacy* (pp. 26–43). London: Palgrave Macmillan.

Brunner, S. (2012). *Remnants of a Shattered Past: A Journey of Discovery and Hope*. Dublin: Abbot Press.

Churchill, W. (2004). *Kill the Indian, Save the Man: The Genocidal Impact of American Indian Residential Schools*. San Francisco, CA: City Lights Press.

Corrigan, K. (2014, August 5). Pilgrimage Through Historic Armenia Stirs Emotions. *Glendale News-Press*. Retrieved December 17, 2020, from www.latimes.com/socal/glendale-news-press/news/tn-gnp-pilgrimage-through-historic-armenia-stirs-emotions-20140805-story.html

Dadrian, V. (2003). *The History of the Armenian Genocide: Ethnic Conflict from the Balkans to Anatolia to the Caucasus*. New York, NY: Berghahn Books.

Der Yeghiayan, G. (1989). *Conversations in Silence*. Washington, DC: The Millennium Institute.

Der Yeghiayan, G. (2008). *The Presence of the Past: Embracing the Land of Our Ancestors. Pilgrimage to Cilicia, Cappadocia & Western Armenia*. Regents Park: Eastgate Institute.

Diler, F.G. (2014). *Armenian Resistance to Erasure, Disappearance and Denial*. Retrieved October 23, 2017, from http://nancykricorian.net/2014/11/armenian-resistance-to-erasure-disappearance-and-denial/

Eyerman, R. (2001). *Cultural Trauma: Slavery and the Formation of African American Identity*. Cambridge: Cambridge University Press.

Eyerman, R. (2004). The Past in Present: Culture and the Transmission of Memory. *Acta Sociologica, 47* (2), 159–169.

Fröhlig, F. (2013). Re-Visiting the Site of the Former Soviet Prison Camp in Tambov. *Journeys, 14* (1), 68–88.

Garbis, C. (2007). The "Religion" of Genocide: A Uniting Force Stronger than the Armenian Church and Language, *The Armenian Weekly, 73* (6), *Armenian Genocide Insert: Controversy and Debate*, 17.

Gitlitz, D.M., & Davidson L.K. (2006). *Pilgrimage and the Jews*. Santa Barbara, CA: Praeger.

Halbwachs, M. (1992). *On Collective Memory*. Chicago, NY: University of Chicago Press.

Haley, A. (1994). *Roots*. New York, NY: Vintage Books.

Hirsch, M. (2008). The Generation of Postmemory. *Poetics Today, 29* (1), 103–128.

Hirsch, M. (2012). *The Generation of Postmemory: Writing and Visual Culture After the Holocaust*. New York, NY: Columbia University Press.

Hirsch, M., & Nancy K.M. (2011). Introduction. In M. Hirsch, & N. K. Miller (Eds.), *Rites of Return: Diaspora Poetics and the Politics of Memory* (pp. 1–20). New York, NY: Columbia University Press.

Hoffman, E. (2004). *After Such Knowledge: Memory, History, and the Legacy of the Holocaust*. New York, NY: Public Affairs.

Hovannisian, R., (ed.). (1986). *The Armenian Genocide in Perspective*. Piscataway, NJ: New Transaction Books.

Hovannisian, R. (1992). *The Armenian Genocide: History, Politics, Ethics*. New York, NY: St. Martin's Press.

Irwin-Zarecka, I. (2008). *Frames of Remembrance: The Dynamics of Collective Memory*. Piscataway, NJ: Transaction Publishers.

Karanian, M. (2015). *Historic Armenia after 100 Years: Ani, Kars, and the Six Provinces of Western Armenia*. Berkeley, CA: Stone Garden Press.

Kasbarian, S. (2018). The Politics of Memory and Commemoration: Armenian Diasporic Reflections on 2015. *Nationalities Papers: The Journal of Nationalism and Ethnicity, 46* (1), 123–143. https://doi.org/10.1080/00905992.2017.1347917

Kelner, S. (2010). *Tours that Bind: Diaspora, Pilgrimage, and Israeli Birthright Tourism*. New York, NY: New York University Press.
Keshgegian, F.A. (2006). Finding a Place Last Night: Armenian Genocidal Memory in Diaspora, In O. B. Stier, & J. Shawn Landers (Eds.), *Religion, Violence, Memory, and Place* (pp. 100–112). Bloomington, IN: Indiana University Press.
Korkmaz, A. (2021). "Our Sacred Native Land": Armenian Roots Tourism in Eastern Turkey. *Études arméniennes contemporaines*, *13*, 49–78.
Lehrer, E.T. (2013). *Jewish Poland Revisited: Heritage Tourism in Unquiet Places*. Bloomington, IN: Indiana University Press.
Manoogian, M.M., & Bakalian, A. (2017). Intergenerational Transmission in Armenian Families: A Focus on Travels to Anatolia by Diasporans. *Journal of the Society for Armenian Studies*, *26*, 150–160.
Nersoyan, H. (1990). *An Armenian Pilgrimage: From Istanbul to Aghtamar*. New York, NY: Ashod Press.
Riegl, A. (1996). The Modern Cult of Monuments: Its Essence and Its Development. In N. S. Price, M. Kirby Talley, Jr., & A. Melucco Vaccaro (Eds.), *Historical and Philosophical Issues in the Conservation of Cultural Heritage* (pp. 69–83). Los Angeles, CA: Getty Conservation Institute.
Sarafian, A. (2001). The Absorption of Armenian Women and Children into Muslim Households as a Structural Component of the Armenian Genocide. In O. Bartov, & M. Phyllis (Eds.), *In God's Name: Genocide and Religion on the Twentieth Century* (pp. 209–221). New York, NY: Berghahn Books.
Sarkisian, Z. (2000). *Homage*. (Unpublished poem). [On file with the author of this chapter].
Somerville, M. (2013). *Water in a Dry Land: Place-Learning through Art and Story*. New York, NY: Routledge.
Suny, R.G. (2015). *"They Can Live in the Desert but Nowhere Else:" A History of the Armenian Genocide*. Princeton, NJ: Princeton University Press.
Thompson Fullilove, M. (2004). *Root Shock: How Tearing Up City Neighborhoods Hurts America, and What We Can Do About It*. New York, NY: A One World/Ballantine Book.
Tošić, J., & Palmberger, M. (2016). Introduction: Memories on the Move – Experiencing Mobility, Rethinking the Past. In J. Tošić, & M. Palmberger (Eds.), *Memories on the Move: Experiencing Mobility, Rethinking the Past* (pp. 1–16). Basingstoke, New York, NY: Palgrave Macmillan.
Turan, Z., & Bakalian, A. (2015). Diaspora Tourism and Identity: Subversion and Consolation in Armenian Pilgrimages to Eastern Turkey. In A. Gorman, & S. Kasbarian (Eds.), *Diasporas of the Modern Middle East* (pp. 173–211). Edinburgh: Edinburgh University Press.
Turan Hoffman, Z. (2014). Diaspora Tours and Place Attachment: A Unique Configuration of Emotion and Location. In H. Jones, & E. Jackson (Eds.), *Stories of Cosmopolitan Belonging: Emotion and Location* (pp. 141–156). New York, NY: Routledge.
van den Berghe, P. (1981). *The Ethnic Phenomenon*. Amsterdam: Elsevier.
Varjabedian, H. (2009). *The Poetics of History and Memory: The Multiple Instrumentalities of Armenian Genocide Narratives*. (Unpublished PhD Dissertation). University of Wisconsin-Madison.
von Bieberstein, A. (2017). Treasure/Fetish/Gift: Hunting 'for Armenian Gold' in post-Genocide Turkish Kurdistan. *Subjectivity*, *10*(2), 170–189. https://doi.org/10.1057/s41286-017-0026-x

2 Refugee Literary Space

Silences, Intergenerational Trauma, and Resilience

Shahab Nadimi

Introduction

The Middle East has witnessed almost a century of political turbulence since World War II, including the Arab–Israeli conflict dating back to 1948, the Yemen Civil War in the 1960s, the Lebanese Civil War (1975–1990), the Iran – Iraq War (1980–1988), and Iraq's invasion of Kuwait in 1990. The collateral effects of the war manifest as traumatic experiences, imposing psychological and physical tolls on the collective memory of survivors and subsequent generations. The Arab Spring, a series of pro-democracy protests that spread from Tunisia to other Arab countries in the early 2010s, continues to add on the affected nations' work of reconstructing a meaningful past, a process which, in turn, has a crippling impact on the collective health of several generations. In armed conflict areas, children experience high rates of physical and mental disorders, including post-traumatic stress disorder (PTSD), distress, hunger, functional impairment, poverty, separation anxiety disorder, and toxic stress (Samara et al., 2020; Dimitry, 2012; Ellis et al., 2019). Importantly, these traumatic experiences extend from the omnipresence of intergenerational trauma, increasing the area's visibility as a hot spot of refugeeism while leaving invisible marks on future generations in the Middle East. Memories of displacement and postwar experiences can be expressed privately and publicly through cultural representations that present important sites of reflection. As Hirsch (2001) notes, "postmemory" can be conceptualized as "reclaiming of memory." She continues to contend that

> postmemory most specifically describes the relationship of children of survivors of cultural or collective trauma to the experiences of their parents, experiences that they 'remember' only as the narratives and images with which they grew up, but that are so powerful, so monumental, as to constitute memories in their own right.
>
> (Hirsch, 2001, p. 16)

Over the past decades, refugee exodus and subsequent discursive debates surrounding their positionality within sociopolitical and economic structures have been complicated by economic inequality, ecological devastation, extreme nationalism, race, gender-based violence, tribalism, and theocracies (Deckard et al.,

DOI: 10.4324/9781003385820-3

2019; Bhabha, 1994). Refugee experience is frequently deemed as traumatic and of ambivalent nature; a moment of continual fluctuation between relief and suffering, hope and grief, protection and exposure across the ecology of spaces. Such continual moments, as it is often argued, affect only the refugees at the point of intervention. However, intergenerational trauma constitutes multilevel consequences, leaving indelible signs on collective memory and group consciousness. Furthermore, intergenerational trauma is not exclusively bound to a singular regional spatiality but is connected to multiple spaces and places passed on to subsequent generations through temporal distances. Intergenerational trauma also vacillates between past and present through fragmented memories that defy language and inflict the literature by and about refugees. Given these complexities of trauma narrativization, fragmented memory, and forgetting as a voluntary coping mechanism, how refugee fiction can offer a space to reconstruct past trauma, facilitate healing, and disrupt intergenerational trauma remains a warranted question.

This chapter examines Azareen Van Der Vliet Oloomi's *Call Me Zebra* (2018), Rawi Hage's *Cockroach* (2008), and Ava Homa's *Daughters of Smoke and Fire* (2020) addressing the impact of intergenerational trauma on descendants' well-being and how these narratives can serve as mechanisms of working through trauma and support resilience and resistance. It is argued that the refugee literary space constitutes a negotiated dynamic between textual narratives and past traumas. Furthermore, this space enables commonalities as emergent in the universal experience and rhetoric of trauma, displacement, and silence. This claim is evidenced by the novelists sharing some of the experiences of their respective protagonists in their childhood.

Alexander (2012) asserts that incidents "are not, in and of themselves, traumatic" (p. 8). Rather, they are characterized as traumatic by those affected, who articulate their pain. This requires a social process to define trauma, involving both the carrier groups (the collective agents) and the public. Narration is the primary tool for this process, carried out through various forms of discourse, such as political speeches, news articles, religious sermons, academic works, casual conversations, films, and literature. (Madigan, 2020, p. 46). Within these modes of discourses, literary and cultural productions mediate trauma and play a central role in distributing social understanding in a given interval. In this sense, a narrative constitutes a central means for refugees through which to discern transgenerational experiences for themselves and the public. That is, the narrative functions as "cultural remembrance" and, as Erll and Rigney (2006) note, literature is a mode of communication for cultural memories that contributes to how societies recall their past.

Arguably, putting the traumatic experience into a coherent logical language is nearly impossible as survivors cannot articulate and witness their own "lacuna" (Agamben, 1999, p. 38). However, as survivors' experiences illustrate, creative forms of retelling and narrative representations contribute to empowering survivors in the present, and allow them to depart from a constant search for past truth (Van der Kolk, 2014, p. 219; Jensen, 2019, p. 19; Kurvet-Käosaar, 2020, p. 311). In reference to the altered relationships to past and meaning, Jensen (2019) argues that articulating past experiences through "representative narratives, whether metaphoric or otherwise," contributes to healing and "enact a search for recognition, justice, and meaning" (p. 19). In exploring intergenerational trauma and collective memory, the three refugee novels this chapter presents highlight how past experiences continue to induce traumatic symptoms long after the incident and serve as a vehicle of cultural memory. Therefore, an analysis of representative literary works demonstrates how the narrativization of past silence indirectly marks the shared experiences of the present rather than disjoining them from the past. Subsequent generations, as Eyerman (2001) posits, reconstitute their collective identity through an engagement with the past to confront traumatic events. Eyerman (2001) premises that the representation of trauma "forms the primal scene in the process of collective identity" (p. 221).

As the past continues to be reimagined and reconstructed, the emphasis on the complex nexus of history, truth, memory, and representation becomes particularly pertinent to the understanding of intergenerational trauma. To that end, Hinton and O'Neill (2009) offer a thorough analysis of how individuals and society remember devastating events in the aftermath of genocide, focusing on how discourses about the monolithic "truth" and "representation" are reproduced. Within this context, Sanford's essay (2009) explicates the themes of forgetting and silencing the past, focusing on the government's hegemonic narrative. She (2009) contends that excavating the individual and collective memory in post-genocidal contexts constitutes a new political space contesting hegemonic metanarrative that "negates subaltern subjectivity and buttresses official histories of denial" (pp. 29–38).

Past/Present Dynamics and the Existential Anxiety in *Call Me Zebra*

Oloomi's much-lauded *Call Me Zebra* (2018) recounts the story of Zebra, a refugee from Iran who calls herself the last survivor in the line of anarchists, atheists, and autodidacts. As the Iran–Iraq War escalates, her parents escape from the traumatizing war to New York with 5-year-old Zebra. On their journey to New York, they experience hunger, poverty, death, fatigue, horror, and displacement. She witnesses the death of her mother when she is crushed under the wreckage of an abandoned house in search of food. After the death of her father, who taught her to love literature, she leaves New York for Barcelona in a quixotic search for the meaning of life, where she meets Ludovico Bembo, a displaced Italian.

The protagonist in this novel has an ill-fated origin; a history that is marked by war, death, mass murder, repression, and colonialism. Through the prism of memory and flashback narrative, Zebra, "a literary terrorist," is plunged into the reminiscence of her "voluble and troubled nation" (Oloomi, 2018, p. 5). She reflects on her father's monologue transcribed verbatim from memory upon her birth: "ill-omened child, I present you with the long and the short of our afflicted country, Iran: Supposed Land of the Aryans" (Oloomi, 2018, p. 4), where world conquerors compete over weak prey. Such a history – a repository of traumatic events – is passed among generations and to Zebra from her father through retelling and narrative. It is through a sequence of traumatic events – the murder of her great-grandfather, the failed Constitutional Revolution,[1] and the false narrative rendered as historical truth – that plunge Zebra into a world of existential anxiety and incomprehension. These historical traumas, as Caruth (1995) notes, suggest the collapse of straightforward understanding (p. 153).

As the novel proceeds, after World War II, Mohammad Reza Shah Pahlavi (1941–1979) who calls himself the "King of Kings" took the throne and began a set of reforms and policies toward the country's modernization. The narrator writes, "It was just a matter of time before the people rose against the King of Kings" (Oloomi, 2018, p. 6). Zebra was born only a few years after the "Revolution broke out," a terrifying period in which the King and the Islamic clergy spilled each other's blood[2] (Oloomi, 2018, p. 7). The Hosseini, as her father notes, were persecuted by both sides, the Pahlavi and Islamic clergy (Oloomi, 2018, p. 7). The narrative demonstrates how the memories of war and violence forge traumatic symptoms long after the events and extend a collective remembrance of "fear, guilt, avarice, grief, or remorse" (Oloomi, 2018, p. 7). As Zebra reflects, "like everyone else in this trifling universe, we Iranians are a sum of our sorry parts" (p. 7). The traumatized Zebra, as Caruth (1995) proposes, "carr[ies] an impossible history within them, or they become themselves the symptom of a history that they cannot entirely possess" (p. 5). History becomes the focal point of the conflict between past and present. While history is shown as a false narrative, Zebra embarks on a pilgrimage trying to subvert the official history and memory and thus expose "the artful manipulation of historical time through the creation of false narratives rendered as truth" (Oloomi, 2018, p. 6).

Oppressive ideological practices, within the political structure of both regimes, contribute to producing a space of untouched silences, adding layers of generational trauma to that of the ongoing individual trauma. These "silent events" (Parktal, 2012; Pennebaker & Banasik, 1997), "lacunae," and "frozen currents" (Menyhért, 2014, pp. 5–6) are "a series of unprocessed collective traumas in cultural memory that imposes cultural trauma upon individual traumas" (Menyhért, 2020, p. 247). While *time* is an important factor in working through trauma and reconstructing memories, the discourse of *space* is equally crucial to reshape and recover silent events, frozen and unspeakable recollections. In highlighting spatiality as inherently connected to memory, Sywenky (2015) remarks that the literary space of post-totalitarian states has the potential to reconstruct official history. The act of rereading memories of collective displacement from an intergenerational point of view becomes a reservoir for healing past trauma (p. 39). To that end, Zebra's father, a self-taught multilingual translator, plays the role of a powerful carrier of cultural memory. He reflects that Iran, as a contested site of power, memory, and ideological conflicts, "was no longer a place to think. Not even the Caspian was safe. We had to flee. We had to go into exile. We departed: numb, astonished, bewildered" (Oloomi, 2018, p. 10). The political and historical space of Iran represents an engendered site of collective trauma. The structural narrative of the novel illustrates how the space of frozen memory and deep silenced voices are connected to multiple spatial imaginations. Zebra seems to be caught in a triangle of dynamics of the past, the present, and the future. As a symbolic resolution, she undertakes a series of physical and metaphysical journeys, thus confronting and reconstructing "the New World" (Oloomi, 2018, p. 66). Since the narrator's childhood, her father[3] has taught her to love nothing except literature, "the only magnanimous host there is in this decaying world"

(Oloomi, 2018, p. 8), contesting the official narrative through literature and philosophical musing; memory becomes a space of belonging and preservation for Zebra where she can "survive the history's bloodshed" and a space to "share the truth of it with the world" (Oloomi, 2018, p. 8). She validates past generations as persecuted and repressed and foresees future generations being prosecuted for seeking truth. The fear of repression and loneliness is deeply ingrained in the collective memory of the Hossienis, affecting Zebra's generation. Researchers have rightly argued that the discourse of cultural memory cannot only be framed by trauma. As Huyssen (2003) notes, "to collapse memory into trauma . . . would unduly confine our understanding of memory, marking it too exclusively in terms of pain, suffering, and loss. It would deny human agency and lock us into compulsive repetition" (p. 8). Collective cultural memories can be reconstructed and transmitted through literary works that reshape the contour of metanarratives. Zebra reflects on the roles of memory and memorization in storytelling, concepts taught to her by her father. Her father left her a notebook with a note: "Ill-fated child, last of the Hosseinis! Add to history's pile of ruins the uselessness of our suffering" (Oloomi, 2018, p. 38). While the notebook suggests a new trajectory mapped by her father, Zebra engages in the process of producing a manifesto: a form of world-making and literary cartography. In doing so, she informs her mentor of her intention to compose a manifesto: "A Philosophy of Totality: The Matrix of Literature," which is Zebra's answer to Morales' question of whether methodologies serve a specific purpose. This is evidence she offers "through memorization" (Oloomi, 2018, p. 30). Furthermore, this can be connected to her prior reflections on the purpose of memorization and its twofold nature: reestablishing the literature's tradition of orality and preserving the repository of humanity from being lost (Oloomi, 2018, p. 11). Her notebooks appear as palimpsest text, allowing for rereading and rewriting the traces of the past. For Zebra, "memorization is [her] only recourse against loss" (Oloomi, 2018, p. 11). Zebra's introspective reflection challenges the official narratives in Iran and the world's hypocrisy. She finds refuge in literature to endure the world's cruel absurdities.

Raised in a culture of grief, displacement, and political turbulence, Zebra embarked on a "Grand Tour of Exile," leaving New York for Barcelona, Girona, and Albania, traveling across oceans to make sense of her world. She suffers from existential anxiety, the sense of being lost, and the urge to belong. She is compelled to narrate the story of her transcendental homelessness in which her life is centered around "the void of exile" (Oloomi, 2018, p. 282). Zebra's frequent references to the concept of "void" are of significance, suggesting a web without center, a blank page, an indefinite, and a world of incompleteness. Zebra muses:

> This incompleteness, this gap, was widened by the cruel facts of my life, its elusive calamity, the cultural assassination of my ancestors, the psychological massacre of exile, the physical and transcendental homelessness that has marked my life. But don't worry, I am an irregular genius who is in the process of synchronizing her multiple minds in order to acquire the privilege to rise in the morning and say *a great and coherent yes to life.*
> (emphasis in original, Oloomi, 2018, pp. 289–290)

Zebra exhibits a shattered-yet-fluid architecture of identity for which she aims to develop a navigational tool or a cognitive map that allows her to locate herself and represent the unrepresentable space of social totality. Influenced by Albert Camus's philosophy, Zebra muses over Camus's words:

> Everything is strange to me, everything, without a single person who belongs to me, with no place to heal this wound . . . I am not from here – not from anywhere else either. And the world has become merely an unknown landscape where my heart can lean on nothing.
>
> (Oloomi, 2018, p. 282)

As her Italian friend, Ludo, breaks up with her, she ponders if the Grand Tour of Exile faded away. However, her memory and philosophical musings, once a space of guidance, keep offering a new form of spatiality, and this time they are combined with "love" (Oloomi, 2018, p. 284). She reflects that "the Grand Tour of Exile has reproduced itself" (Oloomi, 2018, p. 287) and Zebra's previous declaration of her "antilove" is overshadowed by the hope that turns it into "the greatest key and the greatest riddle" (Oloomi, 2018, p. 292).

Oloomi's novel incorporates a variety of interactive forms, between various times and places – fictional, autobiographical, bildungsroman, historical, and testimonial narratives – suggesting the complex structure of intergenerational trauma that underlies the surface of the text. Oloomi employs an assemblage of experimental writing, with techniques of repetitions, brief fragments, philosophical musings and cultural references, and flashbacks to "reassess the past and to reinterpret the intertextual codes inscribed on personal consciousness by society and culture" (Henke, 1999, p. xv), a strategy which, it can be argued, equally repositions her character Zebra as an active subject to overcome her embittered past.

Although intergenerational trauma has created a devastating impact on Zebra's mind, including existential anxiety, voluminous loneliness, the feeling of being lost and eternally displaced, and alienation. Zebra weaves together the memories of her past to the present to confront the present world and search for the meaning of life. Therefore, the novel allows the reader to see how intergenerational trauma is mediated through cultural narratives linking collective memory to historical and spatial distances which contributes to a more global understanding of trauma against the representational incapability of public memories such as ceremonial events, museums, and monuments.

Rawi Hage's *Cockroach: Itineraries of Movement across Time, Space, Feeling, and Species*

Hage's novel, *Cockroach* (2008), is grounded in the bona fide experience of refugees and immigrants affected by civil war, pain, poverty, and non-belonging. *Cockroach* provides a fictional representation of intergenerational trauma, registered in the cultural memory of a generation whose past experiences continue to permeate today's existence. The novel portrays the story of a half-human narrator, who came to Montreal, from a war-torn city of, likely, Beirut around 1982. After being rescued by two police officers from a suicide attempt, he is required to go through a rehabilitation process, which includes attending weekly therapy sessions. Through his therapy treatments with Geneviève, an educated but naive psychotherapist, his memories of traumatic past experiences, including chaotic wars, the death of his sister for which he feels responsible, and parental neglect, are slowly disclosed. Later, he develops a romantic relationship with Shohreh, an Iranian refugee who had been raped, tortured, and imprisoned after the Iranian Revolution of 1979.

The Lebanese Civil War, which started in 1975, has caused a myriad of mental health problems among the inflicted population, including, but not limited to, depression, suicidal thoughts, and PTSD (Samara et al., 2020). In the absence of mental health funding, resources, and specialist staff in the Arab world, mental health problems are likely to continue with the next generation[4] (Okasha et al., 2012, pp. 52–54). Hage's protagonist in *Cockroach* is one of the victims of the postwar period in Lebanon, a historical and spatial duration that can be posited as a site of intergenerational collective trauma. As the plot unfolds and the narrator's past is revealed through flashbacks, the reader learns that he lived in a war-torn city during the Civil War, experiencing violence and tribalism. The murder of his sister by her husband, Tony, exacerbates his traumatic experiences. However, these experiences are "not restricted to his past or his homeland: his trauma is ongoing in Canada, aggravated by conditions of poverty, racism, and abjection, as well as the mechanisms of normalization and assimilation he is regularly subjected to" (Kraus, 2020, p. 109). The novel, in this sense, offers a narrative of spatiality, a category in which historical collective memory, place, and time constitute a conceptual framework to explore traumatic experiences.

The structure through which traumatic events underlie each chapter of the novel can be observed in the narrator's therapeutic discussions. The narrative structure corresponds to the spatial framework of each chapter in which past, present, and memories of old and new spaces are fused in the protagonist's mind. As Sakr (2019) argues:

> The old and the new spaces are simultaneously present in the narrator's consciousness, imaginatively and actually, contrapuntally orchestrating the two voices of trauma on a textual level whereby the place names in Beirut are silenced in the double act of forgetfulness and textual erasure while Montreal spaces are repeatedly named with a compulsive obsessive insistence.
>
> (p. 92)

In this spatial dichotomy, his memories are split between his home and the new setting of Montreal. His memory of home follows the paradigms of forgetting, absenting, or silencing: "I forget about my father, my mother, and the lightless nights I spent with my sister playing cards, dressing up toy soldiers" (Hage, 2008, p. 227). The narrator's desire to forget is articulated within such erased images, nameless places, and silenced words, suggesting collective amnesia. Some of his memories of home as a space of collective trauma are denied, thus representing a psychological escape. However, they continue to haunt his existence in Montreal. The narrator feels trapped and excluded between these spatial categories. In Montreal's cold world, his existence is split, blurring boundaries between human/non-human, reality/illusion, oppressed/oppressor, and inclusion/exclusion, belonging to neither yet existing in his consciousness. The narrator reflects:

> How can I explain all of this to Genevieve? How can I tell her that I do not want to be part of anything because I am afraid I will become an invader who would make little boys hunger, who would watch them die with an empty stomach? ... But how, how to exist and not to belong?
>
> (Hage, 2008, p. 210)

There is a significant shift here in that while Genevieve tries to recover his memories, the narrator's precarious situation becomes the focal point of his *raison d'être*. His frustration with Genevieve's lack of understanding encapsulates his profound sense of non-belonging and makes it impossible to be heard and seen. In this sense, the novel's textualized memories have an empowering potential to understand the complex layers of traumatic experiences anew and "provide hermeneutic resources not only for self-understanding but also for social change, in the struggle against traumatizing structural violence" (Meretoja, 2020, p. 31). As the novel unfolds, the only cultural and social community the narrator shares his stories of displacement and refugeehood is a group of his friends who are victims of violence and political turbulence of their home country – Shohreh, Reza, and Farhoud, all of whom embody a degree of shared identity and commonality. However, he sarcastically attacks and portrays other ignorant immigrants as the "Third World elite" who look upon themselves as "royalty when all they are is the residue of colonial power" (Hage, 2008, p. 159). He does not feel any affinity with the "filth of the planet" (Hage, 2008, p. 159). He is aware of his positionality in an environment where "filthy living spaces" coexist and he despises being involved with other forms of living species (Hage, 2008, p. 52). In his transformation into a cockroach, he is told by a giant insect who appears to him:

> You are one of us. You are part cockroach. But the worst part of it is that you are also human. ... Now go, and be human, but remember you are always welcome. You know how to find us. Just keep your eyes on what is going on down in the underground.
>
> (Hage, 2008, p. 203)

One of the key contentious moments of the traumatized narrator's life is marked by his transformation into a cockroach as he attempts to survive the abyssal history, racism, and poverty. The narrator's mutation into a cockroach suggests that the act of transformation is not only symptomatic of traumatizing socioeconomic conditions but is also a (logical–moral) resistance to his sense of being as he recounts that he is "split between two planes and aware of two existences, and they were both mine. I belong to two spaces, I thought, and I am wrapped in one sheet" (Hage,

2008, p. 119). Living under such an anxiety-inducing circumstance results in his acting abnormally. The above passage marks a post-traumatic/schizophrenic framework caused by the hard-hitting impacts of various social, political, economic, and cultural discourses from which he, as a refugee, is excluded (Libin, 2013; Molnár, 2019; Sakr, 2019; Forget, 2019). The spatiality and temporality of the giant cockroach's existence,[5] although ambiguous, projects a "new-yet-uncanny" condition. In this new spatial geography, the narrator is presented with a pathway imbued with a feeling of empathy and inclusion. Although his sense of unhomeliness causes some sort of disorientation, confusion, and loss, he realizes that living in such a spatial heterogeneity – which includes home (Lebanon), Montreal, and the transnational underground life with its distinct sociopolitical relations – marks his liminal position where different narratives of past, present, and future are simultaneously reproduced and blurred.

The figure of the cockroach in the body of a narrator remains inaccessible, incomprehensible, and mysterious as he reminds himself that "I can escape anything. I am a master of escape and . . . the master of underground" (Hage, 2008, p. 23). Like Zebra's reflections in *Call Me Zebra*, the narrator's private introspection on the notion of escape in *Cockroach* can be linked to past experiences that underlie intergenerational trauma passed on to him through his childhood and collective historical memory: "as a kid, I escaped when my mother cried, when my father unbuckled his belt, when my teacher lifted the ruler high above my little palm" (Hage, 2008, p. 23). The trope of "escape" constitutes a strategic vehicle for the narrator to find a refuge from the brutality of the external world, to resist the silencing of collective memories and search for the meaning of life. The escape narrative appears as a key component of forgetting policies by shaping the itineraries of movement across time, space, feeling, and species. As such, the novel not only investigates the relationship between collective historical traumas and spatiality but also explores the capacity of narrative agency in articulating traumatic experiences that are inaccessible. As Libin (2013) concludes, Hage's novel caters to a gateway from personal trauma to national trauma and beyond that transcends historical and geographical boundaries (p. 78). Hage's fictional exploration of historical, intergenerational, and personal traumatic experiences is an attempt to enlarge our understanding of narrative trauma as a significant site of reflection.[6]

Decolonizing the Past and Universal Belonging in *Daughters of Smoke and Fire*

Ava Homa's debut novel *Daughters of Smoke and Fire* (2020) chronicles intergenerational trauma inflicted on the collective Kurdish psyche. For centuries, the Kurds have been subjected to genocide, uprootedness, and oppression across borders, spaces, and cultures for which the novel's focus spans the last half of the century specifically. Leila, a Kurdish woman, dreams of becoming a filmmaker to spotlight Kurdish oppression internationally while searching for her brother, Chia, an aspiring human rights lawyer motivated by their father's quest for justice. Leila's search for Chia becomes her focus amid her own uncertain future. To that end, the novel showcases how intergenerational trauma persists through the protagonist's parental trauma and the power differential perpetuated by the state's policies in Kurdistan. The locus of the characters' trauma stems from their "struggle" to reconnect to their origins and construct their identities against the insecurity of the present (Tancke, 2011, p. 1).

At the beginning of the prologue, Leila appears as "a woman alone on a mountain at dusk" (Homa, 2020, p. xiii), an unknown helpless woman contemplating suicide. However, this invisible figure brings the reader's attention to her anguish, loathing, and the desire of burning down all the injustice she has suffered shouting, "*basa bas*" translating to "It's enough. Enough" (Homa, 2020, p. xiii). The prologue introduces the struggles of marginalized subjects like Leila, who find it hard to narrate their anguish and invisibility. At 5, Leila sees a nightmarish TV scene that ties her to decades of generational trauma: "Saddam Hussein gassed Halabja this morning. Within a few minutes, five thousand Kurdish civilians died in an aerial bombardment of mustard gas and nerve agents" (Homa, 2020, p. 9). While witnessing bodies "collapsed on the outskirts of town, trying to cross the mountains running to imagined safety" (Homa, 2020, p. 10), Leila breaks down to a desperate shivering. As a witness to a historical catastrophe, such a traumatic scene triggers deep trauma in her psyche and connects her to memories of the past as well as future silences that await her.

Far from its expeditious physical annihilation, the legacy of the genocidal Anfal campaign[7] characterizes a psychic postgenerational legacy of war trauma. This genocidal campaign culminated in the massacre of thousands of civilians, the extensive destruction of the Kurdish rural spaces, and, subsequently, forced displacement (Bozarslan et al., 2021, p. 8). Leila's father was among the survivors of the genocidal policies that forced many to escape Southern Kurdistan in Iraq (Homa, 2020, p. 109). Some refugees were herded into resettlement camps, while others were hosted by Kurdish families in Iran (Homa, 2020, p. 45). Leila's exposure to this traumatic genocide is witnessed secondarily and substantially transmitted through her father's silenced past. As she grows up, the connection between history and present trauma becomes visible to Leila. She witnesses her father's chronic depression and lack of support after his release from the Evin prison. Her mother's neglect furthers her traumatic upbringing. Specifically, the manifestation of intergenerational trauma is also inherent in children's given names during and after the Anfal. The naming system signifies a sociocultural relation with the spatial–temporal boundaries. Leila reflects: "Baba had wanted to name me Nishtman, Kurdish for homeland" (Homa, 2020, p. 16). But since *Nishtman* was on the list of forbidden names by the government, Leila became her name. Moreover, Chia means *mountain* and Shiler stands for a *Fritillaria imperialis*, that is, the *Crown Imperial*. These types of names resonate human–ecology relations that embody not only sociocultural, historical, and psychological implications, but the desire for peace, harmony, and recognition of the Kurds.[8] As a teenager, Leila's Kurdish identity made her a refugee and an outsider in the Agambenian sense. (1998). As the novel unfolds, Leila and Chia realize their Kurdish identity has been altered by a contested political environment. Kurdistan exemplifies "the state of exception" in the modern political system (Agamben, 1998). The state's policies toward such spatial territory is to create an extrajudicial space to expel, subjugate, and dominate Kurdish subjects (Soleimani & Mohammadpour, 2020, p. 664). According to the UNHCR Annual Report (2024), Iranian Kurds, among other ethnic minorities, remain one of the most suppressed groups in the country, with individuals persecuted, arrested, and sentenced to death for their political affiliation or belief (p. 10).

One example of these policies involves educational institution's reshaping of history by altering the narrative surrounding Kurdish history and enforcing the new history with "official agent[s] of the government" whose responsibility was to report non-compliant students and teachers (Homa, 2020, p. 26). In her country, Leila exemplifies the figure of *homo sacer* whose social and political life have been stripped away as the result of unequal political, economic, and cultural relations perpetuated by the state's policies in Kurdistan (see Agamben, 1998; Soleimani & Mohammadpour, 2020). Having been impacted by policies of assimilation and control, Leila remembers the prevailing horror Chia faces at school as follows: "at a young age, our alienation from Kurdish history and literature from our roots, identity, and inevitably our parents began, escalating with each year that passed" (Homa, 2020, p. 24). Leila's confrontation with this reality is shaped by educational policies that push her further into shame, guilt, and disappointment. This is evident in her failure to enter university and enhance her interpersonal relations, while Chia is enrolled in political science at the University of Tehran.

The difficulties and contradictions that the characters encounter during their lives deepen the psychological repercussions within society as narrated by Chia that "the intentional underdevelopment in our region creates economic marginalization that severely inhibits us from participating in Iranian public life" (Homa, 2020, p. 70). Traumatic experiences, such as marginalization, deprivation from learning their mother tongue, and rejection from "mid- and high-level government post[s]" (Homa, 2020, p. 69), shape their trauma within society and connect the children to a long history of exclusion, collective suffering, and denial of basic rights. Chia's palpable awareness of this circumstance suffuses his testimonial activist writings. As the novel unfolds, we are taken back to the scene of "a woman alone on a mountain at dusk" (Homa, 2020, p. xiii) where Leila escapes from one of the significant traumatic episodes of her life, when her mother "was too immersed in carnal joy to notice her daughter" (Homa, 2020, p. 91). Dressed in red lingerie, Leila's mother "was indeed talking lovingly. To a naked woman's tiny penis" (Homa, 2020, p. 91), which prompted Leila to run away to the mountain. This triggers Leila's blurred memories of the chant-like voice of her mother late at night over the phone. Such a traumatic episode profoundly saddens her and pushes her toward attempted suicide. The aftermath of the event is depicted as unnarratable, and the painful scene takes the reader to the hospital. Leila's relationship with her father becomes strained in the hospital when the skeptical father who feels betrayed accuses her of being a whore. Her mother, on the other hand, only thinks of the potential damage to Leila's virginity. Such maladaptive parenting and domestic violence add to Leila's anguished psyche, raising questions about society's ethics, truth, responsibility, and memory.

Trauma fiction is often associated with temporal jumps and sudden interruptions in space and time. The novel's experimental narrative technique emanates from such an interruption that problematizes linear temporality. The aftermath of the affair is specifically marked by such a disruption in time and place. Relocation to Tehran seems to be a coping mechanism and a crucial step for Leila to alleviate the embittered relationship with life, meaning, body, and justice. Leila's access to mental health support in Tehran allows her to acknowledge her conflicting feelings. She begins "sessions with a therapist, who had explained that Mama's narcissism and Baba's chronic depression meant they hadn't deliberately . . . damaged [her]" (Homa, 2020, p. 131). She then reflects that trauma "was a Kurdish heritage, passed down through generations" (Homa, 2020, p. 131). She also finds herself a source of income and joy in an independent bookstore where she pursues her long yearning to make films "to tell our stories" (Homa, 2020, p. 40). Leila's attachment to classic books and movies stems from "extracting meaning from them" (da Silva et al., 2016, p. 29). Leila and Chia inherit the desire to piece together the puzzle of their fragmented past, absences, and repressed silences passed down by older generations. Chia's activism, driven by his pursuit of justice and law career aspirations, leads to his incarceration and eventual disappearance.

The author's experimental narrative reconstructs parallel memories of resistance and resilience. After Chia's incarceration, Leila attempts to navigate her intertwined suffering of past and present using Chia's journal entries, diary, poems, and letters (Homa, 2020, p. 176). With the help of her friend, Shiler, who chose to become a Peshmerga,[9] they spread "Chia's words" to prove his innocence. Shiler once warned her that "you'll be the first culprit in their eyes if his writings go viral" (Homa, 2020, p. 175). Although partially successful in drawing international attention, this increased anxiety and danger as Leila reluctantly agrees to marry Karo, their friend arrested with Chia, so they can move to Canada. Leila's displacement furthers her uprootedness and unbelonging to her country; however, this provides her with a cosmopolitan identity that serves as a universal diasporic belonging. She reflects, "I lifted my face and palms to the sky. I wasn't alone, I saw them. People in Rwanda, Bosnia, plantations, and indigenous residential schools in North America were standing shoulder to shoulder with the Kurds" (Homa, 2020, p. 173). The novel constitutes a continuous dialogue between textual narratives and trauma events embedded in collective memory. Homa deconstructs and decolonizes the official narrative of history to recontextualize the repressed voices and memories of the victims of the totalitarian state. Such decolonization and reconstruction dynamics further suggest a healing practice from the past trauma that Homa inherited. She sees transformation in turning anguish, loss, and rejection into narrative agency and self-expression in a world where she is no longer alone but belongs to other communities with their fair share of trauma. This is evident toward the end of the novel where Leila's film challenges the stereotypical image of Kurds as "victim" and "persecuted." They are now "presented as champions" after their fight against ISIS (Homa, 2020, p. 297). Leila's media narrative reconstructs the voices and memories of the oppressed, holding the potential to generate a universal collective understanding (Bond & Craps, 2020, p. 11).

Conclusion

The refugee literary space negotiates between the hegemonic narrative of the past silences and new social construction that informs new trajectories in recovering the narrative agency and self-expression. Such a literary discourse, as demonstrated in the three representative refugee fictions, weaves together not only personal memory but also that of transnational communities, providing them with a universal diasporic identity and belonging. Despite the politics of forgetting as manifested in various forms of escape, oppression, disruption, and silence, the presented novels highlight the way that temporal and spatial heterogeneity prompts simultaneous different memories which, in turn, necessitate distinct narratives.

In this sense, Zebra's experience of intergenerational trauma is thus manifested in her fractured identity with a sense of existential anxiety and incomprehension. As part of her intergenerational identity formation, she carries an unpossessed history along the present time to register the world. Zebra finds narratives as a space of universal belonging to share and reconstruct the official narrative. Similarly, the narrator's memory in *Cockroach* lies in the paradigms of forgetting, absenting, or silencing which pushes him into spatial categories of past and present. Frustration, lack of positionality, and unhomeliness, among others, mark his liminal position in a way that he forms an escape narrative across time, space, feeling, and species. Finally, Leila's parental trauma and the power differential maintained by the state's policies leave a powerful impact on Leila's consciousness that connects her belonging to a long history of exclusion, collective suffering, and denial of basic rights. Despite the complexity of trauma representation, silenced past, and incoherent narratives, refugee fiction, while occupying an interstitial space between local and global, offers a space to reshape and reconstruct past trauma, thus contributing to the healing process of the protagonists' experiences of intergenerational trauma.

Notes

1 The Constitutional Revolution of Iran between 1905 and 1911 led to the establishment of a parliament during the Qajar dynasty.
2 However, the uprising against the Shah's authoritarian regime was not just simply a power struggle between the Islamic clergy and the state's forces. What led to the revolution encompassed a complex network of relations, including social class, race, gender and so forth. For further information, see Axworthy (2013).
3 Zebra's father has been often referred to as the Autodidact, Anarchist, and Atheist.
4 This is particularly evident in the Arab war-inflicted countries which struggle for political, social, and economic stability.
5 On the discursive representation of trauma, Hage (2011) notes "I used a despicable insect as a metaphor for the ever-resilient mover for whom the architecture of human boundaries is nothing more than a stroll through the pipes and the underground, whose closeness to the ground mocks the idea of an afterlife, a being who defies upward mobility and its clouds of rewards" (p. 235).
6 By the end of the novel, the narrator finds himself in a liminal position, split between different worlds, human and non-human regarding his transformation into a cockroach. However, the traumatized narrator overcomes his apolitical character by murdering Shaheed, the Iranian diplomat and rapist, in retaliation for his beloved Shohreh.

7 An operation led by Iraq's Ba'athist regime aiming at ethnic cleansing of the Iraqi Kurds beginning in the 1960s,
8 For more information, see A. M. S. Haji and L. K. Barany (2023).
9 The Peshmerga refers to the Kurdish military forces who are responsible for the security and protection of the Kurdish people.

References

Agamben, G. (1998). *Homo Sacer: Sovereign Power and Bare Life*. Redwood City, CA: Stanford University Press.
Agamben, G. (1999). *Remnants of Auschwitz: The Witness and The Archive*. Brooklyn, NY. Zone Books.
Alexander, J. C. (2012). *Trauma: A Social Theory*. Cambridge: Polity.
Axworthy, M. (2013). *Revolutionary Iran : A History of the Islamic Republic*. Oxford: Oxford University Press.
Bhabha, H. (1994). *The Location of Culture*. London, New York: Routledge.
Bond, L., & Craps, S. (2020). *Trauma*. London; New York: Routledge.
Bozarslan, H., Gunes, C., & Yadirgi, V. (2021). *The Cambridge History of the Kurds*. Cambridge: Cambridge University Press.
Caruth, C. (1995). Recapturing the Past: Introduction. In C. Caruth (ed.), *Trauma: Explorations in Memory* (pp. 3–12). Baltimore, MD: The Johns Hopkins University Press.
da Silva, T. L. G., Donat, J. C., Lorenzonni, P. L., de Souza, L. K., Gauer, G., & Kristensen, C. H. (2016). Event Centrality in Trauma and PTSD: Relations Between Event Relevance and Posttraumatic Symptoms. *Psicologia: Reflexão e Crítica:* [Psychology: Research and Review], *29*(1), 1–7.
Deckard, S., & Shapiro, S. (2019). *World Literature, Neoliberalism, and the Culture of Discontent*. Berlin: Springer International Publishing.
Dimitry L. (2012) A Systematic Review on the Mental Health of Children and Adolescents in Areas of Armed Conflict in the Middle East. *Childcare Health & Development*, *38*(2), 153–161. https://doi.org/10.1111/j.1365-2214.2011.01246.x
Ellis, B. H., Winer, J. P., Murray, K., & Barrett, C. (2019). Understanding the Mental Health of Refugees: Trauma, Stress, and the Cultural Context. In R. Parekh, & N. H. T. Trinh (Eds.), *The Massachusetts General Hospital Textbook on Diversity and Cultural Sensitivity in Mental Health* (pp. 253–273). Humana, Cham: Springer. https://doi.org/10.1007/978-3-030-20174-6_13
Erll, A., & Rigney, A. (2006). Literature and the Production of Cultural Memory: Introduction. *European Journal of English Studies*, *10*(2), 111–15.
Eyerman, R. (2001). *Cultural Trauma: Slavery and the Formation of African American Identity*. Cambridge: Cambridge University Press.
Forget, A. (2019). The Vengeful Refugee: Justice and Violence in Cockroach. In K. Majer (Ed.), *Beirut to Carnival City: Reading Rawi Hage* (pp. 103–119). Leiden: Brill.
Hage, R. (2008). *Cockroach*. Toronto: Anansi.
Hage, R. (2011). On the Weight of Separation and the Lightness of Non-Belonging. In J. Bland, (Ed.), *Finding the Words: Writers on Inspiration, Desire, War, Celebrity, Exile, and Breaking the Rules* (pp. 227–235). Toronto: McLelland & Stewart.
Haji, A. M. S., & Barany, L. K. (2023). Kurdish Personal Names and Identity: How the Kurds Think of Their Personal Names. *Journal of Duhok University*, *26*(1), 1–17.
Henke, S. (1999). *Shattered Subjects: Trauma and Testimony in Women's Life Writing*, Basingstoke: Palgrave Macmillan.
Hinton, A. L., & O'Neill, K. L. (2009). *Genocide: Truth, Memory, and Representation*. Durham, NC: Duke University Press.
Hirsch, M. (2001). Surviving Images: Holocaust Photographs and the Work of Postmemory. *The Yale Journal of Criticism*, *14*, 5–37.

Homa, A. (2020). *Daughters of Smoke and Fire: A Novel*. New York, NY: Harper Perennial.
Huyssen, A. (2003). *Present Pasts: Urban Palimpsests and the Politics of Memory*. Redwood City, CA: Stanford University Press.
Jensen, M. (2019). *The Art and Science of Trauma and the Autobiographical: Negotiated Truths*. Basingstoke: Palgrave Macmillan.
Kraus, B. (2020). The Roach's Revenge: Suicide and Survival in Rawi Hage's. *Cockroach. ARIEL: A Review of International English Literature*, *51*(1), 105–129.
Kurvet-Käosaar, L. (2020). Trauma and Life-Writing. In C. Davis, & H. Meretoja, (Eds.), *The Routledge Companion to Literature and Trauma* (pp. 305–316). London, New York: Routledge.
Libin, M. (2013). Marking Territory: Rawi Hage's Novels and the Challenge to Postcolonial Ethics. *English Studies in Canada*, *39*(4), 71–90.
Madigan, T. (2020). Theories of Cultural Trauma. In C. Davis, & H. Meretoja, (Eds.), *The Routledge Companion to Literature and Trauma* (pp. 45–53). London, New York Routledge.
Menyhért, A. (2014). Introduction. In A. Menyhért, B. Györe, & G. Szabolcsi (Eds.), *Trauma, Gender, Irodalom. A társadalmi nemi szerepek jelentősége a traumatikus tapasztalatok irodalmi értelmezésében* [*Trauma, Gender, Literature. The Importance of Social Gender Roles in the Literary Interpretation of Traumatic Experiences*] (pp. 5–6). Budapest: ELTE Eötvös Publishers.
Menyhért, A. (2020). Trauma Studies in the Digital Age. In C. Davis, & H. Meretoja (Eds.), *The Routledge Companion to Literature and Trauma* (p. 247). London, New York: Taylor & Francis.
Meretoja, H. (2020). Philosophies of Trauma. In C. Davis, & H. Meretoja, (Eds.), *The Routledge Companion to Literature and Trauma* (pp. 23–35). London, New York: Taylor & Francis.
Molnár, J. (2019). The Psycho-Spatial Continuum in Cockroach. In K. Majer (Ed.), *Beirut to Carnival City: Reading Rawi Hage* (pp. 74–84). Leiden: Brill. https://doi.org/10.1163/9789004417304_006
Okasha A., Karam E., & Okasha T. (2012). Mental Health Services in the Arab World. *World Psychiatry*, *11*, 52–54. https://doi.org/10.1016/j.wpsyc.2012.01.008 pmid: 22295010
Parktal, A. (2012). Lost Chances and Prosperous Present? The Traumatic Past and Estonian Life Today. *Journal of Loss and Trauma*, *17*(4), 350–357.
Pennebaker, J.W., & Banasik, B.L. (1997). On the Creation and Maintenance of Collective Memories: History as Social Psychology. In J.W. Penebaker, D. Paez, & B. Rimé (Eds), *Collective Memory of Political Events: Social Psychological Perspectives* (pp. 3–19). Mahwah, NJ: Erlbaum.
Sakr, R. (2019). Heterotopia and Its Discontents: Exploring Spatial, Social, and Textual Liminality in Rawi Hage's Cockroach. In R. Rimstead, & D. Beneventi (Eds.), *Contested Spaces, Counter-narratives, and Culture from Below in Canada and Québec* (pp. 88–106). Toronto: University of Toronto Press.
Samara, M., Hammuda, S., Vostanis, P., El-Khodary, B., & Al-Dewik, N.I. (2020). Children's Prolonged Exposure to the Toxic Stress of War Trauma in the Middle East. *The British Medical Journal*, *371*, 1–6. https://doi.org/10.1136/bmj.m3155
Sanford, V. (2009), What is an Anthropology of Genocide? In A.L. Hinton, & K.L. O'Neill (Eds.), *Genocide: Truth, Memory, and Representation* (pp. 29–53). Durham, NC: Duke University Press.
Soleimani, K., & Mohammadpour, A. (2020). The Securitisation of Life: Eastern Kurdistan under the Rule of a Perso-Shi'i State. *Third World Quarterly*, *41*(4), 663–682.
Sywenky, I. (2015). Memories of Displacement and Unhomely Spaces: History, Trauma and the Politics of Spatial Imagination in Ukraine and Poland. In S. Mitroiu (Ed.), *Life Writing and Politics of Memory in Eastern Europe* (pp. 25–44). London: Palgrave Macmillan.

Tancke, U. (2011). "Original Traumas": Narrating Migrant Identity in British Muslim Women's Writing. *Postcolonial Text*, *6*(2), 1–15.
UN Human Rights Council. (2024). *Report of the Special Rapporteur on the Situation of Human Rights in the Islamic Republic of Iran*. Retrieved June 10, 2024, from www.ohchr.org/en/documents/country-reports/ahrc5562-situation-human-rights-islamic-republic-iran-report-special.
Van der Kolk, B. (2014). *The Body Keeps the Score: Brain, Mind, and Body in the Healing of Trauma*. New York, NY: Penguin.
Van der Vliet Oloomi, A. (2018). *Call Me Zebra*. Boston, MA: Houghton Mifflin Harcourt.

3 Intergenerational Transmission of Traumatic Experiences among Palestinian Refugees

Fayez Mahamid and Dana Bdier

Introduction

Trauma-related disorders with distressing or disabling effects on one's personality and social interactions can be caused not only by directly experiencing or witnessing a traumatic event but also by indirect exposure through relating or communicating with the victims. Phrases such as trauma transmission and indirect-, unconscious-, secondary-, or empathic-traumatization have been used to describe the phenomenon (Karenian et al., 2011). Moreover, trauma can be transmitted either at a personal or collective level and frequently cross-generationally (Mindiashvili & Kutsia, 2021).

Global conflicts and mass violence have forced millions to leave their homeland and seek refuge in new communities across the world, marking their group consciousness forever. In post-migration settings, refugees attempt to create narratives that allow them to make sense of the past as they adjust to life and negotiate places of safety and growth, both within their own exiled communities and in their new host communities, and these narratives in turn often transmit trauma over generations (Matos et al., 2021).

Palestinians of all ages who live in refugee camps in Palestine or in neighboring countries have grown up with a national narrative of collective trauma. They face daily violence, lack of security, fighting, and find themselves to be refugees behind closed borders after the Palestinian catastrophe Nakba[1] (see Figure 3.1). Until now, many of the families in refugee camps in Lebanon, Jordan, Syria, the West Bank, and Gaza Strip hold on to the keys of their long-lost past after 75 years of refugee experience and migration and three generations later (Mahamid, 2020).

Focusing on the unique characteristics of Palestinian refugees can offer a more nuanced perspective when addressing the transmission of trauma among Palestinian communities. Collectiveness is an important and central characteristic of Palestinian society and culture; Palestinian individuals possess collective selves as their mental health and adjustment are highly dependent on their societies and family's approval and support. Given these socioeconomic and ethnocultural characteristics, examining collective trauma among Palestinian refugees offers a perspective different but complementary to the experiences of other racial, ethnic, and cultural groups who have gone through similar experiences.

DOI: 10.4324/9781003385820-4

Figure 3.1 First generation of Palestinian refugees during Nakba (Abdallah, 2009).

Background and Context

Toward the end of 1948, the land known to the world as Palestine was split into three geopolitical units: one being the newly formed state of Israel, while the other two remaining lands of Palestine were labeled as the West Bank and the Gaza Strip. This contentious division of land and the forcible expulsion of Palestinians from areas seized by Israel in 1948 is known to all Palestinians as the catastrophe Nakba and is a label which remains in use today. The devastation of the Nakba is both singular and continuous, as it impacted and continues to affect the way Palestinians react to their surroundings, how they carry out normal everyday activities, and how they function as a nation (Veronese et al., 2019).

The Nakba also constituted a founding event for the Palestinian refugees. It shattered their long-lived societal and political structures, rendering more than half of Palestinians penniless and denying their sources of living – most significantly their land. Nakba undermined individual and collective identities, and created new sub-identities (Lentin, 2013). Many Palestinians experienced a profound sense of guilt and shame for failing to prevent the loss of their homes and land, and the concomitant sense of dignity, security, and belonging (Wolfe, 2012). Their sense of self-efficacy as Arabs and Palestinians was damaged (Peled, 2016).

After Nakba, many of the forcibly displaced Palestinians resettled in camps as provisional small towns of tents, erected in a hurry, to give shelter to around 470,000 individuals, including those displaced in Palestine and those who fled and resettled in neighboring countries such as Lebanon, Syria, and Jordan (see Figure 3.2). Of those 470,000 forcibly displaced Palestinians, 280,000 refugees settled in the western region, including the east Jerusalem area, and about 190,000 people fled to the Gaza region. Between 1953 and 1955 alone, 8 large and stable living areas for those who were displaced were built in the Gaza region and 20 in the West Bank and Jerusalem region. These became stable camps with small houses, one to two rooms, and small streets. In 1967 when Israel occupied Golan,

Figure 3.2 Early refugee camp in the mid-1950s (Abdallah, 2009).

Sinai, West bank, and Gaza, approximately 325,000 Palestinians again fled out of the country to resettle in Jordan (Salem et al., 2020).

Today, Palestinians are the largest refugee population in the world with high prevalence of war-related trauma (Altawil et al., 2023). The horrors of war-related trauma impact both mind and body and supersede the dimensions of time, feelings of belonging, and personal safety (Mahamid et al., 2023). Nonetheless, empirical research and clinical observations have shown that consequences related to witnessing traumatic war events are not bound to the persons being immediately exposed to the event, but by also witnessing the lasting effects on significant others in their surroundings such as family, friends, and caregivers (Davidson & Mellor, 2001; Van Ijzendoorn et al., 2003). This phenomenon, as is described primarily by psychological research literature, has been described by a variety of terms, such as transgenerational trauma, intergenerational trauma, trans-generative trauma, and traumatic countertransference (Veronese et al., 2022).

Because the Nakba shattered Palestinians' expectations of history, time was frozen at the moment of loss and suspended until the inevitable restoration of the normal as perceived by the Palestinians. Hence, although the Nakba has, since the 1960s, been a foundational experience in the narrative of Palestinian national revival, the latter's overwhelming political objectives precluded coping with the painful aspects the Nakba exposed, such as the Palestinians' helplessness, which kept burying its traumatic core in the Palestinian collective memory (Sa'di, 2002).

Several studies (Mahamid, 2020; Veronese et al., 2021; Giacaman et al., 2011) have shown the effect of trauma on both individuals and large groups in the Palestinian context. Trauma at the collective level becomes known as "chosen trauma." The word "chosen" is not seen as self-election, but as a collective and unconscious connection between members of the larger group. The trauma within the large group, along with the trauma sufferers and those who have had the trauma passed onto them, are seen to comprise whole generations, rather than the generational distinctions within one family (Mahamid & Berte, 2020b). Collective trauma can be understood to be a radical change, such that the individuals cannot immediately resolve the pre-traumatic and post-traumatic dimensions of identity (Aydin, 2017).

A recent study by Mahamid (2020) focusing on refugee children in Palestinian camps in the West Bank of Palestine explored collective trauma among the third generation of Palestinian refugees' children. Findings revealed that children in today's Palestinian camps suffer from collective trauma, and they consider the 1948 Nakba as a "losing" experience that has affected all generations of Palestinian refugees. An investigation by Abu el Hija (2018) sought to explore the relationship between the effects of war-related trauma that second-generation Palestinians were exposed to and the trauma experienced by first-generation Palestinian refugees during the Nakba. The results support a significant positive correlation between the traumatic experiences of first-generation parents and the transmission of the Nakba trauma to the second generation. Additionally, it was found that the Nakba trauma and negative worldview beliefs toward the second generation of Palestinians negatively impacted their mental health and cultivated feelings of revenge and anger. As stated in multiple studies (Kellermann, 2001; Punamäki, 2001; Amir & Lev-Wiesel, 2001), it is common to see such transmitted trauma as both having an immediate influence on the mental health of individuals and establishing more long-term mental health effects. Such experiences leave individuals with an overwhelming sense of helplessness and loss of control due to feeling unsafe and horrified (Mahamid & Berte, 2020b).

Theories of Trauma Transmission and Palestinian Refugees

Several theoretical frameworks are useful in explaining the link between trauma experienced by one generation and the way it affects the next generation. The field of trauma transmission has long been influenced by psychoanalytically oriented theories connecting emotions to conscious. According to these theories, emotions that could not be consciously experienced by the first generation of Palestinian refugees would appear in the children of the second generation by unconsciously absorbing the repressed and insufficiently worked-through Nakba experiences of survivor parents (Kellermann, 2001).

According to attachment theory, psychological transmission of trauma refers to the multiplicity of bonds between a caregiver and child as a means of signaling contentment and distress, and requires both the caregiver and child to engage fully in a system of psychological resonance which tends to become a more natural interaction as the child grows older (Mahamid & Veronese, 2021). Palestinian refugee children who experience psychological transmission of trauma often develop a conscious understanding of the events which initiated the initial trauma. The unconscious effects of trauma are related to people's ability to release tension or move forward after negative experiences which in turn affects how the brain handles the situations that follow. This suggests that when individuals experience insecurity and distress in early life, the brain stores their responses and once they find themselves in similar situations again, their brain triggers the same initial response learned early on in life (Hopper, 2003). Unconscious effects, however, persist, and are accompanied by unconscious obligations such as extreme self-protection and survival strategies transmitted to them by their parents, but they exist juxtaposed with the conscious understanding (Mahamid & Berte, 2020a).

The family systems and communications models of trauma transmission focused on conscious and unconscious transmission of parental traumatization. These transmissions almost always take place in a family environment, which is assumed to present a major impact on the children. Though families who are survivors of the Nakba certainly differ from one another in many ways, the more pathological families describe themselves as "tight little islands," whereby children only interact with immediate family members and other survivors (Milshtein, 2009). In such close quarters, parents are fully committed to their children and children are overly concerned with their parents' welfare, each trying to shield the other from painful experiences (Strazzari & Tholens, 2010). Through mutual identifications, parents live vicariously through their children, and children live vicariously in the horrific past of their parents. Considering these powerful family dynamics, it is not surprising that problems related to individuation and separation (Sayigh, 2020) and attachment (Banat et al., 2018) among parents are often observed among children.

The modulated disclosure and unfiltered speech model refer to a child-centered communication strategy in which first-generation adult parents' talk to their children about their traumatic experiences from the past using age-appropriate language that is sensitive to the child's emotional needs (Johnston, 2006). Unfiltered speech refers to the situation in which there is incongruence between the story lived and the story told, whereby parents are unaware that their own implicit communication about the past and their symptoms of trauma create discrepancies between what the parents think the child knows and what the child actually knows (Dalgaard et al., 2016). This could explain the collective memory of trauma in narratives of third and fourth generations of refugees.

Mental Health Issues among Palestinian Refugees

Mental health problems are common among Palestinian refugee populations, exacerbated by living situations, the impact of forced migration, poverty, discrimination, and social exclusion (Yassin, 2018). The psychological effects associated with experiences of daily life in refugee camps can enhance feelings of helplessness, grief, anxiety, depression, somatization, shame, anger, shattered assumptions, sensitivity to injustice, and survivor guilt. Feelings of extreme isolation, humiliation, and immense loss are also common among Palestinian refugees. Some feelings among refugees may become existential as it relates to the loss of loved ones, the homeland, culture, identity, hope, trust, meaning in life, and faith in a justified world (Thabet et al., 2017).

Several studies report mental health problems among Palestinian refugees. Alduraidi and Waters (2018) explored perceived health and depressive symptom severity in Palestinian refugees. Results showed that 43% of participants had moderate to severe depressive symptoms, 42% lived in poverty, and 20% had fair or poor health. Thabet et al. (2016) investigated mental health problems and family coping strategies among Palestinians refugees in the Gaza Strip, and found that 52.6% had anxiety and 50.6% had depression. Females scored higher on anxiety and depression levels than males. Palestinian refugee children were found to be at greater risk for mental disorders and psychosomatic complaints as evidenced by Wilson et al. (2021) who examined psychological distresses among 106 Palestinian refugee children aged 11–17 in the West Bank, as compared to children living in non-conflict affected settings. Studies such as these suggest that Palestinian refugees suffer from high levels of psychological trauma and distress compared with other refugee populations (see Figure 3.3).

Figure 3.3 Hope for the future in a drawing of a child from Jabalina refugee camp in Gaza Strip (UNRWA, 2016).

Coping Strategies and Implications

Coping reflects the broad process of an individual's ability for self-regulation when it comes to emotions, behaviors, cognition, physiology, and environment (Thabet et al., 2017). The coping mechanism of Palestinian refugees in the face of collective trauma is influenced by their social networks and the intricate dynamics they ascribe to those relationships. Social support and networks play a pivotal role as they provide individuals with diverse information. This information promotes the belief that others genuinely love and care for them, instills a sense of appreciation, and reinforces the notion that they belong to a network of human connections and mutual commitment (Mahamid et al., 2021). In a study conducted in the Amari refugee camp in Palestine, Johnson (2007) was able to demonstrate the close interconnections between talk and action modes and that in many situations, the two were hard to separate, thus building a network around the nature of coping. In working to effectively deal with collective traumatic experiences, active social networks in Palestinian camps were shown to help varying generations of Palestinian refugees (Mahamid & Veronese, 2021). This could be understood as indicating that while individuals strive for independence, the importance of social support and networks can amplify the perception of their actions during resistance, portraying them as acts of heroism (Afana et al., 2020). In addition to social networks and social support, religion was also seen to be an effective coping strategy as religion affords explanatory mechanisms, including meaning, purpose, and specific etiologies (Mahamid & Bdier, 2021). It also provides healing and coping mechanisms for distressful situations. Palestinian refugees rely heavily on religion as a component of their self-identity. Positive religious coping has been found to greatly influence the Palestinians' refugees' understanding of the world, in much the same way that it provides meaning to a reality of suffering, making it more coherent and, in turn, more tolerable (Mahamid & Bdier, 2021). Also, in a study that aimed to explore type of coping strategies used to overcome the stress and trauma as well as the relationship to mental health problems and ways of coping in face of stress and adversities among Palestinian refugee families in the Gaza Strip, the results showed that Palestinian families coped with stressful situations by reframing, acquiring social support, and seeking spiritual support, in which religious coping strategies were characterized by the belief that it is God's wish and by attending religious meetings (Thabet et al., 2017).

Continuing education is another important coping strategy that Palestinian refugees use to deal with collective trauma. The experiences of displacement and prolonged conflict are decisive factors in pushing Palestinian refugees toward education (Koldas, 2011). Education has both helped them adapt to the new life of exile and kept alive the prospects of returning home. It is no surprise that refugees attach great significance to obtaining an education, for it is a survival strategy. Education for Palestinian refugees is used as a remedy, to make up for the loss of land and property, understand precisely what happened and why, and as a means to rescue what was left and to rebuild themselves. In other words, using Freire and Macedo (2005) famous phrase, "they used the words to understand the world"

(p. 58). In a study targeting Palestinian refugees in the West Bank of Palestine, participants considered education to be a source of hope and a positive coping strategy to deal with difficult living conditions they experienced. Moreover, parents encourage their children to pursue education to secure a better future (Mahamid, 2020).

As a means of coping, Palestinian refugees look to build a national narrative and a collective identity. Those who share common past experiences focus on using a constant collective meaning-making process to make sense of their present. They undertake a collective effort of finding goals, values, and a sense of efficacy that works to strengthen their ability to endure hardships (Rmeileh, 2021). A collective identity that follows a collective traumatic event or events may formulate the construction of social identity, highlighting its purpose, values, efficacy, and collective worth. With the passing of time, the effects of trauma on collective identity increase, but the focus begins to shift from the loss to the future-oriented goals derived as lessons learned from the trauma, and as such, the collective memory of the trauma becomes incorporated into the community's collective identity and becomes transgenerational (Veronese et al., 2020).

Another possible coping strategy for Palestinian refugees is hope, as it is a significant predictor of life satisfaction, positive affect, negative affect, and flourishing (Satici, 2016). Hope refers to the cognitive set that is based on a reciprocally derived sense of successful agency (goal-directed determination) and pathways (planning of ways to meet goals), and is consistently related to better outcomes in physical health, psychological adjustment, and psychotherapy (Marques et al., 2015). In a study by Mahamid and Berte (2020b) where hope for the future and coping strategies among Palestinian refugees were explored, findings showed that hope for the future for Palestinian refugee children was based on their desires to live in freedom and peace, return to their homeland, continue their education, and get married and have a family. In another study targeting Palestinian refugees, hope narrated as a source for making a change and having a better life in the future, by being optimistic and having goals for the future despite the hard life conditions (Wilson et al., 2021).

In a study designed to test coping and resilience resources among Palestinian refugees, Mahamid (2020) found that Palestinian refugees appeared to demonstrate a high level of resiliency, positive self-efficacy, and responsibility to deal with difficult and stressful events, despite poor quality of life and collective traumatic experiences they have had. This suggests that Palestinian refugees are resilient individuals, characterized as having high levels of hope, subjective well-being, psychological well-being, life satisfaction, happiness, self-efficacy, self-regulation, and ability to cope with various domains in life (Mahamid et al., 2021).

Conclusion

The tragedies of the Nakba, within the context of the Israeli–Palestinian conflict, shape the respective foundational narratives of victimhood, nationalism, and rebirth. The loss of lands belonging to Palestinians in the 1948 Nakba is not to be looked at using a quantitative or qualitative scale, as this event represents historical injustice that galvanizes modern national struggles among Palestinians (Thomas, 2015).

To better conceptualize the historic trauma in Palestine, great-grandparents, grandparents, and parents have related their experience to a wide range of historic and cumulative traumatic events. These include recurring shock due to massacres, invasions, detention, and torture, as well as long-term entrapment and occupation. The horrors of house demolitions, forced relocation, and living as refugees only add to the trauma. Economic hardships may come in the form of competition between brands and forced financial dependency on Israel. These conceptualizations have also brought on loss of native language and identity; and lack of safety due to continuing military and domestic violence among Palestinians (Barron et al., 2016).

Living through traumatic experiences can have long-lasting effects, which not only affect the victim but are also transmitted across generations. A vast range of emotional and psychological symptoms may be transmitted over generations as many clinical studies (Abu el Hija, 2018; Farina et al., 2020) have reported. These symptoms often include a strong distrust of the world, unclear boundaries, ever-present fear of danger, chronic sorrow, separation anxiety, inability to communicate, and impaired parental function.

The transgenerational effects of trauma appear through a wide variety of mechanisms. Such mechanisms include impacts to parenting and family functioning, disconnection and alienation from extended family, association with parental physical and mental illness, and impact on attachment in relationships with caregivers. These effects are further exacerbated by the process of vicarious traumatization where children witness the ongoing effects of the original trauma, which a parent or other family member has experienced or continues to be exposed to with regard to high levels of stress and trauma, including multiple bereavements and other losses (Rogers, 2021).

It can be concluded that among Palestinian refugees, there is evidence to suggest that a parental trauma history and intergenerational traumatic experiences faced by first generations influenced refugee children negatively and led to their psychological distress. However, the mechanisms by which the transmission is mediated are yet to be exactly determined. Theoretically, disruptions in attachment representations, intra-family communication, and parental symptom level have all been proposed as potential mediating mechanisms (Dalgaard et al., 2016).

Moreover, the difficult and challenging circumstances in Palestinian camps act as catalysts, perpetuating the enduring effects of trauma over a long period of time. Palestinians living in internally displaced camps suffer from incursion and attacks by Israeli soldiers and settlers daily, and this continues to increase the effect of ongoing trauma in people who live in camps and among children in particular. Additionally, the unfavorable economic situation in Palestinian camps, along with the diminishing assistance provided by the United Nations Relief and Works Agency (UNRWA) and other organizations addressing human, social, and psychological matters in these camps, contribute to a highly complex and ongoing situation.

Note

1 Palestinian catastrophe (Nakba) occurred when more than 700,000 Palestinian Arabs – about half of prewar Palestine's Arab population – fled or were expelled from their homes, during the 1948 Arab–Israeli war. The term Nakba also refers to the period of war itself and events affecting Palestinians from December 1947 to January 1949 (Mahamid & Veronese, 2021).

References

Abdallah, S.L. (2009). UNRWA photographs 1950–1978: A view of history or shaped by history? I would have smiled. Photographing the Palestinian refugee experience. *Hal Open Science*. Retrieved November 3, 2023, from https://shs.hal.science/halshs-02540691/document

Abu el Hija, A. (2018). *Intergenerational transmission of parental Nakba related trauma experiences among the Palestinians living in Israel* (Doctoral dissertation, University of Konstanz). KOPS – The Institutional Repository of the University of Konstanz. Retrieved October 3, 2023, from http://nbn-resolving.de/urn:nbn:de:bsz:352-2-1x8e2v3pfnpur5

Afana, A.J., Tremblay, J., Ghannam, J., Ronsbo, H., & Veronese, G. (2020). Coping with trauma and adversity among Palestinians in the Gaza strip: A qualitative, culture-informed analysis. *Journal of Health Psychology*, 25(12), 2031–2048. doi: 10.1177/1359105318785697

Alduraidi, H., & Waters, C.M. (2018). Depression, perceived health, and right-of-return hopefulness of Palestinian refugees. *Journal of Nursing Scholarship*, 50(2), 163–171. doi: 10.1111/jnu.12363

Altawil, M.A.S., El-Asam, A., & Khadaroo, A. (2023). Impact of chronic war trauma exposure on PTSD diagnosis from 2006–2021: A longitudinal study in Palestine. *Middle East Current Psychiatry*, 30, 14, 1–8. doi: 10.1186/s43045-023-00286-5

Amir, M., & Lev-Wiesel, R. (2001). Does everyone have a name? Psychological distress and quality of life among child holocaust survivors with lost identity. *Journal of Traumatic Stress*, 14(4), 859–869. doi: 10.1023/A:1013010709789

Aydin, C. (2017). How to forget the unforgettable? On collective trauma, cultural identity, and mnemotechnologies. *Identity*, 17(3), 125–137. doi: 10.1080/15283488.2017.1340160

Banat, B., Entrena-Durán, F., & Dayyeh, J. (2018). Palestinian refugee youth: Reproduction of collective memory of the Nakba. *Asian Social Science*, 14(12), 147–155. doi: 10.5539/ass.v14n12p147

Barron, I., McInnes, J., & Abdallah, G. (2016). Intergenerational trauma framework for programme efficacy studies: Child trauma recovery in occupied Palestine. *Critical and Radical Social Work*, 4(2), 217–230. doi: 10.1332/204986016X14601003012367

Dalgaard, N.T., Todd, B.K., Daniel, S.I., & Montgomery, E. (2016). The transmission of trauma in refugee families: Associations between intra-family trauma communication style, children's attachment security and psychosocial adjustment. *Attachment & Human Development*, 18(1), 69–89. doi: 10.1080/14616734.2015.1113305

Davidson, A.C., & Mellor, D.J. (2001). The adjustment of children of Australian Vietnam veterans: Is there evidence for the transgenerational transmission of the effects of war related trauma? *Australian and New Zealand Journal of Psychiatry*, 35(3), 345–35. doi: 10.1046/j.1440-1614.2001.00897.x

Farina, A.S., Kremer, K., Maynard, B., Mancini, M., Hershberger, L., & Boyd-Ramirez, A. (2020). Intergenerational trauma among families in El Salvador: An exploratory study. *Journal of Child & Adolescent Trauma*, 13(4), 515–525. doi: 10.1007/s40653-020-00310-4

Freire, P., & Macedo, D. (2005). *Literacy: Reading the word and the world*. Hadleigh, MA: Bergin and Garvey.

Hopper, E. (2003). *Traumatic experience in the unconscious life of groups: The fourth basic assumption: Incohesion: Aggregation/massification or (ba) I: A/M* (Vol. 23). London and New York: Jessica Kingsley Publishers.

Giacaman, R., Rabaia, Y., Nguyen-Gillham, V., Batniji, R., Punamäki, R.-L., & Summerfield, D. (2011). Mental health, social distress and political oppression: The case of the occupied Palestinian territory. *Global Public Health*, *6*(5), 547–559. doi: 10.1080/17441692.2010.528443

Johnston, J.R. (2006). A child-centered approach to high-conflict and domestic-violence families: Differential assessment and interventions. *Journal of Family Studies*, *12*(1), 15–35. doi: 10.5172/jfs.327.12.1.15

Johnson, P. (2007). Tales of strength and danger: Sahar and the tactics of everyday life in Amari refugee camp, Palestine. *Signs: Journal of Women in Culture and Society*, *32*(3), 597–619. doi: 10.1086/510543

Karenian, H., Livaditis, M., Karenian, S., Zafiriadis, K., Bochtsou, V., & Xenitidis, K. (2011). Collective trauma transmission and traumatic reactions among descendants of Armenian refugees. *International Journal of Social Psychiatry*, *57*(4), 327–337. doi: 10.1177/0020764009354840

Kellermann, N. P. (2001). Transmission of holocaust trauma-an integrative view. *Psychiatry: Interpersonal and Biological Processes*, *64*(3), 256–267. doi: 10.1521/psyc.64.3.256.18464

Koldas, U. (2011). The Nakba in Palestinian memory in Israel. *Middle Eastern Studies*, *47*(6), 947–959. doi: 10.1080/00263206.2011.619354

Lentin, R. (2013). *Co-memory and melancholia: Israelis memorialising the Palestinian Nakba*. Manchester: Manchester University Press.

Matos, L., Costa, P.A., Park, C.L., Indart, M.J., & Leal, I. (2021). 'The war made me a better person': Syrian refugees' meaning-making trajectories in the aftermath of collective trauma. *International journal of Environmental Research and Public Health*, *18*(16), 8481. doi: 10.3390/ijerph18168481

Mahamid, F., Bdier, D., & Chou, P. (2021). Traumatic life events and psychological well-being among Palestinian adolescents: The mediating role of resilience. *Journal of Concurrent Disorders*, *3*(3), 105. doi: 10.54127/GTBR1644

Mahamid, F., & Berte, D.Z. (2020a). Happiness, sadness, and hope for the future in narratives of Palestinian refugee children. *International Journal of Mental Health and Addiction*, *18*(6), 1638–1651. doi: 10.1007/s11469-020-00303-2

Mahamid, F., & Veronese, G. (2021). Psychosocial interventions for third-generation Palestinian refugee children: Current challenges and hope for the future. *International Journal of Mental Health and Addiction*, *19*(6), 2056–2073. doi: 10.1007/s11469-020-00300-5

Mahamid, F.A. (2020). Collective trauma, quality of life and resilience in narratives of third generation Palestinian refugee children. *Child Indicators Research*, *13*(6), 2181–2204. doi: 10.1007/s12187-020-09739-3

Mahamid, F.A., & Bdier, D. (2021). The association between positive religious coping, perceived stress, and depressive symptoms during the spread of coronavirus (COVID-19) among a sample of adults in Palestine: Across sectional study. *Journal of Religion and Health*, *60*(1), 34–49. doi: 10.1007/s10943-020-01121-5

Mahamid, F.A., & Berte, D.Z. (2020b). Portrayals of violence and at-risk populations: Symptoms of trauma in adolescents with high utilization of social media. *International Journal of Mental Health and Addiction*, *18*(4), 980–992. doi: 10.1007/s11469-018-9999-0

Mahamid, F.A., Veronese, G., & Bdier, D. (2023). Fear of coronavirus (COVID-19) and mental health outcomes in Palestine: The mediating role of social support. *Current Psychology*, *42*, 8572–8581. doi: 10.1007/s12144-021-02395-y

Marques, S.C., Lopez, S.J., Fontaine, A.M., Coimbra, S., & Mitchell, J. (2015). How much hope is enough? Levels of hope and students' psychological and school functioning. *Psychology in the Schools*, *52*(4), 325–334. doi: 10.1002/pits.21833

Milshtein, M. (2009). The memory that never dies: The Nakba memory and the Palestinian national movement. In Litvak, M. (Ed.), *Palestinian collective memory and national identity*. New York, NY: Palgrave Macmillan. doi: 10.1057/9780230621633_3

Mindiashvili, N., & Kutsia, N. (2021). Collective trauma in refugee literature (based on almanacs-14 Gigabytes and halleluiah). *International Journal of Innovative Technologies in Social Science, 4*(32), 1–8. doi: 10.31435/rsglobal_ijitss/30122021/7695

Peled, A. (2016). Descending the khazooq: "Working through" the trauma of the Nakba in emile habibi's Oeuvre. *Israel Studies, 21*(1), 157–182. doi: 10.2979/israelstudies.21.1.157

Punamäki, R. L. (2001). From childhood trauma to adult well-being through psychosocial assistance of Chilean families. *Journal of Community Psychology, 29*(3), 281–303. doi: 10.1002/jcop.1018

Rmeileh, R. (2021). *"Sumud is to qlways be one hand": Culturally informed resilience among Palestinian refugee men in Lebanon* (Unpublished master's thesis). University of Oslo.

Rogers, R. G. (2021). *Intergenerational transmission of war trauma among Afghan refugees in Canada* (Doctoral dissertation, The Chicago School of Professional Psychology). ProQuest Dissertations Publishing. Retrieved September 29, 2023, from www.proquest.com/docview/2619233441?pq-origsite=gscholar&fromopenview=true

Sa'di, A. H. (2002). Catastrophe, memory and identity: Al-Nakbah as a component of Palestinian identity. *Israel Studies, 7*(2), 175–198. doi: 10.1353/is.2002.0016

Salem, M., Raab, K., & Wagner, R. (2020). Solid waste management: The disposal behavior of poor people living in Gaza strip refugee camps. *Resources, Conservation and Recycling, 153*, 1–9. doi: 10.1016/j.resconrec.2019.104550

Satici, S. A. (2016). Psychological vulnerability, resilience, and subjective well-being: The mediating role of hope. *Personality and Individual Differences, 102*, 68–73. doi: 10.1016/j.paid.2016.06.057

Sayigh, R. (2020). Self-recording of a national disaster: Oral history and the Palestinian Nakba. *Journal of Holy Land and Palestine Studies, 19*(1), 1–13. doi: 10.3366/hlps.2020.0225

Strazzari, F., & Tholens, S. (2010). Another Nakba: Weapons availability and the transformation of the Palestinian national struggle, 1987–2007. *International Studies Perspectives, 11*(2), 112–130. doi: 10.1111/j.1528-3585.2010.00397.x

Thabet, A.M., Thabet, S.S., & Vostanis, P. (2016). The relationships between mental health problems and family coping strategies among Palestinian in the Gaza Strip. *British Journal of Medicine and Medical Research, 17*(8), 1–11. doi: 10.9734/BJMMR/2016/27747

Thabet, A.M., Thabet, S.S., & Vostanis, P. (2017). Coping and mental health problems among Palestinian refugee families. *Journal of Psychological Cognition, 2*(2), 149–156. Retrieved October 2, 2023, from www.alliedacademies.org/journal-of-psychology-and-cognition/

Thomas, S.A. (2015). Collective memory of trauma: The otherization of suffering in the Israeli-Palestinian conflict. *Berkeley Undergraduate Journal, 28*(1), 192–222. doi: 10.5070/B3281025776

UNRWA. (2016). *Draw Your Dream for Gaza in 2020*. Retrieved November 3, 2023, from www.unrwa.org/newsroom/features/draw-your-dream-gaza-2020

Van Ijzendoorn, M.H., Bakermans-Kranenburg, M.J., & Sagi-Schwartz, A. (2003). Are children of Holocaust survivors less well-adapted? A meta-analytic investigation of secondary traumatization. *Journal of traumatic stress, 16*(5), 459–469. doi: 10.1023/A:1025706427300

Veronese, G., Mahamid, F.A., & Bdier, D. (2022). Subjective well-being, sense of coherence, and posttraumatic growth mediate the association between COVID-19 stress, trauma, and burnout among Palestinian health-care providers. *American Journal of Orthopsychiatry, 92*(3), 291–301. doi: 10.1037/ort0000606

Veronese, G., Pepe, A., Diab, M., Jamey, Y.A., & Kagee, A. (2021). Living under siege: Resilience, hopelessness, and psychological distress among Palestinian students in the Gaza Strip. *Global Mental Health, 8*, E40. doi: 10.1017/gmh.2021.37

Veronese, G., Pepe, A., Sala, G., Yamien, I., & Vigliaroni, M. (2019). Positive experience, psychological functioning, and hope for the future as factors associated with mental health among young sub-Saharan internally displaced people (IDP): A quantitative pilot study. *International Journal of Mental Health, 48*(3), 165–187. doi: 10.1080/00207411.2019.1635849

Veronese, G., Sousa, C., Cavazzoni, F., & Shoman, H. (2020). Spatial agency as a source of resistance and resilience among Palestinian children living in Dheisheh refugee camp, Palestine. *Health & Place, 62*, 102304. doi: 10.1016/j.healthplace.2020.102304

Wilson, N., Turner-Halliday, F., & Minnis, H. (2021). Escaping the inescapable: Risk of mental health disorder, somatic symptoms and resilience in Palestinian refugee children. *Transcultural Psychiatry, 58*(2), 307–320. doi: 10.1177/1363461520987070

Wolfe, P. (2012). Purchase by other means: The Palestine Nakba and Zionism's conquest of economics. *Settler Colonial Studies, 2*(1), 133–171. doi: 10.1080/2201473X.2012.10648830

Yassin, N., Taha, A.A., Ghantous, Z., Atoui, M.M., & Forgione, F. (2018). Evaluating a mental health program for Palestinian refugees in Lebanon. *Journal of Immigrant and Minority Health, 20*(2), 388–398. doi: 10.1007/s10903-017-0657-6

4 Holocaust Survivors, Siberians, Refugees, Veterans – Memory and Choice of Jewish Returnees from the USSR to Poland (1945–2024)

Lidia Zessin-Jurek

Introduction

Drawing from oral testimony of Polish Jewish witnesses, this chapter[1] explains why former Holocaust refugee children and youth chose divergent memory paths to remember their dislocation and survival. In addition to the impact of social factors, the chapter leans into the importance of the *individual choice* exercised by people affected by the refugee trauma. Social memory frameworks provide a dynamic and persuasive matrix for processes of personal memory (e.g., Halbwachs, 1925; Schwartz, 1996; McLean & Syed, 2015). They change over time and may be fragmented or multiple at any given place and moment, even for groups that share similar past experiences. The chapter demonstrates how refugee survivors navigated this multiplicity and chose to join (or not) a mnemonic community. Equally important, although only outlined in this text, is the question of how different memory affiliations impacted transmission of trauma to the next generations.

The protagonists of this study are Polish Jewish children and youth who escaped Nazi persecution in 1939 and lived under Soviet rule during the war. Theirs is a unique experience of fleeing the Germans and then surviving Soviet starvation, disease, and abuse of authority, followed by extended displacement in various parts of the world in the postwar period. Of various places were refugees resettled after the war, this chapter zooms in on Poland. This focus on one postwar space allows for a more adequate discussion (in a single chapter) of the issue of the multiplicity of self-narratives, as well as the role and limitations of choice in generating differences in memory.

In memory transmission, children and youth play a stronger filtering role in their families and communities than adult participants of the same events. Although their interpretations of the past are initially susceptible to external (e.g., parental, institutional) influences (Zerubavel, 1996), they later longitudinally transform these interpretations. Eva Hoffman (2004) used the term "hinge generation" to refer to the children of the Holocaust survivors who, even if often burdened by memorial guardianship, possessed greater leeway to transform the familial experience of violence into new "sets of relations with the world" (p. 103). The generation of children who experienced war constitutes still another type. Drawing on Rumbaut's work (2004) on immigrants' cohorts, they might be more accurately described as

DOI: 10.4324/9781003385820-5

the 1.5-generation. Like the hinge generation, they too have a lengthy time and no lack of social opportunities to transform their trauma.[2] But this process occurs by working through their own memories of loss in addition to those inherited from their parents.

The memories of young refugee returnees differed depending on diverse memory frameworks – mnemonic communities – in which they were immersed and chose to function. Interpreting one's own past in terms of the available mental and cultural representations is a well-established trope in the social construction of trauma theories and the sociology of memory (Alexander, 2009; Confino, 1997; Olick & Robbins, 1998). These locally available interpretative lenses account for differences in the social constructs of victimhood. What is particularly remarkable about the surviving Polish Jewish refugees is that social geography, while undoubtedly influential, cannot fully explain the marked differences in self-understanding(s) of this group. The survivors in the East splintered into groups who saw themselves as (1) victims of the Germans, (2) victims of the Soviets, (3) victims of both totalitarian systems, (4) victims of Poland, (5) refugees affected by bad times and bad luck (Zessin-Jurek, 2022), and more. Importantly, those who think of themselves mainly as, for example, "Stalin victims" could have been found in various places, that is, in the United States, Israel, or Poland.

What, then, besides the dominant (and evolving) memory macroframes influenced these refugees' positions vis-à-vis the relevant narratives of collective trauma? The community impacts on a smaller than national scale too; it depends on whether one was surrounded by a sizable Jewish minority or relatively isolated from it. In relation to the latter point, this chapter introduces another important factor behind the diversity of mnemonic trajectories among refugee survivors. This factor is particularly important for the younger generation, as it involves the transition to adult autonomy. Namely, this chapter highlights the category of *choice* as a crucial co-determining factor in whether the former refugee children joined the mnemonic community centered around collective trauma. While it is clear that the choice was tied to both national and community memory frameworks, it also included an element of personal sovereignty. Those who decided (i.e., chose) to stay in Poland after the war are viewed by sociologists primarily through the prism of far-reaching assimilation (Koźmińska-Frejlak, 2022). Such an identity choice was crucial in the otherwise mostly mono-ethnic country that Poland became after the war, and in which antisemitism was palpable. However, being a social construct, collective memory is an element of constant negotiation and contestation (Olick & Robbins, 1998). Listening to the voices of refugees allows for an inquiry into the extent of contestation of the dominant macroframes and helps recognize the mnemonic agency of refugee survivors.

Historical Context: Survivors in the East and Their "Cascading Displacement"

Some refugees (and their parents) suffered more under the Soviets than did others. Most of the Jews who escaped from the Germans by fleeing to the East later experienced deportation to Siberia, while others managed to avoid it. Although the latter were still afflicted by hunger and (their parents') constant fear of the Gulag, they viewed their experience as that of wartime refuge, not deportation, and Soviet exile mainly in terms of "luck" and "escaping the Holocaust." Before looking at the different memory trajectories of Polish Jewish survivors, I would like to offer my own understanding (in a somewhat "normative" historical practice) of what they experienced by highlighting one common element of their stories, that is their multistage refugeeism, as outlined below.

The Polish Jews considered in this chapter experienced a series of displacements after the German invasion of Poland on September 1, 1939. Hundreds of thousands sought refuge in eastern Poland, occupied by the USSR on September 17, 1939. However, they were deported to places of isolation and labor camps in the remote taiga a few months later, part of the Soviet scheme of de-Polonization and "securitization" of the borderland. After Germany attacked the USSR in 1941, most Poles under Soviet authority, including the Jewish Poles, were released to contribute to the Allied War effort against the Wehrmacht (in Italy). They tried moving south toward the Central Asian Soviet republics where the Polish Army was to be formed. Because the army had quotas that strongly discriminated against Jews, most of them remained in the USSR until the war's end.

Jewish refugees were repeatedly displaced during and after the war. The journey that began in the autumn of 1939 continued long after the war, irrespective of where they eventually settled. The post-1945 dislocation was less dramatic than the flight from the Germans and the Soviet deportation as it took place in peacetime and was subject to regularities of the more linear and positive mechanisms of integration as new settlers with personal security more ensured. Alas, this general rule was tainted with the unwelcome homecoming (Rice, 2017) and serious instances of antisemitic violence at the hands of civilians some suffered upon their return (Gross, 2007). When reestablishing themselves in Poland, Jewish refugees also struggled with a painful sense of absence of their communities, and, contrary to the popular local stereotype of the Communist Jew, many had a strong distaste for the Communist system they had suffered under as Soviet deportees.

For these reasons, most of those who resettled in Poland subsequently left the country once again and were soon dispersed throughout the world. The number of returnees from the East comprised a total of 250,000 Polish Jews (adults and children), but it had declined drastically in the 1940s as the result of mass emigration from Poland. In the United States, Australia, and Israel, but also Poland, they lived alongside fellow Jews who had survived the Holocaust in the camps and in hiding, and who gradually acted as witnesses to the German genocide. The refugee survivors, too, were asked in their oral testimonies to bear witness to the families lost in the Shoah. Their own experience of having been uprooted from their Polish home, then going through Siberia, followed by the Central Asian years and a postwar new beginning – that is their transitioning from one refugee situation to another – remained on the margins of historians and memory keepers' interest. Seeking a way to address their complex cascading displacement, many refugee survivors wrote memoirs instead of talking about it.

Mnemonic Macroframes: Holocaust, Gulag, Refugeeism

Recently, the written testimonies provided by Polish Jews made their way into new historical scholarship which charts the complex refugee trajectory (Adler, 2020) and raises questions about the related complications of its memorialization. A decade ago, John Goldlust (2012) and Atina Grossmann (2016) called for research to refocus and address the trauma of Jewish survivors in such a way as to include the unique experiences of refugee survivors. The challenge lies in placing the traumas of these refugees on the memory map, where the suffering of those who had been confined to ghettos and in concentration camps took center stage and eventually the form of a "cosmopolitan memory" (Levy & Sznaider, 2002). For a long time, the greater suffering of the direct Holocaust victims posed a challenge to the memory of Jewish surviving refugees. Genocide against the Jews was the first powerful macroframe of collective memory against which they positioned themselves, in Poland and beyond.

While all the Polish Jews were affected by the loss of their families and most of their prewar universe, the trauma of the surviving refugees from the East involved the cumulative experience of cascading displacement and Soviet rule, rather than the direct experience of the German genocide machine. Both were associated with deprivation, hunger, disease, and often slave labor, but the adult refugees' sense of loss was accompanied by a sense of guilt from having "run away" and "abandoning" others to much more deadly and dehumanizing German methods: "My parents died in the ghetto. I feel guilty about leaving them behind," said Marianna (VHA June 1998). And this is a frequent statement by a generation of young refugee survivors.

The second macroframe which provides a relevant point of reference for Jewish refugees in Poland had more of a national than cosmopolitan character. Poland developed a relatively rich and mostly grassroots memory culture of deportations to Siberia – first dissident, and then official (Zessin-Jurek, 2015). Since the 1980s, deportations have been commemorated as one of the greatest hardships of the Polish nation. This Soviet repression affected several hundred thousand Poles. Although 30% of the deportees were Jews, this group is hardly mentioned in local commemorations adorned with Catholic symbolism. My earlier work points out the rejection, or at least the significant omission, with which the local memory culture of Siberia treated Jewish co-deportees and later co-refugees in Central Asia (Zessin-Jurek, 2021). This culture also completely failed to consider the specific meaning of Soviet exile for the Jews: deportations to slave labor camps in the USSR saved many of these Polish citizens from almost certain death under German occupation.

Here, the goal is not to further analyze the majoritarian Polish frame. This "national" gaze on the Jewish exiles sometimes tolerated them as contributing memoirists, but more often wrongly accused them of having gone to the USSR out of sympathy for Communism. The focus below is on what the former Jewish child refugees made of this Polish frame and what place(s) they found for themselves in relation to the two dominant memory landscapes. To answer this question means to incorporate voices of refugee survivors that have thus far been rarely heard;

namely, those who have navigated their trauma through the complexities of their social setting not in Western countries, but in Poland.

Outside Poland, the appellation of "refugee" for a long time took the central position in descriptions of Polish Jewish experience in the Soviet Union. This third powerful mnemonic macroframe obfuscated two potential identifiers mentioned earlier: a victim of Nazism or Communism. During various stages of their serial dislocations, Jews were considered refugees, initially by the Soviets and later by the International Refugee Organization, the Red Cross, the Joint, and the United Nations Relief and Rehabilitation Administration. The case was similar in their new countries of resettlement in the West. Their self-recognition as refugees was due to a sense of having been on the move since the beginning of the war, and was further reinforced through their belonging to communities that administratively viewed them this way. As George (Zessin-Jurek, Personal Interview, henceforth: "Z-J, PI", Tiburon, November 2022) and Sam (Z-J, PI, online, December 2021) recount, Polish Jews arrived in the United States with papers of stateless refugees after the war. Not only did they fit the paradigm of Jewish refugees from Europe finally arriving in the United States after Americans had largely refused to let them in for the previous decade, which determined the fate of this community. The refugee appellation also fit into the Cold War Western refugee paradigm that viewed refugees as people from countries under Soviet control (Keely, 2001; Bradley, 2014).

Importantly, this official categorization as postwar refugees was not in conflict with the self-perception of Polish Jews immigrating to the West. Their refugee status was in line with their own sense of ongoing need for protection from oppression and persecution. Sam, who lives in the United States, recalls that, after being transported from the USSR to the west Polish city of Katowice (instead of his hometown of Brzesko), his family's decision to leave Poland was determined by fear for their lives: "The Jewish dentist where I had a visit was murdered the next day. My parents decided to leave Poland, if only illegally through the green border with Czechoslovakia" (Z-J, PI, online, February 2021). Such threats justified their presence in the new host society and respective choices to resettle in the new host countries. Reuniting with family who survived the war was undoubtedly an important reason for migration, but breaking free from an oppressive Europe (and their homeland) was equally significant. Therefore, alongside independent post-traumatic psychological determinants, their memories of multilayered persecution and refugeeism played a role on the community level, too.

When the wartime fate of European Jews was finally acknowledged in the form of the Holocaust memory culture that has developed strongly since the early 1990s, some former Jewish deportees to Siberia also embedded their own fate in the wider cosmopolitan framework of antisemitic persecution and survivorship. Conscious carving out a place for themselves in the collective trauma of the Holocaust unlocked their witnessing. This resulted in the recent boom of memoir literature by this group, published mainly in North America and including accounts by those who were children at the time and by children of survivors (Zessin-Jurek, 2022). In addition to the refugee and Holocaust frames, some survivors emphasized Soviet oppression. Hardly ever, though, did they inscribe their memory in the collective trauma of the repeated Russian oppression of the Polish people. Since few surviving refugees remained in Poland, the number of sources (written or spoken) available toward research into the memory of the latter group is comparatively limited. Nevertheless, the interviews[3] conducted for this study, along with testimonies previously collected in Poland by organizations preserving Jewish memory (Shoah Foundation Visual History Archive, henceforth: "VHA" and Centropa) in the 1990s and 2000s, feature a variety of responses to displacement and are a rich trove for consideration (here 25 are quoted).

In Poland: "Refugees" in Their Own Country?

Unlike in Western countries, the "refugee framework" was hardly present in the mnemonic landscape of postwar Poland. Jewish refugees who returned and remained in Poland found themselves in very different conditions of coming to terms with persecution. For security reasons and in view of the dominance of the Communist narrative in Poland, it was initially better to forget the Soviet persecution (and other harassment, as will be shown later in the text). Under Communism, deportees were encouraged to reveal only that they had spent the war years in the USSR and returned as fortunate "repatriates." After Communism collapsed, the labels applied to Poles who had been in the USSR underwent significant changes, but refugeeism (*uchodźstwo*) was not an option to define their experience.

Upon their return to Poland, Jewish refugee survivors were rarely able to reoccupy their family homes. In many cases, their homes had been razed (like in Warsaw), and even when they remained standing, the local population did not want to give them up. The Jewish refugees, like other Poles arriving from the USSR (and like them "homeless" because they were residents of eastern Polish lands which the USSR annexed), were thus settled in unfamiliar localities. "Repatriation transports" directed them from the USSR to the lands in the west vacated by the Germans and newly given to Poland (e.g., Wrocław, Szczecin). Returnees also ended up in the localities where there had previously been a significant German population, such as the cities of Łódź and Gdańsk. It is not easy to reconcile the formal state terminology of "homecoming" or "repatriation" with the realities of this postwar migration. While a slightly provocative research optic, I would argue that going to Poland, as resettling anywhere else after the war, often meant the perpetuation of the refugee condition for returnees from the USSR.

This common pattern of "repatriation" is repeated in the majority of biographies of young refugees who remained in Poland and recently agreed to talk about their past. Miriam (Z-J, PI, Gdańsk, May 2021) and her mother, originally from Częstochowa in central Poland, settled in distant Gdańsk after they came back from the USSR. Similarly, Henryk (VHA, Gdańsk, May 1997) from Nowy Targ lived on the very other edge of Poland in Gdańsk, that is 700 km away from original home. Alina (Z-J, PI, Żary, June 2022), from Ostrołęka near Warsaw, settled in Żary near the German border. Otylia (Z-J, PI, Łódź April 2022), from southern town of Jarosław, moved to centrally located Łódź. To illustrate the experiences of families such as these, Otylia's story is considered below.

In October 1939, 8-year-old Otylia (b. 1931) left the town of Jarosław on foot with her family as a result of early deportations by the Germans, who were pushing Jews into the Soviet-occupied zone of newly divided Poland. Her family first found shelter with peasants they had previously befriended on the other side of the new border and later lived as refugees at the outskirts of Lviv. They were deported again, this time by the Soviets, to forced labor camps in Siberia in the summer of 1940. They were then released in 1941 under "amnesty" negotiated by the Polish government-in-exile with Soviet authorities. Moving toward Iran, around 100,000 Polish deportees later left the USSR with the Polish army. But many more, including most Jews, remained in the USSR as refugees until the end of the war, facing hunger and epidemics. Otylia's family eventually returned to Poland in 1946 as "repatriates," but their house in Jarosław had been seized by new Polish tenants, so they left for Łódź in central Poland where Otylia would spend her entire adult life. The family settled in Łódź precisely because they were *not* from there and felt safer in a bigger city. The period of a vibrant postwar Jewish community in Łódź did not last long, however. For the aforementioned reasons, the Jewish minority was shrinking rapidly. Otylia's family too, repeatedly considered immigrating to Israel, but their imperative, as was the case for most Jewish families in the post-Shoah period, was to stay together. Otylia's brother decided to stay in Łódź, and this dissuaded the rest of the family from leaving. It was only after the death of their parents that the siblings separated, and their sister left for the United States.

In Łódź, they started from scratch and lived together for several years in one room, but the family never compared their circumstances with the good quality of life they had before the war, when Otylia's father had owned a "colonial store" and later a restaurant in the market square in Jarosław. Instead, they felt fortunate in Łódź compared to their wartime refugee experiences. Otylia's peer, the direct survivor and historian, Shimon Redlich, also from eastern Poland, felt similarly about the move to Łódź. Despite exchanging the Galician town of Brzeżany, surrounded by vegetation for a gray textile metropolis, he was pleased with the level of security he regained after wartime turmoil: "Jews usually settled in large urban centers. Cities, unlike small townships, offered them better economic conditions and a greater sense of security" (Redlich, 2012, p. 64). In the end, Łódź, even if not their hometown, was a city in their country of origin and although Redlich would eventually leave for Israel, for Otylia, Łódź became her final home. She married a local Catholic and retained little of her Jewish culture. For Jews originating from the small towns of former Galicia, the formerly Austrian region of Poland, and raised surrounded by the Russian or Central Asian languages, the Polish industrial city of Łódź was like a foreign space. Nevertheless, Otylia and her family never thought of their lives there as an extension of their wartime *refugee* experience, even if it met much of the normative definition (they were not familiar with) of this perennially contested concept, as explained below.

The cornerstone of international refugee law is displacement and seeking refuge from persecution. It includes subjective factors such as experiencing "fear" ("Article 1, Refugee Convention, 1951"). In relation to the Polish Jewish community who survived in the USSR, the terms "persecution" and "fear of persecution" apply to various sources: initially, they fled from Nazis (who later murdered their families) and subsequently most of them experienced violence at the hands of the Soviet regime. In Poland, still threatened by local antisemitic assaults, they would usually resettle in new host societies, far from their original home. Since this last stage of their cascading displacement clearly belongs to the prolonged *refugee* story and fear remained an important motive, I propose categorizing it in these terms.

From Andrzej's account (VHA, Szczecin, April 1997), we learn that, like the Jews who left Poland and were nostalgic about home, many of those who lived there after the war also initially associated with *landsmannschaften*[4] that united residents of their former localities in Poland (e.g., the association of Warsaw Jews in Szczecin). Former child refugees often recount that they never revisited their hometowns and never saw their childhood homes again, although these were, after all, perfectly within their reach, on the territory of the same country (Włodek, VHA, Sopot, March 1997). Dora, increasingly emotional toward the end of her statement, said: "My son promised me that he would take me there [Tomaszów Lubelski – ed.], but time has passed so quickly. I wish before I die, I could still see the place where my mother planted trees" (VHA, Bielawa, November 1996).

Otylia did venture to visit her family's former home when, as a young adult, she found herself in Jarosław during a training trip. Twenty years after the war's end, she still remembered the topography of the town, and her feet instinctively led her to the family apartment. When she tried to explain who she was – omitting her Jewish origin which she believed no longer played any role in her life – the inhabitants of the tenement chased her away, shouting that only Jews had lived there before the war and that she should not show her face there again.

Otylia recalls crying breathlessly. That was the first and only time when she got to express a longing for her lost family home and interrupted childhood. The path of assimilation she chose, and how she wove the memory of her childhood displacement into it, was a process of settling into a home after her earlier experience of homelessness. This explains why Otylia, recounting this emotional scene in Jarosław, expressed her belief that the verbal aggression to which the residents had subjected her was not because she was Jewish. "After all, they could not have known. They were afraid of me because I was a stranger, possibly a thief," she asserted (Z-J, PI, Łódź, April 2022). Behind this assertion (or hope) lies Otylia's assimilation into a society that left her little opportunity to maintain her Jewishness. This limited condition, however, did not disempower the refugee survivors like her. On the contrary, they sought and found other ways to reengage with their displacement and wartime loss. The following section discusses their mnemonic strategies and agency.

Chosen Memory Frames: Siberian Deportees, Wartime Refugees, Veterans, Survivors

Shortly after the war, Otylia's father deposited a testimony at the Jewish Historical Institute in Warsaw. It is a story of expulsion by the Germans (1939), deportation by the Soviets (1940), and resettlement outside their proper home in Poland (1946).[5]

His account, written in Yiddish, is clearly about their Jewish fate. In 1996, Otylia was asked to give her own account to the USC Shoah Foundation Institute Visual History Archive. Her testimony includes details about her Jewish family, Siberia, and her assimilation into Polish culture. In 2021, she testified again, this time for Polish filmmakers producing a documentary about deportees to Siberia. Like several other Polish interviewees, Otylia recounted the conditions of deportation in cattle cars and the hardships of life in Siberia. The filmmakers who conducted the interview were unaware of her Jewish origin and did not ask any questions about exile as remembered by a member of a minority group who, although deported to Siberia, had thereby escaped the Holocaust. They did not exhibit this type of curiosity (and/or lacked the relevant knowledge) when asking the questions. When asked by myself why she had not mentioned this important fact, Otylia could not explain, but presumably felt that this aspect of her experience was better left out as if doubting the egalitarianism of the Polish memory frame in which the interview about Siberian deportations was embedded.

Otylia told her story as a representative of the Siberians' Association (Związek Sybiraków), which she joined in 1989, shortly after its establishment. While the Association numbers are decreasing, after the collapse of the Soviet Union, its many local branches began enrolling Poles who had been deported by the Soviets deep into the USSR. The membership records contain names of Jewish deportees, although they may not be immediately obvious to the untrained eye, since many women changed their names after marriage and men often Polonized first and last names. Józef explains it very simply: "I had to change my name after the war. I did it because I wouldn't get far with a Jewish name, I did it because I had to live somehow" (VHA, Szczecin, April 1997).

The Siberians' Association was one of the mnemonic communities which belatedly offered Jewish refugees a way to reengage with their childhood displacement. Despite the Catholic symbolism that permeates this organization, Otylia, Miriam, Alina, and many others decided they had a rightful place there. Have they been welcomed? This seems to have been the case for those with whom I spoke, although the question itself did not surprise them in the least: "Well yes, I don't flaunt my Jewish background there, but I don't hide it either," said Otylia (Z-J, PI, Łódź, April 2022). The question of affiliation with the Siberians' Association did not come up in interviews conducted in the 1990s by the Shoah Foundation. Above all, the interviewers were interested in the affiliation of the surviving refugees with the Jewish realm in Poland. Even when someone said they belonged to the Siberians' Association, this information was not explored further (VHA, Interview with Zygmunt, Kraków, April 1997). Just as American documentary producers were not interested in the Polish side of Otylia's remembering, Polish ones were not interested in (or even aware of) the Jewish side of it. The results of this witnessing were largely a matter inherent in the interviewing method – which is always the joint product of both parties involved in a conversation, "shaped and organised by asking and answering questions" (Mishler, 2009, p. VII).

Among principles organizing social boundaries, such as participation, self-identification, and ascription (Korycki, 2023), Otylia could choose the first two and practiced them as a "Polish Siberian deportee, member of the Łódź branch." The third one – ascription – was beyond her choice. Otylia heard occasional echoes of antisemitic discourse within the Siberians' Association. One of the most common was the motif of so-called Judeo-Communism and the belief that Jews were responsible for Soviet deportations (allegedly denouncing their Catholic neighbors). Otylia tried to counter the spread of such insinuations via anonymous submissions to the association's bulletin (titled: "My, Sybiracy" [We, the Siberians]).

"Siberian" was not the only appellation to opt for in post-1989 Poland. The democratic authorities ended with the term "repatriates" and initially honored all those who were taken to the Soviet Union as "war veterans," bringing them recognition and some minor social benefits. This definition was later revoked since the Siberian deportee children had not fought in the army against Germany. In the first decade of the 21st century, in accordance with Poland's changing historical policy, the deportees were redesignated as "repressed persons." In 2021, 80 years after the events, those still alive received financial compensation of around $45 for each month of their Soviet repression (from the Polish state, not Russia nor Germany). While they were the subjects of these shifting memory policies and labels, those Jewish survivors who affiliated with the Siberians' Association rarely thought of themselves as refugees. This former feeling, as some of them told me, changed only with the February 2022 Russian invasion of Ukraine. For the first time in 80 years, war has again reached their country's borders. As Otylia put it:

> The sight of refugees, including mothers and children, brought to my mind scenes of my family fleeing Jarosław from the Germans. You see, these people are now also taking shelter in Lwów, Przemyśl, as we were then. Well, and Russia again. . . . They are again deporting this conquered population to Siberia, once again turning other kids' childhoods into a nightmare.
>
> (Z-J, PI, Łódź, April 2022)

Wartime refugeeism – as indicated earlier – was hardly available as a collective memory framework in Poland but was nevertheless a prism through which many former refugee children (unlike Otylia) viewed their past. Due to the absence of the refugee frame in the cultural repertoire of existing collective memories, they remembered their experience primarily in a private and unaffiliated capacity. This included those who did not feel positioned or empowered to self-define as victims of the Holocaust or the Gulag. For one, many saw their suffering in the USSR as the fate of everyone there, not specifically Jews, and thus were far from claiming a (unique) Holocaust framework of memory. Second, they believed that the USSR had inadvertently saved many Jewish lives and so were not ready to join the exclusively victimological memory culture of Siberia as professed by other Poles (Z-J, PI with Marian, Warsaw, December 2021).

For these reasons, in video testimonies collected in the 1990s and 2000s (only some of which are quoted in this chapter), the majority of former refugee children living in Poland recall the past "simply" in terms of the loss of their prewar world, loss of loved ones, and matter-of-fact descriptions of their hungry time in the USSR. They remembered their Soviet exile privately and did not seek validation for it in the collective refugee narrative nor did they attempt to categorize themselves, although the interviewers sometimes hinted at "who" they might feel. Lila, for example, was told, "You are a Child of the Holocaust because you fled to the USSR from the Germans" (VHA, Warsaw, August 1998). Marek stressed that the most important lesson of his story was the hardships of displacement presented through the eyes of a child and understanding what they did to that child. When near Samarkand, he had become an orphan. Within ten days, three members of his family died of typhus: first his older brother, then their mum: "Mum was someone without whom one could not imagine life. I was nine years old and my sister was seven and the youngest was five years old, Chaja. We sat around our unconscious father and called 'Daddy, don't leave us.'" But he died too: "Listeners will hopefully learn about the psyche of the child, what kind of soul it has, and how it lives through tragedies. Because these things create a sort of armor that can only be pierced with difficulty" (VHA, Kraków, September 1996). It was only after 1989 that Jewish friends from the Soviet orphanage passed through Marek's apartment in Poland to reminisce about the wartime hardships in a small trusted collective, without fitting them into any macro framework.

Another important reason to remember their childhood and youth experience as taking refuge during wartime was the fact that some families indeed fled eastward twice, first in 1939 after Germany invaded Poland, and then again, even further to the east, in 1941, when Germany attacked the USSR. Bianka, who was born in Central Asia, said that although her father returned from the USSR in a state of extreme exhaustion similar to that of prisoners from German camps (she uses the term denoting KZ-syndrome "musulman"), neither she nor her family ever inscribed their fate in the collective Polish trauma of Soviet repression: "I can't imagine going to the Siberians' Association with our memory issues." She explained that this organization's reactivation came relatively late (1989) and was reactivated by "a nationalist who collaborated for a time with the Communist security apparatus and was the author of an antisemitic text in 1968." Many interviewees were supportive of the dissident Solidarity movement in Poland (1980s), which was also addressing the subject of Siberia (as one of the biggest anti-regime taboos). In the 1990s, however, they usually discontinued these affiliations due to the increasingly "clerical nature of the Solidarity milieu" (VHA, Interview with Zula, Kraków, April 1997; VHA, Interview with Włodek, Sopot, March 1997) and later refrained from joining the Siberians' associations, which were viewed similarly. Bianca asserted, "personally, I don't know anyone among Jews who belongs to or identifies with the Siberians" (Z-J, PI, Warsaw, February 2023). She is professionally involved in Jewish culture and is part of a self-conscious intellectual Jewish minority in Warsaw. Despite her affiliation with the Jewish community, she neither belongs to the organization that seeks to bring together her generation, called Children of the Holocaust. She believes that what her family survived is most accurately described as "the war," rather than "Siberia" or "the Holocaust."

The minority community in Warsaw includes, however, also former Jewish refugees who do emphasize that their wartime fate was most strongly linked to the tragedy of the Shoah. Their trauma was caused primarily by the German genocide, especially in situations which meant they lost their parents in occupied Poland. Józef was a teenage refugee who was in the East on his own and who lost most of his Warsaw family and friends under the German occupation. Acclaimed novelist, he later wrote poignantly about his bare feet and empty stomach in the USSR (Hen, 1990), but the main theme of his reflections about the past – as he also admitted in a conversation (Z-J, PI, Warsaw, November 2014) – was the Holocaust (Hen, 1991). As a result, he became an important figure in Poland's cultural memory of the Shoah. In terms of trauma, his son, Maciej, confirms:

> It was certainly a difficult exam in life, a kind of school for survival and for preserving the reflexes of civilization in difficult, sometimes extreme conditions – but if traumatic, it was certainly overshadowed by the trauma of the Holocaust. This is how I saw it, observing my parents' behavior and listening to their stories. Yes, they experienced hunger, poverty, homelessness, wandering; my father sometimes risked terrible consequences by escaping twice from work battalions, but all this cannot be compared with the shock they felt when they found out what was happening in Poland at that time. This is how they conveyed it to me.
>
> (Z-J, PI, online, June 2022)

One final framework into which Jewish survivors in the East could integrate their memory – and at the same time one of the more welcoming and earliest – was a variety of associations with the phrase "war veteran" in their names. A sizable number of mostly male youngsters (including Józef) returned from the USSR to Poland as soldiers of the Soviet-controlled army and were later awarded various medals for fighting against Germany. Some survivors sat for interviews with military decorations adorning their lapels. Adam achieved great recognition in the small town of Kudowa as both a community activist and an accomplished member of a veterans' organization (VHA, Kudowa Zdrój, September 1997). Henryk remained in the army for some time but was eventually discriminated against and forced to return to civilian life (VHA, Gdańsk, May 1997). His obituary (2014) lists his rank first as a "retired colonel," followed by "Sybirak" (Siberian). Michał can boast several military medals (Centropa, Legnica, July 2004); all these men were teenagers when they set off on their refugee journey and were sent to Siberia, and young men when they were drafted into the army. In the postwar period, and for some time they enjoyed veterans' allowances as members of the Association of Fighters for Freedom and Democracy, the official Polish Veterans' Union as presently called.

The memory of the war cultivated in this environment was less about victimhood, and more about heroism and fighting for freedom. Its members, and at the same time the coauthors of this collective story, were first deportees, but later actual participants in the combat. In 1991, another organization was created that used the word "combatant" more symbolically. From its very beginning, the Association of Jewish Combatants and Victims of World War II was open to all survivors, whether from ghettos, camps, the underground, or the USSR. The association proved to be very popular among the surviving Jewish refugees, but not everyone joined. When asked why he had not joined, a former refugee survivor, Zygmunt replied: "I am not a veteran. I didn't fight, but was fought against, as a child" (VHA, Kraków, April 1997). Alina, who was Zygmunt's age, as well as Marian, Feliks (Centropa, Warsaw, November 2005), and Anna (Centropa, Warsaw, November 2005), who were a few years older than him, were members, but not because they had returned to Poland as soldiers. Instead, they chose to belong because they understood the association's significance differently. Their sheer survival against all odds – as children and in the USSR – "was an act of resistance against the oppressors" (Z-J, PI with Alina, Żary, June 2022). Their age or status as a soldier did not play a key role here.

An additional noteworthy point is that among the former refugee children and youth interviewed in Poland, there are both individuals with no affiliation at all and others who have decided to join not one but several organizations dealing with the past. Taking advantage of the multitude of post-1989 associations and exercising their right to decide, Alina and Miriam, for example, enrolled in both the Association of Jewish Veterans and the Siberians' Association. Many interviewees reported seeking comfort in Jewish cultural organizations later in their lives in free Poland. Statements from two former refugee children, Lila and Minna (VHA, Szczecin, April 1997), suggest that they gravitated to Jewish organizations not so much to address their wartime trauma or join the collective representation of the past tragedies that befell them (the Holocaust or Siberia), but to reestablish the link with Jewish life and connect with long-lost Jewish culture:

> After the death of my husband, a Catholic, I felt a calling to belong. I don't know, it was just like that. I became very involved in the Jewish community. It gives me a lot of satisfaction, and I started to feel a sense of belonging. I have the same friends as before, the Aryans (*sic!* – ed.), and they support me. Fortunately, I belong to an environment of decent people.
> (VHA, Interview with Lila, Warsaw, August 1998)

Affiliation – Identity – Mnemonic Choice

Displacement is not only a matter of losing one's home. It is not just about dealing with the grief that ensues but is also a matter of striving for a new place and belonging in the world (Malkki, 1995). When their previous communities are destroyed, people look for alternative ways to think about their social relationships (Leydersdorff, 2014). Shared beliefs and perspectives on the past represent one of the basic elements of group formation and the expression of social identity (Tajfel, 1982). In recounting their past, former refugees would often do so in the most socially acceptable way or avoid public statements altogether.

Lacking a socially acceptable collective memory frame corresponding to their sense of the past, the majority of the Polish Jewish interviewees did not mention remembering their displacement in any affiliated, public way. As cited above, Bianka could not have imagined "going to the Siberians" with her memory of

Jewish wartime experiences. Indeed, the group of Jewish survivors who feel affinity with other Polish Siberians constitutes perhaps the most intriguing and least researched community. While the number of such former Jewish refugees is limited, it is not insignificant. For example, at least a dozen names of refugee survivors appear on the association's list of one local branch, namely that in Łódź, including one of the branch's founders, Adam Ochocki.

For Jewish refugees who – unlike Józef or Bianka – lived outside Warsaw and were rather detached from the Jewish community in their daily professional lives, speaking of their experiences as Polish Siberians constituted a valid and rare way to embed their past in a collective narrative. Their adjusted story, repeated many times, grew into *archival memory* (Hoffman & Hoffman, 1994). With repeated retelling, the story increasingly conforms to expectations, and certain aspects that are deemed unnecessary to the narrative are gradually omitted as irrelevant. Such is the case of Jewish identity in Otylia's story as she recounted it for the Polish filmmakers. In the quest to belong to some *imagined community* or an *imagined identity* (Megill, 1998), what people omit is as important as what they repeat.

Joining the Polish community of memory involved repressing the memory of their triple persecution as Jews at the hands of the Nazis, the Soviet regime, and their fellow Poles. This type of confrontation with the past entailed significant memory work by the refugee survivors, including the defensive mechanism of repression and chosen mechanism of silence. Alois Hahn (2000) distinguished between memory (*Gedaechtnis*) and memorization (*Erinnerung*). In his proposition, memory is a selective psychological process over which we have little influence, and it rests in the realm of psychology. Memorization – closer to historical studies – is a process of further but more conscious selection or choice. The conscious thematization of some topics from the past rather than others is linked to the present ever-changing situation of the "rememberers" and the extent to which the current context gives them the freedom or prompts them to engage with the past.

The division into memory and memorization resembles the idea by Charlotte Delbo (1995) who distinguished between a process of *normalizing memory* that is adaptive and seeks meaning and one of *deeper memory* that is locked in the body and refuses to submit to narrative ordering. Otylia's emotional response to returning to her birthplace and being chased away suggests her Jewish identity was deeply tied up in experiences of antisemitism, even if she refused to interpret the scene as antisemitic. Her refusal to denounce her fellow Poles demonstrates a strong conscious commitment to her chosen national identity. Remembering her childhood according to the dominant national narrative – that of Siberians' Association – helped consolidate this identity choice. One can understand that for reasons of security and belonging, most of the generation of former child refugees who stayed in Poland did not delve into the oppressive Christian heritage.

This selective amnesia has had the effect of weakening Jewish identity and limiting their ability to mourn for the families and the world lost in the Holocaust. For those affiliated with the Siberians, the transmission of family history focused primarily on the Soviet experience and fully attributed their sense of victimhood to

Communist totalitarianism. This included emphasizing the strength of spirit, overcoming Siberian cold and hunger, and the fortunate collapse of the Soviet-imposed system in 1989. Bearing witness is often accompanied by the subconscious elimination of one's otherness to present oneself to other people as relatable (Fassin & Rechtman, 2009; McLean & Syed, 2015). This is then followed by a more conscious self-definition on the principle of "strategic essentialism" (Spivak, 2012), chosen as a common ground for integrating into a community or conforming to the prevalent collective representation of victimhood (Helms, 2013).

Had the Jewish refugee survivors in Poland given themselves over to contemplating the full extent of their experiences, that is, as the central targets for annihilation by the Germans in addition to having suffered repression under the Soviets and discrimination by Christian Poles, the resulting trauma would very likely have both stigmatized and alienated them. It would have impeded their (re-)integration in the postwar era. The Jews' status as the primary victims of Nazi oppression represented unwelcome competition with the reality of many Catholic Poles having been abused under German occupation. For that reason, many Jewish refugees avoided emphasizing what differentiated their experiences from those of other Poles during World War II. They chose to remember the past privately or in terms of the dominant Polish memory frames (as veterans or Siberians). But where surrounded by a stronger minority, as in Warsaw, they were more likely to choose to participate in collective Jewish mourning for the losses suffered in the Holocaust.

As part of the Siberians' narrative, the personal story of refugee survivors could finally be publicly recognized, accepted, and embedded in the now safe narrative of the Soviet victim in the post-1989 Poland. Contrary to the narrative of the Holocaust victims, the former did not endanger them. But it demanded a kind of selective memory on several levels which correspond to the popular German formulation: *Verbieten-Verschweigen-Verdrängen*. The full dimension of their wartime experience was marginalized: (1) by external *prohibition* for political reasons until 1989, (2) by *silencing* under a Polish majority focused on their own suffering that they viewed separate from that of the Jews and (3) by the internal *suppression* for fear of social exclusion.

Assimilation into the majoritarian memory culture has led many refugee survivors to either lose or never strongly develop a sense of Holocaust victimhood. Thus, they have filtered and not passed on this specific trauma to the next generation. On the one hand, the affiliation with Siberians may have alleviated, mitigated, or "spared" subsequent generations the burden of the Holocaust integrational trauma (which Otylia's children and grandchildren no longer carried). On the other hand, the embraced grief as an effective resource for change was also lost.

Conclusion

This chapter underscores the fact that, despite the longitudinal influence of national context (part of structural determination), the multidimensional experience of Polish Jewish refugees was not reduced to one simplified narrative; for example, that of the repressed Jewish or Polish nation, that of the Holocaust or the Gulag victimhood. The multiplicity of the adopted mnemonic trajectories was not caused solely by variables in the refugees' experience, nor was it only the product of social community setting (social constraints) or chosen degree of pursued assimilation. While it is crucial to understand the collective conditions under which narrative commitments are made, ultimately it is individuals who remember. Although the refugee group studied here shared a critical juncture of their individual life cycles, they did not yield "a memory generation" and one "intergenerational trauma," even within one country. As this study shows, shared experiences, do not translate one-to-one into a singular victim identity. Narratives are important, and they are constructed and chosen within social limits. In both acts – of construction and choice – former refugees performed an important deliberate agentic role, extending as far as implicating the next generation in fundamentally different contexts of collective memory.

This lack of mnemonic consensus and mnemonic likeness should not be viewed as a deficit. Instead, the multiplicity testifies to the mnemonic prowess of individuals who, in the midst of many social determinants, as this chapter illustrates, have managed to retain some, if limited, capacity to make their own intimate choices regarding which memory path(s) to follow. This meant sometimes opposing the reductive homogenization, and sometimes accepting the prevalent organizing logic of victimhood along ethnonational collectives. The protagonists of this study did not surrender their role as choosing actors. The task of historians working with witnesses is to avoid the temptation to impose their interpretations (epistemological violence) and allow those who were victims to tell and preserve the story according to their chosen narrative. As for further recommendations arising from this study, they would be to work on securing the conditions for memory pluralism, especially for refugee and minority communities as they are entering their respective majoritarian frameworks of social memory: to ensure that the social framework favors the most natural ways, rather than forcing (as has too often been the case here) limited choices about how to remember a difficult personal past.

Notes

1 This text has been written as part of the ERC-Project "Unlikely Refuge? Refugees and Citizens in East-Central Europe in the 20th Century" (grant agreement No 819461).
2 This study thus primarily analyzes testimonies of 1.5-generation and supplements these in two instances with statements from younger interviewees (born during the war).
3 For the comfort of interview participants, the chapter author is only using their first names, which are altered in many cases. The key to the altered identities used as sources in this study as well as recorded interviews are available upon request (and subject to confidentiality) from the author.
4 Landsmannschaften–Jewish associations formed according to their members' place of birth or former residence in Eastern Europe. Also organized by German resettlers from the East after the war.
5 Personal Testimony of the Survivor, Relacje Ocalałych [Survivors' Testimonies], Archive of the Jewish Historical Institute, 1948. Name withheld due to relationship with the privileged interviewee. Testimony is on file with the chapter author.

References

Adler, E.R. (2020). *Survival on the Margins*. Cambridge, MA: Harvard University Press.
Alexander, J.C. (2009). The Social Construction of Moral Universals. In: Alexander, J.C. (Ed.), *Remembering the Holocaust. A Debate* (pp. 3–104) Oxford: Oxford University Press.
Bradley, M. (2014). Rethinking Refugeehood: Statelessness, Repatriation, and Refugee Agency. *Review of International Studies*, *40*(1), 101–123. https://doi.org/10.1017/S0260210512000514
Centropa. (n.d.). Retrieved November 29, 2023, from www.centropa.org/en/our-archive-library-rescued-memories
Confino, A. (1997). Collective Memory and Cultural History: Problems of Method. *The American Historical Review*, *102*(5), 1386–1403. https://doi.org/10.2307/2171069
Delbo, C. (1995). *Auschwitz and After*. New Haven, CT: Yale University Press.
Fassin, D., & Rechtman, R. (2009). *The Empire of Trauma: An Inquiry into the Condition of Victimhood*. Princeton, NJ: Princeton University Press.
Goldlust, J. (2012). A Different Silence: The Survival of More than 200,000 Polish Jews in the Soviet Union during World War II as a Case Study in Cultural Amnesia. *Australian Jewish Historical Society Journal*, *21*(1), 13–60.
Gross, J.T. (2007). *Fear: Antisemitism in Poland after Auschwitz*. New York: Random House Trade Paperbacks.
Grossmann, A. (2016). Remapping Survival: Jewish Refugees and Lost Memories of Displacement, Trauma, and Rescue in Soviet Central Asia, Iran, and India. In Raphael, Gross. (Ed.), *Simon Dubnow Institute Yearbook* 15 (pp. 71–98). Göttingen: Vandenhoeck & Ruprecht. https://doi.org/10.13109/9783666369452.71
Hahn, A. (2000). *Konstruktionen des Selbst, der Welt und der Geschichte* [Constructions of the self, the world and the history]. Frankfurt: Suhrkamp.
Halbwachs, M. (1925). *Les cadres sociaux de la mémoire* [The Social Frameworks of Memory]. Paris: Librairie Félix Alcan.
Helms, E. (2013). *Innocence and Victimhood*. Madison, WI: University of Wisconsin Press.
Hen, J. (1990). *Nikt nie woła* [There is no-one calling]. Warsaw: Wydawnictwo Literackie.
Hen, J. (1991). *Nowolipie*. Warsaw: Iskry.
Hoffman, A.M., & Hoffman, H.S. (1994). Reliability and Validity in Oral History: The Case for Memory. In Jeffrey, J., & Edwall, G. (Ed.), *Memory and History: Essays on Recalling and Interpreting Experience* (pp. 107–136). Lanham, MD: University Press of America.
Hoffman, E. (2004). *After Such Knowledge*. New York: Public Affairs.
Keely, C. (2001). The International Refugee Regime(s): The End of the Cold War Matters. *The International Migration Review*, *35*(1), 303–314.
Korycki, K. (2023). *Weaponizing the Past. Collective Memory and Jews, Poles, and Communists in Twenty-First-Century Poland*. New York and Oxford: Berghahn.
Koźmińska-Frejlak, E. (2022). *Po Zagładzie. Praktyki asymilacyjne ocalałych jako strategie zadomawiania się w Polsce (1944/45–1950)* [After the Holocaust. Assimilation practices of survivors as strategies for settling in Poland (1944/45–1950)]. Warsaw: Jewish Historical Institute.
Levy, D., & Sznaider, N. (2002). Memory Unbound: The Holocaust and the Formation of Cosmopolitan Memory, *European Journal of Social Theory*, *5*(1), 87–106. https://doi.org/10.1177/1368431002005001002
Leydersdorff, S. (2014). When All is Lost: Metanarrative in the Oral History of Hanifa Survivor of Srebrenica. In Cave, M., & Sloan, S.M. (Eds.), *Listening on the Edge: Oral History in the Aftermath of Crisis* (pp. 17–32). Oxford: Oxford University Press.
Malkki, L. (1995). Refugees and Exile: From "Refugee Studies" to the National Order of Things. *Annual Review of Anthropology*, *24*, 495–523. https://doi.org/10.1146/annurev.an.24.100195.002431

McLean, K. C., & Syed, M. (2015). Personal, Master, and Alternative Narratives: An Integrative Framework for Understanding Identity Development in Context. *Human Development*, *58*(6), 318–349. https://doi.org/10.1159/000445817

Megill, A. (1998). History, Memory, Identity. *History of the Human Sciences*, *11*(3), 37–62. https://doi.org/10.1177/095269519801100303

Mishler, E.G. (2009). *Research Interviewing: Context and Narrative*. Cambridge, MA: Harvard University Press.

Olick, J.K., & Robbins, J. (1998). Social Memory Studies: From "Collective Memory" to the Historical Sociology of Mnemonic Practices, *Annual Review of Sociology*, *24*, 105–140.

Redlich, S. (2012). *Na rozdrożu. Żydzi w powojennej Łodzi 1945–1950* [At the crossroads: Jews in post-war Łódź 1945–1950]. Łódź: IPN.

Refugee Convention. (July 28, 1951). *United Nations, Treaty Series*, *189*, 152. Retrieved December 4, 2023, from www.refworld.org/docid/3be01b964.html

Rice, M. (2017). *"What! Still Alive?!": Jewish Survivors in Poland and Israel Remember Homecoming*. Syracuse, NY: Syracuse University Press.

Rumbaut, R.G. (2004). Ages, Life Stages, and Generational Cohorts: Decomposing the Immigrant First and Second Generations in the United States. *International Migration Review*, *38*(3), 1160–1205.

Schwartz, B. (1996). Memory as a Cultural System: Abraham Lincoln in World War II. *American Sociological Review*, *61*(5), 908–927.

Shoah Foundation Visual History Archive (VHA). (n.d.). Retrieved November 29, 2023, from https://vha.usc.edu/home

Spivak, G. (2012). *In Other Worlds: Essays in Cultural Politics*. London and New York: Routledge.

Tajfel, H. (1982). *Social Identity and Intergroup Relations*. Cambridge: Cambridge University Press.

Zerubavel, E. (1996). Social Memories: Steps to a Sociology of the Past. *Qualitative Sociology*, *19*, 283–299.

Zessin-Jurek, L. (2015). Forgotten Memory? Vicissitudes of the Gulag Remembrance in Poland. In Mitroiu, Simona. (Ed.), *Life Writing and Politics of Memory in Eastern Europe* (pp. 45–65). London: Palgrave Macmillan.

Zessin-Jurek, L. (2021). A Matzeva Amid Crosses: Jewish Exiles in the Polish Memory of Siberia. In Friedla, K., & Nesselrodt, M. (Eds.), *Polish Jews in the Soviet Union* (pp. 236–260). Boston, MA: Academic Studies Press.

Zessin-Jurek, L. (2022). Whose Victims and Whose Survivors? Polish Jewish Refugees between Holocaust and Gulag Memory Cultures. *Holocaust and Genocide Studies*, *36*(2), 154–170. https://doi.org/10.1093/hgs/dcac029

5 In the Aftermath of Silence

An Intergenerational Burden of Recognition in Postgeneration Holodomor Survivor Literature

Elise Westin

Introduction

How do *the postgenerations of genocide* contribute to the construction of memory of their ancestors' experiences? How do they speak the "unspeakable" (Schreiber Weitz, 2012), and what resulting capacity exists for them to "work through" (LaCapra, 2014) trauma on behalf of their ancestors? What are the consequences of their participation in these mnemonic practices? These are some of the questions that Melnyczuk (2012) addresses as to the silences of Holodomor survivors among the Ukrainian community in Western Australia, thus working to fill the void in testimonial literature for Ukrainian–Australians. However, her actions embody an inherited survivor debt. As a second-generation survivor, Melnyczuk takes on the burden of this survivor debt, using publications to gain recognition on behalf of her community. This chapter draws on Hirsch's (2012) concept of "postmemory" to describe how *the postgenerations* represent new possibilities for working through trauma. Through the lens of postmemory, the chapter explores Melnyczuk's construction of a 'silent witness trope,' and the way she uses her texts to gain wider public recognition of the Holodomor. The analysis aims to shed light on intergenerational processes of trauma in the Ukrainian–Australian experience, in terms of a postcolonial and a postgenocidal pathology of recognition among postgeneration Holodomor survivors.

Based in Western Australia, Melnyczuk grew up with frequent contact with the Ukrainian community in Perth and dedicated her academic career to researching the Holodomor. As Melnyczuk's parents were Holodomor survivors, her works could be considered both the result of extensive academic research and second-generation survivor testimony. Melnyczuk's parents migrated to Australia from Germany after World War II and spent time in a migrant camp before settling in Western Australia. This family history prompted Melnyczuk's interest in the Holodomor from a migrant perspective. In 2004, she commenced a Ph.D. at Notre Dame University in Fremantle with a thesis investigating the memories and outcomes of Ukrainian migrant refugees in Western Australia who had experienced the Holodomor firsthand (Melnyczuk, 2010). Her thesis resulted in the publication of *Silent Memories, Traumatic Lives: Ukrainian Migrant Refugees in Western Australia* (2012), a monograph that discusses common experiences of Ukrainian migrants to Western Australia and includes short excerpts from interviews with survivors. These interviews were also used in Melnyczuk's more recent coedited publication, *Holodomor: Silenced Voices of the Starved Children* (2018), a collection of 40 firsthand accounts of the Holodomor by survivors who migrated to Western Australia. Melnyczuk has dedicated more than a decade to researching the event, becoming one of a very small group of Holodomor scholars publishing in Australia.

This chapter first explains the Holodomor as an event that was inherently traumatic for the population of Ukraine and provides background information on the formation of the post–World War II community of Ukrainians in Australia. It then moves to a discussion of the concept of a "pathology of recognition" and how this can be recognized in Melnyczuk's *Silent Memories, Traumatic Lives* (2012) as a process for gaining greater recognition from the general public on behalf of Melnyczuk's ancestors and community. Following this discussion, the chapter addresses Melnyczuk and Webster's 2018 text, and her efforts to end the silence for future postgeneration survivors of the Holodomor. Finally, the chapter concludes with a discussion of the intergenerational impact of the Holodomor on *the postgenerations*. It covers the ways in which *the postgenerations* work through their familial trauma discursively, the marks this process leaves upon them, and finally, the challenges that *the postgenerations* face in light of the 2022 Russian invasion of Ukraine.

Background

With the exception of a small number of scholars who deny the existence of the Holodomor, it is unanimously agreed that the 1932–1933 Great Famine in Ukraine resulted from Soviet policies under Joseph Stalin. In 1928, Stalin announced his First Five-Year Plan, which focused on rapid industrialization and the collectivization of agriculture. Many Ukrainian farmers resisted collectivization, equating it to a return to serfdom (Applebaum, 2017, p. 56). To break village community structures, the Kremlin divided villagers into social strata: wealthier peasants or *kurkuls* ("kulaks" in Russian), middle peasants or *serednyaks*, and poorer peasants or *bidnyaks* (Marples, 1984, p. 561). The so-called *kurkuls*, according to this newly introduced definition, as illustrated in Marples (1984), were eventually branded as class enemies, but, in reality, the term was used to target all peasants who opposed the Communists, regardless of their economic status (Fitzpatrick, 1993, p. 745; Snyder, 2010, p. 25). During collectivization, armed brigades forcibly confiscated land and property, evicting families who were then sent to remote areas such as northern Russia, the Urals, Siberia, or Kazakhstan without food or shelter (Snyder, 2010, p. 26). Many died in transit or soon after, while others formed settlements that became forced labor camps (Snyder, 2010, p. 26).

As agricultural productivity diminished due to the elimination of "kurkul" farmers and state mismanagement, urban populations were prioritized over rural ones (Kessler, 2001, p. 481). Roadblocks and internal passports were introduced to prevent starving villagers from entering cities or leaving their regions (Kessler, 2001, p. 482; Naimark, 2010, p. 73). Relief from starvation was further prevented by the Soviet authorities' refusal to accept offers of food relief to Ukraine from outside the Soviet Union (Naimark, 2010, p. 73). Between 1932 and 1933, millions died in Ukraine, Kazakhstan, and other parts of the Soviet Union.[1] The planned nature of the famine, excessive food requisitioning, refusal of aid, and internal passport system suggest an intent to commit mass murder in the Ukrainian countryside. However, the Holodomor's classification as genocide remains debated and its victims largely unrecognized internationally.

Less than a decade later, World War II claimed approximately 20–27 million Soviet lives, including civilians and military personnel (Bideleux & Jeffries, 2007, pp. 419–420; Plokhy, 2015, p. 282). Over 3 million Ukrainians were displaced as laborers, prisoners of war, deserters, or refugees (Dyczok, 2000). After World War II, all but 200,000 of these displaced persons were repatriated against their will to the Soviet Union under the Yalta agreement, considered traitors, and sent to NKVD camps or resettled for hard labor (Dyczok, 2000, pp. 56–62).[2] Some migrated from Germany through illegitimate means, such as bribery, forged documents, or false affiliation with Polish families, who, as non-Soviet citizens, could migrate more freely. While stories of survivors using each of these methods surface in conversations with their descendants, these were rarely documented, officially or otherwise, due to fear of repercussions. However, when the International Refugee Organization (IRO)[3] came into effect in 1948, the policy of forced repatriation shifted to resettlement abroad, as the risks associated with repatriation became acknowledged (Isajiw & Palij, 1992, p. xvii). Many Ukrainian migrants changed their names in Australia to assimilate. Officially documented as "Russians," they were socially referred to as "wogs," "enemy aliens," "Balts," or "New Australians" (Melnyczuk, 2012, p. 209). As the Ukrainian migrants struggled to find common ground with Australians who remained largely ignorant of their experiences, they often kept to their own community. Meanwhile, their retraumatization because of war, displacement, and loss of identity continued to inhibit their ability to deal with the past.

Silence on the topic of the Holodomor was experienced by survivors both within Ukraine and in Ukrainian diaspora communities. Glenn (2004) argues that "like speech, the meaning of silence depends on a power differential that exists in every rhetorical situation: who can speak, who must remain silent, who listens, and what those listeners can do" (p. 9). Silence was a state-enforced policy within Ukraine until the fall of the Soviet Union, due to memory intervention tactics that sought to prevent the act of witnessing (Starovoyt, 2018, p. 321). Etkind et al. (2012) call this "discursive cleansing," whereby witnesses are silenced, so-called evidence that disproves historical events is falsified, and references to such events are retroactively erased (p. 16). In the Ukrainian community in Western Australia, there was a more internalized silence around the topic of the Holodomor. Melnyczuk (2012) refers to this as a "code of silence," resulting from international ignorance of the Holodomor, a desire to protect survivors' families and themselves, a result of fear and shame, and a desire to "look to the future" (p. 191). She notes that "[t]his internalised code of silence was also enforced by external influences, by the Stalinist-era Soviet Government's repressive tactics and the fear they engendered and also by the silence maintained by international governments on the famine" (Melnyczuk, 2012, p. 191).

These silences had an impact on *postgeneration* survivors of the Holodomor in the community. According to Glenn (2004), "whatever its shape, the form of silence (its delivery) is always the same. But the function of silence – that is, its effect upon people – varies according to the social context in which it occurs" (p. xii). In an attempt to understand the silences in her family's past, in her *Silent Memories, Traumatic Lives* (2012), Melnyczuk shapes survivors as silent witnesses, contextualizing these witnesses as a consequence of a lack of treatment for their trauma, along with a lack of international recognition (p. 233). The latter is reinforced in the testimonies of her interviewees, one of whom notes:

> Having the truth of these times revealed today has been a mixed blessing. On one side it is a relief to finally have an accounting of all the suffering that was inflicted upon the Ukrainian people. On the other is a great sadness that has come with being aware that some of the scholars who have undertaken the task of researching the Holodomor think that we who lived through it have forgotten, since we have been reluctant to speak of it to outsiders. How can such people, many of whom have lived in free lands their entire lives, possibly understand the fear we must first overcome before stepping forward with our stories? They forget that all knowledge and written records of this tragedy were completely suppressed for so many years. Silence ensured survival, and that has been a very hard habit to break.
>
> (Maria, as cited in Melnyczuk and Webster, 2018, p. 155)

By contextualizing silence in relation to the lack of international recognition, Melnyczuk demonstrates something similar to a pathology of recognition. According to Oliver (2001),

> [i]t is only after oppressed people are dehumanized that they seek acknowledgement or recognition of their humanity. More perverse is that they seek recognition of their humanity from the very group that has denied them of it in the first place.
>
> (p. 26)

Even if recognition is achieved, the oppressive power structure remains (Oliver, 2015, p. 476). As a *postgeneration* survivor, Melnyczuk seeks public recognition of her community's humanity, historically denied to the Holodomor compared to some other genocides.

"Postmemory," as defined by Hirsch (2012), describes the connection the subsequent generation has to their ancestors' trauma through familial stories and behaviors (pp. 3–6). For *postgeneration* Holodomor survivors, the temporal and experiential distance allows them to voice their ancestors' experiences while addressing their own identity construction. Melnyczuk (2012) herself argues:

> When I began my research, I found that as a child of Ukrainian migrants, I was not alone in my ignorance of the events that befell my parents in their

early years. Many survivors did not share their memories with their families, preferring to separate completely their new lives from their old, partly to protect their children from painful truths and partly to protect themselves.

(p. 7)

Thus, Melnyczuk aims to break familial silences and seek public recognition from a *postgeneration* perspective.

A Pathology of Recognition in *Silent Memories, Traumatic Lives* (2012)

Published by the Western Australian Museum, *Silent Memories, Traumatic Lives* (2012) is the first book-length publication to tell the story of Holodomor survivors who migrated to Western Australia after World War II. The text describes experiences of the Holodomor, displaced persons camps in Europe, and challenges while migrating to Australia. Illustrated with over 100 historical and personal photographs, it is divided into chronological sections: "The Holodomor Years," "Survival," "Life after the Holodomor Years," "Long Term Effects of the Holodomor," and "Manmade Famine as Genocide." Melnyczuk (2012) constructs a silent witness trope to address public ignorance about the Holodomor. She integrates official documentation and survivors' voices, refuting denialism and arguing that the Holodomor was an act of genocide. Her text demonstrates that *postgenerations* can gain recognition where their ancestors could not, giving authority to survivors' voices that had been overlooked. The use of the silent witness trope in each of Melnyczuk's texts represents a form of dialogue with a general readership. Melnyczuk (2012) argues that silence is "both a cause and an effect" of delayed recognition of the Holodomor (p. 194). A lack of knowledge of the existence of atrocities of such magnitude as the Holodomor can invite the question that recurs throughout Melnyczuk's writing: if it was so horrible, and if so many people were killed, why did we not know about it? The silent witness trope demonstrates the ways in which victims struggle to speak *the unspeakable*. Schreiber Weitz (1990, cited in Caruth, 1995) describes this dilemma of bearing witness as follows:

> People have said that only survivors themselves understand what happened. I'll go a step further. We don't . . . I know I don't . . . So there is a dilemma. What do we do? Do we not talk about it? Elie Wiesel[4] has said many times that silence is the only proper response but then most of us, including him, feel that not to speak is impossible. To speak is impossible, and not to speak is impossible.
>
> (p. 154)

Melnyczuk (2012) also notes the place of fear in silencing witnesses in the preface of her text:

> In Soviet Ukraine, giving voice to the truth about the famine years was punishable by imprisonment or execution, and many survivors never lost the

fear that they, or any family left in Ukraine, would suffer if they spoke out. More than 75 years later, most of those who participated in this study still felt that fear to some extent, but all faced it down to share the stories of their lives with me.

(p. 7)

She presents her work as an exception to this silence, in which the silent witness is given a voice, so that the public can finally learn about the Holodomor.

The introduction of historical and legal documents is a technique adopted by Melnyczuk (2012) to support her claim that the Holodomor constitutes genocide. In particular, her chapter entitled "Manmade Famine as Genocide" (p. 237) begins with the definition of *genocide* as it was coined by Raphael Lemkin and as it was recognized and ratified in the 1948 Convention on the Prevention and Punishment of the Crime of Genocide by the United Nations. The chapter proceeds to compare the death toll of the famine in Ukraine with other genocides (p. 239) and Soviet policies supporting the argument that the Holodomor was an intentional act of genocide (pp. 241–242). The use of these documents points to a pathology of recognition in Melnyczuk's work. In fact, within her chapter on the Holodomor as genocide, she notes that

the events of the Holodomor have been subject to academic, political, and popular debate for many years, a debate no doubt fuelled by the continuing refusal of the Soviet Union and later Russia to take responsibility for the deaths of millions of Ukrainians.

(p. 241)

To show readers the unreliability of the denialist stance, Melnyczuk references the US Senate Commission into Ukraine (pp. 243–244), documents from the Soviet archives that evidence the consequences of the famine (pp. 244–249), and physical evidence of mass graves (p. 249).

Melnyczuk also draws on the voices of survivors themselves as a form of evidence, using interviews as a starting point for reconstructing the experiences of Holodomor survivors. In particular, *Silent Memories, Traumatic Lives* (2012) contains short excerpts from these to support her arguments on the enduring legacy of the Holodomor. Using the voices of the survivors themselves gives her historical study a human focus. This may represent an attempt to restore humanity to those who have suffered the dehumanizing effects of genocide. Traditionally, studies that draw on official documentation and other academic scholarship have dominated English language literature on the Holodomor.[5] Such a corpus of literature may further silence the voices of survivors in an attempt to supplement these witness accounts with official documentation and scholarly commentary. Despite this having been the dominant approach, there is arguably no more appropriate way to understand Stalinism than through the individual, personal and intimate experiences that Soviet ideology worked so hard to repress. Melnyczuk's approach to understanding history places emphasis on individual survivors, positioning them at the center of the Holodomor experience.

Melnyczuk also evokes the voices of survivors in her community to counter perceptions of guilt among the target group victimized by Soviet propaganda and the "kurkul" myth. This kurkul myth represented those labeled kurkuls as class enemies responsible for hoarding the wealth of rural communities. Melnyczuk (2012) notes the experience of one of her interviewees who was labeled a "kulak":

> One survivor, Halena, had barely spoken to her husband of her experiences in Ukraine, and her silence seemed to stem from feelings of guilt. . . . Her family had been labelled kulaks and it seemed that this left her with a long-lasting feeling of shame and a belief that somehow she and her family were bad people for having owned property, horses, and farm animals.
>
> (p. 194)

Where propaganda is used to cultivate guilt or shame among a target group, a shared experience of remaining silent often manifests, reducing their perceived authority to bear witness, even when their individual experiences align with those of other victims. Instead, they are traumatized by their perceived perpetration against their own community. However, *the postgenerations* are in a position to question the productive capacity of silence, especially when probing into these experiences can be far more useful for aiding the wider public's understanding of the past. This form of examination can extend to the complexities of positioning around perpetrators and bystanders, for example, the roles of "kapos" in concentration camps, where they were at once both victim and perpetrator. By examining the gray areas of victimhood, these *postgenerations* can effectively engage in meaningful conversation around traditionally unspoken roles in atrocity.

Ending the Silence in *Holodomor: Silenced Voices of the Starved Children* (2018)

While a form of dialogue exists in *Holodomor: Silenced Voices of the Starved Children* (2018), it engages with *the postgenerations* of the Holodomor, perhaps more than the broader public. Melnyczuk (in Melnyczuk & Webster, 2018) responds to the silences these generations experienced in their familial memories as descendants of survivors. She does so by providing them with the original testimonies from her interviews – the words of firsthand witnesses of the Holodomor who testify to experiences comparable to *the postgenerations'* own family members.

Holodomor (Melnyczuk & Webster, 2018) was published by Carina Hoang Communications – a small publisher with a focus on migrant experiences. It contains interviews formatted into individual narratives, emphasizing survivors' voices as authorities on their experiences. Each testimony is illustrated with a hand-drawn image of a Holodomor memorial. Some testimonies are separated by black pages with a quote in white text and the source on the right. Dividing these pages is a frosted, clear page, reminiscent of wax paper in old photo albums. Every copy is signed and numbered by the author, giving the book an heirloom-like quality.

The content of Melnyczuk and Webster's *Holodomor* (2018) also resembles a legacy that can be shared among members of *the postgenerations*. The introduction by Melnyczuk provides an explanation of how the book came into existence, including the influences of scholars and her own community. In investigating the history of the Ukrainian community in Western Australia, she poses the following questions: "Why didn't we know about this? Why didn't the world talk about it? Why was this major episode of history not being taught to students alongside the story of the Holocaust?" (p. viii). In doing so, she alludes to the aim of the book, which on some level seems to be to fill these silences for *the postgenerations*; Melnyczuk describes her collection of eyewitness testimonies as being "for posterity." To shed light on unspoken postgenerational silences, she describes the "legacy" and "inheritance" of certain behaviors among the postgenerations, such as an attitude toward food that comes from its scarcity in the memory of Holodomor survivors. She describes how this legacy is passed on intergenerationally and demonstrates her own affected attitude toward food wastage. Through this specific example, she alludes to the more general trauma that is inherited by *the postgenerations* in her community in Western Australia.

The book's dedication to Melnyczuk's mother is described in the introduction and this theme of family runs throughout its testimonial contributions. For example, one of Melnyczuk's interviewees, Volodymyr Ischenko, mentioned:

> I am glad my own grandchildren never experienced this. We tell them about the famine and how it was a genocide, but they don't understand – they didn't live through it. Food is readily available here in Australia, and unless you have experienced a time without it you have no true way of understanding the effects. I know the other pensioners at the Ukrainian Club understand. We can mention the famine, but that is all.
>
> (p. 10)

Another survivor, Anna Jowanowich, stated that "[e]ven today I struggle to tell my own grandchildren about these times and would much prefer that they read about it themselves so that I didn't have to relive it" (p. 15). Another still, named Maria, uses her testimony to appeal to her children to listen to her story:

> My own children . . . have never cared to hear about those times. It is just so unreal in comparison to their own experiences. . . . I suppose in one sense that is a blessing to be thankful for; but, with me now revealing my own part of the story, perhaps they will understand.
>
> (pp. 155–156)

These testimonies thus emerged in dialogue with *the postgenerations*, justifying past familial silences, while attempting to break them.

A similar attempt to break down familial silences exists in intergenerational Holocaust texts. In Peter Morley's documentary film, *Kitty: Return to Auschwitz* (1979), Kitty Felix Hart revisits the concentration camp in which she was imprisoned during World War II with her adult son to describe her experiences. Horowitz (1997) describes Hart's dual purpose of revisiting her memories of the past: first, "so that the camera, in filming Auschwitz, will refute those who claim that the Holocaust 'never happened,' and so that her son, in visiting Auschwitz, will know and understand what his mother endured" (p. 95). Much like in Melnyczuk's *Silent Memories, Traumatic Lives* (2012), Kitty's attempt to refute denialism demonstrates a pathology of recognition, while her attempt to convey knowledge of her experiences to her son aligns with Melnyczuk's purpose in *Holodomor* (Melnyczuk & Webster, 2018).

While *Silent Memories, Traumatic Lives* (2012) is aimed toward the broader public as its readership, *Holodomor: Silenced Voices of the Starved Children* (2018) demonstrates an attempt to end the long-endured familial silences for *the postgeneration* survivors and future generations. *The postgenerations* are ideally situated to give a voice to silent witnesses. Ong (2019) notes that acknowledgment of what is occurring outside of language is fundamental to one's "capacity to 'read' a trauma survivor. . . . Non-verbal language is, after all, a critical part of a survivor's narrative, testifying at times to the aspects that he or she struggles to express in words" (p. 41). The search for language beyond silence arises from *the postgenerations*' quest for answers to silences from their early years and knowledge gaps in their families' histories that have been left unspoken. As Gilbert (2018) notes, silent victims, whether living or dead, motivate outsider witnesses to speak on behalf of victims (p. 166). However, this motivation could also be seen as an inherited survivor burden. The next and concluding section examines the notion of intergenerational trauma as a part of the Holodomor trauma process, and the consequences of this legacy for *the postgenerations*.

Residual Trauma and the Postgenerations

Through academic, literary, and other creative pursuits, postgeneration survivors work to fulfill their perceived duty to gain recognition for the suffering of their ancestors and their community. This survivor debt is a product of inherited intergenerational trauma. Bezo and Maggi (2015) refer to the traumatic intergenerational impact of the Holodomor as "living in survivor mode," whereby the descendants of survivors experience a "constellation of emotions," including "horror, fear, mistrust, sadness, shame, anger, stress and anxiety, decreased self-worth, stockpiling of food, reverence for food, overemphasis on food and overeating, inability to discard unneeded items, an indifference toward others, social hostility and risky health behaviours" (p. 87). This means that, while *the postgenerations* attempt to work through the trauma of their ancestors, they must simultaneously work through their own intergenerational trauma.

Monteith (2018), a third-generation survivor from Sydney, developed an eating disorder, which she believes resonates from her familial memories and a resulting traumatic relationship with food. She notes that

> [w]ithin studies of intergenerational Holodomor trauma, I found parts of us: anxious mistrust, broken communication, "risky health behaviours," food obsession, stockpiling, terror of enfeeblement, mental illness, parents who loved their children but alienated them with the irrationality of their fear and rage.
>
> (Monteith, 2018, para.10)

In terms of working through the intergenerational trauma of genocide by starvation, Yevchenko and Masliuk (2020) evidenced in their word association study that the significance attached to words relating to food and in association with the concepts of life and death diminishes with each passing generation. This demonstrates the possibility of working through such trauma over time, though it may take generations before the effects are felt by the descendants of survivors.

Academic and creative projects offer *postgenerations* an outlet to work through the trauma of their ancestors alongside their own inherited trauma. Melnyczuk (2012) herself wrote that "[m]y decision to base my doctoral studies on the memories and experiences of the Ukrainian migrants to Western Australia, came from a determination to finally reach some understanding of what my parents and their friends lived through" (p. 6). By developing an understanding of the experiences of her family through an investigative process with systemic norms and conventions, Melnyczuk is attempting to work through both their trauma and her own. Similarly, Montieth (2018) found that academia offered

> a way to conceptualise my place and that of my family. Reading histories and social studies, I found patterns to lay across the cycles of dysfunction that had plagued us like bad blood. It was cathartic, to see us fit within that web of survivors and descendants.
>
> (para.9)

When survivors, whether first-generation or *postgeneration*, are able to draw on their own memories and the memories of others, and to freely convert these memories into discourse, they are able to work through trauma discursively.

For Ukrainian–Australians, opening up discourse around these experiences allows for processes of trauma to develop and progress. When the ability to work through trauma is hindered by external or internal obstacles that silence it, survivors can become caught up in actions situated within the realm of acting out trauma. This means repeating destructive behaviors that prevent the ability to work through the past. Given that Ukraine has now acquired independence and that the sovereignty of its government is supported by other nations, many members of *the postgenerations* both within Ukraine and in the diaspora have become empowered with a renewed legitimacy – one that was not afforded their forebears. Almost a century after the events of the Holodomor, *the postgenerations* continue to work through the trauma of the past at a collective level. However, amid the current Russo-Ukrainian war, there is little space for reflection. The efforts of those with familial connections to Ukraine are now focused on succeeding against a powerful adversary. Nevertheless, the war serves to reinforce identities that have emerged among Ukrainian communities in Australia, who are banding together to come to the aid of those forced to flee their homeland. Despite his best efforts, Russian President Vladimir Putin is effectively putting Ukraine on the map in terms of public recognition, and perspectives on the past among the broader public are being reformed. For *the postgeneration* survivors of the Holodomor, the quest for recognition has never been more supported; their stories have never been more believable or believed. As history repeats itself, however, it may become necessary to analyze the effects of retraumatization on those whose initial trauma was postgenerational.

Notes

1 Estimates of victims of the Holodomor in Ukraine range from 2.4 million to 14.5 million; especially Ukrainian politicians have claimed that Ukrainian losses reached 7, 10, or 12 million (Timtschenko, 2017). Scholarly estimates have been more modest. Banerji (2018) estimates that 5–7 million Soviet citizens may have perished in the famine, of which 4.2 million deaths occurred in Ukraine in 1933 and 1.9 million in Kazakhstan, where this number was equivalent to nearly half of its population (pp. 110–111). Plokhy (2015) estimates close to 4 million deaths in Ukraine during 1932–1934 (p. 253). Applebaum (2017) argues that at least 5 million people died of hunger in the Soviet Union, including 3.9 million Ukrainians during 1931–1934 (pp. xxvi, p. 353). Conquest (1986) suggests that 5 million died of hunger in Ukraine during 1932–1933, and 8 million altogether in the Soviet Union (p. 306).
2 The NKVD, or the "People's Commissariat for Internal Affairs," succeeded the OGPU (1923–1934) as the interior ministry of the Soviet Union, and operated from 1934 until 1946. The agency was originally tasked with undertaking police work and overseeing the prisons and labor camps. It is widely known for its part in maintaining the Soviet police state, particularly in the purges of the late 1930s, widely known as the "terror years." It was succeeded by the MGB, or *Ministerstvo gosudarstvennoy bezopasnosti*, which operated from 1946 until 1953, continuing the task of dealing with internal and external security issues, including secret police duties, foreign and domestic intelligence, and counterintelligence.
3 The International Refugee Organization (IRO) was established in April 1946 by the United Nations to assist and protect displaced people and refugees. As Australia aimed to expand its population during this time, it became involved in resettling people from Europe. Between 1945 and 1954, the IRO sponsored over 182,000 displaced people and refugees to resettle in Australia ("National Archives of Australia," n.d.).
4 Elie Wiesel (1928–2016) dedicated his life to bearing witness to the genocide committed by the Nazis during World War II based on his experiences as a Jewish prisoner in the Auschwitz and Buchenwald concentration camps. In 1986, he was awarded the Nobel Peace Prize, and his most notable work was his first book *Night* (1960).
5 See, for example, Conquest (1986), or Kulchytsky (2018).

References

Applebaum, A. (2017). *Red Famine: Stalin's War on Ukraine*. New York, NY: Doubleday.
Banerji, A. (2018). *Writing History in the Soviet Union: Making the Past Work*. New York, NY: Routledge.
Bezo, B., & Maggi, S. (2015). Living in "Survival Mode": Intergenerational Transmission of Trauma from the Holodomor Genocide of 1932–1933 in Ukraine. *Social Science & Medicine*, *134*, 87–94. https://doi.org/10.1016/j.socscimed.2015.04.009.
Bideleux, R., & Jeffries, I. (2007). *A History of Eastern Europe: Crises and Change*. 2nd Edition. New York, NY: Routledge.
Caruth, C. (1995). *Trauma: Explorations in Memory*. Baltimore, MD: John Hopkins University Press.
Conquest, R. (1986). *The Harvest of Sorrow: Soviet Collectivization and the Terror-Famine*. Oxford: Oxford University Press.
Dyczok, M. (2000). *The Grand Alliance and the Refugees*. New York, NY: Palgrave Macmillan.
Etkind, A., Finnin, R., Blacker, U., Fedor, J., Lewis, S., Mälksoo, M., & Mroz, M. (2012). *Remembering Katyn*. Cambridge: Polity Press.
Fitzpatrick, S. (1993). Ascribing Class: The Construction of Social Identity in Soviet Russia. *The Journal of Modern History*, *65*(4), 745–770. https://doi.org/10.1086/244724
Gilbert, C. (2018). *From Surviving to Living: Voice, Trauma and Witness in Rwandan Women's Writing*. Montpellier: Presses Universitaires de la Méditerranée.
Glenn, C. (2004). *Unspoken: A Rhetoric of Silence*. Carbondale, IL: Southern Illinois University Press.
Hirsch, M. (2012). *The Generation of Postmemory: Writing and Visual Culture After the Holocaust*. New York, NY: Columbia University Press.
Horowitz, S. (1997). *Voicing the Void: Muteness and Memory in Holocaust Fiction*. New York, NY: Suny Press.
Isajiw, W. W., & Palij, M. (1992). Refugees and the DP Problem in Postwar Europe. In W. W. Isajiw, Y. Boshyk, & R. Senkus (Eds.), *The Refugee Experience: Ukrainian Displaced Persons after World War II* (pp. xv–xxiv). Ontario: Canadian Institute of Ukrainian Studies Press.
Kessler, G. (2001). The Passport System and State Control Over Population Flows in the Soviet Union, 1932–1940. *Cahiers du Monde Russe*, *42*(2–4), 477–504. https://doi.org/10.4000/monderusse.8464
Kulchytsky, S. (2018). *The Famine of 1932–1933 in Ukraine: An Anatomy of the Holodomor*. Toronto: Canadian Institute of Ukrainian Studies Press.
LaCapra, D. (2014). *Writing History, Writing Trauma*. Baltimore, MD: The John Hopkins University Press.
Marples, D. R. (1984). The Kulak in Post-War USSR: The West Ukrainian Example. *Soviet Studies*, *36*(4), 560–570. https://doi.org/10.1080/09668138408411555
Melnyczuk, L. (2010). *"Remember the peasantry": A study of genocide, famine, and the Stalinist Holodomor in Soviet Ukraine, 1932–33, as it was remembered by post-war immigrants in Western Australia who experienced it*. PhD Thesis, University of Notre Dame Australia.
Melnyczuk, L. (2012). *Silent Memories, Traumatic Lives: Ukrainian Migrant Refugees in Western Australia*. Perth: Western Australian Museum.
Melnyczuk, L., & Webster, P. (2018). *Holodomor: Silenced Voices of the Starved Children*. Perth: Carina Hoang Communications.
Monteith, S. M. (2018). Hunger (or What I Inherited from My Grandmother). *Overland*. Retrieved March 1, 2023, from https://overland.org.au/2018/06/hunger-or-what-i-inherited-from-my-grandmother/comment-page-1/.
Morley, P. (1979). *Kitty: Return to Auschwitz*. Yorkshire: Yorkshire Television Colour Production.

Naimark, N. (2010). *Stalin's Genocides*. Princeton, NJ: Princeton University Press.
National Archives of Australia. (n.d.). International Refugee Organisation – Australian Government agreement. *National Archives of Australia*. Retrieved July 31, 2023, from www.naa.gov.au/students-and-teachers/learning-resources/learning-resource-themes/society-and-culture/migration-and-multiculturalism/international-refugee-organisation-australian-government-agreement.
Oliver, K. (2001). *Witnessing: Beyond Recognition*. Minneapolis, MN: University of Minnesota Press.
Oliver, K. (2015). Witnessing, Recognition, and Response Ethics. *Philosophy & Rhetoric*, *48*(4), 473–493. https://doi.org/10.5325/philrhet.48.4.0473
Ong, N. (2019). The Language of Touch: Rethinking Silence and Trauma in Anil's Ghost. *Philament Journal*, *25*, 29–52.
Plokhy, S. (2015). *The Gates of Europe: A History of Ukraine*. New York, NY: Basic Books.
Schreiber Weitz, S. (2012). *I Promised I Would Tell*. Boston, MA: Facing History and Ourselves.
Snyder, T. (2010). *Bloodlands: Europe Between Hitler and Stalin*. New York, NY: Vintage Books.
Starovoyt, I. (2018). Holodomor Generation: Literary Responses to Collective Trauma. Visnyk of the Lviv University. *Series Philology*, *67*(1), 321–334.
Timtschenko, V. (2017). Stepan Bandera – Held Oder Kollaborateur Hitlers? *Der Mitteldeutsche Rundfunk*. Retrieved March 1, 2023, from www.mdr.de/heute-im-osten/ostblogger/holodomor-diskussion-ukraine-100.html.
Wiesel, E. (1960). *Night*. New York, NY: Hill & Wang.
Yevchenko, I. M., & Masliuk, A. M. (2020). Porivnialnyi analiz kontseptu "khlib" dlia svidkiv holodomoru ta yikh nashchadkiv [Comparative analysis concept "bread" for witnesses of the holodomor and their descendants]. *Psykholohichnyi chasopys* [Psychological Journal], *1*(6), 130–141.

6 "La Sobrevivencia y La Resistencia" (Survival and Resilience)
The Experience of Intergenerational Trauma Transmission in Nicaraguan American Families

Ricardo Phipps and Janethe Peña

Introduction

Scholars of trauma among immigrants and refugees have recognized a distinct dynamic in the experiences of migrants who leave Central American countries, for example, Belize, Guatemala, Honduras, El Salvador, Costa Rica, Nicaragua, or Panama. The similar political histories of these countries are evident in the common factors which drive their migration patterns (Hiskey et al., 2018). Individuals and families leaving their home countries have resettled in neighboring countries in Central America with more stable governments, such as Costa Rica or Panama, or made longer journeys to more affluent nations like the United States. While the migration patterns of Central Americans have been politicized and migrants have been villainized at times (Rumbaut et al., 2019), the overwhelming majority of Central Americans leaving their home countries do so in desperate search of better livelihood for themselves and their families. Most Central American migrants make perilous journeys on foot, buses, trains, in closed compartment vehicles of "coyotes,"[1] or combinations of these means of transportation, making them vulnerable to numerous traumatic experiences during the journey (Frank-Vitale, 2020). Having survived premigration traumas and trauma associated with resettlement in the host country, migrants from Central American countries are at a risk of experiencing long-term traumatic stress. In more recent years, there has been an increased focus in the literature on how trauma associated with immigration has consequences for subsequent generations of migrant families.

Overview of the Central American Political Landscape

Understanding the complex geographical movement of Central American migrants is impossible without considering the historical background that produced the current political landscape in Central America. For several decades, there has been a steady stream of migration from the Northern Triangle, formed by El Salvador, Guatemala, and Honduras, and from Nicaragua (Wood et al., 2010). These four countries have been plagued by explicit colonialism and neocolonialism, civil

DOI: 10.4324/9781003385820-7

wars, gang violence, and drug trade, all of which brought financial benefit to elite groups, but poverty to the remaining population. From the initial European occupation of the Americas until the early 19th century, the territory known as Central America was under Spanish control. Shortly after declaration of independence from Spain in 1821, five former Spanish territories (Guatemala, Honduras, El Salvador, Costa Rica, and Nicaragua) combined to form the Federal Republic of Central America (Millett, 1991). Due to competing interests of the constituent territories and failure to create a truly unified government, the Federal Republic disintegrated in 1840 into five independent countries. To capitalize on natural resources for rapid economic growth, some of the countries hastily invited foreign investors, primarily from Europe and the United States, to grow the fruit industry and build infrastructure, such as railroads. Rather than true partnerships, these independent Central American nations found themselves in exploitative relationships with foreign investors and governments exercising colonial approaches (Martin, 2018). In Guatemala, El Salvador, and Honduras, the indigenous peoples found themselves largely landless, and military conflicts arose as plays for power ensued among foreign investors, the indigenous masses, and the elite families of each country. Across these three countries, the US government and respective investors worked to protect their own interests. In all these cases, many left their countries to escape military violence and to find opportunity since they were barred from landownership and reduced to peasantry at home (Ching, 2016).

An exception to this pattern of development was Costa Rica, which held its first democratic elections in 1869 (Millett, 1991). Costa Rica has had only two brief periods during which military forces tried to overthrow its democratically elected governments, and both attempts were unsuccessful. Since the second uprising in 1948, Costa Rica has maintained democracy without a standing military. Unfortunately, the history of Nicaragua reads more like that of Guatemala, El Salvador, and Honduras, rather than like Costa Rica's history.

Nicaragua and the Sandinista Revolution

Supported by an occupation army called the National Guard, military dictator General Anastasio Somoza assumed power in Nicaragua in 1936, commencing a 43-year rule characterized by dire poverty for much of the population and extensive human rights violations (Quesada, 1998). In 1979, the Sandinista Front for National Liberation staged a revolt against the Somoza government which endured for the next ten years. Somoza's resistance to the Sandinistas was brutal, including aerial bombardment of urban neighborhoods (Foran & Goodwin, 1993). The Sandinistas cultivated a broad support base, including students, artisans, tradespeople, professionals, priests, members of Christian-base communities, and poorer agricultural workers. They promised agricultural development, improvement of health and education, and employment opportunities (Millett, 1991), achieving substantial progress and winning the support of a large contingent of the Nicaraguan people. Those who benefited from the Somoza regime did not support the Sandinistas and waged war against the new government after the Sandinista Revolution, leading to the interruption of much of the progress due to the need for increased military spending.

Eventually, the Catholic hierarchy in Nicaragua abandoned the side of the Sandinistas and began to penalize individual priests who supported Sandinista policies (Foran & Goodwin, 1993). The US government supported the Somoza regime through economic and political boycotts of the Sandinista regime (Cottam, 1992). The Reagan administration funded a counterrevolutionary army, known as the Contras, and formed civilian leadership from the elite Somoza contingent (Foran & Goodwin, 1993). This war in Nicaragua finally ended in 1990, followed by elections and the ousting of the Sandinista government. The war had a devastating impact on the entire Nicaraguan population, with thousands fleeing their homes for safer parts of the country and others leaving the country. It is estimated that 40,000 died during this war and 100,000 were seriously wounded, including 40,000 orphaned children (Millett, 1991). Approximately 600,000 Nicaraguans met the criteria to qualify for war pension in later years. The US government committed economic aid to the new government but never delivered. These circumstances left Nicaragua as one of the most economically challenged countries in the Western Hemisphere at the end of the 20th century, with massive unemployment, high foreign debt, rampant violent crime, substandard education and health care, mental health crisis, substance abuse, and a host of other social problems. The current regime of Daniel Ortega, president since 2007, has left Nicaraguans with another set of challenges. In April 2018, mass protests erupted in the capital city of Managua over Nicaragua's pension system; the protests escalated to the level of demands for Ortega's resignation. Ortega did not resign, and mass migrations to neighboring countries as well as Spain and the United States have continued to rise due to the political and economic climate (Jarquín & Thaler, 2020).

Mass Migration

There are no winners in civil wars, only losses. Nicaraguans on both political sides were affected, and the country was destroyed in the name of social and economic improvement. During the Civil War, rural villages were burned, government buildings destroyed, innocent adults and children killed, and 16-year-old boys (and often younger) were conscripted into military service, leaving many Nicaraguans with few options for a better life besides migrating to safer places (Rodgers & Jensen, 2008). By all accounts, voluntary immigration is a highly stressful process (Suarez-Orozco & Suarez-Orozco, 2001), but many Nicaraguans migrated because of the economic and traumatic experience of the Civil War in Nicaragua. In their case, the migration process was not voluntary, for individuals believed they had no choice but to flee for their lives.

From November 1979 to September 1980, the Carter administration granted blanket admission to Nicaraguans entering the United States, with the largest number fleeing to southern Florida through the Refugee Act (Marquis, 1989). This group was comprised largely of wealthier Nicaraguans, many of whom had been tied to the fallen Somoza regime and felt threatened by the new Sandinista regime.

At the start of the Reagan administration, the policy toward the entry of Nicaraguans changed. From 1980 to 1986, asylum acceptance rates were only around 10% for Nicaraguans, and no Nicaraguans were given refugee status by the US government until 1987.[2] A 1987 US Supreme Court ruling, *INS v. Cardoza-Fonseca*, which involved a Nicaraguan woman in the United States since 1979, established that the standards for halting deportation were too high, thus making it easier for Nicaraguans to receive asylum status at higher rates (Jensen, 2012).

The Reagan administration was determined to send aid to any country that willingly opposed the Soviet Union.[3] As this anti-Marxist doctrine continued to develop, Reagan pledged support to several countries like Nicaragua, which included continued funding of the Contra forces to resist the Sandinistas (Scott, 1997). As the Revolution persisted, the demographics of Nicaraguans seeking safety in the United States shifted from the elite to the less affluent (Kagan, 1996). The Reagan administration took the position that allowing large numbers of working class and peasant Nicaraguans into the United States would limit the number of Nicaraguans available to fight in the Contra forces. Additionally, there was a concern that extending refugee status to large numbers of Nicaraguans might promote individuals from other Central American countries to seek safety in the United States. More recently, the United States has seen an influx of Nicaraguan migrants at the US–Mexican border. According to US Customs and Border Protection, more than 180,000 Nicaraguans have crossed into the United States since the end of November 2022, constituting more migration activity from Nicaragua than at any time in history since the Civil War, due in part to lack of faith in the Ortega government (Bermúdez & Robles, 2022).

The policy of the Reagan administration was to spend money to stabilize Nicaragua, making it unnecessary for Nicaraguan citizens to flee and for the US government to support their resettlement. This left many Nicaraguans who arrived in the United States in a very precarious position, vulnerable to deportation and struggling to find employment due to their legal status. According to the UN, the plight of the Nicaraguan people qualified as a case of refugeeism (Jensen, 2012) because they were facing political persecution. For many years, the US government maintained that the plight of Nicaraguans was motivated more by economic than political factors and withheld legal refugee status. The authors use the term *exiles* in this chapter as an umbrella term to encompass both refugees and asylees.

Immigrant/Refugee Trauma

The experience of documented migration vastly differs from undocumented migration. Nicaraguan exiles traveling without documentation in pursuit of a better life in the United States are known to have experienced a long, treacherous, and challenging journey. Women were disproportionately physically and sexually abused while children faced hunger and frightening geographic conditions. The long journey could also be demanding for men, as they also face the risk of being caught by government officials, robbery, or suffering dehydration and exhaustion from travel (Franco, 2018). When immigrants reach the United States, many have already experienced assault, abduction, and extortion from cartels, gang members, and even law enforcement (Alberto & Chilton, 2019). These experiences can lead to post-traumatic stress disorder (PTSD) and depression. As the migration of Nicaraguans to the United States shifted from largely affluent Nicaraguans to the less financially resourced, the likelihood of migration by land rather than plane increased, resulting in greater vulnerability to in-transit migration traumas.

The experiences of refugees are plagued with mental and physical health challenges. As a refugee arrives to the United States, the premigration trauma is coupled with post-migration concerns. Many refugees experience memory problems and cannot remember dates, historical events, or recent accounts (Herlihy et al., 2012). The immigrant experience does not end by leaving Nicaragua but is amplified as the immigrant must learn to navigate new social norms and to speak the English language. This new experience is the start of post-migration, resettlement trauma. Despite consisting of different stressors from the violence, bloodshed, and killing, post-migration trauma exacerbates symptoms of psychological disorders that refugees are already experiencing.

Resettlement Trauma

The process of immigration for exiles has potentially traumatic factors spanning premigration in the home country to adjusting to life in a new country, often referred to as resettlement trauma (Perez-Foster, 2001). Individuals who depart from their countries due to civil unrest and persecution are often separated from family and friends, losing their social support system. These individuals also may experience financial insecurity and marginalization in the host country due to differences in ethnicity, language, and other cultural factors. Santa-Maria and Cornille (2007) assert that this trauma can be somewhat mitigated when families are able to travel together, but because of the tendency for families from Central America to espouse collectivist values, influential members of the extended family, especially elders, are often left behind in the home country. Several years may pass before families can reunite, if ever, due to immigration laws (Letiecq et al., 2014). In the case of Central American refugee children, Zea et al. (1997) found that those separated from their fathers as older children demonstrated more vulnerability to PTSD than the same younger children, and that separation from both parents affected academic performance and cognitive and emotional functioning.

Although many immigrants and refugees find homes in communities where others from their home country have already resettled so as to connect immediately to a new support system, factors such as language barriers, documentation status, lack of skills, and xenophobia can lead to difficulties securing employment, perpetuating financial challenges (Letiecq et al., 2014). Moreover, and due to a host of factors, resettlement can be different for women than for men. For instance, Balagopal et al. (2021) discussed the influence of machismo on the feelings of powerlessness Latinx men may experience to control certain family and social dynamics in host countries which can lead to problematic external coping mechanisms, such as excessive alcohol consumption or domestic violence. Latinx immigrant women may be at a disadvantage in securing employment compared to men due to being less likely to speak the language of the host country or being more likely to have less or no experience working outside the home in their home countries (Goodman et al., 2017). While certain resettlement challenges, such as securing employment or housing, tend to be shorter term challenges, other long-term challenges, such as family separation and gender role dynamics, do not lessen over time but are exacerbated.

Impact on Subsequent Generations: Intergenerational Trauma

A growing body of scholarly literature supports the notion that trauma directly experienced by individuals affects other members of the family unit in subsequent generations, particularly children of those directly exposed, referred to as intergenerational trauma. Interest in intergenerational trauma first arose as a scholarly research topic concerning subsequent generations of Holocaust survivors (Epstein, 2022). A large number of articles emerged in the scholarly literature in the 1970s in which researchers observed that the second generation and even the third generation of Holocaust survivor families were exhibiting symptoms of PTSD and depression, although they were conceived and born after the persecutions and imprisonments had ended (Yehuda & Lehrner, 2018). According to Yehuda and Lehrner (2018), these studies noted signs and symptoms reported about the offspring of Holocaust survivors, such as over-identification and fused identity with parents, frequent catastrophizing, worry that parental traumas would be repeated, nightmares, guilt, hypervigilance, and interpersonal functioning challenges. Other contexts, including childhood sexual abuse, natural disasters, combat violence, acts of terrorism, and immigration and refugee experiences, have also been studied as circumstances that can make individuals vulnerable to intergenerational transmission of trauma, often described through the lens of secondary traumatization (Fitzgerald et al., 2020; Goodman & West-Olatunji, 2008; Dekel & Goldblatt, 2008; Pierce & Bergman, 2006; Sangalang & Vang, 2017).

The literature also documents intergenerational trauma dynamics caused by collective and historical traumas, such as the enslavement of African peoples in the Americas or the genocide of indigenous peoples in the Americas (Graff, 2014; Brave-Heart & Chase, 2016). According to Fülöp and László (2013), collective trauma is shared by a group of people during one traumatic event, sometimes spread over the span of many years. One generation will transfer the traumatic effects to other generations by keeping the trauma alive. Nicaraguans who experienced Civil War have offspring that will more than likely have their genetic makeup changed due to the parent's post-traumatic responses, known as an epigenetic, non-genomic explanation of intergenerational trauma (Yehuda & Lehrner, 2018). From this perspective of understanding of intergenerational trauma, parental trauma before children are conceived can produce changes in parents' gene expression which can result in offspring demonstrating characteristics of parents' post-traumatic states (Yehuda & Lehrner, 2018). Despite parents' adaptations to survive the stressors of war and migration, the children of Nicaraguan exiles may have the propensity for mental health challenges as well as physical challenges, such as heart disease or stroke, in the long term (Ornelas et al., 2020). Historical trauma is passed down through stories, historical data, and pictures from one Nicaraguan to the next, with the potential for misleading or exaggerated narratives being shaping the point of view of future Nicaraguans (Leslie, 1993; Summerfield & Toser, 1991).

Mechanism of Trauma Transmission across Generations

The initial explanatory theories for intergenerational trauma were psychodynamic and behavioral in nature and leaned heavily upon the display of trauma symptomology in subsequent generations as the effects of exposure to parenting by those who might have been neglectful or hypervigilant as a result of their own traumatization (Botbol et al., 2022). In this understanding of trauma transmission across generations, the stories that families share as well as the stories about which families are silent heavily influence how subsequent generations understand the trauma and how they respond to it. Based on post-apartheid research conducted in South Africa, Frankish and Bradbury (2012) concluded that silence and under-communication by the generation directly involved in a trauma experience could lead the next generation to create narratives about the trauma experience of parents and grandparents that are even more horrific than the reality. This mode of transmission of intergenerational trauma is like the experience of vicarious traumatization in which a secondhand experience of a trauma can lead to symptoms of trauma for that secondhand observer.

Biological understandings of intergenerational trauma transmission have also emerged. In the case of Holocaust survivors, it has been proposed that parental experiences potentially influence how children learn to regulate stress-related pathways early in development. The stress hormone cortisol is typically activated when a person experiences a trauma. Persons experiencing trauma may have elevated post-traumatic levels of cortisol, and in some cases, lower than normal range post-traumatic levels of cortisol develop, making cortisol level a biological indicator of trauma exposure and trauma symptomatology (Yehuda et al., 2001). Cortisol levels have been tracked in the adult children of military combat veterans diagnosed with PTSD, with consistent findings that the cortisol levels of the adult children of combat survivors diagnosed with PTSD were significantly lower than the cortisol levels of the adult children of those not diagnosed with PTSD (Yahyavi et al., 2015). Studies exist which conclude that younger children of mothers who experienced childhood abuse also have lower cortisol levels (Schreuder et al., 2016). As research continues to develop around studying the children of adults with diagnosed PTSD when those children are closer to birth, it becomes easier to attribute trauma symptomatology in the children to biological factors as opposed to interpersonal dynamics between them and their parents. Arguably, explanations of how trauma is transmitted across generations in families should include both the psychodynamic dimensions and biological influences.

Many exiles from countries where rights are suppressed, such as Nicaraguans, experience many of the vulnerabilities described above. Because of their history,

Nicaraguans are fearful that defiance of government entities or representatives (e.g., police, National Guard, politicians), will bring about serious consequences, such as imprisonment or loss of property. For many Nicaraguan exiles in the United States, there is a preference to stay under the radar and have no interaction with any government entity for fear of negative consequences.

Intergenerational Trauma Transmission in Nicaraguan American Families

The impact of the political dynamics of Nicaragua on families who fled due to war following the Sandinista Revolution is diverse and varied. As in the case with any form of trauma, there are many factors which can mitigate or exacerbate vulnerability to traumatization. Some families left Nicaragua with more resources than others. Many families were able to relocate to areas where they already had social support, while others found themselves largely alone and unsupported. Grief, loss, and disconnection from relatives and loved ones in Nicaragua were other significant factors affecting their level of trauma. The children of Nicaraguan refugees born after their parents left the country experience their own unique relationship with the traumatic pasts of their parents, largely filtered by the extent to which their parents or even grandparents have healed from their past experiences.

Avoidance

A common practice of adult trauma survivors in relation to their offspring, both young children and adults, is maintaining silence about the past traumatic experiences (Ritter, 2014). In the case of Nicaraguans, many survivors prefer not to talk about what they experienced, but rather leave those events in the past. By not talking about the traumatic experiences, survivors have a sense that they are protecting their children and grandchildren from horrors of their past which they prefer the next generations to never know about. Many survivors carry guilt and shame about what they had to do to survive or their inability to save others (Luci & Kahn, 2021). Nicaraguans who initially had a close tie to the Somoza family had a very different experience than those who did not. Specifically, those affiliated with the Somoza family likely experienced protections and had resources, which might have made their exit from Nicaragua less perilous. Because of family's hesitancy to talk about the Nicaraguan revolution and war, the children of these refugees often become conditioned to not talking about what happened, not asking questions, while still pondering on the tragic events that affected their loved ones. As Frankish and Bradbury (2012) concluded about the children of survivors of South African apartheid violence, the children of Nicaraguan refugees piece together their own narratives about their parents' stories in the face of silence. These narratives often produce feelings of anxiety and depression in their creators in a similar manner as would be the case if they had directly experienced the events.

Just as many survivors of the Nicaraguan revolution have mixed feelings about visiting Nicaragua many years later, the children of survivors frequently experience a complex range of emotions about spending time in Nicaragua (Basok, 1990). While the homeland represents a place where many relatives and loved ones still live, especially family elders, for many Nicaragua is a constant reminder of how quickly an already unstable situation can worsen. Abject poverty is still a part of the Nicaraguan story in the 21st century, with employment opportunities greatly limited (Perla & Cruz-Feliciano, 2013). It can be challenging for the subsequent generations in Nicaraguan refugee families to be appreciative of the beauty and allure of the country because their perceptions of Nicaragua are so trauma laden.

Attitudes toward the Government

Although many Nicaraguans fled to other parts of the Western hemisphere besides the United States, those who resettled in the United States arrived with mixed emotions about the country in which they were seeking asylum. Because of the long history of US involvement in Central American affairs, it was no surprise that US interests were a factor in what transpired in Nicaragua. Not only did the US government support the Somoza regime against the Sandinista revolutionaries, but US corporations fought for many years to protect their monopolies throughout the region, which contributed to the perpetuation of a class system that kept many agricultural communities in poverty. To many, the Sandinista promise to reverse this trend and empower the poor was dashed by US interference, creating a belief that the US government will always protect its own interests even through unethical means (Hager & Snyder, 2015). As a result, some Nicaraguan American families with roots in the revolution hold the sentiment that the position of the US government toward Central America is unpredictable and any commitments of support are unreliable.

Beyond the mistrust of the US government, many Nicaraguan survivors and their children feel uneasy toward government in general, including the current Nicaraguan government (Saiani et al., 2021). This is tied to the hesitancy of some families to visit their homeland. Subsequent generations who regularly follow news in Nicaragua see policies that are driven by self-interest, reinforcing the image of the country developed from family narratives or family silence. While government programs and subsidies can be helpful at times, this mistrust of government stokes a self-sufficiency that greatly prefers work and income-building ventures that do not heavily rely on government support.

Anxiety about Resources

The Nicaraguan revolution left many individuals on both sides of the Somoza–Sandinista divide in worse situations than they were prior to 1979. Although the Sandinistas' ushered in some gains in terms of health care, education, and employment opportunities, those gains were temporary as the war progressed and resources were diverted to military operations. Lands were confiscated and reallocated to remedy power imbalances (Broegaard, 2005). People in rural communities and those in cities who benefited from the temporary gains soon found themselves living in a country ravaged by war in which homes, farmland, and infrastructure were typically sacrificed and destroyed, leaving survivors struggling to find basic necessities. On the other hand, friends of the Somoza regime also found themselves not able to live the same privileged existence they had known before 1979. Supply of goods from foreign sources was disrupted, and their homes and other property were often targets of attacks or collateral damage in the mass destruction. Rationing of food affected almost all the Nicaraguan populace (Berth, 2021). This dynamic has created a feeling of uncertainty and unpredictability about the future that promotes constant expectation of economic disaster or loss among Nicaraguan exiles to this day. In terms of subsequent generations, children were raised by parents who were hypervigilant about financial struggles even during times of affluence and success due to the strong work ethic refugees brought from Nicaragua. While there is a wisdom to frugality and responsible spending, the Nicaraguan story has created a fear that one's standard of living can drastically change overnight and that one must stay on guard.

Conclusion

The mass resettlement of Nicaraguans in the United States during and after the 1979 Sandinista Revolution is a unique resettlement experience due to the role the US government played in Nicaraguan politics. After fleeing their country to escape political violence, war, and poverty, Nicaraguans who resettled in the United States brought with them a strong work ethic but also trauma. The impact of the separation from Nicaragua has plagued not only the first generation of refugees, but also subsequent generations. This dynamic has shaped how subsequent generations of Nicaraguan–Americans construct narratives about the revolution, communicate within their families about what transpired in Nicaragua, develop attitudes about traveling to Nicaragua, and manage their personal resources. Subsequent generations in Nicaraguan–American refugee families may grapple with negative effects of their family experiences of war in Nicaragua; nonetheless, many manage to overcome the doubt, mistrust, and hypervigilance about disaster and sudden change to achieve their own versions of the "American dream."

Notes

1 The term "coyote" is used to refer to an individual or a group that provides physical assistance and security to migrants from Central and Latin American countries attempting to travel to the United States and cross the border without authorization. They are referred to as "coyotes" because the practice is typically carried out with a predatory cost with migrants subjected to dangerous conditions (e.g., provided transportation in the back of tractor trailers) (Frank-Vitale, 2020).
2 While both refugees and asylees are individuals who are outside their country of nationality and are unable or unwilling to return for credible fear of persecution due to race, ethnicity, religion, political affiliation, or other such factor, refugees are granted this status by a receiving government before entering that country. Asylees are not granted asylum status until already within the receiving country or when at an entry point seeking to enter. Refugees experience a higher level of support from the receiving country; in

the US context, refugees can receive authorization to work, to travel outside the United States and return, and to begin the process for permanent residency in a more prioritized fashion than asylees (Cottam, 1992), making resettlement stressors typically more intense for those with asylee status.

3 The Reagan Doctrine, articulated by President Ronald Reagan in his 1985 State of the Union Address, was a strategy launched by the Reagan administration to slow the global influence of the Soviet Union. It involved the provision of aid to anti-Communist guerrilla and other resistance movements in various parts of the world, particularly in parts of Africa, Asian, and Latin America, including Nicaragua (Beitz, 2019).

References

Alberto, C., & Chilton, M. (2019). Transnational violence against asylum-seeking women and children: Honduras and the United States-Mexico border. *Human Right Review, 20*(2), 205–227. https://doi.org/10.1007/s12142-019-0547-5

Balagopal, G., Davidson, S., Gill, S., Barengo, N., De La Rosa, M., & Sanchez, M. (2021). The impact of cultural stress and gender norms on alcohol use severity among Latino immigrant men. *Ethnicity & Health, 27*(6), 1–19. https://doi.org/10.1080/13557858.2021.1880550

Basok, T. (1990). Repatriation of Nicaraguan Refugees from Honduras and Costa Rica. *Journal of Refugee Studies, 3*(4), 281–297. https://doi.org/10.1093/jrs/3.4.281

Beitz, C. R. (2019). The Reagan Doctrine in Nicaragua. In S. Luper-foy (Ed.), *Problems of International Justice* (pp. 182–195). New York, NY: Routledge.

Bermúdez, A. F., & Robles, F. (2022, December 27). In record numbers, an unexpected migrant group is fleeing to the U.S. *New York Times*. Retrieved November 17, 2023, from www.nytimes.com/2022/12/27/world/americas/nicaragua-us-migration.html

Berth, C. (2021). *Food and Revolution: Fighting Hunger in Nicaragua, 1960–1993*. Pittsburgh, PA: University of Pittsburgh Press.

Botbol, M., Lebailly, T., Laplace, S., & Saint André, S. (2022). A psychodynamic perspective on psychological traumas in children and their psychosocial consequences. *World Social Psychiatry, 4*(2), 106–111. https://doi.org/10.4103/wsp.wsp_21_22

Brave-Heart, M., & Chase, J. (2016). Historical trauma among indigenous peoples of the Americas: Concepts, research, and clinical considerations. *Wounds of History*, 270–287.

Broegaard, R. J. (2005). Land tenure insecurity and inequality in Nicaragua. *Development and Change, 36*(5), 845–864. https://doi.org/10.1111/j.0012-155X.2005.00438.x

Ching, E. (2016). *Stories of Civil War: A Battle Over Memory*. Chapel Hill, NC: University of North Carolina Press.

Cottam, M. L. (1992). The Carter Administration's policy toward Nicaragua: Images, goals, and tactics. *Political Science Quarterly, 107*(1), 123–146.

Dekel, R., & Goldblatt, H. (2008). Is there intergenerational transmission of trauma? The case of combat veterans' children. *American Journal of Orthopsychiatry, 78*(3), 281–289. https://doi.org/10.1037/a0013955

Epstein, H. (2022). *Children of the Holocaust: Conversations with Sons and Daughters of Survivors*. Lexington, MA: Plunkett Lake Press.

Fitzgerald, M., London-Johnson, A., & Gallus, K. L. (2020). Intergenerational transmission of trauma and family systems theory: An empirical investigation. *Journal of Family Therapy, 42*(3), 406–424. https://doi.org/10.1111/1467-6427.12303

Foran, J., & Goodwin, J. (1993). Revolutionary outcomes in Iran and Nicaragua: Coalition fragmentation, war, and the limits of social transformation. *Theory and Society*, 209–247.

Franco, D. (2018). Trauma without borders: The necessity for school-based interventions in treating unaccompanied refugee minors. *Child and Adolescent Social Work Journal, 35*(6), 551–565. https://doi.org/10.1007/s10560-018-0552-6

Frank-Vitale, A. (2020). Stuck in motion: Inhabiting the space of transit in Central American migration. *Journal of Latin American and Caribbean Anthropology, 25*(1), 67–83. https://doi.org/10.1111/jlca.12465

Frankish, T., & Bradbury, J. (2012). Telling stories for the next generation: Trauma and nostalgia. *Peace and Conflict: Journal of Peace Psychology, 18*(3), 294–306. https://doi.org/10.1037/a0029070

FüLöp, É., & LászLó, J. (2013). Emotional processes in elaborating a historical trauma in the daily press. *Narratives and Social Memory: Theoretical and Methodological Approaches*, 46–60.

Goodman, R., & West-Olatunji, C. (2008). Transgenerational trauma and resilience: Improving mental health counseling for survivors of Hurricane Katrina. *Journal of Mental Health Counseling, 30*(2), 121–136. https://doi.org/10.17744/mehc.30.2.q52260n242204r84

Goodman, R. D., Vesely, C. K., Letiecq, B., & Cleaveland, C. L. (2017). Trauma and resilience among refugee and undocumented immigrant women. *Journal of Counseling & Development, 95*(3), 309–321. https://doi.org/10.1002/jcad.12145

Graff, G. (2014). The intergenerational trauma of slavery and its aftermath. *Journal of Psychohistory, 41*(3), 181–197.

Hager Jr, R. P., & Snyder, R. S. (2015). The United States and Nicaragua: Understanding the breakdown in relations. *Journal of Cold War Studies, 17*(2), 3–35. https://doi.org/10.1162/JCWS_a_00546

Herlihy, J., Jobson, L., & Turner, S. (2012). Just tell us what happened to you: Autobiographical memory and seeking asylum. *Applied Cognitive Psychology, 26*(5), 661–676. https://doi.org/10.1002/acp.2852

Hiskey, J. T., Córdova, A., Malone, M. F., & Orcés, D. M. (2018). Leaving the devil you know: Crime victimization, US deterrence policy, and the emigration decision in Central America. *Latin American Research Review, 53*(3), 429–447. https://doi.org/10.25222/larr.147

Jarquín, M., & Thaler, K. M. (2020, May 1). Two years after Nicaragua's mass uprising started, why is Daniel Ortega still in power? *Washington Post*. Retrieved November 17, 2023, from www.washingtonpost.com/politics/2020/05/01/two-years-after-nicaraguas-mass-uprising-started-why-is-daniel-ortega-still-power

Jensen, A. (2012). *Fleeing North: An examination of U.S. Refugee and Asylum Policy Towards Nicaragua*. Master's thesis, College of Saint Benedict and Saint John's University. Digital Commons. Retrieved November 15, 2023, from https://digitalcommons.csbsju.edu/polsci_students/2

Kagan, R. (1996). *A Twilight Struggle: American Power and Nicaragua, 1977–1990*. New York, NY: Free Press.

Leslie, L. (1993). Families fleeing war: The case of Central Americans. *Marriage & Family Review, 19*(1–2), 193–205. https://doi.org/10.1300/J002v19n01_11

Letiecq, B. L., Grzywacz, J. G., Gray, K. M., & Eudave, Y. M. (2014). Depression among Mexican men on the migration frontier: The role of family separation and other structural and situational stressors. *Journal of Immigrant and Minority Health, 16*(6), 1193–1200. https://doi.org/10.1007/s10903-013-9918-1

Luci, M., & Kahn, M. (2021). Analytic therapy with refugees: Between silence and embodied narratives. *Psychoanalytic Inquiry, 41*(2), 103–114. https://doi.org/10.1080/07351690.2021.1865766

Martin, J. (2018). *Banana Cowboys: The United Fruit Company and the Culture of Corporate Colonialism*. Albuquerque, NM: University of New Mexico Press.

Marquis, C. (1989, July 16). Nicaraguan exile community forges new life in S. Florida. *The Miami Herald*, 1A.

Millett, R. (1991). Central America: Background to Crisis. In Jan Knippers Black (Ed.), *Latin America, It's Problems and its Promise: A Multidisciplinary Introduction* (2nd ed.) (pp. 317–345). New York, NY: Routledge.

Ornelas, I. J., Yamanis, T. J., & Ruiz, R. A. (2020). The health of undocumented latinx immigrants: What we know and future directions. *Annual Review of Public Health, 41*, 289–308. https://doi.org/10.1146/annurev-publhealth-040119-094211

Perez-Foster, R. (2001). When immigration is trauma: Guidelines for the individual and family clinician. *American Journal of Orthopsychiatry, 71*(2), 153–170. https://doi.org/10.1037/0002-9432.71.2.153

Perla, H., Jr., & Cruz-Feliciano, H. (2013). The twenty-first century left in El Salvador and Nicaragua: Understanding apparent contradictions and criticisms. *Latin American Perspectives, 40*(3), 83–106. https://doi.org/10.1177/0094582X13480932

Pierce, M., & Bergman, A. (2006). Panel reports: Intergenerational transmission of trauma: What we have learned from our work with mother and infants affected by the trauma of 9/11. *International Journal of Psychoanalysis, 87*(2), 555–557. https://doi.org/10.1516/FH80-9YDH-CMQF-1VKV

Quesada, J. (1998). Suffering child: An embodiment of war and its aftermath in post-Sandinista Nicaragua. *Medical Anthropology Quarterly, 12*(1), 51–73. https://doi.org/10.1525/maq.1998.12.1.51

Ritter, M. (2014). Silence as the voice of trauma. *American Journal of Psychoanalysis, 74*(2), 176–194. https://doi.org/10.1057/ajp.2014.5

Rodgers, D., & Jensen, S. (2008). Revolutionaries, barbarians, or war machines? Gangs in Nicaragua and South Africa. *Socialist Register 2009: Violence Today, 45*, 220–238. https://eprints.lse.ac.uk/28421/

Rumbaut, R. G., Dingeman, K., & Robles, A. (2019). Immigration, Crime, and the Criminalization of Immigration. In S. J. Gold & S. J. Nawyn (Eds.), *Routledge International Handbook of Migration Studies* (pp. 472–482). New York, NY: Routledge.

Saiani, P. P., Ivaldi, E., Ciacci, A., & Di Stefano, L. (2021). Broken trust: Confidence gaps and distrust in Latin America. *Social Indicators Research*, 1–13. https://doi.org/10.1007/s11205-021-02796-3

Sangalang, C. C., & Vang, C. (2017). Intergenerational trauma in refugee families: A systematic review. *Journal of Immigrant and Minority Health, 19*(3), 745–754. https://doi.org/10.1007/s10903-016-0499-7

Santa-Maria, M. L., & Cornille, T. (2007). Traumatic stress, family separations, and attachment among Latin American immigrants. *Traumatology, 13*(2), 26–31. https://doi.org/10.1177/1534765607302278

Schreuder, M. M., Vinkers, C. H., Mesman, E., Claes, S., Nolen, W. A., & Hillegers, M. H. (2016). Childhood trauma and HPA axis functionality in offspring of bipolar parents. *Psychoneuroendocrinology, 74*, 316–323. https://doi.org/10.1016/j.psyneuen.2016.09.017

Scott, J. M. (1997). Interbranch rivalry and the Reagan Doctrine in Nicaragua. *Political Science Quarterly, 112*(2), 237–260. https://doi.org/10.2307/2657940

Suarez-Orozco, C., & Suarez-Orozco, M. M. (2001). *Children of Immigration*. Cambridge, MA: Harvard University Press. https://doi.org/10.2307/j.ctvjz82j9

Summerfield, D., & Toser, L. (1991). "Low intensity" war and mental trauma in Nicaragua: A study in a rural community. *Medicine and War, 7*(2), 84–99. https://doi.org/10.1080/07488009108408972

Wood, C. H., Gibson, C. L., Ribeiro, L., & Hamsho-Diaz, P. (2010). Crime victimization in Latin America and intentions to migrate to the United States. *International Migration Review, 44*(1), 3–24. https://doi.org/10.1111/j.1747-7379.2009.00796.x

Yahyavi, S. T., Zarghami, M., Naghshvar, F., & Danesh, A. (2015). Relationship of cortisol, norepinephrine, and epinephrine levels with war-induced posttraumatic stress disorder in fathers and their offspring. *Brazilian Journal of Psychiatry, 37*(2), 93–98. https://doi.org/10.1590/1516-4446-2014-1414

Yehuda, R., Halligan, S. L., & Grossman, R. (2001). Childhood trauma and risk for PTSD: Relationship to intergenerational effects of trauma, parental PTSD, and cortisol excretion. *Development and Psychopathology, 13*(3), 733–753. https://doi.org/10.1017/S0954579401003170

Yehuda, R., & Lehrner, A. (2018). Intergenerational transmission of trauma effects: Putative role of epigenetic mechanisms. *World Psychiatry, 17*(3), 243–257. https://doi.org/10.1002/wps.20568

Zea, M., Diehl, V., & Porterfield, K. (1997). Central American youth exposed to war and violence. In J. Garcia & M. Zea (Eds.), *Psychological Interventions and Research with Latino Populations* (pp. 39–55). Boston: Allyn & Bacon.

7 Intergenerational Trauma among Refugees in Africa and the African Diaspora

Mario J. Azevedo and Tiffany D. Caesar

Introduction

The chapter examines intergenerational trauma among refugees in Africa and draws parallels between them and other African diaspora communities such as African Americans. These two groups have exhibited similar challenges starting from the onslaught of slavery to continuing disparities in health, education, and other forms of institutional racism.

The parameters of critical refugee analysis are considered by the global principles intrinsic to the Geneva Conventions of 1951 and 1954 and subsequent human rights declarations, among others, by the United Nations High Commissioner for Refugees (UNHCR), the International Organization for Migration (IOM). This chapter is premised on six goals: (1) adopting an adequate definition of the related key concepts, such as refugee, trauma and post-traumatic stress disorder, liberation war, settlements and camps, diaspora, transatlantic slave trade, refoulement, and repatriation; (2) readdressing the post-1945 international conventions and regulations on the rights of refugees; (3) analyzing African Americans' experience to understand their colonial refugee experience and approach to aid refugees in Eastern and Southern Africa; (4) examining the root causes of the international, regional, and national conditions that lead to asylum-seeking and refugee status in Eastern and Southern Africa; (5) exploring prospects on refugees' state in these respective areas; and (6) providing recommendations for the mitigation of refugee conditions and thus setting directions of future research.

In terms of methodology, diverse refugee experiences are surveyed in this chapter over time and space in Africa and the African diaspora with consideration to the impact of (neo)colonialism on intergenerational trauma and the cultural and linguistic differences that have complicated trauma, coupled with the centuries-old stereotypes and myths on both sides of the Atlantic. In addition, the chapter demonstrates how national and international conflicts, violence, and health calamities represent a long history of intergenerational trauma, aggravated by racist colonial and current policies and practices. In Africa, these processes are often exacerbated by chronic interethnic hostilities, leaders' rampant corruption, and dictatorial tendencies along with economic disparities. By focusing on three spaces of oppression – political unrest, unpredictable cases of pandemics throughout history, and unacceptable law enforcement practices – it is argued that there is a state of refugee permanence among Africa-descended refugees. Indeed, after displacement, some never return to their homeland, or attain citizenship in the new homelands to which they choose to migrate. While assimilation is often thwarted by continuous injustices that impact people's liberty, national and international laws remain oblivious to refugee/immigrant rights and freedoms. In addition, at *prima facie*, political systems create continued multilayered trauma and post-traumatic stress disorders (PTSDs), compelling those such as Dr. Joy DeGruy (2005) to introduce the concept of "post-traumatic slave syndrome" (PTSS). This chapter aims to illustrate these refugee experiences as sampled from Mozambique, Uganda, South Africa, Ethiopia, Zimbabwe, Sudan, South Sudan, and Malawi, drawing, as appropriate, parallels and contrasts with the plight of African diaspora.

Challenges Inherent in the Literature on Intergenerational Trauma

Most studies on trauma tend to be historical and are based on experiences from the Holocaust that in turn cannot be translated to all refugee populations. For example, they move away from potential or real traumatic circumstances, including war, political and religious persecution, and genocide, which has been the case among the Rwandans and Burundians, and instead prefer to cover areas usually bordering the countries in Africa.

Comprehensive studies on trauma and its impact on future generations require an interdisciplinary approach as well as collaboration with refugees themselves, and their educated kin, who can speak the local languages of the communities they purport to study, while considering the indigenous culture(s). Notably, one of the contributors to this chapter is a former refugee in East–Central Africa, who as a Fulbright scholar, visited several refugee camps in Mozambique, Malawi, and Zimbabwe, conducted research on refugees in Uganda, and published a book *Tragedy and Triumph: Mozambique Refugees in Southern Africa* (2002). This academic and human perspective combined enables researchers to gain the trust of the people they study. Therefore, *cultural competence* is a *sine qua non* condition to study refugee issues, specifically in multilingual Sub-Saharan Africa, a region that was colonized, exploited, and denigrated by the Europeans and the Arabs.

Although literature indicates that certain life events, such as war, killing of loved ones, and catastrophic natural disasters result in PTSDs, some social and behavioral scientists, biologists, geneticists, and neuroscientists remain skeptical whether the psychological and physical impact of trauma experienced by the first generation may be passed on to the next and even the *third generation of blood-related individuals, families, and the communities* with whom they interact (Isobel & Edwards, 2017, pp. 1–3, emphasis by the chapter authors). Furthermore, complexities as to trauma research can be identified in five additional research areas: (1) transmission pathways that allow the transfer of the harmful impact from one generation to another within the same family and related community; (2) preventive steps that help avoid traumatic experiences; (3) curative or intervention strategies that mitigate psychological and physical harm inflicted on people by traumatic occurrences they witness or experience; (4) varying definition offered by experts, coupled with the parochial disciplinary-specific approaches; and (5) at times, subjective interpretations of the outcomes in the field of trauma itself. These issues are exacerbated when refugee trauma and living conditions in camps, (re)settlements are studied *in situ*, using qualitative and quantitative (mixed) methods. In fact, complete (but not definitive) studies are frequently hindered by political, cultural, and linguistic (in)sensitivities, coupled with the general remoteness of geographical spaces allocated to successful asylum seekers and internally dispersed persons.

Intergenerational or transgenerational trauma is sustained trauma, manifesting in the form of PTSD or through other abnormal situations that persist over time within family or kin community. This type of transmission is also known as *relational trauma*. If and when relational trauma occurs, it is noticeable early in life, often through alterations of normally expected behavior, as a result of "maltreatment, abuse, and neglect experiences from parents and others, as well as the serious and pervasive disruptions in care-giving as a consequence of parental mental illness, substance use, or abrupt separation" (Isobel et al., 2018, p. 2). Unresolved by the parent(s), the intergenerational or transgenerational trauma experiences become "processes by which parents with unresolved trauma transmit to their children via specific interactional patterns, resulting in the effects of trauma being experienced without the original trauma experience or event" (Isobel et al., 2018, p. 2).

Those who suffer from such disorders, including the parents and other affected family members, are often unable to express these verbally or non-verbally, particularly to strangers. As Isobel et al. (2018) further explain,

> The uniqueness of intergenerational trauma therefore lies in its existence as a relational process. Rather than an event or events, intergenerational trauma is both an antecedent and outcome of traumatic attachment, . . . Once transmitted, the trauma has its own consequences and individual affects as per all psychological and interpersonally developed traumas including vulnerability to further transmission . . . to subsequent generations.
>
> (p. 2)

Yet, as is the case with qualitative studies, O'Neil et al. (2018) remind: "There are extreme variations in the lasting effects from childhood abuse from heightened stress responses resulting from aversive childhood experiences. In adult survivors of childhood abuse or hypercortisolism it results in a lack of response or dysregulated trauma" (p. 7). Emotional dysregulation "refers to the inability of a person to control or regulate their emotional responses to provocative stimuli. It should be noted that all of us can become dysregulated when triggered" ("Psychological Care and Healing Center," 2022, para.1).

In other words, in the first generation, the symptoms may be noticeably abnormal mental and/or physical (somatic) behaviors, such as inability to care for the children and impairment resulting from substance abuse, making it difficult to cope with the demands of life. In the next generation, however, the inherited disorders may manifest as low self-esteem, difficulty in maintaining sound and permanent relations, and other unusual symptoms and behaviors, which, even though "invisible" in the second generation, might persist in the third generation, and beyond. Most of the initial studies on the impact of trauma focused on victims and survivors of the Holocaust and on the Indian aborigines in the United States. However, in the third generation, although not visible, parents' non-easily discernible traumatic behavior may well be present as asymptomatic to a non-trained observer.

In fact, as if in a chain reaction, "traumatic events can be embedded in collective, cultural memory, and passed on by the same mechanisms through which culture itself is transmitted, as well as being individually passed from parent to child," which might "exhibit the hidden symptoms among two previous generations that seem to resist change in individual therapy, suggesting an epigenetic contribution" (Isobel et al., 2018, pp. 2, 6). This type of transmission of traumatic experiences to the next generations is critical to the present study of Sub-Saharan African refugees, most of whom are displaced by wars. Indeed, it is known that "Families who generations ago experienced trauma upheaval from war, residential schooling, oppression and racism as in the black Diaspora, natural disasters, and similar events, may experience various effects and enactments of the trauma passed on from parents to children" (O'Neil et al., 2018, pp. 2–3).

The Root Causes of Political Unrest and Understanding Africa's Refugee Predicament

Africa in the Context of the Global Refugee Population

According to the World Health Organization, in 2020, about 30 million people – mostly displaced by political and economic reasons, including refugees and asylum seekers – lived in Africa. This number represents almost one-third of the world's refugee and displaced population estimated at 100 million ("Concern Worldwide," 2023, para.1). These estimates are in contrast to the 1.9 million in 1951, 2.4 million in 1970, 12.1 million in 2000, and 14.3 million stateless people in 2014 (Sangalang & Vang, 2017, pp. 1–2). During the last 40 years of its independence from Europe, political instability and consistent warfare have been endemic in Africa. Civil wars ravished Rwanda and Burundi, liberation wars erupted in Mozambique and Angola in 1975, and the intermittent state of violence wreaked havoc in the DRC during the last 15 years, as well as in Sudan, South Sudan, Liberia, Central African Republic, Sierra Leone, South Africa prior to the end of the apartheid regime during the 1990s, and in Nigeria during the 1967–1970 Biafran War.

Concomitantly, refugees have been a constant fixture in Africa; in the 1960s, 300,000 Angolese refugees sought asylum from the former Congo-Leopoldville and 160,000 from Rwanda in Burundi, Congo, Tanzania, and Uganda. Similarly, from Guinea-Bissau, 60,000 refugees were hosted by Senegal; 150,000 Sudanese became refugees in the Central African Republic; 20,000 Mozambicans were hosted by Tanzania; 30,000 Ethiopians crowded the refugee camps in Sudan; and 65,000 from the former Belgian Congo, now the Democratic Republic of Congo, fled wars abroad in Burundi, the Central African Republic, Sudan, Uganda, and Tanzania (Carlin, 1989, pp. 81–82).

Recent African refugees have come from South Sudan, DRC, Burundi, Ethiopia, and Somalia, and a great majority – about 1,709,900 in 2021, surpassing Ethiopia that had 704,000 refugees, mainly from Somalia, Eritrea, Sudan, and South Sudan – are hosted by Uganda due to its open-door policy (Momodu, 2016). Comparably, Uganda – Africa's largest refugee host that provides refuge to over 1.5 million people – trails only Turkey that hosts 3.7 million refugees, followed by Pakistan with 2.1 million. Generally, in Sub-Saharan Africa, some 6.3 million refugees remain scattered around ("UNHCR Refugee Statistics," 2023; "UNHCR Türkiye Operational Update," 2023).

In many former colonies, violence also erupted as part of liberation movements which, for example, devastated Zimbabwe in its guerrilla warfare against the Ian Smith regime in former Southern Rhodesia during the 1970s–1980s. While Namibia, former South-West Africa, fought against Apartheid South Africa in the 1980s, the Ethiopian violent struggle against Eritrea lasted from 1961 to 1991 followed by a civil war from September 12, 1974 to 1991. The former Spanish Sahara waged war against Morocco, and in Somalia, the "failed state" or "the state without a state" is the portal of the unending deadly debacle since 1992, resulting in the deaths of hundreds of people annually.

Critical Definitions, Historical Antecedents, and Current Knowledge of Trauma

As per the 1951 Refugee Convention, core to the concept of *refugee* is that it designates a person who flees war, violence, conflict, and has crossed an international border to find safety in another country, and thus being protected by national and international law (UNHCR, 1950). In 1969, this was clarified in Article 1 of the Organization of African Unity (OAU), now the African Union (AU), as follows:

> [T]he term "refugee" shall also apply to every person who, owing to external aggression, occupation, foreign domination or events seriously disturbing public order in either part or the whole of his country of origin or nationality, is compelled to leave his place of habitual residence in order to seek refuge in another place outside his country of origin or nationality.
>
> (OAU Convention, 1969, September, p. 5)

The AU – in line with UNHCR definitions – states that "an international migrant" is different from a refugee in that s/he is a person who "changes his or her country of usual residence, irrespective of the reason for migration or legal status, for either a short or a long-time period" ("USA for UNHCR, the UN Refugee Agency," 2023). Concomitantly, the word "resettlement" connotes "the selection and transfer of refugees from a country in which they have sought protection to a third country that has granted them permission to stay" for either a long-term or permanent residence status, assuring the protection of refugees ("USA for UNHCR, the UN

Refugee Agency," 2023). According to international law, settled refugees are not to be subjected to *refoulement* or forced return, and are provided access to rights similar to those enjoyed by citizens, while giving them an opportunity to eventually become citizens of the resettlement country ("USA for UNHCR, the UN Refugee Agency," 2023).

While refugee status tends to be temporary, and repatriation means the return of a refugee to their original home, which, according to the UN and the AU, must be a decision of the individual and not based on forced return, often called *refoulement*. Governments and international organizations are, therefore, requested to assist those refugees that desire to return home or to assimilate in the new place of refugee residence (UNHCR, 1950). Article 5.1 of the OAU Convention (1969), trying to prevent any ambiguity, also notes the importance of repatriation and emphasizes that it must be voluntary. Refugees may be repatriated for several reasons, including (1) if the prevailing conditions change in the country they fled (since most refugees leave their country under duress in order to escape individual persecution); (2) when their status is reexamined should the situation change); (3) when the host state encourages repatriation if it can no longer afford the burden the refugees represent; and 4) when refugees might be forced to return to their country of origin because of various other national or international pressures. Additionally, a person may be repatriated if he/she becomes involved in subversive or violent activities in the country of asylum (OAU Convention, 1969, September, pp. 9–10).

Relatively few comprehensive studies exist on (intergenerational) trauma among refugees, a bulk of which exclusively focus on Middle Eastern refugees and displaced persons. Expectedly, even fewer studies are available that address refugees in Africa and the Americas. To add to this, more recent studies use methodologies that often gloss over the role and impact of culture, language, collective behavior, close familiar relationships, and extended family systems. Beyond these deficiencies, as Sangalang & Vang (2017) note, the study of "refugee practices is scattered and contains wide variations in approaches for examining intergenerational trauma" (pp. 745–746). Nevertheless, research on the impact of slavery on African Americans in the United States, and the way in which intergenerational trauma is conceptualized through the prism of post-traumatic slave syndrome by Dr. Joy DeGruy can serve as points of departures.

Most scholarship on trauma among African refugees and their offspring comes from general observations about those living outside the continent of Africa. Indeed, Sangalang and Vang (2017) remark, "Much of the existing literature on refugee families has centered on Holocaust survivor families, more distantly removed from war-related traumas and issues of immediate resettlement," such as Vietnamese, Cambodians, Syrians, Egyptians, Moroccans, Lebanese, college students, and refugees in Sweden, and thus have emphasized "the traumatic experience of imprisonment, torture, rape, kidnapping, near-death, and forced separation" (pp. 752, 750). However, there is *the Black Holocaust* that started in the 1600s in the first settlements in Virginia, a colony that passed laws making Black people, and only Black people, slaves for life. Like with the Jewish Holocaust, within slavery, there are experiences among African slaves as refugees that include dehumanization and vilification, rape, slave labor, mass incarceration, medical experimentation, mass murder, and long-lasting psychological effects on survivors and their descendants ("America's Black Holocaust Museum," 2023).

In military and autocratic regimes, rape is used as weapon to punish opponents and recalcitrant citizens who protest publicly or silently as it was the case with African American women in the United States during slavery. African women are currently fighting for their rights in spaces that still consider them to be objects and socially and physically inferior to men. The negotiation of gender politics is also witnessed extensively in the refugee camps and settlements. As Luckham (1994) notes:

> Not only are military and security bureaucracies themselves largely male institutions, they coopt women, they embody ideological relations between male (for example, as military wives, prostitutes and ancillary workers) into divisions of labor which cater to their needs. They embody ideological relations between male protectors and female protected, reinforcing the social and political marginality of women within the state – all the more so under military and authoritarian governments, whose sole base in armed forces has almost by definition excluded women from key power positions.
>
> (p. 23)

Another problem related to African refugees is that much of the existing literature focuses on "trauma-informed care rather than . . . on trauma-related symptoms as indicators of a mental disorder" ("Substance Abuse and Mental Health Services Administration," 2014, pp. 1–2). Horowitz (1989 defines trauma

> as a sudden and forceful event that overwhelms a person's ability to respond to it, recognizing that a trauma needs not to involve actual physical harm to oneself; an event can be traumatic if it contradicts one's worldview and overpowers one's ability to cope.
>
> (as cited in "Substance Abuse and Mental Health Services Administration," 2014, p. 1)

The type of trauma that "persists" is distressing, and interferes with a person's daily life and relationships, commonly known as a post-traumatic syndrome disorder (PTSD) (Legg & Leonard, 2020, p. 4), associated with such risk factors as previous trauma, physical pain or injury, and lack of adequate support following a traumatic incident.

Furthermore, many studies on trauma originate from qualitative studies that suffer from subjectivity and convenience sampling. Often, African women refugees are excluded from a mental health perspective. Generally, trauma scholarship prefers studying men over women or children, including the experiences of next generation of refugees. Thus, when, for example, treatment is provided to a refugee population, screening, diagnosing, and special care must assess the common and different exposures of men, women, and children regarding violence, including pre- and post-migration cases. Sangalang et al. (2019) stress that more emphasis should be placed on refugees' mental health status both during the premigration and post-settlement period because of the critical difference between the terms refugee and non-refugee migrants. Recent trauma scholarship also shows limited concern for trauma-related experiences after relocation and post-settlement (Sangalang et al., 2019). Onyut et al. (2009) alert that "data on the prevalence of diagnosed common mental health disorders, including PTSD among post-conflict populations in Africa, is still scanty" (p. 5) and is compounded by methodological inconsistencies, including translations of questionnaires and interview metrics that are not always specified.

One exception is Boothby and Abubacar (1991) who documented the children of the former Portuguese colony's refugees during the 1970s and 1980s in Malawi, Zimbabwe, South Africa, and Zambia as experiencing trauma and nightmares in the host refugee camps, worsened by ethnic differences. Many children were born in camps, complicating the problem of defining the source of trauma. The issues of overcrowded conditions and related coping mechanisms have not received much attention in the literature with Mozambique parents and their children in Southern African refugee camps, but the painful experiences of asylum-seeking and resettlement ordeals continue to haunt them – the occurrence that can be characterized as *detrimental* as aggravated by the lack of freedom of movement, "closed social circle, fear, resulting in much anxiety from shock, pain, exploration, acceptance, and reemergence" (Azevedo, 2002, pp. 6–7).[1]

Sangalang and Vang (2017) evidence that

> [e]ffects of refugee parents' trauma on children and offspring were diverse yet mostly negative. More than half of the study findings . . . suggest an increased risk of adverse psychological outcomes and vulnerability to psychological stress within the next generation of refugee families. Adverse outcomes included PTSD, mood, anxiety disorder symptoms, psychological pain or burden in relation to parental trauma and greater risk of abuse and neglect.
>
> (p. 753)

A gender study conducted among Congolese refugees in Uganda by Ainamani et al. (2020) reveals that

> refugees were highly exposed to war-related traumatic events when experienced dangerous flight as the most common event for both men (97 percent) and women (97 percent), with the overall PTSD of 94 percent among women, their condition exacerbated by rape, compared to 84 percent among men.
>
> (p. 1)

The study also showed that "The dose-response effect differed significantly between men and women, with women showing higher PTSD symptoms severity when experiencing low and moderate levels of potentially traumatizing event types"

(Ainamani et al., 2020, p. 1). Research by Ainamani et al. (2020) is in contrast to the events in refugee settlements in Uganda, Nakivale, Isingor District in Southwestern Uganda, which found that 73% of DRC study participants had witnessed episodes of death and mutilated bodies, 69% shelling bomb attacks, 68% weapon injury, 60% the torching of houses, 60% caught in cross-fire or sniper attacks, through which the DRC women had experienced more "potentially traumatizing events than the men between March and June of 2013" (Ainamani et al., 2020, p. 1).

More specifically, women stood as greater victims of sexual violence in numbers, suggesting "high conditional risk for PTSD development" (Ainamani et al., 2020, p. 8). Although the study found that no significant difference between men and women in terms of susceptibility to high levels of potentially traumatic events, both tended to eventually develop PTSD. Women, who had experienced what is known as *building block effects* "presented higher PTSD symptoms severity than men with low to moderate levels of trauma exposure," because the former seemed to be more vulnerable to experiencing sexual violence, which often becomes continuous rather than just a singular "post-traumatic event stressor" (Ainamani et al., 2020, p. 8).

Experts distinguish different types of PTSD symptoms. While *Criterion A* comprises the state of experiencing or witnessing a traumatic event, such as natural disasters, a serious accident, a terrorist act, war or combat, rape, or violent assault, *Criterion B* – called Re-Experiencing the traumatic event – refers to "intrusive memories, distressing dreams, flashbacks, or distress in psychological reactions upon exposure to cues of the trauma" ("American Psychiatric Association," 2013, p. 271). *Criterion C* focuses on avoidance of the disorders from trauma. Other symptoms include memory alterations, mood recalling the trauma, and swings in what is called "psychological arousal and reactivity" ("American Psychiatric Association," 2013, p. 271). All these symptoms are frequently bundled together as Re-Experiencing, Avoidance, and Hyperarousal ("Substance Abuse and Mental Health Services Administration," 2014, p. 82). Importantly, Acute Stress Syndrome (ASS) is detectable almost immediately and is therefore difficult to differentiate from PTSD.

However, research on refugees and vulnerable populations emphasize that minors tend to show higher rates of trauma than non-transnational youth. Indeed, Miller et al. (2019) remark, "while youth are incredibly resilient, trauma and toxic stress can persist in poor health outcomes that persist throughout life, even though there are clinical ways of mitigating them" (p. 2). In fact, the trauma experienced by refugee children is critical, and, according to Miller et al. (2019), out of 30 million children and youth displaced under the age of 18 years, 17 million had experienced violence or conflict in their own country, while some 13 million were potentially able to secure refugee status (p. 1). Likewise, a study by Yousef et al. (2021) conducted among Syrian university students found that war was the greatest violent trigger of PTSD, especially among the poorest living at very low income who saw war. Among 833 students, the results illustrate showed that 86% experienced at least one violent event, resulting in a prevalence of 28.2%, with 46.3% forced to engage in unwanted sex; about 0.32% had experienced internal displacement, followed by those who had witnessed childhood trauma or violence and those adults who had seen violence (Yousef et al., 2021, p. 19).

Comparing Somali and Rwandan women, Barbieri et al. (2019) reported that Somali women had the lowest PTDS sum score, whereas the Rwandan women had a high rate of trauma, and experienced the same high number of events as the Somali men in PTDS score. Furthermore, Somali refugee women had higher indicators of ill-health than their Rwandan counterparts. Regarding rape, the scores were lower (4.2%) for both Somali and Rwandan women, with sexual incidents at 6.0%, forced prostitution at 2.1% (but affecting Rwandan women slightly more), forced circumcision at 4.1% (mainly among the Somali), and sex for food or security at 1.4% (Barbieri et al., 2019, p. 6). Furthermore, in the Nakivale's Ugandan settlement, Onyut et al. (2009) compared Somali women ($n = 516$, all Muslim except for one, with 90.5% Somali Christians) and 906 Rwandan women (90.5% Christians). Somali women scored higher than the men in both the arousal symptoms of PTSD and anxiety. Men had a higher PTSD prevalence but reported less substance abuse. Among the Rwandans, men had a higher score in the number of lifetime traumatic events and a higher PTDS sum score (Onyut et al., 2009, p. 21). On behalf of the World Peace Foundation, de Waal (2015) remarks as to the Somali settled in Uganda in 2003 and the Sudanese youth[2] running from the civil war in Sudan during the 1980s that they were victims of inhumane events, such as hunger and starvation, threat of being eaten by animals, pursuit and death inflicted by the army, and fear of being victims of genocide (pp. 1–10).

Only about half of the Somali boys reached the United States. One of them, Jacob Atem, who had temporarily settled in Kenya's Kakuma Camp, stressed that

> yes, there were some who struggled adjusting to America. When we first got here, a lot of us were diagnosed with PTSD. That doesn't justify whatever crimes they did but it's a part of the baggage we came with – depression, anxiety. It was a struggle for some.
> (as cited in Jensen, 2018, pp. 1–18)

Mayor (2005) further explicates:

> Results showed that the children scored well on measures related to functioning at school and with peers. However, they tended to score less well on measures of general and mental health, family activities, and family cohesion. A fifth of the boys had a diagnosis of post-traumatic stress disorder and were more likely to have lower (worse) scores on all scales of the child health care.
> (p. 1)

Among the Somali, 73.5% had witnessed dead or mutilated bodies, while 69.3% saw shelling or bomb attacks on their people, including, of course, parents and loved ones ("Unite for Sight," 2010, pp. 1–4).

Regarding refugee children in sub-Saharan Africa, according to *Unite for Sight* (2010), "second generation refugee children are at high risk of suffering from behavioral conditions, such as substance abuse and eating disorders. Fortunately, not all children who experience war trauma develop mental illness or behavioral problems" (p. 2). However, because of the cumulative stressors that they have experienced, African refugee children are also at a high risk of developing emotional and behavioral problems. Children may have arrived at refugee camps alone, often having witnessed the death of a parent or loved one and having experienced or witnessed violence or torture. Refugee children are particularly vulnerable to developing mental health problems when they are frequently separated from their parents or guardians, or their parents may be too overwhelmed or otherwise unable to attend to their emotional needs ("Unite for Sight," 2010, paras. 2–4). With an emphasis on refugee girls aged 13–19 and their experiences of violence, domestic abuse, and mental disorders in the Nakivale settlement, Uganda, Ivanova et al. (2019) showed through the 260 interviews, a majority of participants from DRC and Burundi and 93% of them girls, as follows: out of 30 girls, 11 had experienced forced sexual intercourse during the conflict in their respective countries; 27 of the 260 had undergone female circumcision; and 30% had never visited a health center. Otherwise, 2.8% of the refugee girls in Uganda suffer from anxiety due to fear of losing their jobs, death of relatives, alcohol, and experience other forms of mental disorders, with most never going to the mental facilities. Overall, some 4,297 cases of violence were reported by the UNHRC in Uganda settlements during January–November 2019, with 87% of the survivors being women and 13% children. Although the Ugandan government had mental hospitals in some of the settlements, few refugees attempted to avail themselves of the existing institutions (Ivanova et al., 2019, pp. 2–11).

Studies on the frequency of trauma among African refugees in the United States confirmed that the level of Potentially Traumatic Event Exposures (PTEs) is high for both men and women from East Africa in the new Western environment. The problem, however, is the analytical methodology, particularly the discrepancies between sampling and metrics protocols. Shook et al. (2018) stress the prevalence of high frequency of PTEs among the East African refuges in the United States, particularly in Southern California, and conclude that, categorically, it cannot be inferred whether males or females tend to experience a higher level of trauma (pp. 8–9). "Individuals who experience more trauma also tend to experience more severity across the board, although the level of distress does not appear to be significantly greater for one gender to the other" (Shook et al., 2018, (p. 1), the tendency that has been reported for Sudanese and the Somali refugees as well. Schauer et al. (2003) conducted in-depth interviews with 3,371 Africans, among others, from Sudan, Uganda, DRC, Zimbabwe, and Burundi from 1,842 households, focusing on forced migrants' experiences. They found traumatic stress was to be so profound that most resistant individuals' reaction was indicative of a psychological breaking point beyond which refugees could not withstand the pressure resulting from the stressors of being forcibly displaced. In addition, Schauer et al. (2003) concluded that

> the three most commonly endorsed lifetime traumatic events were suddenly/unexpected death of someone close (n=112; 72.26 percent), physical assault

(n=83; 52.87 percent), and combat trauma (n=77; 49.68 percent). The proportion of study participants with exposure to sexual trauma was 24.20 percent (n=38).

(pp. 5–6)

Most asylum seekers – principally from Mozambique, Malawi, Eswatini (former Swaziland), and Zimbabwe – in South Africa expect to live better lives in urban than in rural areas. However, traumatic disorders remain and include anxiety, panic, nausea, vomiting, shortness of breath, heart palpitations, fear of death, depersonalization and de-realization. Women are also subjected to numerous physical and psychological stressors. An interview conducted in Durban, South Africa, in 2018, revealed that trauma for women results in a higher PTSD risk. Another study model confirmed greater PTSD resulting from sexual trauma (Mhlongo et al., 2018).

It can be argued that the resettlement period is critical for developing PTSD symptoms for both adult refugees and their children, especially among those who experience severe torture, which, contingent upon the number of refugees and the environment where they live, may be between 3% and 63%, and considered to be an independent variable for "medical psychological illness in refugees of war" ("Refugee Health Technical Assistance," 2001, para.3). Indeed,

it is during the period of resettlement where stress may be higher as the refugees find the time to recall other traumatic events in their lives, when resettlement agencies and health care workers might start to reverse the effects of trauma across the span by providing culturally sensitive care that gives the refugee support.

("Refugee Health Technical Assistance," 2001, para.4)

However, the plight of young refugees may worsen given their vulnerability to psychological problems, including anxiety and PTSD, clinically proven to be as high as 40%. This condition may result in a prevalence of PTSD 15–50% among female refugees, but at a lesser degree for male refugees, arising from resettlement conditions (Gwozdziewycz & Mehl-Madrona, 2013, p. 2). It is further argued that war and rape affect more adolescents and early adults, with rape constituting "the highest risk" since half of the young victims are aged 13–20 or younger and three quarters between 13 and 26 when they are raped. Furthermore, Gwozdziewycz and Mehl-Madrona (2013) observe:

[T]he period of greatest psychological vulnerability is also in reality the period of greatest traumatic exposure, for both young men and young women. . . . Rape and combat might thus be considered complementary social rites of initiation into the coercive violence at the foundation of adult society. . . . They are the paradigmatic forms of trauma for women and men.

(p. 13)

Barbieri et al. (2019) sampled 120 African refugees in Italy, who attempted to get treatment, and their study found that that 79% had met the DSM-5 criterion for PTSD, 38% for ICD-11 PTSD, and 30% for ICD-11 CPTSD. Complex post-traumatic syndrome disorder (CPTSD) is linked to "complex trauma," conceptualized "as a repeated, prolonged interpersonal traumatic event exposure" (Barbieri et al., 2019, p. 10). However, few studies have been conducted on African refugees in the Western world regarding their experience of displacement or potential torture, and "other [possible] gross violations of human rights" (Barbieri et al., 2019, p. 10). *Nevertheless, Barbieri et al. (2019) showed that the longer the Africans stayed in that country, the fewer post-traumatic problems they encountered* (chapter authors' emphasis). Therefore, the following question is warranted: Could this be the norm with Africans becoming refugees in the Western world?

Africans and African Americans as Refugees: The Legacy of Slavery and Its Stressors

The first African slave was taken to the United States in 1619. Thereafter, the institution of slavery continued to shape the American culture indefinitely as it concerns the marginalization of people of color (Hannah-Jones, 2019). Consequently, because of ongoing oppression, inequities, discrimination, and violence inflicted on peoples of African descent or the Black diaspora in the United States, several authors have described African Americans as a colony resembling the refugee populations on the African continent and elsewhere. Although laws, policies, and amendments have been created to protect African Americans' rights since the Emancipation Proclamation of January 1, 1863, racism in the United States has prevailed to the point where this group remains without an "optimal citizenship" and therefore represents a refugee population that has constantly been in search of full citizenship.

To that end, during slavery when African Americans fled to places such as Canada, they were labeled as "fugitives," or as individuals "who escaped from slavery in the period before and including the Civil War" ("Britannica," 2023, para.1). Harriet Tubman, the conductor of the Underground Railroad, once stated: "We would rather stay in our native land, if we could be as free there as we are here" (as cited in Gallagher, 2022) Once enslaved Africans were able to reach freedom, they had no desire to go back to slavery (Gallagher, 2022). The Fugitive Slave Law of 1850 made it clear that

> "[n]o person held to service or labor in one State, under the laws thereof, escaping into another, shall, in consequence of any law or regulation therein, be discharged from such service or labor." The North lost its appeal to runaway slaves as Southern bounty hunters inflicted the constitution on anyone who decided not to abide by the US law and return their runaway slaves. Most southerners believed that abolitionists in the North were the problem causing many southern states to lose a good number of resources.
> (Campbell, 1970, p. 23)

Even after 1865 with the passing of the 13th Amendment that abolished slavery, a faction of US citizens continued to prevent African Americans from accessing "freedom."

Moreover, African Americans have been referred to as refugees in the United States due to their limited status to acquire full citizenship because of the lack of laws and policies to enforce it. In February 1865, after the ending of the Civil War, the Congress created the *Bureau of Refugees, Freedmen, and Abandoned Lands* – commonly known as the *Freedmen's Bureau* – to "assist black and white Southerners left destitute by the Civil War" (Hine et al., 2010, p. 317). An estimated 750,000 Americans died in the Civil War, and 50,000 of them were Black men (Hine et al., 2010, p. 279). The Congress understood that formerly enslaved Black people were displaced from the South, and, due to the ongoing aggression by white people in opposition of the newly formed laws, Black people became a vulnerable group. A standard definition of a refugee group is people who must leave their home area for their own safety or survival. A refugee's home area could be a country, state, or region. People become refugees for many reasons, including war, oppression, natural disasters, and climate change ("USA for UNHCR, the UN Refugee Agency," 2023). Historian Abigail Cooper approximated that over 200 refugee camps sprang up during the Civil War due to many African Americans fleeing the Confederacy (Goodman, 2020). Although Black people's transition to full citizenship was assisted, the *Freedmen's Bureau* was understaffed and lacked the resources to help millions of newly emancipated people. Many resources were promised to African Americans during the Reconstruction, such as land, but the promise was revoked because white landowners felt violated (Hine et al., 2010, p. 208).

Blackmon's *Slavery by Another Name* (2009) elucidates how the practices of slavery continued after its abolishment; Peonage Laws, Pig Laws, Convict Leasing, Sharecropping, and terrorist acts in the form of white supremacist groups, such as the Ku Klux Klan, created an atmosphere to "criminalizing black men for profit and to maintain a racial status quo" that led to the current prison industrial complex that is overpopulated by Black people (Blackmon, 2009).[3] The final strike against Reconstruction occurred with the creation of the Compromise of 1877, which gave power back to the people that opposed emancipation in the first place (Hine et al., 2010, p. 360). This contributed to the last federal troops being withdrawn from the South which was the only protection that freed Blacks could depend on (Hine et al., 2010, p. 363). Throughout African American history there is a lack of laws and legislations not fully actualized, thus leaving the US Black population as just an occupied space of *citizen on paper* versus citizens with accessible rights *fully protected* by law. Contemporarily, banned books, the termination of affirmative action, attacks on diversity, equity, and inclusion (DEI) programs demonstrate the same past pattern of revocation of laws as it concerns African Americans maintaining their rights as citizens in the United States. Even internationally, the African diaspora is included as the sixth region of the African Union to include all African descended people, even those who were forcefully removed from their homeland (Edozie, 2014). The colonial forces uprooted millions of African people in the transatlantic slave trade through violence, this would establish African descended people globally as a long-standing refugee population. The trauma experienced from hundreds of years of forced displacement caused continued illness that has even been studied epigenetically in African diasporic populations (DeGruy, 2005).

In addition, there is the trauma of Black maternal necropolitics that occurs to Black mothers who experience the loss of their children due to police brutality to give an example of other challenges that impact Black populations full integration into a country (Caesar et al., 2022).

As a consequence of policies and legislation not fully executed for African Americans, institutionalized racism continues to impact all areas of their life, including education, housing, health, business, and employment. Currently, Americans are recognizing the reemergence of the Reparations Movement. African Americans are asking for resources to assist them to live effectively in the United States due to the continuous disruption in policies and legislation that has promised support. Currently, San Francisco is leading the way with their Reparations proposal to provide support for Black people. The draft of the San Francisco Reparations Plan by the San Francisco African American Reparations Advisory Committee discusses an extensive plan to assist Black people due to "The genetic, psychological, financial, and racial trauma experienced by Black Americans through US chattel slavery as one of the greatest crimes against humanity perpetuated by our nation" ("San Francisco Reparations Plan," 2022, p. 3). Even Black political thought leaders, human rights activist, and educators Queen Mother Moore and W.E.B Dubois both named psychological issues that occur to Africans in the diaspora trying to adapt to a Western hegemonic structure that is not culturally inclusive. Queen Mother Moore called it oppression-psycho neurosis and Du Bois named it double-consciousness (Umoja, 2019; Du Bois, 1968). Frantz Fanon also addresses the disintegration of African descended people's psychological health when constantly bombarded with colonial standards (Fanon, 1952). Both, Queen Mother Moore and W.E.B Du Bois were fighting for various forms of reparations for African descended people in the Americas due to the continued violence and racism experienced.

Public health also provides a great example of African Americans being treated as second-class citizens as demonstrated in Washington's *Medical Apartheid* (2006). Washington (2006) conceptualized "Black Iatrophobia" as the fear Black people have against doctors due to years of abuse and involuntary usage in deadly experiments as Guinea pigs. For example, in the Tuskegee Syphilis Study experiment, Black men from the depression era to the 1970s were infected without their knowledge or consent and denied treatment even after a cure had been found (Washington, 2006; Ekundayo, 2007). Furthermore, Nobel Peace Prize winner Toni Morrison based her book *Beloved* on a slave woman, Margaret Garner, who killed her kids to protect them from the trauma of slavery (Morrison, 1987; Taylor, 2016).

These aforementioned examples of cruelty and insanity continue to affect Black people. For instance, according to the Centers for Disease Control and Prevention (CDC) (2023), "Black women are three times more likely to die from a pregnancy-related cause than White women" (para.3.) COVID-19 pandemic added to the challenges that Black women encountered and Clark (2022) notes that

> [t]he rate of women who died during pregnancy or shortly after birth increased significantly during the first year of the COVID-19 pandemic, according to new data from the National Center for Health Statistics. As a

result of the pandemic, Black women continued to experience maternal death at rates more than twice the national average.

(para.1)

Thus, the following question remains warranted: Why are Black mothers dying at an exponential rate if there was true health equity? Many argue that Africans Americans are still treated like the 1619 slaves without access to sustainable health care.

Furthermore, America has a Black Refugee Tradition that is not only steeped in the residue of the transatlantic slave trade, but the "U.S. deportation of undocumented migrants is also anti-black" (Gallagher, 2021, para.2). Between 2019 and 2020 alone, more than 6,700 people whose country of origin was in Africa or the Caribbean were deported (Gallagher, 2021). There was also the huge ordeal with over 15,000 Haitian migrants who camped in Texas because US policies did not see their humanity after crossing from Mexico ("National Conference of Black Political Scientists," 2021). Specifically, refugees from the Caribbean islands, notably Black Haitians, reported inhumane treatment at the Texas Border (Garcia) in reference of their racial belonging as Black. In *A Call to Action: Justice for Haitian People at the U.S. Border* (2021), various social justice and academic organizations, such as the National Conference of Black Political Scientists (44 in *toto*), came together to discuss the challenges of Black Haitians treatment at the border in 2021 ("National Conference of Black Political Scientists," 2021).

In fact, America has continued the legacy of treating Black people like unwanted refugees. Such scholars as DeGruy have significantly contributed to provide Black people with strategies to deal with the impact of slavery and ongoing racism. She defines post-traumatic slave syndrome (PTSS) as "a theory that explains the etiology of many of the adaptive survival behaviors in African American communities throughout the U.S. and the Diaspora" (DeGruy, 2023, para.2). In turn, DeGruy suggests ways of healing the trauma that can be effectively used by any refugee community in Africa and the African diaspora. DeGruy (2005) shares three symptoms associated with post-traumatic slave syndrome "vacant esteem, present anger, and racist socialization" (p. 183). She proposes a series of strategies for treating cases of permanent trauma that includes building self-esteem, alleviating stress factors, reprogramming mindset to one of value to counter the racist propaganda of inferiority and more (DeGruy, 2005, 2009). Her research provides a great avenue that can help African refugees face the trauma of colonial legacy.

Adult Refugees and Children's Resilience to Trauma and Its Stressors

Despite the fact that trauma and PTSD are threats to one's physical and mental well-being, some at risk individuals can withstand expected outcomes, thus testifying to resilience or positive coping strategy. Ungar (2008) defines resilience as follows:

In the context of exposure to significant adversity, whether psychological, environmental, or both, resilience is both the capacity of individuals to navigate their way to health-sustaining resources, including opportunities to experience feelings of well-being, and a condition of the individual's family, community and culture to provide these health resources and experiences in culturally meaningful ways.

(p. 225)

Beyond inner strength and resoluteness, many African refugees cope with disorders by using their religious faith or spirituality, and rely on their cultural traditions, ethnic cohesion, and the extended family, which help them find and accept the meaning of a painful event, hoping for a better future, while assimilating the enlightenment usually provided by education (Gladden, 2012, pp. 177–196). For African refugees, a reliance on the intervention of the ancestors and the cohesiveness of their ethnic group are two major assets and sources of resilience, strength and well-being common to all Sub-Saharan Africa. Thus, it is most likely true that "despite the negative experiences during different phases of migration, not all refugees develop mental health problems. Instead, despite the risks, some refugees manage to be resilient" (Ungar, 2008, p. 225). Incidentally, in Africa, most personal mental problems are bound up with post-traumatic stress disorders, as revealed in the following figures by Njenga et al. (2006): 39.3% PTSD, 52% depression, 60% anxiety, and 72.2% somatization disorder or physical symptoms such as pain and shortness of breath caused by distress (pp. 38–39).

In Mozambique, and notably in South Africa throughout the Truth and Reconciliation Commission, community involvement seems to be working as a saving process (Pham, 2016, p. 2), strengthened by friendships, participation in cultural local events, and intentionally reinforced solidarity with community agents to provide emotional support for resilience. This is also the case particularly with Sudanese refugees' targeted assistance from company agents, schools, interest groups, churches, organizations that provide help to young African refugees, and trusted researchers. Furthermore, refugee children, primarily in East Africa,

> cope well under the stress of war and experience fewer effects of trauma if they are able to retain a positive attachment to their mother [and from the extended family], if the parent (e.g., mother) can continue to project a sense of stability, permanence, and competence to their children.
>
> (Pham, 2016, p. 46)

This study concluded that "the vast majority exposed to violent life-threatening events do go on to develop post-traumatic stress disorder. . . . Many experience short-level subclinical stress reactions but these symptoms often abate spontaneously" (Pham, 2016, p. 11).

Based on focus group interviews with 15-year-olds and older refugees between 2000 and 2022, the same tendencies were observed among the Congolese, Somali, Sierra Leonean, Rwandan, and Zimbabwean refugees, indicating that the second generation of refugees have more resilience tools than their parents and the older generations. These predispositions can help much older Africans who witnessed war or were combatants in the African guerrilla wars against the colonizers, as was the case in Mozambique, Angola, Guinea-Bissau, Sudan, South Africa, and Eritrea, where the excessive requirements to win the war quickly affected fighters, including women. The record on guerrilla liberation wars seems to indicate gender behavior that was detrimental to women. Female guerrillas were often beaten up, accused of being prostitutes, and constantly bullied, which the guerrilla leaders denied categorically. In the case of Zimbabwe, for example, the treatment of women by men was often brutal, particularly when they tried to resist men's advances at night; such experiences are recounted by a female guerrilla, now a Member of Parliament in Harare, Zimbabwe, who also recalls her father's mental problems stemming from his joining the war. Those memories, the daughter recounts, have continued to haunt him and her, even after Zimbabwe's liberation in 1980 (Muzenda, 2019, pp. 1–28).

This former female guerrilla fighter continues to reveal that when she arrived at the headquarters of ZANU and ZAPU in Southern Mozambique from where the war was being waged inside Zimbabwe, the male guerrillas, and the leaders, instead of welcoming them, they constantly harassed, raped, and ridiculed them: "You are those young ladies [they uttered with disdain] sent with tubes in their vaginas to kill us" (Muzenda, 2019, p. 20). As to the trauma of her father as a guerrilla fighter, she recounts poignantly: "I remember years back when my father was startled by the bursting sound of a plastic tube I would pump with air . . . he would jump" (Muzenda, 2019, p. 20). She continued to recall the traumatic experience:

> After reading more about PTSD and all the psychological trauma that comes with war, I think my father *and his siblings* [i.e., the family and the second and following generations that had also joined the struggle] could have been suffering from it [or the same stressors].
> (Muzenda, 2019, p. 20, chapter authors' emphasis)

Another guerrilla said:

> There were many types of abuse on both sides . . . Prisoners also received electric torture, with electric wires often attached to their sexual organs. Many tortured blood. Guerrillas suspected of rebellion were executed by a firing squad. Some of the executions took place publicly and *were witnessed by children.*
> (Muzenda, 2019, p. 20, chapter authors' emphasis)

Muzenda (2019), a film recreating the ordeal, had to be removed off the screen quickly.

Testing Intergenerational Cases of Trauma and Intervention Strategies

As emphasized earlier, an effective intervention requires culturally competent and trained individuals who can gain the trust of the traumatized refugee "patients," and when the need arises for consultation and treatment, they seek, voluntarily if possible, assistance from official caregivers at the appropriate health center, keeping in mind that refugees usually do not come from the middle class. Instead, often illiterate and uneducated members of the lower class, most refugees tend to spring from deprived rural areas. As also emphasized by O'Neil et al. (2018), intervention interviews and the administration of clinical treatment, particularly children, should involve the family. A set of "dyads," such as patient/therapist, wife/husband, girl/stepfather should be considered. Whenever possible, respected members of the community that mediate the effectiveness of an intervention may be used, and strict confidentiality should be maintained throughout the process (O'Neil et al., 2018, p. 1).

Therefore, it is of paramount importance that opportunities are created for refugees, particularly for those who experience horrendous trauma, to meet and share their experiences, just as the members of Anonymous Alcoholics or cancer survivors do as a support system in the United States. The gatherings, which can be called reunions or refugee trauma recovery clubs or councils, could play a cathartic and purgative role in mitigating the impact of trauma, thus benefitting the children who bear hidden but intense memories of war, persecution, rape of relatives, and natural disaster, and the anxiety they might have experienced during seeking asylum. The proposed gatherings would not be completely comparable to the Truth and Reconciliation Commissions in post-apartheid South Africa (1996) and in Sierra Leone following the Civil War (1999) based on the premises that (1) reconciliation would not apply to people who did not mistreat each other as refugees but as fellow citizens, and (2) refugees are brought together with the hope of returning home one day or remaining in the resettlement by choice as citizens, as is often the case among refugees in Uganda.

An additional strategy to turn the younger generation away from trauma memories is the provision of daily or weekly recreation opportunities. The role of sports and games, particularly football, or soccer in the United States, cannot be overestimated: in fact, give one soccer ball to a group of kids in Africa, you will see them play the game almost the entire day, unless they have other chores they are forced to attend to. This behavior applies not only to teenagers and young adults in Africa, but also often to mature refugees. What African children need is a place, with or without goal nets, to play football, and they will forget all the misery they continue to endure as refugees, regardless of whether or not they are from the same ethnic group or country. Naturally, this effort requires resources, but not the resources the host governments and the international community could not afford.

Most importantly, many mixed methodological studies of trauma follow the Harvard University model (Harvard Trauma Questionnaire or HTQ) that contains 17 major variables of trauma stressors. Indeed, the content of the 17-item instrument has been criticized as not being comprehensive enough in view of the various stressors that may trigger a physical and/or an emotional response in refugee adult individuals and children, querying as to whether one experienced or witnessed the event or only heard about it. As one expert points out,

> While this has been a useful tool, it is clear that the breadth and depth of trauma for refugees is far greater than 17 events. For example, in more

recent work, sixty-seven Vietnamese and Kurdish refugees endorsed 612 war-related traumatic events during in-depth interviews to assess the role of traumatic events and thus providing "a comprehensive Trauma Inventory."
("Refugee Health Technical Assistance Center," 2011, para.1)

Overall, the types of outcomes in refugee studies hinge on the methods of data collection and sample size, as well as the nature of the subsequent analysis, which can make the expected results weak or strong, or be both internally reliable and externally generalizable.

On the one hand, quantitative studies involving children and adolescent refugees suggest that the best "potential" mediators of traumatic health and behavioral consequences are family and parents. On the other hand, qualitative studies tend to be

exploratory in nature and [draw] attention to the way in which parental trauma [is] transformed and infused with meaning for the next generation. Theory-driven empirical investigations that test other potential mechanisms of impactful transmission of biological, individual, and society pathways, for example, should continue to be explored in future research.
(Sangalang & Vang, 2017, p. 753)

Overall, many refugee studies fall short on considering the following: (1) cultural values, which remains a critical point the authors of this chapter also underline, (2) the context of the mental and physical disorders attributable to trauma, and (3) biometrical perspective, and thus, summarily, contributing to "viewing PTSD as purely medical pathology of the individual inherently depoliticizing and de-contextualizing the socio-political conditions which shape trauma" (Joseph et al, 2022, para.7).

Conclusion: PTSD Future Pathways in Refugee Settlements

If the political and economic conditions remain almost the same as during the past 70 years or more, generations of Africans will continue to experience the same traumatic moments for decades to come. Indeed, wars, political and economic corruption, rape, hunger, civil unrest, and protracted conflicts continue to perpetuate refugee exodus and the permanence of psychological and physical disorders, which are constitutive of symptoms such as anxiety, nightmare, depression, abuse, mood alterations, substance abuse, assaults on others, headaches, fatigue, palpitating hearts, digestive problems, numbness episodes, jumpy feelings and denials.

Eliminating war, rape, and torture should be the top priority of focus for academicians, psychologists, sociologists, and public health practitioners in an attempt to provide a better response to the rising problem that cripples mentally and physically millions of innocent Africans. More studies are needed on African refugee settlements, relying less on missionary expatriates or the shifting whims of the international community. Likewise, attempts at uncovering latent problems in refugee camps and settlements remain of primary importance, and the experience of the occupants ought to be taken seriously through studies that use qualitative, quantitative, or mixed social science techniques and gather adequate random samples to allow Africans to generalize and teach life-long lessons to their young students at African schools and universities.

Currently, the literature is sparse and remains oblivious to the cultural underpinnings and context on which African advancement should be based. Nevertheless, academicians, national health ministries, and universities can take inspiration from African diasporic studies conducted by African Americans and mental health professionals to advance discussion on intergenerational trauma.

Indeed, few studies have specifically focused on how Africa should handle the daily life problems and the death threats to its people which, in turn, manifest in psychosomatic disorders that continue to deem Africans unreliable partners internationally. It is argued that instead of an overreliance on guidelines by the international community, relevant policies and protocols that improve both urban and rural areas should be developed, and greater attention should be on effective counseling at health centers and educational facilities. For a systemic improvement of the mental and physical health of refugees in settlements across Sub-Saharan Africa, it is worth quoting the "10 Pearls" recommended by Miller et al. (2019) to improve the mental and physical health of the refugees in the settlements scattered across Sub-Saharan Africa: (1) focusing on practice- and strength-based approach to care; (2) creating an immigrant-friendly health care; (3) promoting trusting relationships with the health care environment; (4) enhancing opportunities for public discussion of politically difficult subjects; (5) recognizing the impact of trauma on the developing brain and its various manifestations while screening for trauma and associated mental conditions; (6) treating trauma and its associate symptoms appropriately; (7) utilizing a two-generational approach to care; (8) knowing the local resources and making sure they are effective; (9) recognizing that trauma may not end after migration; and (10) advocating for patients both in and outside the clinical environment (p. 5).

In addition, experts such as Hutchinson et al. (2012) caution that trauma and its grip in victims are vaguely used and defined, noting that "The literature suggests that refugee resilience moves beyond the Western individualized notion of resilience (also called a Dominant of Western deficits model)" (Hutchinson et al., 2012, p. 8) to a more communal perspective that does not define refugee people as helplessly traumatized victims.

Similarly, Gladden (2012) reminds us that "the most common coping skills [have] included faith/religion or other belief systems, social support and cognitive reframing or finding meaning in the situation" (p. 177). This applies well to Africa and the African diaspora and is further articulated by DeGruy's work on post-traumatic slave syndrome as a way of understanding systematic colonial trauma and the ways in which one can holistically heal. By the same breath, Kalt et al. (2013) also conclude:

> In services, screening, and treatment, attention must be paid to common exposures to violence, particularly sexual violence against women and

torture. Voluntary sexual health screening and care programs for female and male asylum seekers are critical. Similarly, greater attention must be given to the risk of postmigration violence, with specific recognition of community, intimate partner, and family violence.

(p. 16)

The UNHRC and related UN agencies have received both praise and condemnation, given the fact that their refugee assistance has not only helped refugees threatened by wars and persecution, but also contributed to Africa's dependence on international assistance. In fact, countries such as Uganda and Ethiopia have been handicapped by the fact that the international community has fallen short of the assistance it has promised to the traumatized refugees and succeeding generations. In this context, Zachary Lomo, a Ugandan university professor and lawyer, remains one of the most outspoken critics of the UN and the Uganda's government policies and practices. Lomo (2006) writes that "The UNHCR's policies in Africa create huge obstacles for refugees to realistically reclaim their lives after experiences of loss and trauma" (2006, p. 40). Uganda has changed its policies on the refugees and, over the past five years, has emphasized self-sufficiency and the integration of refugees into the Ugandan nation as citizens. Furthermore, in Uganda and in most Sub-Saharan Africa, repatriation has been voluntary in most cases, thus following the UNRC policies that no one should be forced to return to the country of origin unless he/she decides to do so.

Nevertheless, the International Organization for Migration (IOM) that is a part of the United Nations system is rarely mentioned when searching funding for interventions on behalf of traumatized refugees, especially on health issues. Yet, IOM makes available a number of financial and logistic opportunities to refugees that choose to repatriate. IOM also maintains several regional offices in Africa and provides services, including movement, emergency, post-crisis programs, immigration health, migration and sustainable development, regulation of migration, facilitation of migration, and general program support for a total assistance budget of $256,805,900 (fiscal year 2020–2021) (IOM, 2022, p. 10). According to the IOM Abridged Annual Report for 2022, over "31.1 million people, including internally displaced persons, refugees, and migrants" were assisted with their resources (IOM, 2022, p. 1). By highlighting international organizations' crisis response in refugee communities can equip and empower more local institutions to aid people in Africa and the African diaspora impacted by the continued legacy of intergenerational trauma.

Notes

1 Cf. Onyut et al. (2009).
2 Forty thousand orphaned Lost Boys of Sudan sought asylum in Kakuma refugee camp in Kenya.
3 Cf. Joseph-Gabriel (2014).

References

Ainamani, H., Elbert, H., Olama, D., & Hecker, T. (2020). Gender Differences in Response to War-related Trauma and Posttraumatic Stress Disorder – a Study among the Congolese Refugees in Uganda. *BioMed Central Psychiatry, 20*(17), 1–9. https://doi.org/10.1186/s12888-019-2420-0

American Psychiatric Association (APA). (2013). *Diagnostic and Statistical Manual of Mental Disorders.* 5th edition. Arlington, VA: American Psychiatric Association.

America's Black Holocaust Museum (ABHM). (2023). *What Is the Black Holocaust in America?* Retrieved from www.abhmuseum.org/about/what-is-the-black-holocaust/

Azevedo, M. J. (2002). *Tragedy and Triumph. Mozambique Refugees in Southern Africa, 1977–2001.* Portsmouth, NH: Heinemann.

Blackmon, D. (2009). *Slavery by Another Name: The Re-Enslavement of Black Americans from the Civil War to World War II.* First Anchor books edition. New York, NY: Anchor Books.

Barbieri, A., Visco-Comandini, F., Alunni Fegatelli, D., Schepisi, C., Russo, V., Calò, F., Dessì, A., Cannella, G., & Stellacci, A. (2019). Complex Trauma, PTSD and Complex PTSD in African Refugees. *European Journal of Psychotraumatology, 10*(1–16), 1700621. https://doi.org/org/10.1080/2008198.2019.1700621

Boothby, N. U., & Abubacar, P. S. (1991). *Children of Mozambique: The Cost of Survival.* [working paper]. Washington, DC: U.S. Committee for Refugees and Immigrants.

Britannica (2023). *Fugitive Slave: United States history.* Retrieved from www.britannica.com/topic/fugitive-slave

Caesar, T., Melonas, D., & Jones, T. (2022). Mothering Dead Bodies: Black Maternal Necropolitics. *Meridians, 21*(2), 512–537. https://doi.org/10.1215/15366936-9882174

Campbell, S. W. (1970). *Slave Catchers: Enforcement of the Fugitive Slave Law, 1850–1860.* Chapel Hill, NC: University of North Carolina Press.

Carlin, J. L. (1989). *The Refugee Connection: A Lifetime of Running a Lifeline.* London: Macmillan.

Centers for Disease Control and Prevention (CDC). (April 6, 2023). *Working Together to Reduce Black Maternal Morality.* Bethesda, MD: NIH. Retrieved from www.cdc.gov/healthequity/features/maternal-mortality/index.html

Clark, M. (February 25, 2022). Increase in Maternal Mortality During COVID Underscores Need for Policy Changes. *Georgetown University McCourt School of Public Policy.* Retrieved from https://ccf.georgetown.edu/2022/02/25/increase-in-maternal-mortality-during-covid-underscores-need-for-policy-changes.

Concern Worldwide. (2023). *The 10 Largest Refugee Crises to Know in 2023.* New York. Retrieved from www.concern.net/news/largest-refugee-crises

DeGruyuy, J.A. (2023). *Post Traumatic Slave Syndrome.* Retrieved December 29, 2023, from www.joydegruy.com/post-traumatic-slave-syndrome

DeGruy, J. A. (2005). *Post Traumatic Slave Syndrome: America's Legacy of Enduring Injury and Healing.* Milwaukie, OR: Uptone Press.

DeGruy, J. A. (2009). *Post Traumatic Slave Syndrome: America's Legacy of Enduring Injury and Healing: The Study Guide.* Portland, OR: JDP Publisher.

de Waal, A. (2015). *The Real Politics of the Horn of Africa: Money, War and the Business of Power.* Malden, MA: Polity Press.

Du Bois, W. E. B. (1968). *The Souls of Black Folk: Essays and Sketches.* New York: Johnson Reprint Corp.

Edozie, R. K., & Gottschalk, K. (2014). *The African Union's Africa: New Pan-African Initiatives in Global Governance.* East Lansing, MI: Michigan State University Press.

Ekundayo, B. (2007, March 7). Medical Apartheid. *ColorLines.* Retrieved from www.colorlines.com/articles/medical-apartheid.

Fanon, F. (1952). *Black Skin, White Masks.* New York: Grove Press.

Gallagher, S. (2021, April 7). The Black Refugee Tradition. *Black Perspectives*. Retrieved from www.aaihs.org/the-black-refugee-tradition/.
Gallagher, S. (2022, February 14). Enslaved Black Americans Crossed Borders To Find Freedom. Today's Asylum Seekers Want To Do The Same. *The Washington Post*. Retrieved from www.washingtonpost.com/outlook/2022/02/14/enslaved-black-americans-crossed-borders-find-freedom-todays-asylum-seekers-want-do-same/
Gladden, J. (2012). The Coping Skills of East African Refugees: A Literature Review. *Refugee Survey Quarterly*, *31*(3), 177–196. https://doi.org/10.1093/rsq/hds009
Goodman, L. (2020, February 14). Between Bondage and Freedom: Life in Civil War Refugees Camps. *Brandeis Now*. Retrieved from www.brandeis.edu/now/2020/february/civil-war-refugee.html
Gwozdziewycz, N., & Mehl-Madrona, L. (2013). Meta-Analysis of the Use of Narrative Exposure Therapy for the Effects of Trauma Among Refugee Populations. *Permanent Journal*, *17*(1), 70–76. https://doi.org/10.7812/TPP/12-058
Hannah-Jones, N. (2019, August 14). Untold. 1619: The Legacy of Slavery in America. *The New York Times*. Retrieved from www.nytimes.com/interactive/2019/08/14/magazine/1619-america-slavery.html
Hine, D. C., Hine, W. C., & Harrold, S. (2010). *The African-American Odyssey*. Volume II, 5th Edition. London: Pearson.
Hutchinson, M., & Dorsett, P. (2012). What Does the Literature Say about Resilience in Refugee People? Implications for Practice. *Journal of Social Inclusion*, *3*(2), 55–78. https://doi.org/10.36251/josi.55
International Organization of Migration (IOM). (2022). *International Organization of Migration Abridged Annual Report for 2022*. Retrieved December 28, 2023, from https://publications.iom.int/books/abridged-annual-report-2022
Isobel, S., Goodyear, M., & Foster, K. (2018). Preventing Intergenerational Trauma Transmission: A Critical Interpretive Synthesis. *Journal of Clinical Nursing*, *28*(7–8), 1–14. https://doi.org/10.1111/jocn.14735
Isobel, S., & Edwards. C. (2017). Using Trauma Informed Care as a Nursing Model of Care in an Acute Inpatient Mental Health Unit: A Practice Development Process. *Journal International Journal of Mental Health Nursing*, *26*(1), 1–3. https://doi.org/10.1111/inm.12236
Ivanova, O., Masna Rai, M., Mlahagwa, W., Tumuhairwe, J., Bakuli, A., Nyakato, V., & Kemigisha, E. (2019). A Cross-Sectional Mixed-Methods Study of Sexual and Reproductive Health Knowledge, Experiences and Access to Services Among Refugee Adolescent Girls in the Nakivale Refugee Settlement, Uganda. *Reproductive Health*, *16*(35), 1–11. https://doi.org/10.1186/s12978-019-0698-5
Jensen, B. (2018, November 3). Lost Boy from Sudan. How He found his True Calling in America. *NPR*. Retrieved December 30, 2023, from www.npr.org/sections/goatsandsoda/2018/11/03/663152469/how-a-lost-boy-from-sudan-found-his-true-calling-in-the-u-s
Joseph, S., Tanous, O., Hosny, N., & Koga, P.M. (2022, January 27). Whose Trauma? De-Colonizing Post-Traumatic Stress Disorder and Refugee Mental Health Frameworks. *Harvard Medical School Center for Primary Care*. Retrieved December 30, 2023, from https://info.primarycare.hms.harvard.edu/perspectives/articles/whose-trauma-
Joseph-Gabriel, A. K. (2014). Slavery by another Name: A Film Review. *Palimpsest*, *3*(1), 86–88.
Kalt, A., Hossain, M., Kiss, L., & Zimmermann, C. (2013). Asylum Seekers, Violence and Health: A Systemic Review of Research in High-Income Host Countries. *American Public Health Association*, *103*(3), 1–22. https://doi.org/10.2105/AJPH.2012.301136.
Legg, T., & Leonard, J. (2020, June 3). What is Trauma? What to know? *MedicalNews Today*. Retrieved December 29, 2023, from www.medicalnewstoday.com/articles/trauma

Lomo, Z. (2006). Refugees in East Africa: Developing an Integrated Approach. In Dorina A. Bekoe (Ed.), *East Africa and the Horn: Confronting Challenges to Good Governance* (pp. 37–57). Boulder: Lynne Rienner Publishers. https://doi.org/10.1515/9781685853570-005

Luckham, R. (1994). The Military, Militarization, and Democratization in Africa: A Survey of Literature and Issues. *African Studies Review, 37*(2), 13–75. https://doi.org/10.2307/524766

Mayor, S. (2005, June 11). Lost Boys of Sudan Have Emotional Problems. *British Medical Journal, 330* (7504), 1350.

Mhlongo, M., Tomita, A., Maharaj, V., & Burns, J. (2018). Sexual Post-Traumatic Stress among African Refugees and Migrants in South Africa. *South African Journal of Psychiatry, 24*, 1208. https://doi.org/10.4102/sajpspsychiatry.v24.i0.1208.

Miller, K., Brown, C., Shramk, M., & Svetaz, M. (2019). Applying Trauma-Informed Practices to the Care of Refugee and Immigrant Youth: 10 Clinical Pearls. *Children (Basel), 6*(8), 94–97. https://doi.org/10.3390/children6080094

Momodu, S. (2016). *Africa Most Affected by Refugee Crisis. Africa Renewal.* Retrieved December 29, 2023, from www.un.org/africarenewal/magazine/december-2016-march-2017/africa-most-affected-refugee-crisis

Morrison, T. (1987). *Beloved.* New York: Alfred Knopf.

Muzenda, M. (2019, April 18). The Invisible Trauma of Women in Zimbabwe's Liberation Struggle. *This Is Africa.* Retrieved December 29, 2023, from https://thisisafrica.me/politics-and-society/the-invisible-trauma-of-women-in-zimbabwes-liberation-struggle/

National Conference of Black Political Scientists (NCOBPS). (September 22, 2021). *A Call to Action: Justice for Haitian People at the U.S. Border.* Retrieved from www.ncobps.org/a-call-to-action-justice-for-haitian-people-at-the-u-s-border

Njenga, F., Ngugthi, A., & Kangethe, R. (2006). War and Mental Disorders in Africa. *World Psychology, 5*(1), 38–39.

OAU Convention Governing the Specific Aspects of Refugee Problems in Africa (September 10, 1969). *United Nations, Treaty Series No. 14691.* Addis Ababa, Ethiopia. Retrieved from https://au.int/sites/default/files/treaties/36400-treaty-36400-treaty-oau_convention_1963.pdf

O'Neil, L., Fraser, T., Kitchenham, A., & McDonald, V. (2018). Hidden Burdens: A Review of Intergenerational Historical and Complex Trauma, Implications for Indigenous Families. *Journal of Child and Adolescent Trauma, 11*(2), 173–186; https://doi.org/10.1007/s40653-016-0117-9.

Onyut, L., Neuner, F., Ertl, V., Shauer, E., Odenwald, M., & Elbert, T. (2009). Trauma, Poverty and Mental Health Among Somali and Rwandese Refugees Living in an African Refugee Settlement – an Epidemiological Study. *Conflict and Health, 3*(6), 1–16. https://doi.org/10.1186/1752-1505-3-6

Pham, B. H. (2016). A Sociological Study of East African Refugee and Mothers' Experiences of Trauma and how it affects Parenting. Dissertation, Antioch University, 1–190.

Psychological Care and Healing Center (PCH). (2022, June 2). *What is Emotional Dysregulation?*

Psychological Care and Healing Center. (n.d.). CA. Retrieved from www.pchtreatment.com/who-we-treat/emotional-dysregulation/

Refugee Health Technical Assistance Center (RHTAC). (2001). *Traumatic Experiences of Refugees.* Retrieved from www.refugeehealthta.org/physical-mental-health/mental-health/adult-mental-health/traumatic-experiences-of-refugees/

San Francisco Reparations Plan (SFReparationsPlan). (December 2022). *Draft San Francisco Reparations Plan.* San Francisco, CA: San Francisco Human Rights Commission Staff. Retrieved from https://sf.gov/sites/default/files/2023-01/HRC%20Reparations%202022%20Report%20Final_0.pdf

Sangalang, C., Bacerra, D., Michell, F., Lechanga-Pena, S., Lopez, K., & Isok, K. (2019). Trauma, Post-Migration Stress, and Mental Health: A Comparative Analysis of Refugees and Immigrants in the US. *Journal of Immigrants Minor Health*, *21*(5), 909–919. https://doi.org/10017/s1093–0826–2209.

Sangalang, C. C., & Vang, C. (2017). Intergenerational Trauma in Refugee Families. *Journal of Immigrant Minor Health*, *19*(3), 745–754. https://doi.org/1007/s1080-016-0498-7I.

Schauer, M., Neuner, F., Karunakara, U., Klaschik, C., Robert, C., & Elbert, T. (2003). PTSD and the "Building Block" Effect of Psychological Trauma Among West Nile Africans. *European Society for Traumatic Stress Studies Bulletin*, *10*, 5–6.

Shook, B., Tetum, C., Parker, J., & English, B. (2018). Pre-Migration Trauma Experiences of East African Refugees in the United States. *American International Journal of Contemporary Research*, *8*(1), 12–22.

Substance Abuse and Mental Health Services Administration (SAMHSA) (2014). *Trauma-Informed Care in Behavioral Health Services. 57 Treatment Improvement Protocol (TIP) Series, Department of Health and Human Services*. Rockville, MD: Center for Substance Abuse Treatment. Retrieved November 25, 2023, from www.ncbi.nlm.nih.gov/books/NBK207201/pdf/Bookshelf_NBK207201.pdf

Taylor, N. (2016). *Driven Toward Madness: The Fugitive Slave Margaret Garner and Tragedy on the Ohio*. Athens, OH: Ohio University Press.

Umoja, A. (2019). Queen Mother Moore: Matriarch of the Captive Nation. *Black Perspectives*. Retrieved December 29, 2023, from www.aaihs.org/queen-mother-moore-matriarch-of-the-captive-african-nation/

Ungar, M. (2008). Resilience across Cultures. *British Journal of Social Work*, *38*(20), 218–235. https://doi.org/10.1093/bjsw/bcl343

UNHCR. (June 2023). *Türkiye Operational Update 2023*. Retrieved December 29, 2023, from https://reliefweb.int/report/turkiye/unhcr-turkiye-operational-update-june-2023-entr#:~:text=3.7%20million,other%20nationalities%20and%20stateless%20persons

UNHCR. (October 24, 2023). *Refugee Statistics*. Retrieved December 29, 2023, from www.unhcr.org/refugee-statistics/

UNHRC. (1950). UNHCR Statute, Art. 8.c, Adopted by the UN General Assembly on 14 December 1950, Resolution 428 [V]). Retrieved December 30, 2023, from www.unhcr.org/sites/default/files/legacy-pdf/3b66c39e1.pdf

Unite for Sight. (2010). *Mental Health in Refugee Camps and Settlements*. Retrieved December 29, 2023, from https://ghu.uniteforsight.org/certificate-in-refugee-healthcourse2 module-2

USA for UNHCR, the UN Refugee Agency. (2023). Retrieved November 26, 2023, from www.unrefugees.org/

Washington, H. A. (2006). *Medical Apartheid: The Dark History of Medical Experimentation on Black Americans from Colonial Times to the Present*. New York, NY: Harlem Moon.

Yousef, L., Ebrahim, O., Alnahr, M., Mohsen, F., Ibrahim, N., & Sawah, B. (2021). War-Related Trauma and Post-Traumatic Stress Disorder among Syrian University Students. *European Journal of Psychotraumatology*, *12*, 1954774. https://doi.org/10.1080/20008198.2021.1954774

8 Marginalization as Traumatization

Developmentally Based Trauma Framework for Intergenerational Transmission of Trauma in Somali Refugees

Muna Saleh and Hyojin Im

Introduction

Refugee families face multiple sources of distress during resettlement that impede family resilience and social integration, stoking a risk for transmission of trauma across generations. Such adversities range from unprocessed past traumas causing lingering impacts on relationships and coping, to challenges in accessing services and resources exacerbated by cultural and language barriers, and to ongoing pressures for acculturation and integration. Although many refugee families are highly resilient and adjusted to the host community, some may remain vulnerable to further traumatization during resettlement, experiencing social alienation and marginalization. While classical and current refugee trauma theory and practice underscore the primacy of individual traits and discrete events in informing refugee psychopathology, over the past two decades there has been growing evidence implicating post-resettlement stress and systemic factors in contributing to psychological distress (Alemi & Stempel, 2018; Gleeson et al., 2020). Specifically, systemic stressors such as marginalization and discrimination have been linked to worse social, economic, and health outcomes for refugees (Kira et al., 2023; Lincoln et al., 2021).

Despite the consensus on the role of systemic factors in contributing to traumatization for some refugees, current methods for addressing these challenges frequently medicalize traumatic stress and focus largely on individual and familial interventions targeting distressing symptoms (Kira et al., 2014; Summerfield, 1997). Aside from limiting theoretical explanations for trauma observations, such narrow focus obscures clinical practice with refugees who have experienced trauma, in that it often fails to consider additional or more pertinent sources for their distress. This same individualistic and clinical model for refugee trauma is also dominant in the intergenerational transmission of trauma (ITT) literature, where the process of transferring trauma from one generation to the next is understood from biological, behavioral, or psychodynamic perspectives.[1] Much less understood are how the marginalization of refugees places them at risk for transmitting trauma cross-generationally. This gap may be attributed to the fact that relatively little is known about how cumulative trauma sequelae are associated with structural challenges that lead to marginalization of refugee families.[2] Consequently, there is an

DOI: 10.4324/9781003385820-9

under theorization of the process of marginalization and its role in the proliferation of trauma and the ITT process.

Kira et al. (2013; 2014) developed the Development-Based Trauma Framework (DBTF) to broaden the concept of trauma to include historically neglected sources of traumatization (i.e., structural factors) and to expand conceptualization of trauma to include collective traumas based on marginalized identities. The DBTF is especially useful in that it overcomes the limitations of individualized notions of trauma and is inclusive of both individual traits and collective and systemic factors that are implicated in trauma or stress generation (Kira, 2022).

In this chapter, we use *marginalization* as a form of systemic trauma and employ the DBTF framework to explore the nexus of marginalization and the proliferation of individual trauma and the emergence of collective identity trauma in post-resettlement contexts. Specifically, in using the DBTF, we describe the process in which marginalization contributes to the ITT for refugees as well as potential mechanisms for transmission. We examine the case of Somali refugees resettled in Minnesota in the United States – a group with multiply marginalized identities – to illustrate the implication of structural traumatization for family functioning, social capital, and coping resources.

Consequences of the Marginalization Process for Resettled Refugee Families

The concept of marginalization is commonly used in the refugee literature to describe the intersectionality of refugee identity, policy, and social and physical spaces.[3] Its focus extends from the concept and goal of refugee *integration* endorsed by host societies. Unlike inequality or other related concepts, *marginalization* has been characterized as both a process and condition (Alakhunova et al., 2015). As a process, marginalization refers to the strategies used to create and replicate inequality (Andersson, 2003; Bynner, 1997). As a social condition, marginality refers to the social space (e.g., class, race, gender) an individual occupies (Alakhunova et al., 2015). Although marginalization is differentiated by inequality, the constructs are closely related, with those in privileged social groups maintaining power in architecting the social categories relegated to living at the margins (Bea & Poppe, 2021). While many conceptualizations of marginalization can be found throughout the literature, it is generally accepted as a multidimensional concept resulting in the exclusion of certain social groups from the social, cultural, and economic spheres of society (Fangen, 2010). Although initially analyzed in 1994 (Hall et al., 1994), the concept has been traced back to other sociological concepts concerned with group classification and the social construction of those groups, often resulting in the creation of social realities (Bourdieu, 1984). A consequence of social classification is the hierarchical organization of constructed social groups. Unlike the traditional hierarchical structure where rank is ordered from top to bottom, in the marginalization process the normed social identities and their experiences are centered, while marginalized social identities/experiences are pushed and contained to the *margins* of the center. The marginalization process culminates with the social exclusion of the marginalized, as well as their *overinclusion* in social control systems (Foucault, 1977; Hellenbach et al., 2017; Nicosia et al., 2013; Muller, 2012). The ramifications of social exclusion include the exacerbation of mental distress, physical health problems, social isolation, unemployment, disrupted social networks, impeded accruement of social/human capital, overrepresentation in child welfare (Berridge, 2007) and criminal justice systems (Crenshaw, 2011), and other related economic and social problems (Banulescu-Bogdan, 2020).

Like other marginalized groups, refugees at the perimeter of society must grapple with the social, economic, and health costs associated with their marginality. Previously, social alienation in post-resettlement has been identified as especially important in explaining symptoms of mental distress (Kirmayer et al., 2011; Lindencrona et al., 2008). A critical review by Hynie (2018) underscores the importance of considering social determinants of mental health alongside premigration characteristics. However, much of the effort in addressing these post-resettlement stressors remains on supporting individual refugees to adopt modifications through self-help (Easton-Calabria & Omata, 2018), mutual assistance (Tomlinson & Egan, 2002), or mental health and psychosocial interventions (Nosè et al., 2017). The capacity for systems, specifically policies, to marginalize certain categories of identities have been implicated in the development of social welfare policies and criminal policies. Marginalizing policies tend to replicate and sustain inequalities among groups, often leading to prolonged peripheralization by delineating which constructed identities have access to social welfare benefits (Burnham et al., 2005; Carbone, 2011; Constance-Huggins, 2011; Grossman & Friedman, 2011). Consequences of marginalization include devastated coping with psychosocial challenges and the development of newer mental health problems across marginalized identities (Krieger et al., 2008; Lindencrona et al., 2008). For refugees specifically, their exposure to traumatic stress prior to resettlement makes them especially vulnerable to the negative effects of marginalization given refugees' reduced capacities for effective coping (Im, 2021).

While understanding the effects of marginalization on refugee well-being is an important starting point, research detailing how the marginalization *process* unfolds for refugees is still unclear. For refugees, the marginalization process may become facilitated in several ways including through social and economic welfare policies and in part by the chronic exposure to post-resettlement stress brought on by the resettlement program and related structural factors. The unique legal categorization of refugees, compared with other migrant classes, offers refugees special entitlements to specific social welfare benefits as well as a largely uncomplicated path toward citizenship in the United States. However, the refugee resettlement policy also creates a distinctive socioeconomic and marginalizing environment for refugees characterized by structural impediments to achieving long-term integration (Brown & Scribner, 2014; Kreisberg et al., 2022). The discontinuity of the resettlement program with other refugee-serving systems is also notable for its propensity to proliferate marginalization (Im & Swan, 2021). Although refugees arrive in the United States with relatively higher human capital compared to other migrants (Capps et al., 2015), once resettled, they experience more unfavorable economic outcomes than both the native-born population and other migrant classes (Capps et al., 2015; Evans & Fitzgerald, 2017). This trend has been attributed to the difficulties transferring credentials to American systems (Desiderio, 2016), discrimination, and the narrow focus of the resettlement policy in achieving early self-sufficiency (Brown & Scribner, 2014). Decades after resettlement, refugees continue to experience lower income levels than the native-born population (Kreisberg et al., 2022), highlighting the protracted nature of refugee marginalization.

Resettlement policies related to the dispersal of refugees may also proliferate marginalization. Dispersal policies tend to relocate refugees in low-quality housing in high-poverty neighborhoods (Sichling, 2021), reinforcing marginality (Chaskin & Joseph, 2011; Hughes, 2021; Saugeres, 2011) and increasing vulnerability to social alienation and discrimination (Hynie, 2018). Specifically, the placement of refugees in high-poverty neighborhoods has been linked to an increased risk for experiencing traumatization at both individual and collective levels (Beiser & Hou, 2016; Xu, 2017). Relatedly, the principle of rapid self-sufficiency inherent in the United States resettlement policy, and related refugee benefit programs, significantly contribute to the type and quality of employment available, as well as the short and long-term earnings of refugees (Haffejee & East, 2019), fortifying their marginalization in the labor market (Kreisberg et al., 2022; Shutes, 2011. Historically, generous and long-term social benefits available to refugees have been implicated in the successful adjustment of refugee newcomers in the United States (e.g., Vietnamese refugees under McCain Amendment).[4] Despite the positive impact of cash assistance for refugee well-being, refugee cash and medical assistance have become more restrictive and limited since the 1990s, decreasing from a limit of 36 months in 1980 to 8 months in 1991 (Bruno, 2011) possibly contributing to the marginalization of refugees, such as Somalis, who initially arrived in the United States in 1991. Despite the well-documented evidence of resettlement policies contributing to the marginalization of refugees and its impact on mental health, a predominant emphasis in refugee ITT literature tends to focus, instead, on individual- or family-level factors which we outline in the following section.

Implicated (and Neglected) Mechanisms in the ITT Literature

Meta-analyses comparing the prevalence of mental health problems consistently reveal refugees experience higher rates of mental disorders than non-refugees (Blackmore et al., 2020; Porter & Haslam, 2005). Along with problems related to individual-level adjustment to the host community, refugee families are also at increased risk of experiencing family and intergenerational conflict. The prevalence of family conflict and the ITT have been identified as contributing to rates of prolonged mental health problems for the generation arriving as refugees and those born post-migration (Timshel et al., 2017). In addressing the ITT process, the primary focus continues to revolve around the identification of individual-level traits, familial characteristics, and cultural barriers. These values reflect epistemologies rooted primarily in psychiatric and psychological traditions (Summerfield, 2004), which tends to over-implicate individual and premigration characteristics in trauma transmission. While these are important factors in discerning the experiences of refugees navigating resettlement, psychiatric and developmental models of refugee trauma offer a limited view of how the process unfolds for individuals undergoing forced migration and resettlement in marginalizing contexts.

Weighting the effects of premigration trauma is crucial in refugee trauma treatment, as exposure to this type of trauma is strongly correlated with refugee psychopathology, and linked to a range of negative psychosocial outcomes that extend to subsequent generations (Bogic et al., 2015). Long-term effects of ITT result in several adverse effects, ranging from psychiatric symptomatology and common mental disorders (East et al., 2018) to physical health symptoms (Subica & Link, 2022). Although the concept of ITT has been around for more than half a century and enjoys wide consensus on its existence, its full conceptual clarity – especially regarding the *process* of transmission – is still relatively unclear (Yehuda & Lehrner, 2018). Points of contention largely center around whether secondary traumatization occurs through epigenetic mechanisms or through psychodynamic or behavioral pathways. Even less studied are the structural mechanisms involved in the process (Flanagan et al., 2020; Kelstrup & Carlsson, 2022).

In refugee studies specifically, evidence for the ITT process is even more scant. The extant literature has implicated cultural, familial dynamics, and individual psychopathology variables to explain the process of ITT. Precipitates for transmission is typically focused on discrete events, rather than on past, present, and ongoing stressors. In a systematic review of ITT in refugee families, Sangalang and Vang (2017) highlighted the presence of specific populations for which current understanding of refugee ITT is based. Many of the studies included in the review were conducted exclusively with descendants of Holocaust survivors. Although this population has and continues to experience, varied levels of marginalization in the United States, the lack of heterogeneity in the populations studied presents challenges for discerning how non-white and more recently resettled refugees undergoing marginalization experience the ITT process. This point becomes emphasized considering that a majority of the studies included in the review conforms to a paradigm pattern that considers non-structural factors traditionally implicated in refugee trauma studies and omits systemic factors (i.e., state-perpetrated violence) that have been previously shown to contribute to refugee psychopathology (Kira et al., 2014). When explaining the transmission of trauma, most studies focused on parent- or child-level mental health variables, as well as family-level variables. Although one study (Lev-Wiesel, 2007) did explore the concept of collective trauma, the systematic review revealed a common but narrow conceptualization of refugee trauma in the literature, constituted mainly of single-event and premigration exposure to stress.

While Sangalang and Vang (2017) examined methodologies and findings common in the ITT literature, a systematic review by Flanagan et al. (2020) identified implicated *mechanisms* of the ITT process in refugee families. The consistent findings from the Sangalang and Vang (2017) and Flanagan et al. (2020) reviews suggest common themes around the effects of parental trauma on children's well-being. Flanagan et al. (2020) found insecure attachments, maladaptive parenting styles, diminished parental emotional availability, decreased family functioning, accumulation of family stressors, dysfunctional communication styles within families, and parental symptom severity were implicated mechanisms of the ITT process for refugees. The review included one study specifically conducted with Somali refugees in the United States (East et al., 2018) examining maternal past traumas and current mental health impacts on their children who have not experienced trauma exposure directly. The study found no association between past trauma and child well-being, but did find that parental post-traumatic stress disorder (PTSD) and depressive symptoms significantly mediated the effects of past trauma on children's well-being, challenging the position that parental trauma indirectly affects child well-being.

The reviews by Sangalang and Vang (2017) and Flanagan et al. (2020) illustrate the over-implication of discrete events as qualifiers as trauma contributing to both psychopathology and transmission in the literature. These explanations are extended to accounting for the process of ITT in refugee families, whereas developmental delays and dysfunction in children and adolescents are derived from impediments to parent–child attachments (Dalgaard et al., 2016; Han, 2006; Van Ee et al., 2012), parental mental health (East et al., 2018), levels of family functioning (Dalgaard & Montgomery, 2017), family systems (Vaage et al., 2011), and maladaptive parenting styles (Field et al., 2013). Additionally, the literature takes a perspective of trauma characterized by individual experiences, rather than a collective experience. Consequently, interventions both at the psychosocial and clinical levels focus on individual psychological traits, and passively on considerations of ongoing and systemic stressors.

Although trauma is a multifaceted construct (Stein et al., 2016), trauma studies, broadly, are largely informed by the Diagnostic and Statistical Manual of Mental Disorders (DSM)[5]. This congruence with psychiatric epistemologies is supported by empirically grounded evidence for the physiological implications of trauma exposure. In contrast to individualized explanations, a structural/systemic assessment of trauma etiology and sequelae is needed to address what other factors may contribute to both the chronicity and intensity of individual-level traumatization and transmission (Kira et al., 2014). This involves (a) appraising how refugee-serving industries and receiving societies contribute to and proliferate traumatization through their interactions with refugees and (b) examining how the US refugee resettlement program interfaces with other service providers to proliferate the marginalization of multiply marginalized identities. The latter part requires identifying points in the policy that promote a holistic integration of services, and, contrastingly, where services and systems are siloed. For example, the self-sufficiency clause guiding the current policy may work well in placing refugees initially in locales with available jobs, but may fail to consider levels of racism, discrimination, xenophobia, and the cultural incongruency of social care systems to address the needs of new populations. To help contextualize how marginalization may proliferate traumatization and ITT in refugee communities, in the next section we introduce the DBTF before moving to a discussion on how we may apply it to Somali refugees resettled in the United States.

The Developmentally Based Trauma Framework (DBTF): Theorizing Marginalization as a Contributor in the ITT Process for Refugees

Trauma symptomatology is commonly attributed to single-event and premigration exposure to stress events. However, this view inhibits our understanding of the long-term effects of ongoing and chronic stress experienced in the resettlement context. By viewing stressors and traumatic experiences as largely unidimensional, we miss potential sources of traumatization and the effects of cumulative trauma on clinical presentations. In refugee studies, traumatic stress has been largely dichotomized – and thus conceptualized – as the stress encountered premigration and post-resettlement. This pre and post dichotomization may be considered an extension of the work conducted with trauma typologies. Specifically, Terr's (1991) influential work dividing childhood trauma into two basic types to distinguish the nature of the trauma exposure has been further developed by trauma researchers. In Terr's typology, Type I traumas result from the exposure to discrete events, while Type II traumas are a result of chronic and repeated exposure to external events. Building on Terr's work, Solomon and Heide (1999) propose dividing Type II traumas into Type II and Type III, where Type III would account for chronic and repeated exposure to discrete events starting at an early age.

The typologies proposed by Terr (1991) and Solomon and Heide (1999) have advanced understanding of the nature of trauma by their consideration of trauma exposure's developmental effects as well as the implications of its chronicity for later symptomatology. However, these typologies conceptualize trauma as discrete events, and do not expand on exposure to other trauma types, such as those from systemic sources. Kira et al. (2013) have built on the trauma typology work to propose the bidimensional DBTF framework to overcome this limitation. In addition to Types I through III traumas, the DBTF introduces Type IV traumas, and expands on Type III traumas (see Table 8.1). Consistent with other typologies of trauma, the DBTF framework categorizes Type I traumas as single events that have occurred once, and have since ceased (such as a car accident or witnessing a violent event, most closely related to current DSM criterion A for PTSD; Kira, 2022). Type II traumas are discrete events that have repeatedly occurred but have since stopped (e.g., repeated exposure to torture or violence refugees experienced in their home countries). Whereas Type I and Type II traumas describe traumas that have ceased, Type III traumas describe those stressors and traumas that are ongoing, such as discrimination, racism, and social ostracism. The DBTF uses a slightly different definition of Type III trauma than earlier definitions. Instead of viewing Type III traumas as beginning early in life and continuing later in life, the DBTF categorizes Type III traumas as "the cumulative effect of the sequence of all direct and indirect traumatic events on one or more of the different areas of functioning across the lifespan" (Kira, 2022, p. 89). In the DBTF, Type IV traumas are defined as "large scale dynamics that include cumulative stressors and traumas and the [Trauma Proliferation and Stress Generation Model] across the lifespan" (Kira et al., 2018, p. 584). Unlike Types I through III, Type IV traumas are not discrete

Table 8.1 Taxonomy of Severe Stressors

	Physical Traumas		Attachment Traumas		Individuation Traumas			Interdependence Traumas		
Salience	Mortality		Connection, Intimacy		Identity; Annihilation			Group Elimination, Subjugation, and Dominance		
Developmental Task	Safety		Security		Individuation			Affiliation and Interdependence (Belonging, Inclusion, and Exclusion Dynamics)		
	Internal	External	Child	Adult	Personal Identity	Collective Identity	Role Identity	Secondary	Tertiary+	Systemic Violence
Type I	Severe pain	Car accident	Parental neglect	Failed relationships	Rape	Pearl Harbor attack	Serious failure (school, business)	Witnessing murder	Multiply transited	–
Type II	Life-threatening illness, reproductive trauma	Combat	Parental neglect	Failed relationships	Sexual abuse, perpetration-induced trauma	September 11, 2001, war on terror	Dropping out of school, bankruptcy	Domestic violence (child), vicarious trauma (therapist)	–	Genocide
Type III	HIV	Protracted violent conflict, terrorism	Foster care	Failed relationships	Prostitution, human trafficking	Oppression, racism, slavery	Homelessness	Violence, media exposure, globalization	Historical trauma, Cross-generation	Extreme poverty, caste system
Type IV	Multilateral continuous traumatic stress — cumulative traumatic and non-traumatic stress (chronic stress) across life span*									

Source: Reprinted from "Advances in continuous traumatic stress theory: Traumatogenic dynamics and consequences of intergroup conflict: The Palestinian adolescents case" by Kira, I. A., Ashby, J. S., Lewandowski, L., Alawneh, A. W. N., Mohanesh, J., & Odenat, L. (2013). *Psychology, 4*(4), 398). Reprinted with permission.

Note: * Multilateral traumas are those that involve the overlap of two or more of these basic severe stress elements.

events occurring on a continuum, but rather a cumulative stressor that results from exposure to all traumas a person experiences across the lifespan (Kira et al., 2013).

The DBTF demonstrates how trauma/stressors may attenuate or proliferate exposure to continuous and chronic exposure from those trauma/stressors originating from discrete, single, interpersonal events to chronic, ongoing, systemic trauma. The DBTF also overcomes the biases of the individual experience of traumatization by introducing the concept of group traumatization, as well as rejecting the qualifier of single events as precipitates to traumatization. Rather, "the DBTF defines traumatization as a process that can be triggered by stressors with different levels of intensity that range from chronic hassles to severe traumatic complex stressors" (Kira et al., 2013, p. 397). Kira and colleagues have empirically incorporated various stressor and trauma types into the categories included in the DBTF. The DBTF includes two dimensions. The horizontal dimension encapsulates development-based and interpersonal traumas such as identity trauma (individual and collective identity traumas), attachment traumas, physical traumas, and interdependence traumas. According to Kira and colleagues, interdependence traumas include socially made traumas that may be transmitted through networks, and "some traumas [that] reverberate continuously horizontally and/or vertically in the fabric of social networks to spread activation of waves of secondary and tertiary trauma and can continue cross-generationally" (Kira et al., 2013, p. 397). The second dimension of the DBTF includes a vertical dimension, in which stressors occur on a severity and chronicity spectrum. The vertical dimension also includes two types of trauma: Type I traumas and complex traumas (comprising Type II and III traumas). Using this framework, Kira and colleagues also elaborate on the transmission of trauma processes by describing how socially made traumas can be transmitted traditionally either through parent to child or through the collective experience of socio-structural traumas (Kira et al., 2013).

The concept of social (collective) identity stressor/trauma (CIST) may conceptually explain the unique stressor/traumas experienced because of systemic violence (Kira, 2019). Experiences of discrimination and oppression are strongly implicated in contributing to deteriorated mental health (Pascoe & Richman, 2009) and have been theorized as a form of traumatization (Helms et al., 2010). Despite the collective nature of discrimination/oppression experiences, the concept of collective trauma and the social construction of meanings groups attribute to these experiences are less considered. Using the DBTF framework, marginalization may be conceptualized as a chronic, systemic trauma to an individual's collective identity, or a Type IV Collective Identity Trauma (Kira et al., 2014). Systemic trauma refers to social systems and dynamics as perpetrators of trauma and includes socially made traumas such as oppression, racism, and state-perpetrated violence that have the potential to impact mental health and the intergenerational transmission of trauma (Fanon, 1961. By collective, it is meant that individuals share this trauma type with others within their social groups. The key here is that an element of a person's socially constructed identity becomes the basis on which traumatization occurs. Unlike pre-identity traumas, or single-event traumas, a person's group membership determines their vulnerability for experiencing structural violence. According to the DBTF, social structural violence can then "reverberate through secondary and tertiary interdependence and traumatization dynamics to those who belong to the same targeted group" and across generations (Kira et al., 2013, p. 179).

ITT in Marginalized Somali Refugees Resettled in the United States

Somalis comprise one of the world's largest refugee populations, with an estimated 3.1 million Somalis listed as a concern to the UNHCR (UNHCR, n.d.). Since the onset of civil conflict in 1991, Somalis have resettled in over 27 resettlement countries and represent over half of all resettled African refugees in the United States (Anderson, 2017). The protracted conflict and formidable natural disasters in Somalia have produced a continued external exodus of Somalis in addition to the 2.9 million internally displaced (UNHCR, 2022) and continues as one of the world's worst humanitarian crises. Upon resettlement, many Somalis seek out established Somali communities and undergo the process of secondary migration to overcome service gaps and barriers through informal support. Minnesota, for instance, is one such hub for Somalis, where 40% of Somali refugees have resettled, earning it the name "Little Mogadishu."

Despite well-documented resilience prevalent within the community (Chambers, 2017; Liu et al., 2020; Terrana et al., 2022; Uekusa & Matthewman, 2017), Somali refugees grapple with exposure to multiple social risks engendered by displacement. The losses associated with forced migration extend beyond material and human losses for Somalis. As a collectivist society, resettled Somali refugee families with children grapple with losses in social and cultural connections that have been a central component in child-rearing (Heger Boyle & Ali, 2010). Separation from family members, adverse mental health effects, stressors experienced during migration, and exposure to traumatic experiences, all contribute to disruptions in traditional parenting practices. Somali families traditionally endorse multigenerational family structures, which become compromised in the context of forced migration, often resulting in either enmeshed or detached family relationships (Bowie et al., 2017). Refugee families, who eventually resettle in host communities, are commonly single-female-headed households, presenting challenges to the maintenance of traditional and pre-conflict family dynamics. For example, US Census Bureau (2000) data reveals lower levels of intact families, and higher rates of female-headed households among Somalis. Disruptions in coping and resources may also contribute to the observed changes in Somali family structures, such as a shift in families consisting of wide social networks to independent units (Heger Boyle & Ali, 2010).

The resettlement process may significantly contribute to the process of trauma proliferation and ITT for Somalis. Specifically, policy guides sociodemographic variables – such as the quality of the neighborhoods and homes refugees will be resettled into, the quality and network of agencies that serve their needs, access to health care, and opportunities for educational advancement that influence later socioeconomic status – that have been shown to impact the transmission of trauma cross-generationally (Fitzgerald et al., 2020). For example, newly resettled Somali refugee families who experience involuntary housing instability often do so due to issues related to discrimination and economic insecurity that in turn contribute to worsening trauma symptoms (Gillespie et al., 2020). Somali refugees, in particular, report susceptibility to structural barriers – such as lack of access to suitable housing, employment and health care, and experiences with discrimination on the basis of their racial and religious identity – in accessing mental health resources (Terrana et al., 2022).

Somali refugees may be prone to the structural factors that lead to ongoing traumatization and marginalization due to higher rates of mental disorders, chronic poverty, and unemployment fueled by protracted refugee situations (Milner, 2011). While rates of premigration trauma are present across refugee populations, the unique experiences of Somali refugees' post-migration illustrates disparities compared with other refugee groups. Somalis report large-scale disruptions in family structures, including greater marriage problems in the United States, generational and parenting conflicts, and greater perceived difficulties in integrating with the larger host community (Heger Boyle & Ali, 2010). Reasons for family conflict and impeded social acculturation have been reported by Somali refugees to be related to structural factors, such as intervention from social welfare systems and criminal justice systems (Heger Boyle & Ali, 2010), challenging agentic notions of refugee integration.

Proponents of the current US refugee resettlement policy tout the successful integration of refugees overall, citing higher levels of labor market participation (Brell et al., 2020), income levels, and employment rates than US-born counterparts (Capps et al., 2015). However, these statistics are skewed. Although refugees overall perform well on outcome measures, Somali refugees tend to do much worse than other refugee groups (Capps et al., 2015), underscoring their marginality. Somalis in Minnesota experience a poverty rate of 46% with another 29% living near poverty (Minnesota Demographic Center, 2023). This is compared to the overall poverty rate of 9% in the state (Minnesota State Demographic Center, 2023). Additionally, the prevalence rate of diabetes among Somalis in Minnesota is much higher than that of non-Somalis, with the risk of health complications increasing with residential status (Njeru et al., 2016), highlighting the vulnerability of Somali refugees in both health and economic domains.

The extent to which Somali families may experience marginalization may be related back to several possible points, including practical, cultural, and structural causes. Somalis are more likely than other refugee groups to be illiterate in their own language (Capps et al., 2015), making communication with the dominant culture challenging. They are also more likely to experience discrimination due to their Black identity, affecting their mental health (Lincoln et al., 2021; Kirmayer et al., 2011) and proliferating mental distress. Furthermore, as a group, Somalis are much more likely to be younger, compared to other refugee groups (Capps et al., 2015), which may impact time spent in the labor market and earnings. Somalis are overwhelmingly Muslim, which may complicate employment due to the need to take frequent breaks for prayer, positioning them as more likely to experience anti-Muslim bias (Hebbani, 2014). Family dynamics may additionally be a reason for their marginalization since many Somalis are female-headed households, so in addition to refugee status, existing gender politics may impact their ability to participate fully in employment, enroll in English language/education courses to improve future earning odds, secure childcare, and receive social welfare benefits tied to employment.

In their qualitative study examining barriers to the successful adjustment to life in the United States, Chen and Hulsbrink (2019) found that structural barriers compound with individual factors to raise difficulties in achieving self-sufficiency. Similarly, Fee (2019) has implicated the organizational structure of the resettlement program, in influencing how caseworkers provide services to refugees, often feeling compelled to satisfy demands to funders even to the detriment of their clients. In explaining the decline in refugee employment rates, Kreisberg et al. (2022) identify three interrelated structural "weaknesses," including retrenched resettlement funding, the logic of self-sufficiency that push individuals into low wage, undesirable jobs, and the siloed networks of refugee-serving organizations. Studies such as these emphasize the marginalizing effects of the resettlement policy and how it may impede successful resettlement. Structural barriers to refugee resettlement are also compounded by the disparate nature of the United States resettlement program, in which other essential human services (e.g., health care, housing, mainstream social services, schools, and employment) are disconnected from the delivery of resettlement services. The consequences of this include the inability of service providers to adequately support and meet the needs of an especially vulnerable group experiencing unique traumatization. In the sections above, we highlighted some of the systemic sources of trauma for Somali refugees. In the following section, we apply the DBTF to this population and discuss implications for the ITT process.

Application of the DBTF to Somali Refugees at Risk for ITT

Given the scope and nature of the marginalization faced by Somalis during resettlement, the DBTF provides a useful tool to understand the effects of resettlement dynamics and forced migration on the trauma proliferation and ITT of marginalized families. The bidimensionality of the framework allows for flexibility to conceptualize the impacts of all trauma types on the mental health and psychosocial functioning of refugees by considering both its intensity and chronicity as well as the effects of their interaction. The DBTF extends on the potential impacts of systemic sources of traumatization present in the resettlement context that contribute to the proliferation of cumulative stress experiences and its culmination in the transmission of trauma cross-generationally.

Somali refugees report higher exposures to Type I traumas compared with other refugee groups (Gerritsen et al., 2006), although most Somalis report exposure to numerous traumatic events, including rape, witnessing murder and kidnappings, and physical assaults (Im et al., 2020). Reporting Type II traumas also pervade in Somali refugees, who survive prolonged torture experiences, chronic lack of resources and care, and physical pain because of untreated illnesses and continuous exposure to violence (Robertson et al., 2006). Along with repeated discrete traumas, continuous stressors (i.e., Type III trauma) are identified as a strong contributor to the mental health outcomes of Somali families (Ellis et al., 2008; Jorgenson & Nilsson, 2021). For instance, the effects of discrimination, racism and psychosocial stressors have been consistently linked not only to increased depression among Somali adults (Bentley et al., 2012) but also to low in-group status and collective self-worth among youth (Ellis et al., 2022). While facing systemic trauma during resettlement, Somali refugees continue to grapple with untreated past traumas, ongoing stress and trauma from prolonged separation of families, and the ongoing conflict in Somalia (Lincoln et al., 2021). In such regard, Type IV traumas explicates the complex and cumulative dynamics of all the different types of stressors included in the framework, as well as the synergistic effect of systemic traumas before and after resettlement. In the context of marginalization, these experiences are proliferated and may be conceptualized as a Type IV Collective Identity trauma when they threaten not only individual well-being but also collective identities and community capacity for resilience.

Although the available literature on collective identity traumas and their interaction with other trauma types is limited, contextualizing trauma presentations and its intergenerational transmission with broader resettlement dynamics should be a necessary component in treatment with refugee populations. Of particular consideration is how experiences with Type III traumas and the cumulative exposure to systemic stressors can contribute to both the proliferation and initiation of new traumatization. Along with trauma exposure prevalent across refugee populations, Somali families experience exposure to unique and chronic systemic stressors that may exacerbate Type I and Type II traumas, culminating in deterioration in psychosocial functioning and fueling marginalization. For instance, Somalis report more challenges in integrating with the larger host society, and may become especially vulnerable to social protection systems, reflecting the likelihood that intersecting marginalized identities (e.g., being Black, Muslim, and a refugee) shape Somalis' individual and group experiences.

Studies have and continue to consistently find associations between collective identity traumas (e.g., discrimination and marginalization) and worsening health for refugees. However, studies examining the interactions between collective identity traumas and other forms of trauma and its implication for the ITT process are limited. This gap in conceptualizations have major implications for refugee trauma interventions and gesture toward a critical need for empirically driven theories to help guide interventions. The marginalization process for refugees is of concern given the vulnerability of refugees who already endorse complicated trauma profiles pre-resettlement and are most often thrusted into social care systems with marginalizing capacities. The stress garnered from experiences of marginalization is unique from the stress experienced from premigration sources, or traditional post-migration sources such as deteriorated psychosocial circumstances, and thus may contribute significantly to the ITT.

Positioning refugees in relation to their ecological realities requires us to consider the fact that refugees undergo a series of consistent adaptations to their host environment. Somali refugees report challenges with discrimination and marginalization and describe being confronted with threats to their identity. When there is perceived threat to group identity, refugees may be compelled to respond accordingly. For Somali parents who are confronted with threats in the host environment, the lack of parenting resources and social capital may mean an obligation to raise resilient children who will ultimately grapple with similar threats. In the context of an individualist society like the United States, Somali parents increasingly report parenting as particularly challenging (Osman et al., 2016). Instead of attributing intergenerational conflicts to problems specific with the child or forced migration, many Somali families credit the issue almost entirely to Western culture and dynamics, and thus see a need to "rescue [their children] from America" (Phillips, 2023). One strategy for circumventing structural challenges to generational trauma that is increasingly employed by Somalis in the diaspora is the practice of "Dhaqan Celis," which translates directly to "return to culture." Dhaqan Celis refers to the practice of first-generation Somali parents resettled in the West, sending their children back home to Somali, often with traumatizing and dangerous outcomes (Bakaari & Escandell, 2021), with the hope that the child will regain lost identity and regain intergenerational connection (Bakaari & Escandell, 2021).

In the case of Somali refugees who experience considerable levels of Type IV traumas, attention should be given to how structural violence impacts the ITT process as well as related mechanisms. As implied in earlier sections, in the ITT literature, we assume the ITT process is monodirectional – that trauma travels from parent to child. However, trauma can also, at the same time, flow from child to parent and is almost always influenced by contextual factors. Accordingly, when assessing for ITT, it is essential to ecologically position refugees in relation to individual factors (such as premigration trauma), mezzo factors (such as communities in which refugees are dispersed), and structural factors (such as the marginalizing context of a host society and resettlement policies).

Conclusion

The link between marginalization and trauma proliferation is not yet well-defined but using the DBTF to make sense of the experiences of Somali refugees allows for consideration of factors implicated in sustaining traumatization and its transmission to later generations. Scholarly and clinical interest, nevertheless, continues to focus on premigration Type I traumas in the ITT process. While Type I traumas occurring before migration to the host community are an important aspect in later psychopathology, preliminary empirical data supports consideration into the system-level traumas that may both proliferate and moderate trauma dynamics existing in resettlement contexts. Discerning how chronic exposure to systemic violence results in collective and identity-based traumas may help facilitate clinical interventions for providing effective and holistic care. Research refining the conceptual links in the mechanisms implicated in the ITT process may also help introduce competing and critical paradigms to help guide the policymaking process.

While the nature of forced migration results in the deterioration of many psychosocial faculties and resources – such as loss of material resources, coping and mental health – preliminary research has identified family functioning as especially impacted. Theoretically, marginalization may contribute to the intergenerational transmission of trauma in two main ways for Somali refugee families. First, through the proliferation of traumatization due to structural impediments to successful integration, and second, through adjustments to parenting styles as a response to these structural impediments and perceived threats to collective identity. Refugee parents undergoing traumatic experiences endorse higher rates of mental disorders than those without these experiences. For many of these individuals, they often arrive in the United States with little to no previous treatment or intervention for their deteriorated mental health and are continually missed in early screening efforts by refugee-serving agencies once resettled in the United States, becoming mired in welfare systems. These unresolved traumas interfacing with systemic marginalization may result in poor (sensitized) parental emotional regulations which increases the likelihood that their children may also face similar difficulties in regulations. Somali families experiencing marginalization within social welfare systems find themselves grappling with potentially hostile contexts that threaten not only their well-being but also that of their children. Current paradigms guiding trauma treatment may fail to detect resettlement dynamics contributing to trauma proliferation. Use of the DBTF framework may help overcome these limitations and allow for the conceptual flexibility to imagine how these different traumas may converge to produce unique outcomes for refugee families and its repercussions for chronic marginalization cross-generationally.

Notes

1 See, for example, Lehrner and Yehuda (2018), or Weingarten (2004).
2 See Flanagan et al. (2020).
3 See, for example, Goodkind and Deacon (2004), or Sabarini (2012), or Im (2021), or Zetter (2007).
4 See Bruno (2011).
5 For further discussion, see Lafrance and McKenzie-Mohr (2013).

References

Alakhunova, N., Diallo, O., Martin del Campo, I., & Tallarico, W. (2015). Defining marginalization: An assessment tool. *A product of the partnership between four development professionals at the elliot school of international affairs &the word fair trade organization-Asia*. Washington, DC: The George Washington University.

Alemi, Q., & Stempel, C. (2018). Discrimination and distress among Afghan refugees in northern California: The moderating role of pre-and post-migration factors. *PloS one*, *13*(5), e0196822. https://doi.org/10.1371/journal.pone.0196822

Anderson, M. (2017, February 14). African immigrant population in US steadily climbs. *Pew Research Center*. Retrieved from www.pewresearch.org/short-reads/2017/02/14/african-immigrant-population-in-u-s-steadily-climbs/

Andersson, M. (2003). Immigrant youth and the dynamics of marginalization. *Young, 11*(1), 74–89. https://doi.org/10.1177/1103308803011001077

Bakaari, F., & Escandell, X. (2021). Ambivalent returns: Dhaqan celis and counter-diasporic migration among second-generation Somalis. *Global Networks, 22*(1), 51–64. https://doi.org/10.1111/glob.12324

Banulescu-Bogdan, N. (2020). *Beyond work: Reducing social isolation for refugee women and other marginalized newcomers*. Washington, DC: Transatlantic Council on Migration.

Bea, M. D., & Taylor Poppe, E. S. (2021). Marginalized legal categories: Social inequality, family structure, and the laws of intestacy. *Law & Society Review, 55*(2), 252–272. https://doi.org/10.1111/lasr.12553

Beiser, M., & Hou, F. (2016). Mental health effects of premigration trauma and postmigration discrimination on refugee youth in Canada. *The Journal of Nervous and Mental Disease, 204*(6), 464–470. https://doi.org/10.1097/NMD.0000000000000516

Bentley, J. A., Thoburn, J. W., Stewart, D. G., & Boynton, L. D. (2012). Post-migration stress as a moderator between traumatic exposure and self-reported mental health symptoms in a sample of Somali refugees. *Journal of Loss and Trauma, 17*(5), 452–469. https://doi.org/10.1080/15325024.2012.665008

Berridge, D. (2007). Theory and explanation in child welfare: Education and looked-after children. *Child & Family Social Work, 12*(1), 1–10. https://doi.org/10.1111/j.1365-2206.2006.00446.x

Blackmore, R., Boyle, J. A., Fazel, M., Ranasinha, S., Gray, K. M., Fitzgerald, G., & Gibson-Helm, M. (2020). The prevalence of mental illness in refugees and asylum seekers: A systematic review and meta-analysis. *PLoS Medicine, 17*(9), e1003337. https://doi.org/10.1371/journal.pmed.1003337

Bogic, M., Njoku, A., & Priebe, S. (2015). Long-term mental health of war-refugees: A systematic literature review. *BioMed Central International Health and Human Rights, 15*(1), 1–41.

Bourdieu, P. (1984). A social critique of the judgement of taste. *Traducido del francés por R. Nice*. London: Routledge.

Bowie, B., Wojnar, D., & Isaak, A. (2017). Somali families' experiences of parenting in the United States. *Western Journal of Nursing Research, 39*(2), 273–289. https://doi.org/10.1177/0193945916656147

Brell, C., Dustmann, C., Preston, I. (2020). The labor market integration of refugee migrants in high-income countries. *Journal of Economic Perspectives, 34* (1), 94–121. https://doi.org/10.1257/jep.34.1.94

Brown, A., & Scribner, T. (2014). Unfulfilled promises, future possibilities: The refugee resettlement system in the United States. *Journal on Migration and Human Security, 2*(2), 101–120. https://doi.org/10.1177/233150241400200203

Bruno, A. (2011). *US refugee resettlement assistance*. Darby, PA: Diane Publishing.

Burnham, L., Conrad, C., Whitehead, J., Mason, P., & Stewart, J. (2005). Racism in US welfare policy: A human rights issue. *African Americans in the US Economy*, 309.

Bynner, J. (1997). Agenda for youth research in the next century: A British perspective. *Young, 5*(4), 34–49. https://doi.org/10.1177/110330889700500403

Capps, R., Koball, H., Campetella, A., Perreira, K., Hooker, S., & Pedroza, J. M. (2015). *Implications of immigration enforcement activities for the well-being of children in immigrant families*. Washington, DC: Urban Institute and Migration Policy Institute.

Carbone, G. (2011). Democratic demands and social policies: The politics of health reform in Ghana. *The Journal of Modern African Studies, 49*(3), 381–408.

Chambers, S. (2017). *Somalis in the twin cities and Columbus: Immigrant incorporation in new destinations*. Philadelphia, PA: Temple University Press.

Chaskin, R. J., & Joseph, M. L. (2011). Social interaction in mixed-income developments: Relational expectations and emerging reality. *Journal of Urban Affairs, 33*(2), 209–237. https://doi.org/10.1111/j.1467-9906.2010.00537.x

Chen, X., & Hulsbrink, E. B. (2019). Barriers to achieving "economic self-sufficiency": The structural vulnerability experienced by refugee families in Denver, Colorado. *Human Organization*, *78*(3), 218–229. https://doi.org/10.17730/0018-7259.78.3.218

Constance-Huggins, M. (2011). A review of the racial biases of social welfare policies. *Journal of Human Behavior in the Social Environment*, *21*(8), 871–887. https://doi.org/10.1080/10911359.2011.588531

Crenshaw, K. W. (2011). From private violence to mass incarceration: Thinking intersectionally about women, race, and social control. *UCLA Law Review*, *59*, 1418.

Dalgaard, N. T., & Montgomery, E. (2017). The transgenerational transmission of refugee trauma: Family functioning and children's psychosocial adjustment. *International Journal of Migration, Health and Social Care*, *13*(3), 289–301. https://doi.org/10.1108/IJMHSC-06-2016-0024

Dalgaard, N. T., Todd, B. K., Daniel, S. I., & Montgomery, E. (2016). The transmission of trauma in refugee families: Associations between intra-family trauma communication style, children's attachment security and psychosocial adjustment. *Attachment & Human Development*, *18*(1), 69–89. https://doi.org/10.1080/14616734.2015.1113305

Desiderio, M. V. (2016). *Integrating refugees into host country labor markets: Challenges and policy options*. Washington, DC: Migration Policy Institute.

East, P. L., Gahagan, S., & Al-Delaimy, W. K. (2018). The impact of refugee mothers' trauma, posttraumatic stress, and depression on their children's adjustment. *Journal of Immigrant and Minority Health*, *20*(2), 271–282. https://doi.org/10.1007/s10903-017-0624-2

Easton-Calabria, E., & Omata, N. (2018). Panacea for the refugee crisis? Rethinking the promotion of 'self-reliance' for refugees. *Third World Quarterly*, *39*(8), 1458–1474. https://doi.org/10.1080/01436597.2018.1458301

Ellis, B. H., MacDonald, H. Z., Lincoln, A. K., & Cabral, H. J. (2008). Mental health of Somali adolescent refugees: The role of trauma, stress, and perceived discrimination. *Journal of Consulting and Clinical Psychology*, *76*(2), 184. https://doi.org/10.1037/0022-006X.76.2.184

Ellis, B. H., Sideridis, G., Davis, S. H., Cardeli, E., Abdi, S. M., & Lincoln, A. K. (2022). Discrimination and mental health of Somali immigrants in North America: A longitudinal study from 2013 to 2019. *Social Psychiatry and Psychiatric Epidemiology*, *57*(5), 1049–1059. https://doi.org/10.1007/s00127-022-02235-9

Evans, W. N., & Fitzgerald, D. (2017). *The economic and social outcomes of refugees in the United States: Evidence from the ACS* (No. w23498). Cambridge, MA: National Bureau of Economic Research.

Fangen, K. (2010). Social exclusion and inclusion of young immigrants: Presentation of an analytical framework. *Young*, *18*(2), 133–156. https://doi.org/10.1177/110330881001800202

Fanon, F. (1961). *The wretched of the earth*. New York, NY: Grove Press.

Fee, M. (2019). Paper integration: The structural constraints and consequences of the US refugee resettlement program. *Migration Studies*, *7*(4), 477–495. https://doi.org/10.1093/migration/mny016

Field, N. P., Muong, S., & Sochanvimean, V. (2013). Parental styles in the intergenerational transmission of trauma stemming from the Khmer Rouge regime in Cambodia. *American Journal of Orthopsychiatry*, *83*(4), 483–494. https://doi.org/10.1111/ajop.12057

Fitzgerald, M., London-Johnson, A., & Gallus, K. (2020). Intergenerational transmission of trauma and family systems theory: An empirical investigation. *Journal of Family Therapy*, *42*(3), 406–424. https://doi.org/10.1111/1467-6427.12303

Flanagan, N., Travers, A., Vallières, F., Hansen, M., Halpin, R., Sheaf, G., & Johnsen, A. T. (2020). Crossing borders: A systematic review identifying potential mechanisms of intergenerational trauma transmission in asylum-seeking and refugee families. *European Journal of Psychotraumatology*, *11*(1), 1790283. https://doi.org/10.1080/20008198.2020.1790283

Foucault, M. (1977). *Discipline and punish: The birth of the prison*. Harmondsworth, Middlesex: Penguin.

Gerritsen, A. A., Bramsen, I., Devillé, W., van Willigen, L. H., Hovens, J. E., & Van Der Ploeg, H. M. (2006). Physical and mental health of Afghan, Iranian and Somali asylum seekers and refugees living in the Netherlands. *Social Psychiatry and Psychiatric Epidemiology*, *41*, 18–26. https://doi.org/10.1007/s00127-005-0003-5

Gillespie, S., Cardeli, E., Sideridis, G., Issa, O., & Ellis, H. (2020). Residential mobility, mental health, and community violence exposure among Somali refugees and immigrants in North America. *Health & Place*, *65*. https://doi.org/10.1016/j.healthplace.2020.102419

Gleeson, C., Frost, R., Sherwood, L., Shevlin, M., Hyland, P., Halpin, R., & Silove, D. (2020). Post-migration factors and mental health outcomes in asylum-seeking and refugee populations: A systematic review. *European Journal of Psychotraumatology*, *11*(1), 1793567. https://doi.org/10.1080/20008198.2020.1793567

Goodkind, J. R., & Deacon, Z. (2004). Methodological issues in conducting research with refugee women: Principles for recognizing and re-centering the multiply marginalized. *Journal of Community Psychology*, *32*(6), 721–739. https://doi.org/10.1002/jcop.20029

Grossman, J. L., & Friedman, L. M. (2011). *Inside the castle: Law and the family in 20th century America*. Princeton, NJ: Princeton University Press.

Haffejee, B., & East, J. F. (2019). "We're not asking for handouts!" voices of women refugees from Africa on rapid economic self-sufficiency in the United States. *Refugees and Asylum Seekers: Interdisciplinary and Comparative Perspectives*, 290.

Hall, J. M., Stevens, P. E., & Meleis, A. I. (1994). Marginalization: A guiding concept for valuing diversity in nursing knowledge development. *Advances in Nursing Science*, *16*(4), 23–41. https://doi.org/10.1097/00012272-199406000-00005

Han, M. (2006). Relationship among perceived parental trauma, parental attachment, and sense of coherence in Southeast Asian American college students. *Journal of Family Social Work*, *9*(2), 25–45. https://doi.org/10.1300/J039v09n02_02

Hebbani, A. (2014). The impact of religious difference and unemployment/underemployment on Somali former refugee settlement in Australia. *Journal of Muslim Mental Health*, *8*(1). https://doi.org/10.3998/jmmh.10381607.0008.103

Heger Boyle, E., & Ali, A. (2010). Culture, structure, and the refugee experience in Somali immigrant family transformation. *International Migration*, *48*(1), 47–79. https://doi.org/10.1111/j.1468-2435.2009.00512.x

Hellenbach, M., Karatzias, T., & Brown, M. (2017). Intellectual disabilities among prisoners: Prevalence and mental and physical health comorbidities. *Journal of Applied Research in Intellectual Disabilities*, *30*(2), 230–241. https://doi.org/10.1111/jar.12234

Helms, J. E., Nicolas, G., & Green, C. E. (2010). Racism and ethnoviolence as trauma: Enhancing professional training. *Traumatology*, *16*(4), 53–62. https://doi.org/10.1177/1534765610389595

Hughes, C. (2021). A House but not a home: How surveillance in subsidized housing exacerbates poverty and reinforces marginalization. *Social Forces*, *100*(1), 293–315. https://doi.org/10.1093/sf/soaa108

Hynie, M. (2018). The social determinants of refugee mental health in the post-migration context: A critical Review. *The Canadian Journal of Psychiatry*, *63*(5), 297–303. https://doi.org/10.1177/0706743717746666

Im, H. (2021). Falling through the cracks: Stress and coping in migration and resettlement among marginalized hmong refugee families in the United States. *Families in Society*, *102*(1), 50–66. https://doi.org/10.1177/1044389420901393

Im, H., & Swan, L. E. (2021). "We learn and teach each other": Interactive training for cross-cultural trauma-informed care in the refugee community. *Community Mental Health Journal*, 1–13.

Im, H., Swan, L. E., & Heaton, L. (2020). Polyvictimization and mental health consequences of female genital mutilation/circumcision (FGM/C) among Somali refugees in Kenya. *Women & Health*, *60*(6), 636–651. https://doi.org/10.1080/03630242.2019.1689543

Jorgenson, K. C., & Nilsson, J. E. (2021). The relationship among trauma, acculturation, and mental health symptoms in Somali refugees. *The Counseling Psychologist, 49*(2), 196–232. https://doi.org/10.1177/0011000020968548

Kelstrup, L., & Carlsson, J. (2022). Trauma-affected refugees and their non-exposed children: A review of risk and protective factors for trauma transmission. *Psychiatry Researh*, 114604.

Kira, I. A. (2022). Taxonomy of stressors and traumas: An update of the development-based trauma framework (DBTF): A life-course perspective on stress and trauma. *Traumatology, 28*(1), 84–97. https://doi.org/10.1037/trm0000305

Kira, I. A., Alpay, E. H., Shuwiekh, H. A., & Türkeli, A. (2023). A type III continuous trauma perspective on the effects of increased ongoing hostility, discrimination, community violence and poverty on refugees' mental health and cognitive functioning: A longitudinal study. *Journal of Community & Applied Social Psychology, 33*(4), 851–867. https://doi.org/10.1002/casp.2693

Kira, I. A., Ashby, J. S., Lewandowski, L., Alawneh, A. W. N., Mohanesh, J., & Odenat, L. (2013). Advances in continuous traumatic stress theory: Traumatogenic dynamics and consequences of intergroup conflict: The Palestinian adolescents case. *Psychology, 4*(4), 396–409. https://doi.org/10.4236/psych.2013.44057

Kira, I. A., Fawzi, M. H., & Fawzi, M. M. (2013). The dynamics of cumulative trauma and trauma types in adults patients with psychiatric disorders: Two cross-cultural studies. *Traumatology, 19*(3), 179–195. https://doi.org/10.4236/psych.2013.44057

Kira, I. A., Lewandowski, L., Chiodo, L., & Ibrahim, A. (2014). Advances in systemic trauma theory: Traumatogenic dynamics and consequences of backlash as a multi-systemic trauma on Iraqi refugee Muslim adolescents. *Psychology, 5*(5), 389–412. https://doi.org/10.4236/psych.2014.55050

Kira, I. A., Shuwiekh, H., Al-Huwailah, A. H., Lewandowski, L., Alawneh, A. W. N., Abou-Mediene, S., & Aljakoub, J. (2019). The central role of social identity in oppression, discrimination, and social-structural violence: Collective identity stressors and traumas, their dynamics and mental health impact. *Peace and Conflict: Journal of Peace Psychology, 25*(3), 262. https://doi.org/10.1037/pac0000363

Kira, I. A., Shuwiekh, H., Kucharska, J., Fawzi, M., Ashby, J. S., Omidy, A. Z., & Lewandowski, L. (2018). Trauma proliferation and stress generation (TPSG) dynamics and their implications for clinical science. *American Journal of Orthopsychiatry, 88*(5), 582–596. https://doi.org/10.1037/ort0000304

Kirmayer, L. J., Narasiah, L., Munoz, M., Rashid, M., Ryder, A. G., Guzder, J., & Pottie, K. (2011). Common mental health problems in immigrants and refugees: General approach in primary care. *Canadian Medical Association Journal, 183*(12), E959–E967.ki

Kreisberg, A. N., De Graauw, E., & Gleeson, S. (2022). Explaining refugee employment declines: Structural shortcomings in federal resettlement support. *Social Problems*, spab080. https://doi.org/10.1093/socpro/spab080

Krieger, N., Chen, J. T., Waterman, P. D., Hartman, C., Stoddard, A. M., Quinn, M., & Barbeau, E. M. (2008). The inverse hazard law: Blood pressure, sexual harassment, racial discrimination, workplace abuse and occupational exposures in US low-income Black, White and Latino workers. *Social Science & Medicine, 67*, 1970–1981. https://doi.org/10.1016/j.socscimed.2008.09.039

LaFrance, M., McKenzie-Mohr, S. (2013). The DSM and its lure of legitimacy. *Feminism & Psychology, 23*(1), 119–140. https://doi.org/10.1177/0959353512467974

Lehrner, A., & Yehuda, R. (2018). Trauma across generations and paths to adaptation and resilience. *Psychological Trauma: Theory, Research, Practice, and Policy, 10*(1), 22. https://doi.org/10.1037/tra0000302

Lev-Wiesel, R. (2007). Intergenerational transmission of trauma across three generations: A preliminary study. *Qualitative Social Work, 6*(1), 75–94. https://doi.org/10.1177/1473325007074167

Lincoln, A. K., Cardeli, E., Sideridis, G., Salhi, C., Miller, A. B., Da Fonseca, T., & Ellis, B. H. (2021). Discrimination, marginalization, belonging, and mental health among Somali immigrants in North America. *American Journal of Orthopsychiatry*, *91*(2), 280. https://doi.org/10.1037/ort0000524

Lindencrona, F., Ekblad, S., & Hauff, E. (2008). Mental health of recently resettled refugees from the Middle East in Sweden: The impact of pre-resettlement trauma, resettlement stress and capacity to handle stress. *Social Psychiatry and Psychiatric Epidemiology*, *43*(2), 121–131. https://doi.org/10.1007/s00127-007-0280-2

Liu, J., Mansoor, Y., Johar, J., Kim, S., Sidiqi, A., & Kapoor, V. (2020). Strengths-based inquiry of resiliency factors among refugees in metro Vancouver: A comparison of newly arrived and settled refugees. *Social Science & Medicine*, *263*, 113243. https://doi.org/10.1016/j.socscimed.2020.113243

Milner, J., & Loescher, G. (2011). *Responding to protracted refugee situations: Lessons from a decade of discussion*. [Policy brief]. Oxford: Refugee Studies Center, Oxford Department of International Development.

Minnesota State Demographic Center. (2023). *The economic status of minnesotans: A chartbook with data for minnesota's largest cultural groups*. Saint Paul, MN: Minnesota Department of Administration.

Muller, C. (2012). Northward migration and the rise of racial disparity in American incarceration, 1880–1950. *American Journal of Sociology*, *118*(2), 281–326. https://doi.org/10.1086/666384

Nicosia, N., MacDonald, J. M., & Arkes, J. (2013). Disparities in criminal court referrals to drug treatment and prison for minority men. *American Journal of Public Health*, *103*(6), e77–e84

Njeru, J. W., Tan, E. M., St Sauver, J., Jacobson, D. J., Agunwamba, A. A., Wilson, P. M., & Wieland, M. L. (2016). High rates of diabetes mellitus, pre-diabetes and obesity among Somali immigrants and refugees in Minnesota: A retrospective chart review. *Journal of Immigrant and Minority Health*, *18*(6), 1343–1349. https://doi.org/10.1007/s10903-015-0280-3

Nosè, M., Ballette, F., Bighelli, I., Turrini, G., Purgato, M., Tol, W., & Barbui, C. (2017). Psychosocial interventions for post-traumatic stress disorder in refugees and asylum seekers resettled in high-income countries: Systematic review and meta-analysis. *PLoS One*, *12*(2), e0171030. https://doi.org/10.1371/journal.pone.0171030

Osman, F., Klingberg-Allvin, M., Flacking, R., & Schön, U. K. (2016). Parenthood in transition – Somali-born parents' experiences of and needs for parenting support programmes. *BioMed Central International Health and Human Rights*, *16*(1), 1–11.

Pascoe, E. A., & Smart Richman, L. (2009). Perceived discrimination and health: A meta-analytic review. *Psychological Bulletin*, *135*(4), 531. https://doi.org/10.1037/a0016059

Phillips, M. (2023, February 3). One father's desperate plan to rescue his son from America. *The Wall Street Journal*. Retrieved November 30, 2023, from www.wsj.com/articles/one-fathers-desperate-plan-to-rescue-his-son-from-america-11675436043

Porter, M., & Haslam, N. (2005). Predisplacement and postdisplacement factors associated with mental health of refugees and internally displaced persons: A meta-analysis. *Journal of the American Medical Association*, *294*(5), 602–612. https://doi.org/10.1001/jama.294.5.602

Robertson, C. L., Halcon, L., Savik, K., Johnson, D., Spring, M., Butcher, J., & Jaranson, J. (2006). Somali and oromo refugee women: Trauma and associated factors. *Journal of Advanced Nursing*, *56*(6), 577–587. https://doi.org/10.1111/j.1365-2648.2006.04057.x

Sabarini, T. (2012). *Palestinian refugee identity: Marginalization and resistance in refugee camps in Lebanon*. [Thesis, Ryerson University]. Digital Commons @ Ryerson.

Sangalang, C. C., & Vang, C. (2017). Intergenerational trauma in refugee families: A systematic review. *Journal of Immigrant and Minority Health*, *19*(3), 745–754. https://doi.org/10.1007/s10903-016-0499-7

Saugeres, L. (2011). (Un)accommodating disabilities: Housing, marginalization, and dependency in Australia. *Journal of Housing and the Built Environment, 26*, 1–15.

Shutes, I. (2011). Welfare-to-work and the responsiveness of employment providers to the needs of refugees. *Journal of Social Policy, 40*(3), 557–574. https://doi.org/10.1017/S0047279410000711

Sichling, F. (2021). The housing experiences of Syrian refugee youth in the United States. *Journal of Immigrant and Refugee Studies.* https://doi.org/10.1080/15562948.2021.1980641

Solomon, E. P., & Heide, K. M. (1999). Type III trauma: Toward a more effective conceptualization of psychological trauma. *International Journal of Offender Therapy and Comparative Criminology, 43*(2), 202–210. https://doi.org/10.1177/0306624X9943200

Stein, J. Y., Wilmot, D. V., & Solomon, Z. (2016). Does one size fit all? Nosological, clinical, and scientific implications of variations in PTSD criterion A. *Journal of Anxiety Disorders, 43*, 106–117. https://doi.org/10.1016/j.janxdis.2016.07.001

Subica, A. M., & Link, B. G. (2022). Cultural trauma as a fundamental cause of health disparities. *Social Science & Medicine, 292*, 114574. https://doi.org/10.1016/j.socscimed.2021.114574

Summerfield, D. (2004). Cross-cultural perspectives on the medicalization of human suffering. In Rosen, G.M. (Ed). *Posttraumatic stress disorder: Issues and controversies.* Chichester: John Wiley & Sons Ltd.

Summerfield, D. A. (1997). Legacy of war: Beyond "trauma" to the social fabric. *The Lancet, 349*(9065), 1568. https://doi.org/10.1016/S0140-6736(05)61627-3

Terr, L. C. (1991). Childhood traumas: An outline and overview. *American Journal of Psychiatry, 148*(1), 10–20. https://doi.org/10.1176/ajp.148.1.10

Terrana, A., Ibrahim, N., Kaiser, B., & Al-Delaimy, W. K. (2022). Foundations of somali resilience: Collective identity, faith, and community. *Cultural Diversity and Ethnic Minority Psychology, 28*(4), 533–543. https://doi.org/10.1037/cdp0000536

Timshel, I., Montgomery, E., & Dalgaard, N. T. (2017). A systematic review of risk and protective factors associated with family related violence in refugee families. *Child Abuse & Neglect, 70*, 315–330. https://doi.org/10.1016/j.chiabu.2017.06.023

Tomlinson, F., & Egan, S. (2002). From marginalization to (dis) empowerment: Organizing training and employment services for refugees. *Human Relations, 55*(8), 1019–1043. https://doi.org/10.1177/0018726702055008182

Uekusa, S., & Matthewman, S. (2017). Vulnerable and resilient? Immigrants and refugees in the 2010–2011 Canterbury and tohoku disasters. *International Journal of Disaster Risk Reduction, 22*, 355–361.

US Census Bureau. (2000). *Table FBP-1. Profile of Selected Demographic and Social Characteristics: 2000.* Retrieved from https://www2.census.gov/programs-surveys/decennial/tables/2000/stp-159/national/stp-159-somalia.pdf

United Nations Higher Commission on Refugees. (2022). *Horn of Africa Somalia Situation.* Operational Data Portal: Refugee Situations. UNHCR. Retrieved November 30, 2023, from https://data.unhcr.org/en/situations/horn/location/192

United Nations Higher Commission on Refugees. (n.d.). *Somalia.* Retrieved from www.unhcr.org/countries/somalia

Vaage, A. B., Thomsen, P. H., Rousseau, C., Wentzel-Larsen, T., Ta, T. V., & Hauff, E. (2011). Paternal predictors of the mental health of children of Vietnamese refugees. *Child and Adolescent Psychiatry and Mental Health, 5*(1), 1–11. https://doi.org/10.1186/1753-2000-5-2

Van Ee, E., Kleber, R. J., & Mooren, T. T. (2012). War trauma lingers on: Associations between maternal posttraumatic stress disorder, parent – child interaction, and child development. *Infant Mental Health Journal, 33*(5), 459–468. https://doi.org/10.1002/imhj.21324

Weingarten, K. (2004). Witnessing the effects of political violence in families: Mechanisms of intergenerational transmission and clinical interventions. *Journal of Marital and Family Therapy*, *30*(1), 45–59. https://doi.org/10.1111/j.1752-0606.2004.tb01221.x

Xu, Q. (2017). How resilient a refugee community could be: The Vietnamese of New Orleans. *Traumatology*, *23*(1), 56. https://doi.org/10.1037/trm0000091

Yehuda, R., & Lehrner, A. (2018). Intergenerational transmission of trauma effects: Putative role of epigenetic mechanisms. *World Psychiatry*, *17*(3), 243–257. https://doi.org/10.1002/wps.20568

Zetter, R. (2007). More labels, fewer refugees: Remaking the refugee label in an era of globalization. *Journal of Refugee Studies*, *20*(2), 172–192. https://doi.org/10.1093/jrs/fem011

9 The Long Shadow of the Eritrean Independence Struggle

Transgenerational Transmission of Trauma across Diaspora Generations

Nicole Hirt

Introduction

Eritrea is a small country in the Horn of Africa whose self-definition as a nation relies strongly on a 30-year long independence struggle against Ethiopia. Once an Italian colony, the territory was federated with Ethiopia in 1952 and then annexed by Emperor Haile Selassie in 1962. The Eritrean independence struggle was launched in 1961, and the subsequent years were characterized by violence and destruction. About 1 million people had fled Eritrea by 1991, when the Eritrean People's Liberation Front (EPLF) led Eritrea to independence through a military victory and promised emancipation from suppression and injustice.

However, three decades after Eritrea's independence, the situation in the country is desolate. The leader of the EPLF Isaias Afewerki has ruled the country as its unelected president since its formal independence in 1993, and the political system has become increasingly autocratic over the years. Today, Eritrea is characterized by a complete lack of civil liberties and an absence of the rule of law (Freedom House, 2023). A mandatory and open-ended national service was introduced in 2002 that imposed on the adult population forced labor for the government for a very small renumeration (Hirt & Mohammad, 2013). The militarized command economy has led to economic decline and endemic poverty. The prevailing ideology of collectivism and self-sacrifice, used to justify the often decade-long conscription of Eritreans, is based on the alleged respect for the legacy of the martyrs of the independence struggle (Kibreab, 2018). Eritrean youth are encouraged to follow the example of the governments' portrayal of the gallant fighters who selflessly sacrificed their lives for the nation while living a life full of hardships. However, substantial parts of the youth have chosen to flee the country rather than serving in the national service (Hirt, 2017). Over time, Eritrea has become a diasporic trans-nation with about half of its citizens residing abroad. Many have been exiled for generations, while new refugees have been following suit for the past two decades. However, transnational ties between diasporans and the homeland have remained strong. The government has followed a policy of transnational control and financial exploitation of its citizens abroad since the 1980s and continues to mobilize parts of the diaspora for its purposes (Hirt & Mohammad, 2018).

DOI: 10.4324/9781003385820-10

Accordingly, narratives related to the armed struggle have been passed on, often as postmemories, from the first diaspora-generation to their descendants, many of whom have only a vague imagination of their ancestral homeland. In the political realm, both the Eritrean government and the exiled opposition parties have used the memory of the martyrs to mobilize political support by claiming to represent their legacy (Conrad, 2006; Hirt, 2021).

This chapter explores how the transgenerational transmission of trauma, defined as deeply distressing or disturbing experiences related to the independence struggle, affect both younger diaspora generations who grew up in safe democratic environments and refugees who fled the oppressive regime in Eritrea and were victimized by the repressive system. It draws on the theoretical notion of "postmemory" (Hirsch, 2008) to explain how events of the past, real or imagined, have influenced identity formation and social agency of diaspora-born generations and refugees. It builds on long-term participant observation in Eritrean diaspora communities as well as in Eritrea from the 1980s until the present. The chapter is further informed by more than 100 in-depth interviews conducted with diaspora Eritreans in Germany, Norway, Sweden, and the UK between 2018 and 2021 by the chapter author and an Eritrean co-researcher.[1] These interviews initially focused on transnational repression by the government and diaspora responses, but the present sampling is redirected to explore postmemory and trauma transmission. The chapter author regularly follows Eritrean social media to observe the varying pro- and anti-government narratives and their ideological backgrounds. Accordingly, this chapter is based on a variety of data sources which resulted in a heuristic thought model originating in the question of why many Eritreans resettled in democratic countries, where they enjoy citizenship endorsed by civil and political rights, support a regime that is known for its dismal human rights record ("UNHRC", 2023). The chapter demonstrates the interconnectedness between developments in Eritrea and how various diaspora communities perceive them based on their personal exposure to postmemory and transgenerational trauma transmission. Specifically, it explores how narratives that originate in trauma suffered by specific communities can be transformed into certain narratives by political entrepreneurs to influence political opinions.

The chapter first explains how Eritrea emerged as a diasporic trans-nation even before its recognition as an independent state and how the glorification of the martyrs was used as a tool of political mobilization of the war refugees by the EPLF. It then analyzes post-independence political junctures and how they were perceived and related to the memory of the martyrs in the diaspora and in the homeland. Furthermore, it explains how the government's idealized picture of life in Eritrea presented to the younger diaspora generation differs from the reality as it is being perceived by the national service conscripts, many of whom have opted to flee the country. The conclusion discusses how the politicization of memory influences the interaction between the established diaspora and the current refugees, and how the shadow of the past may have a paralyzing impact on political reform movements that strive for change in Eritrea.

Eritrea's Emergence as a Diasporic Nation during the Independence Struggle

The independence struggle caused the flight of about 1 million Eritreans between the 1970s and the late 1980s when the Eritrean Liberation Front (ELF) and the EPLF fought against the Ethiopian military regime ("World Bank," 1994). People were traumatized by widespread political terror committed by the Ethiopian Dergue regime in the capital Asmara and other cities, while the countryside was devastated by scorched-earth policies of the Ethiopian army and a civil war between the liberation fronts. In 1991, the EPLF achieved a military victory over Ethiopia and Isaias Afewerki declared himself head of the provisional government (Pool, 2001). The EPLF's strategy had relied on two pillars: on the one hand, the fighters were involved in a guerrilla war and tried to live a self-sufficient life in the liberated areas; on the other hand, all Eritreans in exile were under the moral obligation to support the struggle through material assistance to the front. The Marxist EPLF actively organized diaspora Eritreans in mass organizations in the Sudan, Europe, North America, and Arab countries, and indoctrinated them politically (Hirt, 2015a). The leadership skillfully used the "survivor's guilt," which many of the refugees developed having left the country instead of sacrificing their lives for the Eritrean cause (Conrad, 2006, p. 257; Von Nolting, 2002, p. 56). EPLF cadres in the diaspora told them how they could contribute to the struggle by making generous donations, and transnational organizations such as the National Unions for Eritrean workers, women, and youth organized festivals and other fund-raising events. They provided the refugees with a mix of propaganda, Eritrean food, music, and dance to convince them that the EPLF was the only representative of the Eritrean people and the sole representative of a future independent country (Conrad, 2010).

The main support base of the EPLF consisted of ethnic Tigrinya Orthodox Christians, who made up about half of the population, while the other half was predominantly Muslim and ethnically fragmented; many of them had been supporters of the Muslim-dominated ELF and remained so in exile. To unite the people under its own command, the EPLF created a narrative of national unity which denied the existing rifts within Eritrea's society. The country was portrayed as a victim of international conspiracies resulting in annexation by Ethiopia against the will of the people. This narrative ignored the fact that particularly the Orthodox Christians – later the main support base of the EPLF – had initially favored unity with Ethiopia due to their cultural affiliation to the Abyssinian culture and had only started to favor independence under the impression of the Dergue's Red Terror atrocities (Wolde Giorgis, 1989). This narrative also ignored the fact that Muslims had been the initiators of the independence struggle and portrayed them and the ELF as conservative puppets of Arab power interests (Mohammad, 2013; Trevaskis, 1977).

The main task of EPLF's representatives in the diaspora was to spread its own historical narrative among the emerging diaspora communities and convince them of adapting the image of one united Eritrean people fighting together for independence. They also emphasized the importance of each diaspora member contributing support for this effort from abroad (Conrad, 2006, p. 257). The socialist Ethiopian Dergue received military support from the Eastern Bloc because of Ethiopia's strategic importance as a regional power during the Cold War. The EPLF, despite of portraying itself as a socialist movement as well, was only backed by some leftist European NGOs and some church organizations, especially Norwegian Church Aid (Duffield & Pendergast, 1994). Accordingly, the refugees were the key to achieving the EPLF's goal of self-reliance, which had been formulated as a response to its international isolation.

To enhance their readiness to support the struggle, the diaspora communities were supplied with video-taped documentaries that presented an idealized picture of life in the liberated areas where the fighters were active at the military front while struggling for political emancipation under the immediate threat of losing their lives (Connell, 1993; Pateman, 1990). The EPLF leadership skillfully developed a martyr's cult, in which those who had sacrificed their lives for the country received a quasi-religious form of adoration. As a Marxist and thus anti-religious organization, the spiritual feelings of the people were rechanneled into deep feelings of guilt, thankfulness, and obligation toward those who had paid the ultimate price. The political leadership portrayed them as heroes who decided to choose collective self-sacrifice to achieve the liberation of their compatriots. This image also convinced many leftist admirers of revolutionary liberation fronts from democratic countries, who traveled to the liberated areas under the guise of the EPLF and produced publications such as *Never Kneel Down: Drought, Development and Liberation in Eritrea* (Firebrace & Holland, 1985) or *Against All Odds: A Chronicle of the Eritrean Revolution* (Connell, 1993), which glorified the purported uniqueness of the Eritrean liberation struggle.

The dark side of the movement – which had been under the firm leadership of Isaias Afewerki who had rigorously silenced his opponents since the mid-1970s (Pool, 2001) – was rarely discussed. Both the leftist western EPLF supporters and the Eritrean diaspora communities perceived any form of criticism of the leadership as treason against the common cause. After independence, diaspora Eritreans were encouraged to pay a diaspora tax to help rebuilding the war-devastated country (Koser, 2003; Hirt, 2015a). The sacrifices paid by the population inside the country were enormous: about half a million people had died during the decades of war, while about the same number had been internally displaced. Some 450,000 Eritreans lived in Sudanese refugee camps, awaiting resettlement (DADM-Project database). Accordingly, despite the military victory that led to independence, the emerging nation suffered from a collective trauma due to the loss of relatives and the extensive damage caused by the war. Most diaspora Eritreans felt a sense of guilt and obligation toward the EPLF leadership, especially those who had made it to prosperous Western democracies where most of them were leading relatively comfortable lives and acquired the nationality of their respective host countries.

The Politicization of a Collective Trauma: A Nation Built on the Legacy of the Martyrs

Many first-generation diasporans remain in a psychological state of limbo, torn between the emotional ambivalence of appreciating to have found a safe haven alongside the pangs of remorse related to their flight into exile (Von Nolting, 2002, pp. 55–56). While most of them worked and started families, their thoughts often wander to their distant homeland. After independence, only small numbers of diaspora Eritreans returned; most of them preferred the security of their adopted home as compared to the insecurities awaiting them in "free Eritrea." For many diaspora Eritreans, better educational opportunities for their children also played an important role to stay in their respective host countries. As a psychological compensation, some developed obsessive forms of long-distance nationalism (Anderson, 1992), which helped them express their Eritreanness from the security of their democratic new homes. Thus, a second generation of diaspora-born Eritreans grew up in an atmosphere that was heavily influenced by the postmemory of the traumatic experiences of their parents and relatives.

The term "postmemory" was coined in the context of Holocaust survivors and their children and describes

> the relationship that the generation after those who witnessed cultural or collective trauma bears to the experiences of those who came before, experiences that they "remember" only by means of the stories, images, and behaviours among which they grew up. But these experiences were transmitted to them so deeply and affectively as to *seem* to constitute memories in their own right.
>
> (Hirsch, 2008, pp. 106–107)

Postmemory is not obtained through personal experiences, but rather derived from traumatic events experienced by earlier generations, either in person or through the loss of relatives and destruction of their homeland. These experiences affect the generations that come after, who cannot fully integrate them and thus create their own perception of those past events (Codde, 2011, p. 1; Hirsch, 1997, p. 22).

These collective traumas constitute "a social, interpersonal phenomenon, which, when narrated into national identity, can constitute the nation-state's identity" and influence its activities (Lerner, 2019, p. 563). Thus, trauma-affected postmemory can be manipulated by political interest groups, as Volkan (2001) has shown for Serbia, Conrad (2006) for the Eritrean diaspora, Duschinski and Hamrick (2018) for Namibia, and Orjuela (2020) for Rwanda and Sri Lanka. In the case of Eritrea, the government has skillfully used the narrative of the heroic struggle to attract substantial numbers of second-generation diaspora Eritreans in Europe and North America. Festivals and patriotic music have played an important role to create feelings of strong Eritrean patriotism ("Shabait," 2012) and of appreciation toward the freedom fighters, personified by President Isaias Afewerki.

The children of EPLF activists were strongly influenced by the activities of their parents because they were exposed to political propaganda material in the form of videos and songs (Graf, 2018, p. 121). However, some of those children felt rather annoyed by the close-knit and hyper-nationalist EPLF communities, which they experienced as patronizing. Many members of the younger diaspora generations, most of whom are now in their 30s, feel that they are still not recognized as competent enough to have their own opinions regarding Eritrea. One female respondent from the second-generation diaspora living in Germany explained:

> They [first-generation diasporans] do not tell you directly that you must have been ready to sacrifice yourself for your country before you will be entitled to make political decisions [concerning Eritrea], they do not literally say this, but there are some unconscious mechanisms that are applied to intimidate the younger generation because they have not been ready to die for their country Eritrea.
> (N. Hirt, Personal interview, online Zoom, February 2021).

Notably, this observation shows how members of the first generation, who left Eritrea as refugees and became political activists due to their feelings of survivor-guilt, indirectly blame their own offspring for their lacking willingness to make sacrifices. This means they have internalized the EPLF's narrative that only the ex-fighters (symbolized by a small political elite around the president) have the right to rule the country.

However, other second-generation diasporans with similar background do not engage with this aspect of their postmemory to an equal extent, but express outright appreciation toward their EPLF-supporting parents for leaving Eritrea and not returning during the 1990s. This stance is evidenced by another female respondent who revealed:

> I can say that I am proud that my parents have made so many things possible for us here [in Germany], and I often think about what would have been the alternative if we had returned to Eritrea after independence. I am deeply moved by the imagination of having been forced to go through all the horrible things the refugees who escaped Eritrea in recent years had to experience.
> (N. Hirt, Personal interview, online Zoom, April 2021).

This interviewee refers to the developments that took place during the decades after independence, when Eritrea turned from a beacon of hope into one of the most restrictive dictatorships on earth.

The EPLF renamed itself People's Front for Democracy and Justice (PFDJ) in 1994 and worked on a democratic constitution which was ratified in 1997 but never implemented. A year later, the leadership got involved in another disastrous war with Ethiopia over a piece of disputed border land which caused up to 100,000 deaths and resulted in the military defeat of the Eritrean troops in 2000 (Negash & Tronvoll, 2000). During the following years, President Isaias clamped down on political reformers and journalists and established himself as an autocratic ruler in a country where the rule of law is absent (Ogbazghi, 2011). In 2002, a national service without time limit was introduced, and has since been forcing male and female Eritreans to spend their productive lives performing forced labor for the government without the right to choose their place of living or their occupation, and without earning enough income to secure their subsistence

(Hirt & Mohammad, 2013; "UN General Assembly," 2015; Kibreab, 2018). This has resulted in an ongoing mass exodus of young Eritreans, parts of whom manage to reach Europe, often after traumatizing journeys through the Sudan and Libyan refugee camps (Belloni, 2016).

The miserable situation inside Eritrea caused increasing rifts between different diaspora communities, which are split into government supporters and a fragmented opposition composed of former ELF supporters, PFDJ dissidents, and a variety of religious- or ethnic-based organizations (Mohammad, 2021). There is also a human-rights-centered movement of Justice Seekers, but all organizations are prone to internal quarrels and frequent breakups (Mohammad & Tronvoll, 2015). One part of the second diaspora generation is still convinced that the government under Isaias Afewerki has had the right way of conduct since independence and that he was forced to introduce some unpopular measures due to foreign conspiracies. They are under the influence of the Young PFDJ, the youth branch of the ruling party founded in 2004 that operates exclusively in western democracies with the aim of indoctrinating the younger diaspora generation. The legacy of the martyrs is used as a tool to instill pride and feelings of indebtedness into young Eritreans born abroad, and the EPLF/PFDJ government is presented as the only legitimate representative of the people because it achieved independence under immense sacrifices (Hirt, 2021).

Post-Independence Developments through the Lens of the Homeland and the Diaspora

The years after 2002 were characterized by the paralyzation of democratic forces and the installation of the open-ended national service, which affected the Eritrean people in a critical way. The introduction of a Maoist-style militarized command economy resulted in a state of social anomie, in which it is impossible to earn a living through normal economic activities without becoming a draft evader (Hirt & Mohammad, 2013). During the 1990s, education was highly valued among the Eritrean society as a tool for personal development with the hope of achieving a better future. However, in 2003, the government established the remote military camp Sawa as a militarized boarding school where all 12-grade students had to pass their final school year while undergoing military training (Kibreab, 2018). Since then, education has been perceived as a form of punishment, and many students attempted to intentionally fail their exams in order not to be sent to Sawa (Riggan, 2016). These developments also triggered an exodus of young people who first moved to refugee camps in the neighboring countries Sudan and Ethiopia. An undisclosed number migrated further to the Arab Gulf (Hirt & Mohammad, 2023), and tens of thousands reached Europe after crossing the Mediterranean under difficult conditions (Hirt, 2017).

In the diaspora, reactions toward these developments were mixed. On the one hand, the opposition strived to create strong and unified organizations that could form an alternative to the autocratic government. However, its efforts failed due to personal competition, and regional, ethnic, and religious rifts (Mohammad &

Tronvoll, 2015). Concurrently, the government and its transnational organizations created a narrative that presented Eritrea as the victim of international conspiracies with the aim of destroying the country's hard-won independence. When the UN imposed sanctions against the government for its alleged support of Islamists in Somalia in 2009, the leadership mobilized the diaspora to engage in a "resolute nationalist rebuff" by making extra donations and participating in pro-government demonstrations in Europe and the United States (Hirt, 2015a).

Despite the obviously deteriorating situation inside the country, where even the most basic commodities were hard to come by, many second-generation diasporans stuck to the PFDJ's narrative. The regime cleverly used the postmemory of the second generation and the resulting diffuse feelings of guilt to channel their politicization in favor of the regime. PFDJ ideologists stressed the inseparability of the liberation front and the people and created a psychological conflation between Eritrea as a nation, the State of Eritrea as an institution, and the PFDJ under President Isaias as a symbol for the glorious struggle (Conrad, 2010, p. 166). The diaspora is supposed to help defend the country against alleged threats from its enemies, which include the CIA, Ethiopia, and anti-Eritrean traitors (Tesfamariam, 2019).

Meanwhile, the UN Human Rights Council's Commission of Inquiry on Human Rights in Eritrea (COIE) interviewed numerous witnesses and published a report in 2015 which stated that "systematic, widespread and gross human rights violations have been and are being committed in Eritrea under the authority of the Government. Some of these violations may constitute crimes against humanity" ("UN General Assembly," 2015, p. 1). Ironically, the Eritrean Ministry of Foreign Affairs (2014) condemned the report as being part of ongoing international conspiracy and stated that the accusations were an attack, "not so much on the government, but on a civilized people and society who cherish human values and dignity."

This statement mirrors a narrative which implies the unity of the people, the state, and government, which means that criticizing the horrifying deeds of the leadership against its own people is an insult against the very same people (Hirt & Mohammad, 2018). The success of this absurd argumentation among the pro-government segments of the diaspora cannot be explained without recurring to psychological mechanisms that allow the repression of sympathy for the regime's victims. Feelings of compassion are suppressed because they would disturb the idealized image of Eritrea's struggle and the legacy of the martyrs. Thus, sympathy for victims of the regime would also shatter those diaspora Eritreans' identities as proud nationals of a heroic nation. Accordingly, the government's ideologists in the diaspora have successfully used postmemory as a phenomenon that can trigger psychological repression mechanisms regarding the harsh reality in Eritrea. Hollander (2016) has described similar processes as large-group identity formation "on the basis of shared anxieties, fantasies, defenses, myths and memories [that] can be mobilised in response to chosen traumas and chosen glories" (p. 66).

In a similar vein, Koinova and Karabegović (2019) have demonstrated that new diaspora generations can either perpetuate conflict-generated identities, or they can internalize democratic values that shaped their socialization in democratic societies (p. 1819). In the case of the second-generation Eritrean diaspora, there are deep rifts between those who are adhering to the myths of the heroic independence struggle, while others engage in political or civic opposition movements. There is also a large "silent majority" that has preserved their identities as Eritreans, but represents no specific political stand toward and only a vague knowledge of their ancestral homeland.

The Second Diaspora Generation and the Refugees: Two Worlds, One Collective Trauma?

A rift also exists between those people of Eritrean origin who were born or spent their formative years in the diaspora and the refugees who were born and brought up in Eritrea but fled the long national-service, economic deprivation, and the absence of rule of law and civil liberties. They have personally experienced suppression and suffered from the adverse living conditions in Eritrea which are often blatantly denied by the privileged government supporters in the diaspora. These two groups can be referred to as "one Eritrean generation, two worlds" (Hirt, 2015b), even if they are now sharing the same country of residence.

The newcomers often struggle to get a secure residence status, and many have been traumatized by the arduous living conditions they faced not only in Eritrea, but also on their flight routes through the Sahara Desert to Libya, where many of them were held in inhumane conditions in prison camps before they were able to continue their journey (Van Reisen et al., 2023). In Europe, they are exposed to growing xenophobia and feel intimidated by European right-wing politicians (Abdalla, 2017; Campo et al., 2021).

At the same time, the Eritrean government regards the refugees as traitors who illegally deserted the mandatory national service. During their asylum interviews, they are often faced with pro-government translators who warn them "not to speak badly about their country" (Mengis, 2015). Ironically, they can lift their status and become full members of the diaspora once they have been granted asylum and signed the so-called "letter of repentance," in which they declare to regret having left Eritrea and pledge to pay the 2% diaspora tax for the rest of their lives (Hirt, 2015a). As a result, those who fled Eritrea in recent years rarely socialize with pro-government second-generation diasporans due to fundamental differences in the perception of their homeland; yet, if such encounters take place, they can be very stressful. For instance, one female refugee told the chapter author that she had been continuously harassed by pro-government fellow Eritreans at school after they had noticed that she opposed the regime in Asmara, and when she told them about her mother's unjust arrest in Eritrea, they simply called her a liar (N. Hirt, Personal interview, Norway, July 17, 2018).

The refugee generation often finds relief in secluded ethnic, regional, and religious communities (Mohammad, 2021) in contrast to those Eritreans who grew up in the diaspora and whose worldview has been influenced by the secular and nationalistic EPLF ideology that shaped their parents' worldview. The transnational arm of the Eritrean government is aware of the refugees' orientation toward religion, and it has infiltrated Orthodox church communities in the diaspora with false clergymen who take high fees for baptism or marriage services, which are then sent to the government's coffers (N. Hirt, Personal interviews with Eritrean informants in Norway, Germany and the United Kingdom, 2018).

When comparing the Eritrean second-diaspora-generation with those who grew up in and later fled post-independence Eritrea, it becomes evident that both groups are affected by Eritrea's collective trauma stemming from the armed struggle, yet in different ways: those who grew up in the diaspora were impacted by postmemories through their parents, extended families, and EPLF-created narratives of the heroic struggle that influenced their youth and created feelings of blame as an indirect consequence of their parent's survivors guilt. Some of them reacted either by idealizing the armed struggle and developing a sense of appreciation toward the EPLF/PFDJ as the guardian of independent Eritrea, while denying the gross human rights violations committed by the ruling party. Others realized the crimes committed by the regime after discrediting reformers and journalists in 2002. They formed political and civic organizations with the aim to initiate change in Eritrea, yet with little success.

Those who grew up in Eritrea faced a dire reality after the victory of the EPLF in 1991. The devastating border war with Ethiopia from 1998 to 2002 and the consequent societal militarization confronted them with the choice of living as puppets of the regime without personal freedom (Hirt & Mohammad, 2021), or to risking their life while fleeing the country illegally. Once they obtain a safe residence status outside Eritrea, these Eritrean refugees attempt to live the normal lives they were denied in their homeland, and give up hope for a better Eritrea. Many of them perceive the opposition in exile as superfluous and inefficient and focus on working through their personal traumas (N. Hirt, Personal interviews with Eritrean refugees in Norway, Germany and the United Kingdom, 2018 and 2019).

Conclusion

This chapter explored the role of a collective national trauma passed by postmemory from one generation to the next on political opinion formation. Collective traumas experienced by certain social groups can be exploited by political entrepreneurs, in the case of Eritrea, by the EPLF and its successor, the PFDJ, which has ruled Eritrea since independence in 1993. The atrocities that were committed in Eritrea during the 30 years of war between 1961 and 1991 caused approximately 1 million Eritreans to flee, while some 90,000 fighters fought against the Ethiopian army to liberate the country ("World Bank," 1994). Thereafter, the EPLF created a martyr's cult around the fallen heroes and used the survivors' guilt of those who had fled abroad. This was done to mobilize them politically and to indoctrinate them with its own version of Eritrean nationalism.

The second diaspora generation was influenced by this traumatic past – not only through postmemory derived from their parents, but also through transnational agents of the Eritrean regime such as the Young PFDJ. One part of the second-generation diaspora accepted the narrative of a heroic nation under continuous threats by international conspiracies spread by the Eritrean government.

They refuse to acknowledge the grave reality in the country, where young Eritreans have been subjected to decades of servitude in the mandatory national service. An idealized picture of their ancestral home clashes with the experiences of tens of thousands of refugees who reached Europe in the past two decades, fleeing dire living conditions in Eritrea. There is limited interaction between these groups because the presence of the refugees poses a threat to the idealized narrative of the pro-government diaspora communities, who tend to view them as traitors from their privileged position as European nationals.

There are, however, also second-generation diasporans who oppose the regime and engage in opposition movements, while some of them have withdrawn from Eritrean politics altogether. It seems that interaction between the government opponents of the second generation and the refugees is also limited. The latter often congregate in religious-based communities or subnational ethnic or region-based organizations where they interact mostly among themselves (Mohammad, 2021).

Since independence, Eritrea has become a diasporic nation due to the continuous outflow of its younger generation caused by wars, societal militarization, political repression, and economic deprivation. Still, the memory or postmemory of the independence struggle serves as a mechanism to forge commonalities in Eritrean identity, albeit with differing justifications. Government supporters and opponents alike feel pride and appreciation toward the martyrs who made independent Eritrea possible. However, government supporters believe that the small ruling group that consists of former EPLF fighters has earned its legitimization through the military victory over Ethiopia three decades ago. In contrast, government opponents propagate that this group has betrayed the aspirations and the legacy of the martyrs, who gave their lives in the hope to create a better Eritrea.

In conclusion, the politicization of memories (real or imagined) influences the perception of Eritrean reality, and thus the formation of political opinions. Moreover, the interaction between the second-generation diaspora and those who fled the regime in Asmara is negatively impacted by different perceptions of what Eritrea symbolizes and what it means to be Eritrean. Accordingly, the internalization of dissimilar narratives regarding what makes up "Eritrea," and differing life experiences of diaspora-born Eritreans and refugees from Eritrea may have a paralyzing impact on communication and social exchange between different Eritrean communities in exile that, in turn, continues to affect the political reform movements for a democratic Eritrea.

Note

1 I would like to thank my colleague Abdulkader Saleh Mohammad who participated as my co-researcher in the projects "Do Diasporas Contribute to the Persistence of Authoritarian Rule? Responses of Eritrean Citizens Abroad to Transnational Governance" funded by the German Research Association (2018–2020), and conducted several interviews in the frame of the project "Transnational Lives in the Shadow of Repression: Diaspora Youth and the Struggle for Democracy," funded by the Swedish Research Council (2020–2021). The data of all interviewees were anonymized for the sake of the participant's safety.

References

Abdalla, J. (2017). *Europe's Refugee Crisis: Right-Wing Populism and Mainstream Cooption in Germany and France*. New York: CUNY Academic Works.

Anderson, B. (1992). *Long-Distance Nationalism: World Capitalism and the Rise of Identity Politics*. Amsterdam: Centre for Asian Studies.

Belloni, M. (2016). 'My uncle cannot say "no" if I reach Libya': Unpacking the social dynamics of border-crossing among eritreans heading to Europe. *Human Geography*, 9(2), 47–56. https://doi.org/10.1177/194277861600900205

Campo, F., Giunti, S., & Mendola, M. (2021). *The Refugee Crisis and Right-Wing Populism: Evidence from the Italian Dispersal Policy. IZA Discussion Paper No. 14084*. Bonn: IZA – Institute of Labor Economics.

Codde, P. (2011). Keeping history at bay: Absent presences in three recent Jewish American novels. *MFS Modern Fiction Studies*, 57(4), 673–693. https://doi.org/10.1353/mfs.2011.0097

Connell, D. (1993). *Against All Odds: A Chronicle of the Eritrean Revolution*. Lawrenceville, NJ: Red Sea Press.

Conrad, B. (2006). Out of the 'memory hole: Alternative narratives of Eritrean revolution in the diaspora. *Afrika Spectrum*, 41(2), 249–271.

Conrad, B. (2010). *We are the prisoners of our dreams: Long-distance nationalism and the Eritrean diaspora in Germany*. PhD Thesis, University of Hamburg. Retrieved December 16, 2023, from https://d-nb.info/1027573118/34.

DADM Database, Ethiopia-Eritrea. (1950–1993). *University of Central Arkansas*, Retrieved December 3, 2023, from https://uca.edu/politicalscience/dadm-project/sub-saharan-africa-region/ethiopiaeritrea-1950-1993/.

Duffield, M.A., & Pendergast, J. (1994). Without Troops and Tanks. In *Humanitarian Intervention in Ethiopia and Eritrea*. Trenton, NJ: Red Sea Press.

Duschinski, H., & Hamrick, E. (2018). Enduring injustice: Memory politics in Namibia's genocide reparations movement. *Memory Studies*, 11(4), 437–454. https://doi.org/10.1177/1750698017693668

Eritrean Ministry of Foreign Affairs (July 24, 2014). *Press Statement*. Retrieved December 3, 2023, from http://shabait.com/news/localnews/20212-statement-of-the-ministry-of-foreign-affairs.

Firebrace, J., & Holland, S. (1985). *Never Kneel Down: Drought, Development and Liberation in Eritrea*. Lawrenceville, NJ: Red Sea Press.

Freedom House. (2023). *Freedom of the World Report Eritrea 2022*. Retrieved December 3, 2023, from https://freedomhouse.org/country/eritrea/freedom-world/2023.

Graf, S. (2018). Politics of belonging and the Eritrean diaspora youth: Generational transmission of the decisive past. *Geoforum*, 92, 117–124. https://doi.org/10.1016/j.geoforum.2018.04.009

Hirsch, M. (1997). *Family Frames: Photography, Narrative, and Postmemory*. Cambridge, MA: Harvard University Press.

Hirsch, M. (2008). The generation of postmemory. *Poetics Today*, 29(1), 103–128.

Hirt, N. (2015a) The Eritrean diaspora and its impact on regime stability: Responses to UN sanctions. *African Affairs*, 114(454), 115–135.

Hirt, N. (2015b). One Eritrean generation, two worlds: The established diaspora, the new exiles and their relations to the homeland. *Horn of Africa Bulletin*, 27(5), 23–27.

Hirt, N. (2017). Fleeing Repression. Inside Eritrea. In G. Carbone (Ed.), *Out of Africa. Why People Migrate* (pp. 95–118). Milano: ISPI.

Hirt, N. (2021). Eritrea's chosen trauma and the legacy of the martyrs. The impact of postmemory on political identity formation of second-generation diaspora Eritreans. *Africa Spectrum*, 56(1), 19–38. https://doi.org/10.1177/0002039720977495

Hirt, N., & Mohammad, A.S. (2013). 'Dreams don't come true in Eritrea': Anomie and family disintegration due to the structural militarisation of society. *The Journal of Modern African Studies*, *51*(1), 139–168. https://doi.org/10.1017/S0022278X12000572

Hirt, N., & Mohammad, A.S. (2018). By way of patriotism, coercion, or instrumentalization: How the Eritrean regime makes use of the diaspora to stabilize its rule. *Globalizations*, *15*(2), 232–247. https://doi.org/10.1080/14747731.2017.1294752

Hirt, N., & Mohammad, A.S. (2021). Eritrea's self-reliance narrative and the remittance paradox: Reflections on thirty years of retrogression. *Remittances Review*, *6*(1), 17–31. https://doi.org/10.33182/rr.v6i1.1056

Hirt, N., & Mohammad, A.S. (2023). The limits of diaspora: Double vulnerabilities among Eritreans in Saudi Arabia. In Dalia Abdelhady, & Ramy Aly (Eds.), *Routledge Handbook on Middle Eastern Diasporas*. London and New York: Routledge.

Hollander, N.C. (2016). Trauma as ideology: Accountability in the "intractable conflict". *Psychoanalysis, Culture & Society*, *21*(1), 59–80. https://doi.org/10.1057/pcs.2015.67

Kibreab, G. (2018). *The Eritrean National Service. Servitude 'for the Common Good' and the Youth Exodus*. Woodbridge: Boydell & Brewer.

Koinova, M., & Karabegović, D. (2019). Causal mechanisms in diaspora mobilizations for transitional justice. *Ethnic and Racial Studies*, *42*(11), 1809–1829. https://doi.org/10.1080/01419870.2019.1624802

Koser, K. (2003). Mobilizing New African siaspsoras: An Eritrean case study. In Khalid Koser (Ed.), *New African Diasporas* (pp. 111–112). London: Routledge.

Lerner, A.B. (2019). Theorizing collective trauma in international political economy. *International Studies Review*, *21*(4), 549–571. https://doi.org/10.1093/isr/viy044

Mengis, E. (2015). *"Sprich nicht so über dein Land!" "Tigrinya-Dolmetscher in Anhörungen vor dem Bundesamt für Migration und Flüchtlinge* ["Don't Speak about Your Country Like This!" Tigrinya-interpreters in Hearings at the Federal Agency for Migration and Refugees]. Master Thesis, University of Mainz. Retrieved December 16, 2023 from https://openscience.ub.uni-mainz.de/bitstream/20.500.12030/4201/1/100000024.pdf.

Mohammad, A.S. (2021). The resurgence of religious and ethnic identities among Eritrean refugees: A response to the government's nationalist ideology. *Africa Spectrum*, *56*(1), 39–58. https://doi.org/10.1177/00020397209632

Mohammad, A.S. (2013). *The Saho of Eritrea: Ethnic Identity and National Consciousness*. Berlin: Lit Academic Publisher.

Mohammad, A.S., & Tronvoll, K. (2015). *Eritrean Opposition Parties and Civic Organisations*. Oslo: Noref Expert Analysis.

Negash, T., & Tronvoll, K. (2000). Brothers at war. In *Making Sense of the Eritrean-Ethiopian War*. Athens, OH: Ohio University Press.

Ogbazghi, P.B. (2011). Personal rule in Africa: The case of Eritrea. *African Studies Quarterly*, *12*(2), 1–25.

Orjuela, C. (2020). Passing on the torch of memory: Transitional justice and the transfer of diaspora identity across generations. *International Journal of Transitional Justice*, *14*(2), 360–380. https://doi.org/10.1093/ijtj/ijaa005

Pateman, R. (1990). Eritrea. *Even the Stones are Burning*. Trenton, NJ: Red Sea Press.

Pool, D. (2001). From Guerillas to Government. In *The Eritrean People's Liberation Front*. Oxford: James Currey.

Riggan, J. (2016). The struggling State. In *Nationalism, Mass Mobilization, and the Education of Eritrea*. Philadelphia, PA: Temple University Press.

Shabait (2012). Role of music in the Eritrean struggle for independence. *Shabait*. Retrieved December 16, 2023, from www.shabait.com/about-eritrea/art-a-sport/13566-role-of-music-in-the-eritrean-struggle-for-independence.

Tesfamariam, S. (2019). Eritrea: Tail wagging at the UN. *Shabait*. Retrieved December 16 2023, from www. shabait.com/categoryblog/27850-eritrea-tail-wagging-at-the-un.

Trevaskis, G.K. (1977). *Eritrea: A Colony in Transition 1941–1952*. Westport, CT: Greenwood Press.

UN General Assembly, Human Rights Council. (June 4, 2015). *Report of the Commission of Inquiry on Human Rights in Eritrea. UN Document A/HRC/29/42*. Retrieved August 2, 2023, from www.ohchr.org/en/hr-bodies/hrc/co-i-eritrea/report-co-i-eritrea-0.

UNHRC (2023). Human rights situation in Eritrea. *Report of the Special Rapporteur on the Situation of Human Rights in Eritrea: UN Document A/HRC/40/23*. Retrieved August 2, 2023, from https://documents-dds-ny.un.org/doc/UNDOC/GEN/G23/149/13/PDF/G2314913.pdf?OpenElement.

Van Reisen, M., Mawere, M., Smits, K., & Wirtz, M. (2023). *Enslaved, Trapped and Trafficked in Digital Black Holes. Human Trafficking Trajectories to Libya*. Bamenda, Cameroon: Langaa RPCIG.

Volkan Vamik, D. (2001). Transgenerational transmissions and chosen traumas: An aspect of large-group identity. *Group Analysis*, *34*(1), 79–97. https://doi.org/10.1177/05333160122077730

Von Nolting, N. (2002). *Gemeinschaft im Exil: Eritreische Flüchtlinge in Frankfurt am Main* [Society in Exile: Eritrean Refugees in Frankfurt am Main]. Arbeitspapier/Working Paper No. 11. Mainz: Gutenberg Universität Mainz, Institut für Ethnologie und Afrikastudien.

Wolde Giorgis, D. (1989). Red Tears. *War, Famine and Revolution in Ethiopia*. Trenton, NJ: Red See Press.

World Bank. (1994). *Eritrea: Options and Strategies for Growth. In two Volumes. Report No. 12930-ER*. Washington, DC. Retrieved December 16, 2023, from https://documents.worldbank.org/en/publication/documents-reports/documentdetail/543131468770065817/statistical-annex

10 The Elephant in the Room

Experiences of Intergenerational Trauma in Second-Generation Bosnian Americans

Ajlina Karamehić-Muratović and Laura Kromják

Introduction

Following the 1992–1995 war in Bosnia and Herzegovina (hereinafter referred to as "Bosnia"), more than half of its 4.3 million inhabitants were displaced from their homes. Of these, over a million individuals were internally displaced, while the remaining number sought refuge in host countries across the globe. Estimates suggest that the number of Bosnians who resettled in the United States is approximately 300,000–350,000 (Karamehić-Oates & Karamehić-Muratović, 2020). The majority resettled between 1993 and 2006, populating several US metropolitan areas, including Chicago, St. Louis, New York, Atlanta, and Phoenix (Halilovich et al., 2018).

It is well documented that the refugee experience is marked by pre- and post-migration challenges, including those affecting one's mental health long after resettlement. Studies conducted among resettled refugees indicate that they tend to have higher rates of mental disorders, such as depression, post-traumatic stress disorder (PTSD), and anxiety, compared to those who had not been exposed to war. Over nearly three decades, a considerable body of literature has addressed the mental health of Bosnian refugees who resettled in the United States (and other parts of the world). Exposure to war in Bosnia included a series of traumatic events such as witnessing atrocities or being a victim of violence, concentration camps, systematic rape of women, physical and psychological torture, and destruction of homes and all that was familiar. As further supported in the literature, added trauma associated with resettlement in a new country presented Bosnian refugees with enduring mental health challenges. For instance, as early as one year into their resettlement in the United States, Weine et al. (1995) documented a high rate of PTSD among Bosnian refugees, as well as persistent symptoms of PTSD one year after their resettlement (Weine et al., 1998). Subsequently, further evidence of their PTSD and depression symptoms was revealed and it was concluded that several individuals experiencing significant psychiatric symptoms do not seek or receive mental health services, yet rate their health relatively positively (Weine et al., 2000). This suggests that some Bosnian refugees harbor distress in silence and possibly never seek help.

In investigating the mental health of Bosnian refugees who now called the United States their home after being resettled for nine years on average, Craig et al.

DOI: 10.4324/9781003385820-11

(2008) found that this community averaged several traumas in their lifetime and were still experiencing high rates of PTSD, traumatic grief, anxiety, and depression, despite half self-reporting positive well-being. Wartime trauma was also found to be strongly related to PTSD, anxiety, and depression among Bosnians in Idaho, USA, whereby the experience of being a refugee and associated difficulties exacerbated their mental health challenges (Begic & McDonald, 2006). Similarly, Keyes and Kane (2004) noted some positive experiences associated with adaptation but showed that the group of individuals they studied largely "experienced culture shock, loneliness, and feelings of dejection, humiliation, and inferiority as well as psychic numbness, grief, nostalgia, and feeling as if they belonged nowhere" (pp. 824–825). Further, in assessing the utility of the Primary Care Behavioral Health Screener for adult Bosnian refugees (PCBHS-B), Lepper et al. (2017) found that even though the overall incidence of behavioral health problems among Bosnians did not significantly differ from the general population, these refugees scored much higher when it came to PTSD. Specifically, items focusing on intrusive and disturbing thoughts in one's mind and nightmares and memories of negative events were present. War-related nightmares and chronic insomnia were likewise challenges in Miller et al.'s (2002) study looking at Bosnians in Chicago, which in turn limited their capacity to adapt to the new homeland.

Recent studies with Bosnian refugees have continued to find that mental disorders are widespread in the community for years following their traumatic experiences and resettlement (Sichling & Karamehić-Muratović, 2020). Though conducted in the Netherlands, Knipscheer's and Kleber's (2006) study has parallels to Bosnians resettled in the United States when considering long-term mental health. In their study, post-traumatic responses were shown to be a powerful predictor of mental distress among Bosnian refugees, whereby 80% of the community reported above the threshold for post-traumatic reactions. They suggested that Bosnian refugees have "critical mental health condition," where "the level of posttraumatic stress gets even worse when time goes by" (p. 350). Along similar lines, in their systematic review of studies among long-settled war refugees worldwide, Bogic et al. (2015) found that "the risk of having a serious mental disorder is substantially higher in war refugees than in the general population, even several years after refugee resettlement" (p. 35). The same study suggested that refugees from the former Yugoslavia (thus including Bosnia) tended to have the highest rates of depression and PTSD. Bogic et al. (2015) concluded that past traumatic experiences (along with postmigration socioeconomic situation) were the most cited risk factors that predicted mental disorders among long-settled war refugees.

Scholarship points to post-traumatic stress reactions enduring and potentially intensifying over time among resettled Bosnian refugees who now largely identify as Bosnian Americans (Sichling et al., 2021; Sichling & Karamehić-Muratović, 2020). The findings are also significant because Bosnians experienced severe and varied traumatic events in their homeland, placing them at a heightened risk of enduring traumatic memories well into their future lives in their new homelands.

Inheritance of Trauma in the Bosnian American Community

Long-term and enduring trauma among Bosnians who arrived to the United States as refugees, built new lives, acquired jobs and homes, and had children, can have a negative effect on various areas of life, including family interactions and relationships. Early research on Bosnian refugees in the United States found PTSD symptoms to be predictive of relationship distress, such as in terms of marital functioning (Spasojević et al., 2000). Noting the significance of the family unit in Bosnian cultural context, Weine et al. (2004) explored traumatic experiences from a family perspective among a group of Bosnians in Chicago in their initial resettlement. Their study revealed that "when refugee families live with the memories of traumas and losses, the family itself becomes a very important context for narrating memories," and they consequently suggest interventions "such as helping parents and children to share memories in ways that are developmentally timed and build trust" (pp. 158–159). Related themes emerged from Weine et al.'s (2004) study, including the enduring presence of war memories among families, causing both physical and psychological distress. Many individuals opted for silence, avoiding discussions about the war, while their children expressed reluctance to delve into past traumas experienced by either their parents or themselves (Weine et al., 2004). Silence about trauma is not uncommon among refugee groups and is "a natural way for trauma survivors to protect themselves from reliving the traumatic experience" (Sichling & Karamehić-Muratović, 2020, p. 1464). Hence, the traumatic memories of war infiltrate families, altering parent–child dynamics, with silence surrounding trauma fueling a distant relationship. Children grapple with their parents' war experiences, whether through sharing memories and narratives or through silence. In the case of Bosnian Americans, though there is substantial knowledge about the mental health of first-generation Bosnians (Lepper et al., 2017; Xin et al., 2017; Sichling & Karamehić-Muratović, 2020), less information documents the experiences of second-generation[1] Bosnian American youth and how their parents' recollections of war and trauma affect them.

Literature not specific to Bosnian Americans, however, document how indirect traumatization, or exposure to deeply distressing secondhand experiences and narratives, can lead to a range of potential consequences. Children born to parents who were witnesses or victims of violence may experience transgenerational trauma, whereby these younger generations ultimately inherit (un)wanted painful experiences and narratives of older generations through parenting practices, behavior issues, violence, substance abuse, and mental health challenges. As children develop and mature alongside their parents' memories, narratives, or silence regarding war trauma, they may internalize these experiences, leading to transgenerational trauma that frequently manifests in psychological and behavioral challenges well into their adulthood (Aviad-Wilchek et al., 2017; Davidson & Mellor, 2001; Daud et al., 2005). More recently, Karamehić-Muratović et al. (2022, 2023) found that most Bosnian American youth understood that their parents had war trauma, and could speak to the way this premigration trauma continued to affect their parents' lives. Other young individuals reported their parents remaining mostly silent about their past trauma and reluctance to share. Likewise, the same studies documented that some youth reported their mental health challenges, largely not understood by their parents who could not fathom how these youth could have mental health challenges if they had been born in the United States and did not share their respective war experiences. Karamehić-Muratović et al. (2022) study concluded that there was a presence of intergenerational trauma among second-generation youth interviewed, possibly passed down via family dynamics –

> Told by the voices of the youth themselves, not only were the youth in our study exposed to their parents' trauma via narratives of multiple traumas experienced they overheard or direct and indirect behaviors they observed, but the youth interviewed often seemed to resent their parents' attitudes on mental health.
> (p. 1465)

Recently, Sichling et al. (2024) examined ethnic and self-identification of Bosnian youth in the United States, highlighting the generational differences between refugee parents and their children. This study sheds lights on the potential impact of intergenerational trauma on the second-generation youth.

To summarize, while there has been considerable scholarly interest in the Bosnian American community in the past three decades, we have limited insight into the second-generation Bosnian American perspectives, with only a handful of studies delving into their experiences thus far. With many second-generation Bosnian Americans' parents, however, having experienced a sequalae of war trauma, it is unavoidable that youths have been impacted by parents' adverse experiences. Exploration of the transmission of trauma from first- to second-generation Bosnian Americans is beginning to emerge in the literature, though it remains largely uncharted. Hence, the goal of this chapter is to consider the ramifications that first-generation war trauma has had on second-generation Bosnian Americans. The chapter considers oral histories and interviews with youth residing in St. Louis, Missouri, to understand how experiences of war and trauma inherited from the first-generation, primarily parents, have influenced and shaped their lives.

Bosnian Americans in St. Louis, MO

The St. Louis metro area in Missouri in the United States is home to the large Bosnian community. Since fleeing the Bosnian genocide and the arrival of the initial war refugees, the community has garnered recognition as a remarkable model of immigrant integration. Today it is estimated that there are somewhere between 35,000 and 75,000 residents of Bosnian origin living in St. Louis (Gilsinan, 2013; Hume, 2015). The wide range of estimates is due to the difficulty to obtain accurate figures on the native-born children of Bosnian origin because they tend to dissolve in the Census category "White." Estimates are therefore based on the 11,000 refugees from Bosnia initially resettled in St. Louis between the mid-1990s and early 2000s, secondary migration from places such as Germany, Chicago, and New York since the end of the genocide in Bosnia in 1995, and attempts to calculate the number of native-born children (Halilovich et al., 2018).

Local and global scholars have taken significant interest in St. Louis Bosnians, especially given the community's recognition as a model of immigrant integration in the United States (Sichling et al., 2021). Two local projects – *Center for Bosnian Studies* (formerly *Bosnia Memory Project*) and the *Bosnian Family and Youth Study* – have been instrumental in exploring the experiences of Bosnian Americans via research endeavors. The *Center for Bosnian Studies* is a historical and cultural documentation effort directed at establishing an enduring record of the experiences of Bosnian genocide survivors and their families, including second-generation Bosnian Americans. To date, the Center has conducted over 250 in-depth interviews with Bosnian Americans. The *Bosnian Family and Youth Study* is a collaborative project between St. Louis University and the University of Missouri St. Louis, two area universities. Since 2019, it has been conducting comprehensive interviews as part of a longitudinal study focusing on second-generation Bosnian youth aged 15–23. To date, some 62 interviews have been conducted with Bosnian American youth as part of this project. Interviews for both projects are semi structured and focus on various themes, including but not limited to war, family history, experiences of resettlement, adaptation to the United States, identity, and mental health. Oral histories and interviews last anywhere from 30 minutes to 2 hours, are audio recorded, and transcribed.[2] The rest of this chapter is based on interviews conducted as part of these two projects.[3] In the oral histories conducted by the *Center for Bosnian Studies*, code names have been used to protect the identity of the interviewees. In the interviews conducted for the *Bosnian Family and Youth Study*, respondents chose their own alias to maintain confidentiality.

Experiences of Bosnian Americans

Given the goal of this chapter, the four most relevant themes pertinent to trauma that emerged from the youth's narratives include (1) understanding PTSD, (2) silencing the past, (3) trauma and identity construction, and (4) integrating collective trauma.

Theme 1: Understanding PTSD

Recent scholarship points to the continued struggle with multiple traumas from past atrocities and the forced migration Bosnian refugees experienced (Karamehić-Muratović et al., 2022; Sarajlić Vuković et al., 2021; Kartal et al., 2019). Moreover, the "old" trauma from the war and the long-term effects of PTSD have been aggravated by the COVID-19 pandemic and the wars in Ukraine and Gaza (Baćevac, 2022; Dizdarevic & Grebo, 2023) for many Bosnian Americans. Since the PTSD diagnostic criteria in 1980,

> trauma researchers have learned how certain repetitive and pervasive traumatic stressors, even when they may not directly pose a risk to life, can nonetheless present a genuine risk of injury to spirit, psyche, and body – and in particular, to a child's chances for healthy development.
>
> (Hübl, 2020, p. 36)

For Bosnian refugee communities, the clinical notion of PTSD has been a broad concept and a cultural metaphor covering the aftermath of a variety of stressful responses to trauma. Hence, in what follows, an emphasis is on an analysis of refugees' cultural and personal understandings of PTSD and their implication for transmission of trauma. Subjective interpretations rather than the diagnosis of the clinical condition are captured in the following sample interviews to present an understanding of how a traumatic event is perceived.

Ismar (17) explained:

My dad has a lot of PTSD from the war. His leg was blown off, so he has artificial joints and a bunch of other stuff in his leg. And he has shelling in his arms . . . he stays inside most of the days because he is scared of war out of nowhere, so he has really bad PTSD from social crowdings.

He aptly captures that PTSD from the war still affects Bosnians in the diaspora, and the consequences can be severe enough to disrupt familial relationships. Similarly, Željka[4] (29), born to Bosnian Serb parents, recounts that her mother struggles with severe PTSD, and remains vigilant so as not to trigger her:

We always had to be careful with my mom because she didn't like to talk about it [the war]. I know that when she hears certain things or certain songs it says they're off and we have to leave. I remember always being sensitive to that as a kid.

When asked, "how could you tell that your father has PTSD?," Ena (18) stressed:

It would just be like little things that would set him off and he working in construction, it wasn't really easy for him. Like hearing loud sounds. I think after all that he felt tension for the rest of the day. So he would come home, he would start yelling.

The prevalence of PTSD among first-generation Bosnians is also reflected in the narratives of Ismar (17), Željka (29), and Ena (18). Hanifa[5] (36) echoes that for her the parents' PTSD from the war was difficult to understand as a child, resulting in the experiences of disconnectedness and feelings of irritability, only to fully be cognizant of these common symptoms of PTSD as an adult: "I guess since I got older I started realizing what was happening because in the beginning I didn't know." Furthermore, social stigma and cultural neglect surrounding mental health conditions in Bosnian communities continue to compound a generational rift. Eldin[6] (20), born to interethnically married parents in St. Louis, for instance, declared:

Bosnians don't understand the concept of PTSD. They don't understand the concept of sarcasm either. I remember talking to this guy, not even that long ago. And he would tell me "Yeah, I remember every night. Like it plays in my head. Like me shooting this dude off the side of the mountain and watching his body drop. And I have hard time sleeping and I just drink myself to sleep and I wake up and drink another bottle." . . . And my grandma walks by with my mom. He's like "ah, my story, you know?" And everyone's like that. They all got the same traumatic story. And they're all just like, "we're all the same, who cares, it's normal." But it's not, you know. And they just laugh about it instead of getting help.

Eldin (20) accounts for a sense of abnormal "normalcy" that is culturally attributed to the concept of PTSD. While mental health diagnosis seems to be detrimental and discrediting to many Bosnians, the employment of PTSD as a "trope" central to one's traumatic story becomes a validated social determinant to human behavior. Similarly, Hanifa (36), who left her hometown Gradačac with her family at age 3, emphasized, "I think a lot of us don't even understand how PTSD affects us . . . unless you see a therapist. A lot of residents don't see therapists for whatever reasons."

Many factors contribute to why mental health care utilization remains low post-resettlement. Ismar (17) highlights:

[M]ost Bosnians just deal with it [PTSD] in their day to day lives. . . . Depression, anxiety, any of that stuff is not really acknowledged because you can't see it. Unless it's like a physical deficit, then it's really hard to get that known.

The perceived invisibility of PTSD is amplified by the fear of social rejection and socioeconomic marginalization it entails in the host country, which is echoed by Blake (23) as follows: "my dad did not wanna claim as a PTSD. He did not want to have that on his record." As Karamehić-Muratović et al. (2022) note, "it is not unusual for refugees to fear a mental health diagnosis which could lead to them being perceived as 'crazy,' socially isolated, and a burden on the community" (p. 1458). Furthermore, Bosnians tend to embrace collectivist values, "where the focus is on the extended family, maintenance of group well being . . . putting the group before oneself, and maintenance of 'face'" (Karamehić-Muratović et al., 2022, p. 1459). In turn, the cultural dimension of collectivism can have a contrapuntal effect on generational trauma: it can either alleviate or aggravate it, depending on the extent to which validation from a group is important to heal trauma from the war. "When a family or community fails to validate a traumatized person's experiences or to establish a sense of caring and safety after the fact," Hübl (2020) suggests that explicating the subtleties of possible intergenerational healing, "the trauma is less likely to be metabolized with resilience and more likely to express itself in symptoms of post-traumatic stress" (p. 35).

For Hanifa (36), whose only war memory is when they were getting on the bus and she had to separate from her father, the cultural dimension of collectivism is associated with tormenting inheritance and increased mental health stigma:

processing the fact that there was a genocide in your own country, and the people were killing our people because of who they are really like affects you personally . . . it's hard to comprehend that somebody would want to kill you because of who you are. And just knowing that was happening there, affects you in every way.

Her comment aptly illustrates the ensuing post-traumatic stress of past atrocities that continue to shame and victimize her and occlude a coherent sense of self-identification as Bosnian. Alem (17) adds, "Like half his [his father's] family died. And that put a lot of weight on your shoulders." Arguably, war trauma is very much alive within the second-generation who did not experience the war firsthand, and the consequences of the transfer of violent past memories may trigger transgenerationally as explained by Blake (23):

[H]e [his father] puts a lot of anger in the Serbs because he went through all that . . . he gets angry, it's pretty brutal. I hate seeing that side of him. I tried to tell him he can't be like that. Especially with my sister around. My sister does not know anything. She's lived here her whole life because he was born here [St. Louis] . . . in truth, she's the full blooded American.

Parents' continued ethnic hatred and the transmission of traumatic memories through ethnically captured cultural beliefs continue to affect – often radicalize – children's ethnic–racial socialization in the new cultural environment. Along PTSD, parental anger and resentment are confirmed by Anel (18):

He [his father] was always like sad or mad or sometimes it would switch between modes of them . . . the point where he did become an alcoholic, non-stop drinking. I remember when I was 13 years old, I had enough.

This intergenerational cultural dissonance, coupled with PTSD, results in negative outcomes, including emotional detachments in family relationships, psychosocial maladaptation, and risky behavior among first-generation Bosnians as well as the second-generation youth. Max (17) stresses, "drug addiction is a huge crisis with them [Bosnians]," which is viscerally captured by Cristiano's (18) statement of his parents who "have PTSD sometimes and . . . drugs will lead them on, just start doing some things." Ethnic Communities Opioids Response Network-Missouri (ECORN-MO)[7] documents a rising opioid-related death toll among St. Louis-area refugees and immigrants, with overdose mortality exponentially high among the youth. Bosnian Opioid Project director and ECORN-MO co-founder Aldin Lolic notes, "lack of addiction resources for those with limited English language fluency contributes to the opioid problem among local Bosnians . . . parents' reliance upon their children for information presents a serious challenge when their children are taking opioids" (as quoted in Cha, 2023, para.4). Parental postmigratory crisis has both direct and indirect impact on children's difficulties in personality development, their increased levels of anxiety, depression, and predisposition to substance use disorder. Mike (19) recounts:

There was a lot of counselors that I saw as a kid . . . but after the overdose, when I came back to school, I felt I wasn't doing as good in school because of all of the things that I've been putting up with and they were really, really psychologically destroy[ing].

Similarly, Violet (18) narrates, "I had developed anxiety and depression and then I was being bullied a lot. . . . I became very, very suicidal and eventually I made a plan and, I decided to give life one more try."

There is a consensus among researchers of immigrant youth in America that PTSD in parents has been linked with family dysfunction and symptoms in their children, including lower self-esteem, suicidal attitude, and higher disorder rates resembling the behaviors of traumatized parents affected by PTSD, thereby becoming intergenerational (Daud et al., 2005; Bogic et al., 2015). Consequently, if the family has a history of trauma, the new generations may internalize traumatized aspects of their parents, permeating their psychological functioning in the long run and manifesting subtly in everyday functioning. The impact of secondary trauma that extends beyond direct exposure to war trauma becomes evident on the younger generation's self-fulfillment, as aptly captured by Mike (19): "I felt so overburden and . . . I felt like I had the weight of the world and it really was affecting my schoolwork and . . . my GPA isn't anywhere near where I want it." Thorup Dalgaard et al. (2020) remind us that the transmission of traumatic symptoms to the next generations happens when refugees' parental unresolved grief and anxiety stemming from exposure to traumatic events prevent the formation of healthy connections with children. For instance, Violet (18) recalls avoidant behavior and parental detachment:

> I told a counselor what my plan was and . . . she called my mom and my mom didn't handle it well. . . . They didn't understand at all. I thought that they would, because I definitely see them. My parents have some type of depression. My grandpa definitely has PTSD, he has depression and he has anxiety.

Parental unresolved loss and ongoing postmigratory trauma present cumulative psychosocial consequences for both generations, occluding an appreciation of forward-looking attitude both on a personal level and a collective level; against the pressures of a generational rift perpetuated by parents' trauma reenactment, Blakes (23) narrative insightfully captures the youth's cry for a more pro-social prospect: "I mean times are changing. You gotta change too with it. You cannot hold that anger. You have to let that go . . . you think about yourself, your health."

Theme 2: Silencing the Past

Among Bosnian Americans, one of the main tensions in the inconsistent transmission of knowledge about the past is the parental dilemma of whether to silence or voice traumatic memories. Regarding the process of transmission of knowledge – or lack thereof – Danieli (1998a), Bar-On (1996), and Wiseman et al. (2002) asserted that the mode of family communication between survivors of trauma and their family will affect how trauma is transmitted to the next generation. For instance, Jen

(21) recounts, "My dad lost his toes while stepping on a bomb. I assumed it was hard for him to walk again. I didn't know he was in the hospital for so long. He doesn't talk about his therapy or anything." This confirms "conspiracy of silence" as a salient pattern in which family members agree to avoid discussing the past (Danieli, 1998a). Similarly, Ismar (17) states, "we never ask – we always just wait for them [parents] to start talking about it." Max (17) also reveals, "it's mostly when I overhear him [father] talking to other people." This suspension of communication about the past from parents and their progeny has been termed a "double wall of silence" as "parents do not tell, and children do not ask" (Bar-On, 1996, p. 168). The silence surrounding traumatic memories is often driven by a post-traumatic survival mechanism to preserve self-integrity and avoid increased vulnerability to retraumatization. In her study on Swiss Bosnians, Müller-Suleymanova (2023) suggests that "this reluctance to talk might be also explained by the first generation's need to work through their experiences, gain a certain emotional distance from them and come to terms with events that they had previously seemed unimaginable" (p. 1791). To that end, Željka (29) explained, "my parents didn't used to talk about it [the war] as much just because my mom didn't want to relive it. . . . We didn't like to talk about it in front of her because she would have panic attacks so we tried not to." Likewise, Elmin (15) noted, "He [father] doesn't wanna talk about it probably because of the flashbacks." Such aspects of l distancing from past trauma function as protective strategies not only to the survivors' but also to their family's ontology. This ontological comfort enshrined in the protection of silence is echoed by Ley (13): "he [father] doesn't really like talking about it. There was always a lot of fear about death and he just doesn't want to confront that anymore." Too much exposure to human loss and the existential crisis caused by witnessing severe distressing events amplify emotional numbness and the proclivity to repress these traumatic memories in familial dialogue as well. Caruth (1995) reminds us that there is a "crisis of witnessing" with human experiences far beyond the normal cognitive and linguistic capacity to recall. Specifically, "Trauma is not locatable in the simple violent or original event in an individual's past, but rather in the way its very unassimilated nature . . . returns to haunt the survivor later on" (Caruth, 1995, p. 3). Silence may be profoundly conflictual because it attests to the survivors' inability to create a meaningful dialogue around trauma. As a disruptive experience, trauma disarticulates one's subjectivity and, as Sejo (20) explains concerning her mother's definitional struggle, "there are irreparable ruins there." For many, the act of silence becomes a shield against the attacks of intrusive memories that keep creating gaps in existence.

To the question, "Why do you think your parents are secretive about the war?," Kobe (18) revealed, "That's just a part of being a parent and I completely understand that . . . there is that overprotectiveness which is completely understandable because after what they have been through, they don't want to experience more loss." Parents refrain from revealing sensitive topics to keep a psychological integrity and relegate silences for the management of stable family life. Aisha[8] (18) recalls, "I was always interested [in stories of the war]. But I was younger, so I really didn't understand. But I got more detailed information from my parents over the years." In defending their children from overwhelming knowledge and mental damage, "parents would be ready to talk about traumatic experiences later, mostly when children are adults themselves and are old enough to deal with this information" (Müller-Suleymanova, 2023, p. 1791). Furthermore, Ismar (17) narrates, "he [father] tells us stories more so that he can teach us lessons out of them, but he doesn't talk about the brutal things he did or witnessed because you can tell it takes a lot out of him." This is to highlight that by not passing on the burden of war memories, the first generation tries to avoid the resurgence of hate discourse, thus supporting the future orientation of the second generation. Such silences can be interpreted as a "moral imperative" to counter any future expressions of ethnic hatred that fueled the war itself; parental silence reflects that "the most malignant component of the transmission is the raw, unintegrated affect that has never been processed in the parents' generation and, consequently, becomes internalized in the children in another place and time" (Danieli, 1998b, p. 677). This also testifies to the desire to "move on" and integrate into new contexts as no longer overshadowed by the toxicity of past aggression.

Conversely, when unprocessed grief is among the dominant discourses, restorative nostalgia provides a sense of reassurance in the face of present uncertainties. Latifa[9] (35) states:

> [E]very family gathering or everything that we went to that involve Bosnian people, the conversations were identical or similar, and it was before the war and after the war. It was like this in Yugoslavia, and this is how well we got along. And suddenly it happened overnight. And now we're here [the U.S.].

Yugo-nostalgic reminiscences are deployed to overcome conflicting interpretations of the past. Müller-Suleymanova (2023) further contends that these nostalgic articulations offer "a way for second-generation Bosnians to establish and build an attachment to their parents' homeland" (p. 1795). The parents' nostalgically (re) created vision of the Yugoslav past of stability becomes a catalyst to voice an idealized and presentable version of the past, while glossing over memories too heavy to bear transgenerationally. This Yugo-nostalgic framing of memories transfuses into what Hübl (2020) aptly terms as "trauma loyalty," that is, the unconscious group bonds based in a pain narrative. Ismar (17) recounts:

> my parents mostly talk about it when we get back together with old friends who also went through the war – my dad has a lot of war buddies who live in America, New York or New Jersey – so once they come, he starts talking about it, I just sit there and cry and listen, because it's just really hard stuff to listen to.

This suggests that while second-generation Bosnians may only inherit memories of war, the intensity and solidarity with which they invest in the unprocessed collective loss may resemble to that of their parents, thus the trauma becoming transgenerational and cumulative.

Theme 3: Trauma and Identity Construction

After three decades, being a Bosnian, particularly for a younger generation who navigates daily between "here and there" within their own families and communities while grappling with their own developing sense of American identity, remains problematic (Sichling et al., 2024). For instance, Latifa (35), who was 10 years old at the time her family resettled from Berlin to St. Louis, notes, "I think we all had a way to survive this critical teenage time . . . and identity crisis was the single biggest thing I struggled with." Put differently, "While Bosnian identity remains a master status for many first-generation Bosnian parents, for their children growing up in the United States, the line between being 'American' and 'Bosnian' is blurred" (Karamehić-Muratović et al., 2023, p. 77). The identity crisis among the second-generation as they struggle both as a Bosnian and an American can be related to an intergenerational dissonance in *how* to remember and communicate past trauma.

One of the factors complicating the youth's self-identification and perception of the war is bound up with the language as laid out by Latifa (35):

> My parents forbid and I would get in so much trouble if I spoke English at home . . . there were arguments after arguments after arguments about us speaking English. And how we are Bosnian and we cannot forget that no matter how hard we try, we will always be Bosnian.

Along with many cultural aspects, language is a primary denominator of national authenticity, and given the acceleration of the second-generation's fitting in new contexts, their Bosnian language proficiency may erode in comparison to that of their parents. The Americanization of the youth, evident in their preference for using English even at home, affects the family's ability to address and the children's ability to fully understand past trauma, thereby complicating generational dialogue. Eldin (20) explains:

> [M]y Bosnian was way better when I was younger living with my parents growing up. But the moment I went to public schools here in America, I lost a lot of that because I would just talk English and I'd come home and then talk English and I'd forget a lot of the things I knew before.

While the biggest challenge for immigrant youth is to effectively navigate between their home and host cultures, their assumed in-betweenness as "neither Bosnian nor American" is amplified by the emotional unease the loss of heritage language entails (Sichling et al., 2024). To the question of "how the loss of language has affected your relationship with being Bosnian?," Eldin (20) also revealed:

> I'll have Bosnians here [in St. Louis] and they'll be like, "your Bosnian is pretty off." I'll go over there to Bosnia and they'll be like "you sound like a gypsy girl. You sound like one of those refugees." I'll be like, "but I am."

Eldin's narrative is indicative of a "cultural homelessness," and as Spolsky (2012) reminds us, the relationship that the second-generation youth have with the heritage language is strongly linked with emotions and identity. Therefore, for the second-generation Bosnian youth, linguistic heritage as a guarantee for both culturally authentic identities and genuine reconnections with the past is eroding, throwing open vulnerabilities, such as shame and loss of self-respect, inherent in the "refugee" position. Prospectively, Hanifa (36) said:

> [I]n America, you eventually lose that label [of being a refugee.] You start becoming more Americanized and, as the generations go on, that label is going to be completely dissolved, because the third generation Bosnians are probably not even going to speak Bosnian with the way that it's going.

For the Bosnian American youth, navigating two sets of cultures and facing the generational chasm posed by their perceived assimilation as fully Americans add up to the trauma already inherent in the family's universe. Latifa (35) aptly summarizes:

> I remember. Struggling. Not being too Bosnian. Because I did want to be liked and I did want to fit in. . . . I hated that I was Bosnian and I told my mom, why are we Bosnian? I struggled and I hated the identity crisis that I was experiencing because the American friends I had would talk negatively about Bosnians.

For Latifa (35), identity crisis is equaled with "the crisis of fitting-in," and, as also revealed by Müller-Suleymanova (2023), young people feel stigmatized by such negative projections that depict, against the majority host culture, an image of them as a Balkan "Other."[10] Such xenophobic remarks and expressions of prejudice are captured by Eldin (20):

> When I was a kid, you may be made fun of for being Bosnian. They'd come up to me like, "hey, hey. Where's your bomb? I know you're hiding it." . . . They'll have, like, a beeping noise. "Like you hear that" "Like you hear that?"

Likewise, Latifa (35) recalls a bullying instance of this "othering" discourse:

> [C]ertain refugees here in the US have been able to stand out so much that now being Bosnian has an image attached to it. I'll still get that in middle school here when I moved to the United States. Often kids would say things like, "Oh yeah, you're from Bosnia. What did you guys sit on like? Dirt roads, you know, did you sit on dirt at school.

The essentialist construction of the refugee category also impacts future generations, determining who continues to be identified as a "proper" American.

The confrontation with the Balkanist label often happens in the context of Bosnian Americans' "invisible whiteness." Karamehić-Oates and Karamehić-Muratović (2020) note that in America the context of reception for Bosnians, specifically for Bosnian Muslims, was very positive, being white Caucasian and looking like they would fit in aided their integration into the mainstream American culture. Being perceived as white provides advantages, known as "white capital," however, when made known, has been known to be cause for discrimination. Latifa (35) recalls that during her 6th grade at an affordable Christian private high school in St. Louis where Muslims did not have to be a member of the church to attend, she got bullied because of her religion. "Kids didn't accept that I was Muslim and worked their darn hardest to convert me to Christianity." She describes her experience of feeling different because of her religious affiliation, fair skin, and blond hair. Although as a Bosnian Muslim, she was never dark, never Muslim enough, and never foreign enough to be accepted as a refugee by the Western world. Hence, not all forms of whiteness are equally valued. White Bosnian Muslims can leverage their "white capital" to fit in, this privilege is not universal and can lead to inequalities, with non-Western refugees and their progeny facing discrimination. Among the Bosnian American ethnic youth, everyday experiences of "othering" and attempts to come to terms with their own people's ethnic hatred and migrant roots, trauma stories they heard in the flow of family life receive renewed and often distorted and radicalized meanings.

Theme 4: Integrating Collective Trauma

Concentration camp survivor and Bosnian American psychiatrist Esad Boškailo writes, "The goal of healing is to have some semblance of life before the trauma" (Boškailo & Lieblich, 2012, p. 154). Boškailo explicates that although remembering traumatic experiences reopens soul wounds, trauma requires integration into one's life. Regarding the role of prior trauma in subsequent trauma responses and the social transmission of those responses in a family's everyday practices, Danieli (1998a) reminds us that two contrasting perspectives exist: "The *vulnerability perspective* holds that trauma leaves permanent psychic damage that renders survivors more vulnerable when subsequently faced with extreme stress. The *resilience perspective* postulates that coping well with trauma will strengthen resistance to the effects of future trauma" (emphasis added, p. 10). Both perspectives have cumulative effects on the integrationist position of the youth caught between the contradictory forces of remembrance, silencing and/or forgetting within their families. For instance, Mirna (38) recalls how she started to reason about her parents' position on memories early on:

So it's just that exposure very early on in life will shape you for the rest of your life. That's why I had a lot of understanding for my parents for whatever they wanted to do. . . . Just the fact that you want to go somewhere and leave everything must mean that you're struggling to keep us [their children] alive.

Similarly, Jennifer (16) emphasized:

> I don't know a lot about my family history from Bosnia, but at the same time, I do know that it's hard for my dad to talk about it because a lot happened for him and as well as my mom. . . . I do know that they came here for safer place.

Both Mirna (38) and Jennifer (16) account for a retrospective witnessing by acknowledging their parents' suffering. To that end, Hirsch's concept of "postmemory" (2008) seeks to explore how postgenerations remember growing up dominated by inherited memories that carries the pain of others. From an intergenerational point of view, postmemory is not only a recollection "by means of the stories, images, and behaviors among which [the post-generation] grew up" (p. 107), but a progressive reconnection with the past that is ruptured by the magnitude of collective trauma. An integration of traumatic meanings can take place by the second-generation's reliving and validating their parents' firsthand experiences, and thus reestablishing the agency inherent in the legacy of thriving within the family's common universe. Voicing the heterogeneity of refugee adaptation post-resettlement has a sense of coherence in the second generation. Interfamilial involvement through creating felt awareness is important to heal trauma from the war as "until trauma has been acknowledged, felt . . . it will be experienced from without in the form of repetition compulsion and projection and from within as tension" (Hübl, 2020, p. 174). Therefore, the youth's rationalization of parental experiences of trauma and survival can facilitate positive communication in Bosnian American families, strengthening healing prospects and integrationist understanding of cultural identity that transcends ethnic boundaries.

Concomitantly, a shared knowledge and felt awareness of parental trials can create, consciously or unconsciously, a narrative competition between parents and children's experiences. This hierarchical differential between memories in the laudable move to embrace intergenerational remembrance is also explicated by Hirsch (2008) as follows: "To grow up with such overwhelming inherited memories, to be dominated by narratives that preceded one's birth or one's consciousness is to risk having one's own stories and experiences displaced, even evacuated, by those of a previous generation" (p. 107). An illustrative example of inscribing parents' traumatic memories into progeny's own life so that parental experiences gloss over one's own concerns is captured by Erna (18):

> [S]uch extreme things that they [parents] went through like coming to a different country and building a new life and the fact that they literally went through everything imaginable and so my little things, they matter but it doesn't. It doesn't count like they've been through all these other things.

Likewise, Mirna (38) who fled to Rijeka, Croatia in 1993 and lived there for six years before her family came to St. Louis in 1999, recounts:

> [P]eople were noticing my accent and making fun of it . . . as soon as you start speaking, they can figure out that you're a refugee. But I was a small

child. I really didn't have many, many issues. You know, that was the extent of my problems. If you can call it a problem. Really.

Both narratives are a testament to how disparate familial memories are conditioned by the second-generation's gullibility that they have not suffered "enough" so their "their little things," as explicated by Erna (18), escape the label of "real problem." This also reminds us of a *hierarchy of life* which ensures that "certain lives will be highly protected . . . other lives will not even qualify as 'grievable'" (Butler, 2004, p. 32). From this perspective, different generations' trauma stories within refugee families may determine the "value" of individual accounts, thus complicating the youth's moral dilemma of whether to compare their secondhand trauma to the firsthand parental grief. Therefore, a prominent line of research on transgenerational memory objects conflates the suffering of parents with that of their offspring. Notably, van Alphen (2006) challenges that there is a "fundamental continuity" (p. 474) between the experiences of parents and those of their children, revealing that they are different altogether. Weissman (2004) also reminds us, "the difference between memory and postmemory is primarily one of distance rather than substance" (p. 17). Both remarks point out that the universality of collective trauma can be confronted in the transmission process, and while the integration of trauma is crucial to healing within families and communities at large, the extent to which it exposes vulnerability such as "hierarchy of griefs" should also be considered.

Arguably, the memory of resilience is a socially mediated attribution in collective identity, and the second-generation's accounts weaving personal testimonies of human suffering with resilience articulate a versatile mode of being that emerges from discontinuity and "makes use of the bits and pieces here and there and somehow keeps going" (Lifton, 1993, p. 1). Eldin (20) explains:

> [H]e [his father] doesn't give me the full story of anything. He'll tell me things . . . during the war, when they were going through the trails in the woods to flee, no one would have any medicine. His niece would find beans. Like the shape of them would look like pills and give placebos to people. And that's a cool story I remember.

Stories of survival serve as positive copying mechanisms and as sources of strength across generations. Eldin (20) testifies to the ethos of a Bosnian spirit epitomic of resistance and survival, and thus confirming its long-term ontological prospects in the face of any challenges. A wide consensus exists among scholars that narrating personal growth through challenge increases psychological well-being. Using humor to deflect trauma has gained significant attention in transmission studies. The 2012 study of Braga et al. on Brazilian offspring of Holocaust survivors confirms:

> [H]umor may be viewed as a sort of symbolic displacement, at once allowing the survivor to present and repudiate the traumatic experience without

distancing himself or herself from it, creating something of a cushion to lessen the impact of traumatic experience.

(p. 4)

To that end, Mirna (38) aptly illustrates:

> They would turn it [electricity] off for long periods of time and then they would turn it back on for a couple of hours only and then turn it back off. It was funny because when it came on, you would just see people disappear off the streets, and all the washing machines come on and all the TV's and vacuum cleaners and like anything electric would go off and people would try to do things as fast as they could before it disappeared again.

Linguistic resources such as symbolic stories of resilience, jokes, and laughter have a critical role in trauma recovery and the recognition of a common humanity, enabling generational dialogue on past grief, while simultaneously denouncing the violence experienced.

Kobe (18) emphasizes, "I would say that in my family and in Bosnian community a lot of us are strongly united by what we went through in the 90's." His comment indicates that solidary articulations of a shared traumatic past offer a way for second-generation Bosnians to establish an attachment to their parents' suffering. A memorialization of the shared cultural legacy of loss that reconnects with trauma situates collective sufferings within the families' common universe as a reservoir of strength and continuity. Blake (23), for instance, explains:

> [W]hen we are in Bosnia, they'll have ceremonies and memories during the summertime for the people – in our city center, we have a memorial of the people who died in the war. It was all Muslims and it has an English writing and in Bosnian it's basically "here we lie, we have to remember those people that have fought for our land."

Likewise, Željka (29) recounts,

> [H]e [her uncle] managed to get a few letters out to his brother and . . . he was giving him instructions on what to do with his family when he dies. He was always saying, like "when he dies" because he knew he would. My aunt published them actually, I think they're only published in Serbian, but she called them "Letters to My Brother."

These testimonies reveal the empowering "uniqueness" of traumatic experiences whereby validating them through generational remembrance may function as a counternarrative to the intent that once aimed at obliterating the existence of the group, they now hold these memories. Ismar (18) contends, "whatever comes our way we can survive anything, we survived the war, the culture shock. . . . You just gotta be open and brave enough to actually go and push forward." These are testaments to how the focus on the power to draw meaning and positive personal change after suffering can enhance positive reconnection with the painful past and thus to fortify belonging. Insightfully, Latifa (35) recounts that during a longer visit to Bosnia, she felt remorse over rationalizing her family's stories as a "burden" to her.

> I don't know what happened exactly, but I felt sad that so much suffering caused so many people to spread across the world . . . but then I came back [to St. Louis] and I wanted access to everything everyone saw. I wanted to know what they felt and what they saw and who they lost and who died in front of them. And who they had to bury. I wanted all of it.

Latifa's story is illustrative of a perceived sense of self-awakening because of struggle with highly challenging life circumstances known as post-traumatic growth (PTG). Tedeschi and Calhoun (1996) remind us that growth is not necessarily a simple consequence of trauma but rather a destination that one may reach by living a "new" and post-trauma life. Hanifa (36) reflects:

> I think being a refugee child made me stronger because I was able to overcome the obstacles that I had as a kid . . . I learned to thrive and it's either you succeed or you'll completely lose yourself . . . it made me who I am today and I feel like if I didn't go through all of that I wouldn't be the person that I am.

Hanifa's comment demonstrates that PTG is not an end to pain but merely an unintentional experience of growth as a result of the ability to integrate collective trauma into one's life-trajectory. In Hanifa's own words,

> So it's about whether you're going to take control of the situation and use those experiences and become stronger. Or, are you just going to take them and become a victim and go the other direction where you have no control of your life.

This enhanced human agency spawning from the legacy of trauma can be further exemplified by early responsibility taking as a source of strength post-resettlement. Specifically, Aisha (18) narrates:

> I have a younger sister. She was also born here [St. Louis] six years apart. She's having a better life than what I had when I was growing up. Because before, my parents really didn't understand of what to how to speak here. So then, mostly, I didn't get the changes that my sister has now, since they have me to help them.

Aisha (18) displays that "responsibility" speaks to an ability to respond and to weave the threads of a challenging life into a firm pattern of meaning and action.

Being empowered by collective suffering, this propensity to action-taking is viscerally reflected in Kobe's (18) narrative:

> [B]ecause when hearing about the war period and the genocide, the killing, seeing that human beings were absolutely mercilessly slaughtered in the home country, for me, personally, to not take action towards what happened to my people, towards my family, is an injustice on myself and the world itself.

Similarly, Latifa (35) shares how she started to develop witness poetry and "imagining or embodying that person, dead or alive ... not just from [her] standpoint, but from the standpoint of the real victims who do have memories who aren't relying on someone else's story." To feel the problems of their people is to know suffering within their families, but, as revealed by our second-generation interlocutors, this requires a unique appreciation of the "inheritance" that runs through the family, and a compassionate ability to remember and reconnect with trauma that affects all.

Conclusion

Aisha (18), born in St. Louis to Muslim parents from Srebrenica, succinctly captured the essence of the Bosnian American experience by saying "not everyone knows my whole story. They're mostly like, 'your parents live here now and then you're Bosnian American.' It's like, 'no, I have way more behind that.'" This chapter considered the ramifications that war trauma experienced by first-generation Bosnian refugees had on second-generation Bosnian Americans. Oral histories and interviews conducted with Bosnian Americans in St. Louis, MO, suggest that though the Bosnian resettlement and adaptation to the United States three decades later is characterized by many positive experiences and success stories, the lives of Bosnian Americans continue to be affected by war trauma from Bosnia's violent past. Further, there is ample evidence to suggest that individuals who endured the war and its associated trauma are transferring their experiences to their children, born amidst and after war.

The themes explicated in this chapter indicate that in the case of Bosnian Americans, PTSD is almost a "household word" commonly used to denote the aftermath of a variety of stressful responses to trauma following the violence witnessed in Bosnia. Interviewee excerpts included in the chapter point to subjective, cultural, and personal understandings of PTSD and their implication for the transmission of trauma; PTSD in this group is conceptualized as a more collective and lived experience of war, designed to encompass a variety of experiences of a violent past. Thus, the interpretation and understanding of PTSD does not follow a clinical notion and are removed from scientific and diagnostic criteria of diagnosis. PTSD experiences among Bosnian Americans have been shown to disrupt family relationships and hinder communication, leading to feelings of disconnectedness and emotional detachment. There is also evidence that Bosnian American second-generation youth are at increased risk of engaging in risky behaviors, such as substance abuse, due to war- and trauma-burdened parent–child relationships. Regarding "conspiracy of silence," it is evident from our analysis that many Bosnian American families favor this method to cope with past trauma. Remaining silent is exercised as a protective mechanism whereby parents not only shield their children from their own war memories but also allow them to repress their intrusive thoughts and preserve family existence. In certain instances, the "conspiracy of silence" seems to serve the function of preventing ethnic hate discourse, thereby promoting future focus and the "healthy" integration of the second generation. At the same time, untold stories of trauma and painful memories of war, shared only at certain familial events, appear to provide first- and second-generation Bosnian Americans a common bond. Our findings also suggest that trauma associated with war among many first-generation Bosnian Americans has consequences for the identity construction of their second-generation children. As evidenced by Sichling et al. (2024), many Bosnian American youth struggle with their identity and fitting in as they navigate their Bosnian language proficiency indicative of how Bosnian versus American they are. Finally, our findings point to several second-generation Bosnian Americans who rationalize and acknowledge the trauma experienced by the first-generation. While this can promote shared knowledge and felt awareness between the first- and second-generation Bosnian Americans in turn creating a sense of bond, it also adds a hierarchal dimension to suffering whereby second-generation's struggles seem insignificant and unimportant in a grander scheme of things. Together, the themes related to traumatic war experiences and memories gleaned from oral histories and interviews included in this chapter suggest that intergenerational trauma characterizes interactions among first- and second-generation Bosnian Americans, and child–parent relationships specifically.

A generation after the end of the Bosnian war, questions remain about the intergenerational effects of memories of the violent past, particularly for younger Bosnians who have only inherited memories of the war while grappling with their developing sense of Americanness. While first-generation Bosnians bear firsthand memories of trauma, younger Bosnians continue to live separated from their heritage and have a limited understanding of their (grand)parents' experiences. Increasingly, memories of war are changing across generations, and, as the underlying concept of *postmemory* posits, the relationship of the younger generation to their parents' traumatic experiences, which are transmitted to them during childhood through stories, images, and behaviors, seems to constitute memories in their own right (Hirsch, 2008, p. 106). The collective trauma that remains unaddressed and if passed down to the progeny of those who had lived through them invites questions about what happens to traumatic memories now that a new generation of diaspora Bosnians has come of age. How do they deal with these legacies of the violent past? How does this traumatic inheritance define their identities and affect their sociocultural and psychological well-being in new contexts? These questions are timely and critical considering that not only is trauma passed on transgenerationally, but it is also cumulative. Phipps and Degges-White (2014) remind us that "Traumatic stress can be renewed in each generation as members continue to witness the effects of the original trauma experienced by previous generations even when the new generation is shielded from the specifics of the trauma story" (p. 177). Hübl (2020) further contends that "when unresolved trauma is passed on, it may become 'more severe' in successive generations" (p. 16). With that in mind, the Bosnian American second-generation offers a compelling case example to explore the manifestation of intergenerational trauma.

Notes

1 Second-generation Bosnians have been defined elsewhere as "native-born children with at least one foreign-born parent, or children born abroad who immigrated before age 12" (Sichling & Karamehić-Muratović, 2020, p. 13).
2 Detailed descriptions of the methodological approach employed toward the oral histories and the interviews are described at https://griffinshare.fontbonne.edu/bosnia/ and in Sichling and Karamehić-Muratović (2020).
3 We would like to acknowledge and thank both the *Center for Bosnian Studies* and the *Bosnian Family and Youth Study* for generously providing access and use to their oral histories and interview data for this chapter.
4 Interview ID per the oral history repository of the Center for Bosnian Studies at Fontbonne University: FBU-2016-04-19.
5 Interview ID per the oral history repository of the Center for Bosnian Studies at Fontbonne University: BHS-2022-04-01.
6 Interview ID per the oral history repository of the Center for Bosnian Studies at Fontbonne University: AHS-2022-03-02-A.
7 For further information, See Ethnic Communities Opioid Response Network – MO (n.d.) Retrieved May 14, 2024, from https://ecorn-mo.org/about/
8 Interview ID per the oral history repository of the Center for Bosnian Studies at Fontbonne University: AHS-2020-02-08.
9 Interview ID per the oral history repository of the Center for Bosnian Studies at Fontbonne University: FBU-2017-09-14.
10 Todorova (2009) explicates "banal ethnocentrisms" and "barbarism" as often and mistakenly attached to the image of the Balkans.

References

Aviad-Wilchek, Y., Levy, I., & Ben-David, S. (2017). Readiness to use psychoactive substances among second-generation adolescent immigrants and perceptions of parental immigration-related trauma. *Substance Use & Misuse*, *52*(12), 1646–1655. https://doi.org/10.1080/10826084.2017.1298618

Baćevac, S. (2022). Long term PTSD for Bosnian war survivors. *Good Morning America*. Retrieved May 13, 2024, from www.goodmorningamerica.com/news/video/long-term-ptsd-bosnian-war-survivors-84199656

Bar-On, D. (1996). *Fear and Hope: Three Generations of the Holocaust*. Cambridge: Harvard University Press.

Begic, S., & McDonald, T. W. (2006). The psychological effects of exposure to wartime trauma in Bosnian residents and refugees: Implications for treatment and service provision. *International Journal of Mental Health and Addiction*, *4*(4), 319–329. https://doi.org/10.1007/s11469-006-9036-6

Bogic, M., Njoku, A., & Priebe, S. (2015). Long-term mental health of war-refugees: A systematic literature review. *BioMed Central International Health and Human Rights*, *15*, 29. https://doi.org/10.1186/s12914-015-0064-9

Boškailo, E., & Lieblich, J. (2012). *Wounded I Am More Awake: Finding Meaning After Terror*. Nashville: Vanderbilt University Press.

Braga, L. L., Mello, M. F., & Fiks, J. P. (2012). Transgenerational transmission of trauma and resilience: A qualitative study with Brazilian offspring of Holocaust survivors. *BioMed Central Psychiatry, 12*(134), 1–11. https://doi.org/10.1186/1471-244X-12-134.
Butler, J. (2004). *Precarious Life: The Powers of Mourning and Violence*. London: Verso.
Caruth, C. (1995). *Trauma: Explorations in Memory*. London: John Hopkins University Press.
Cha, E. (2023). New coalition aims to curb opioid deaths among St. Louis immigrants and refugees. *St. Louis Public Radio*. Retrieved May 13, 2024, from www.stlpr.org/show/st-louis-on-the-air/2023-09-25/new-coalition-aims-to-curb-opioid-deaths-among-st-louis-immigrants-and-refugees
Craig, C. D., Sossou, M.-A., Schnak, M., & Essex, H. (2008). Complicated grief and its relationship to mental health and well-being among Bosnian refugees after resettlement in the United States: Implications for practice, policy, and research. *Traumatology, 14*(4), 103–115. https://doi.org/10.1177/1534765608322129
Danieli, Y. (1998a). Introduction: History and Conceptual Foundations. In Danieli, Y. (ed.), *International Handbook of Multigenerational Legacies of Trauma* (pp. 1–21). New York: Springer.
Danieli, Y. (1998b). Conclusions and Future Directions. In Danieli, Y. (ed.), *International Handbook of Multigenerational Legacies of Trauma* (pp. 669–690). New York: Springer.
Davidson, A. C., & Mellor, D. J. (2001). The adjustment of children of Australian Vietnam veterans: Is there evidence for the transgenerational transmission of the effects of war-related trauma?. *The Australian and New Zealand journal of psychiatry, 35*(3), 345–351. https://doi.org/10.1046/j.1440-1614.2001.00897.x
Daud, A., Skoglund, E., & Rydelius, P.-A. (2005). Children in families of torture victims: Transgenerational transmission of parents' traumatic experiences to their children. *International Journal of Social Welfare, 14*(1), 23–32. https://doi.org/10.1111/j.1468-2397.2005.00336.x
Dizdarevic, E., & Grebo, L. (2023). Pandemic and Ukraine War Aggravate Suffering for Bosnians with PTSD. *Balkan Insight*. Retrieved May 13, 2024, from https://balkaninsight.com/2023/03/01/pandemic-and-ukraine-war-aggravate-suffering-for-bosnians-with-ptsd/
Ethnic Communities Opioid Response Network – MO. (n.d.) Retrieved May 14, 2024, from https://ecorn-mo.org/about/
Gilsinan, K. (2013). Why are there so many Bosnians in St. Louis?. *The Atlantic Cities*. Retrieved from www.citylab.com/politics/2013/02/why-are-there-so-manybosnians-stlouis/4668/
Halilovich, H., Hasic, J., Karabegovic, D., Karamehić-Muratović, A., & Oruc, N. (January 2018). *Mapping the Bosnian-Herzegovinian Diaspora: Utilizing the Socio-Economic Potential of the Diaspora for Development of BiH*. Sarajevo, Bosnia and Herzegovina: International Organization for Migration/Ministry for Human Rights and Refugees of Bosnia and Herzegovina.
Hirsch, M. (2008). The generation of postmemory. *Poetics Today, 29*(1), 103–128.
Hübl, T. (2020). *Healing Collective Trauma: A Process for Integrating Our Intergenerational and Cultural Wounds*. Louisville: Sounds True.
Hume, S. E. (2015). Two decades of Bosnian place-making in St. Louis, Missouri. *Journal of Cultural Geography, 32*(1), 1–22.
Karamehić-Muratović, A., Sichling, F., & Doherty, C. (2022). Perceptions of parents' mental health and perceived stigma by refugee youth in the U.S. context. *Community Mental Health Journal, 58*(8), 1457–1467. https://doi.org/10.1007/s10597-022-00958-2.
Karamehić-Muratović, A., Sichling, F., Zuko, S., & Vamvas, E. (2023). Neither Bosnian Nor American Parents' Perceptions of Children's Adaptation Experience in the United States. In Karabegovic, D., & Karamehić-Oates, A. (eds.), *Bosnian Studies: Perspectives from an Emerging Field* (pp. 77–98). Columbia: University of Missouri Press.
Karamehić-Oates, A., & Karamehić-Muratović, A. (2020). Borders and integration: Becoming a Bosnian-American. *Global Studies Law Review, 19*(3), 327–352.

Kartal, D., Alkemade, N., & Kiropoulos, L. (2019). Trauma and mental health in resettled refugees: Mediating effect of host language acquisition on posttraumatic stress disorder, depressive and anxiety symptoms. *Transcultural Psychiatry, 56*(1), 3–23. https://doi.org/10.1177/1363461518789538.

Keyes, E.F., & Kane, C.F. (2004). Belonging and adapting: Mental health of Bosnian refugees living in the United States. *Issues in Mental Health Nursing, 25*, 809–831. https://doi.org/10.1080/01612840490506392

Knipscheer, J. W., & Kleber, R. J. (2006). The relative contribution of posttraumatic and acculturative stress to subjective mental health among Bosnian refugees. *Journal of clinical psychology, 62*(3), 339–353. https://doi.org/10.1002/jclp.20233

Lepper, L. E. T., Karamehić-Muratović, A., Salas, J., Pollard, C.A., Karahodzic, E., & Asher, J. (2017). Mental health screening in a Bosnian refugee population using the primary care behavioral health screener-Bosnian translation. *Journal of Clinical Psychology in Medical Settings, 24*(2), 152–162. https://doi.org/10.1007/s10880-017-9499-6.

Lifton, R. (1993). *The Protean Self: Human Resilience in an Age of Fragmentation*. New-York: BasicBooks.

Miller, K. E., Worthington, G. J., Muzurovic, J., Tipping, S., & Goldman, A. (2002). Bosnian refugees and the stressors of exile: A narrative study. *American Journal of Orthopsychiatry, 72*(3), 341–354. https://doi.org/10.1037/0002-9432.72.3.341

Müller-Suleymanova, D. (2023) Shadows of the past: Violent conflict and its repercussions for second-generation Bosnians in the diaspora. *Journal of Ethnic and Migration Studies, 49*(7), 1786–1802. https://doi.org/10.1080/1369183X.2021.1973392

Phipps, R., & Degges-White, S. (2014). A new look at transgenerational trauma transmission: Second-generation latino immigrant youth. *Journal of Multicultural Counseling and Development, 42*(3), 174–183. https://doi.org/10.1002/j.2161-1912.2014.00053.x

Sarajlić Vuković, I., Jovanović, N., Džubur Kulenović, A., Britvić, D., & Mollica, R.F. (2021). Women health: Psychological and most prominent somatic problems in 3-year follow-up in Bosnian refugees. *International Journal of Social Psychiatry, 67*(6), 770–778. https://doi.org/10.1177/0020764020972433.

Sichling, F., & Karamehić-Muratović, A. (2020). 'Makin' it' in the Heartland: Exploring perceptions of success among second-generation immigrant youth in St. Louis. *Journal of Adolescence, 82* (1), 11–18. https://doi.org/10.1016/j.adolescence.2020.05.005

Sichling, F., & Karamehić-Muratović, A., Vamas, E., & Muratović, E. (2021). Perceptions of Bosnians in St. Louis. *International Journal of Intercultural Relations, 84*, 119–129. https://doi.org/10.1016/j.ijintrel.2021.07.003.

Sichling, F., Taylor, M., & Karamehić-Muratović, A. (2024). The true colors of the chameleon: Identities of Bosnian youth in the United States. *Journal of Ethnic and Migration Studies, 29*(2), 1–17. https://doi.org/10.1080/1369183X.2024.2344513

Spasojević, J., Heffer, R. W., & Snyder, D. K. (2000). Effects of posttraumatic stress and acculturation on marital functioning in Bosnian refugee couples. *Journal of Traumatic Stress, 13*(2), 205–217. https://doi.org/10.1023/A:1007750410122

Spolsky, B. (2012). Family language policy – the critical domain. *Journal of Multilingual and Multicultural Development, 33*(1), 3–11. https://doi.org/10.1080/01434632.2011.638072

Tedeschi, R. G., & Calhoun, L.G. (1996). The posttraumatic growth inventory: Measuring the positive legacy of trauma. *Journal of Traumatic Stress, 9*(3), 455–472. https://doi.org/10.1002/jts.2490090305

Thorup Dalgaard, N., Høgh Thøgersen, M., & Riber, K. (2020). Transgenerational Trauma Transmission in Refugee Families: The Role of Traumatic Suffering, Attachment Representations, and Parental Caregiving. In De Haene, L., & Rousseau, C. (eds.), *Working with Refugee Families Trauma and Exile in Family Relationships* (pp. 36–49). Cambridge: Cambridge University Press. https://doi.org/10.1017/9781108602105.004

Todorova, M. (2009). *Imagining the Balkans*. Oxford: Oxford University Press.

Van Alphen, E. (2006). Second-generation testimony, transmission of trauma, and postmemory. *Poetics Today*, *27*(2), 473–88.
Weine, S., Muzurovic, N., Kulauzovic, Y., Besic, S., Lezic, A., Mujagic, A., Muzurovic, J., Spahovic, D., Feetham, S., Ware, N., Knafl, K., & Pavkovic, I. (2004). Family Consequences of Refugee Trauma. *Family Process*, *43*(2), 147–160. https://doi.org/10.1111/j.1545-5300.2004.04302002.x
Weine, S. M., Becker, D. F., McGlashan, T. H., Laub, D., Lazrove, S., Vojvoda, D., & Hyman, L. (1995). Psychiatric consequences of "ethnic cleansing": Clinical assessments and trauma testimonies of newly resettled Bosnian refugees. *The American Journal of Psychiatry*, *152*(4), 536–542. https://doi.org/10.1176/ajp.152.4.536
Weine, S. M., Razzano, L., Brkic, N., Ramic, A., Miller, K., Smajkic, A., Bijedic, Z., Boskailo, E., Mermelstein, R., & Pavkovic, I. (2000). Profiling the trauma related symptoms of Bosnian refugees who have not sought mental health services. *The Journal of Nervous and Mental Disease*, *188*(7), 416–421. https://doi.org/10.1097/00005053-200007000-*00004*
Weine, S. M., Vojvoda, D., Becker, D. F., McGlashan, T. H., Hodzic, E., Laub, D., Hyman, L., Sawyer, M., & Lazrove, S. (1998). PTSD symptoms in Bosnian refugees 1 year after resettlement in the United States. *The American Journal of Psychiatry*, *155*(4), 562–564. https://doi.org/10.1176/ajp.155.4.562
Weissman, G. (2004). *Fantasies of Witnessing: Postwar Efforts to Experience the Holocaust*. Ithaca: Cornell University Press.
Wiseman, H., Barber, J. P., Raz, A., Yam, I., Foltz, C., & Livne-Snir, S. (2002). Parental communication of holocaust experiences and interpersonal patterns in offspring 147 of Holocaust survivors. *International Journal of Behavioral Development*, *26*(4), 371–381. https://doi.org/10.1080/01650250143000346
Xin, H., Karamehić-Muratović, A., & Klein, N. (2017). Examining the effectiveness of physical activity on mental health among Bosnian refugees: A pilot study. *Universal Journal of Public Health*, *5*(2), 76–84.

11 German Perversions of Mental Health Care

Male Afghan Refugees, Deportation, and Carceral Systems during NATO's War in Afghanistan

Paniz Musawi Natanzi

Introduction

This chapter discusses how Germany's mental health policies, implemented in the military–civil infrastructure that German institutions and organizations constructed in Afghanistan during NATO's (North Atlantic Treaty Organization) war and occupation from 2001 to 2021, attempted to humanize deportations and promote "return" among Afghan refugees, in particular bodies marked as male, who applied for asylum in Germany. While the German organization Ipso (International Psychosocial Organization) claimed to "empower" Afghans and support their personal agency in daily life in Afghanistan, male Afghan refugees' embodied experiences suggested that their alleged empowerment was defined by Germany and oriented at its objectives toward Afghan refugees in Germany and the population in Afghanistan. Refugee is used in the chapter to refer to civilian Afghans who did not work in a civil or military capacity for occupying states, came via land and water route to Germany, and applied for asylum in Germany. The signifier "Afghan" refers here to individuals who are legally and politically considered citizens of the nation-state of Afghanistan. While the interlocutors this chapter refers to were refugees in Germany, other men I was in conversation with in Kabul were deported to Afghanistan from Iran and Turkey before they could reach Europe. Moreover, the chapter does not cover the experiences of Afghan residents who were categorized as members of the "host community" because they did not experience refuge/deportation. The chapter builds on empirical research and theorization on race, masculinities, and governance and argues that to view Afghan refugees through the prism of intergenerational trauma obscures how racialization and gendering regulate and control the movement of Afghans placed in intragenerational war. The concept of intergenerational trauma in geographies of intergenerational war focuses on symptoms without tackling the political, economic, and legal structures that confine deported and coercively returned male Afghan refugees and produce racialized men. The imperial architecture consisting of increasingly merging military, foreign, and development policies, which was implemented via multilateral and bilateral entities that funded also the nominally sovereign government, considered male Afghan refugees as liberated men when they lived in Afghanistan. In this

DOI: 10.4324/9781003385820-12

neoliberal setup during the occupation, *German perversions* took various forms: here, specifically, I discuss how they constituted in mental health care where it was promulgated that Afghans have the agency to take responsibility for their present and future, while stripping these men of the freedom to move and transforming their lifeworlds into "operational theatres" to be marketized. The European Union and Germany, and in coordination with the Afghan government, Iran, Pakistan, and Turkey, have used deportations and systemic neglect of male Afghan refugees as punishment for their refusal to obey this order.

Carceral Systems and the Production of Deportable Afghan Men

Since the early 2000s, German Mental Health and Psychosocial Support (MHPSS) programming in Afghanistan was aligned with Germany's increasingly coordinated military, foreign, and development policies. The role of Germany is noteworthy as other foreign and Afghan-led NGOs and consulting firms specializing in MHPSS-related services could not compete at the scale at which Germany operated; MHPSS was incorporated into the work of the German Federal Foreign Office (AA) and Federal Ministry for Economic Cooperation and Development (BMZ). Building on the US "lessons" from military operations which had shown that engaging the occupied decreases the feeling of being occupied, Afghans were trained to implement counterinsurgency operations in a civil and military capacity (Jones, 2008). The same logic was also deployed in the building of civil-run institutions, whereby Afghan mental health care providers were trained how to approach the "social reintegration" of deported and coercively returned male Afghan refugees, as this chapter illustrates.

Refugees in this context are referred to as deported/coercively returned, and while the two are distinct processes, coercion pertains to both "deportation" and "voluntary return." In Afghanistan, men from both groups were "target beneficiaries" of German development projects. Germany and the nominally sovereign government of Afghanistan deployed parallel to concerted development, migration, deportation, and foreign policies rhetorical means to shame the predominantly male refugees for leaving Afghanistan. While deportation was out of refugees' control, they did not have an incentive to "return," unless feeling socially isolated, economically paralyzed, and unable to wait for their situation to change. Alimia (2018) points out that assisted voluntary repatriation programs managed by Pakistan and the United Nations High Commission for Refugees (UNHCR) with the cooperation of Afghanistan have driven "a process of coercive rather than voluntary repatriation or outward migration" for Afghan refugees in the country (p. 415). In Germany, Afghan refugees, many of them cis men, found themselves coerced by state structures that impeded healthy ways of living and working. At the same time, the military occupation perpetuated *German perversions* in Afghanistan: institutions and organizations claimed to foster community cohesion and peace-building through MHPSS, while reorganizing social and political life around the military time of the occupation. Carceral systems[1] produced "good" and "bad" maleness and as such affected how male Afghan refugees/deportees/coercively returned experienced the valuation and devaluation of their labor and bodies. If affect, as Puar (2021) proposes, is "also an object of control as well as a mode of controlling" (pp. 405–406), the men's labor, whose stories are narrated in this chapter when they were refugees in Germany and as deportees and coercively returned to Afghanistan, was mobilized to cater to Germany's demographic and spatial placing of Afghan men.

Whether it was a personal initiative or expected by kin, fleeing toward Europe became constitutive of acting like a man.[2] It was the attempt to become legible in the "conception of the human, Man" (Wynter, 2003, p. 260) by refusing the "inhuman configuration" (Puar, 2017, p. 19) of racializing processes in Afghanistan. Ahmad[3] was 14 years old when his parents sent him with a smuggler via land and sea route to Germany from Afghanistan. According to a 2013 EU directive, as a minor Ahmad required protection and support (European Parliament & Council of the European Union, 2013). While living in a "Heim" (shelter) in Germany, Ahmad went to school. After reacting with aggression during an encounter with other boys, he was referred to a therapist for a year. Looking back on this experience while with his family in Pakistan, Ahmad remembers, "I said I take the help, because I needed it" (P. Musawi Natanzi, Personal interview via phone with Ahmad, Germany, May 2023). Ahmad did well as a student in a "Berufsschule" (vocational school) in Germany and was able to communicate in German. Upon turning 18 in 2017, he had to leave the shelter and go into an "Asylheim" (asylum seeker home), where life got worse as he lost the social support network he established as a teenager. Ahmad worried about his asylum plea not being accepted and failing his mother who had put all her hope and money into him. After finishing his training and completing an internship in a supermarket, his asylum application was rejected. In his 2017 "Ablehnungsbescheid" (rejection letter), it was argued that Afghanistan is safe and his mother's employment in an international non-governmental organization (INGO) and his father's service in the army were used as evidence of stability and safety. This caused Ahmad to lose hope, and he began to socialize with men he referred to as "falsche Leute" (wrong people) (P. Musawi Natanzi, Personal interview via phone with Ahmad, Germany, May 2023). Ahmad describes how he became more aggressive as he felt that no matter how hard he tries to do well and succeed, it was never enough. When the boys started "Prügeleien" (beatings) he joined in, saying that: "At that time I was a bit stupid. I thought it is cool and if I don't help them then I am not a man, this and that" (P. Musawi Natanzi, Personal interview via phone with Ahmad, Germany, May 2023).

In January 2018, now all by himself, Ahmad got into a fight and was sentenced to two years and six months for assault in a "Justizvollzugsanstalt" (JVA, prison) in Bavaria. JVAs are carceral institutions implementing "Jugendstrafen" (juvenile sentences) or "Freiheitsstrafen" (prison sentences) for youth and young adults and are governed by the Ministry of Justice in the respective "Bundesland" (there are 16 states in the Federal Republic of Germany). Male prisoners, aged between 14 and 21 years and above, are assigned to specific carceral institutions in their Bundesland depending on their age and their sentence; some JVAs oversee detainees in "Abschiebungsverfahren" (deportation processings).[4] Ahmad describes behaving very well while in detention, where he also started to work again. He pointed out that he was never sent to the "Bunker" (a colloquial term for solitary confinement). His third and last plea for asylum was rejected while in prison. Ahmad received a letter in which he was told that he would be deported from Germany to Afghanistan. After two years in prison, in January 2021, he was picked up by authorities in prison and taken to the airport. He did not have any money for a lawyer nor was he given time to gather the funds to hire one. He felt like he had failed his family again.

Meanwhile, in Kabul, his mother Farzana,[5] who used to work for an INGO as a development worker, had heard about the services of the German Corporation for International Cooperation (Deutsche Gesellschaft für Internationale Zusammenarbeit (GIZ)). She asked me for help to introduce her son to services offered by Germany for "voluntary returnees" and deportees in Afghanistan (P. Musawi Natanzi, Personal communication with Farzana, Afghanistan, January 2021). The country director of an INGO and Farzana's former employer introduced her in early 2021. At that time, I was working as a consultant for a mental health start-up, registered in Afghanistan as a company and in the United States as a 501(c), and the German Press Agency (dpa) in Kabul. Farzana's employer, Jack, said that she had heard about a female Afghan development worker of the INGO who had been relocated to a state in Central Asia. Farzana asked to be relocated too, but Jack said he could not help her. He also pointed out that she was a survivor of domestic violence (P. Musawi Natanzi, Personal communication with Jack, Afghanistan, January 2021). The INGO had introduced her in the past to a counselor, but Farzana was quite transparent about not finding counseling useful. Farzana wanted to migrate outward (P. Musawi Natanzi, Personal communication with Farzana, Afghanistan, January 2021). In early 2021, Jack gave US$300 to the start-up I was working for, which were paid to an Afghan counselor, who was then hired to provide eight family counseling sessions with three of her six children including Ahmad in the course of two months. Jack then ceased to respond to Farzana's messages.

Focusing on Ahmad's situationality as he arrives as a deportee in Kabul through the lens of intergenerational trauma, and ways in which his mother's wishes, grief, anxieties, and declining health played out in his life, presents at least two epistemological shortcomings. First, the approach ignores Ahmad's continuous experiences of violence as a child, teenager, and young adult refugee between Germany and Afghanistan. Second, it shifts the focus away from the political, social, economic, and ideological structures that treated the bodies of Farzana and her children as carceral bodies who were not permitted to live, work, and thrive outside of the environment they were designated to. Even within their city, Kabul, much of the city's geographies were off limits for them, including residential and work places of foreigners and of the new and old national bourgeoisie behind concrete walls and checkpoints. Farzana knew she was not one of the "chosen" women in Afghanistan, who became showcases of liberal freedom during the military occupation. Instead, she was placed to ranks of women engaged in footwork of neoliberal development who, like thousands of other women, learned about and used the language of gender mainstreaming out of utter precarity in a competitive job market. Farzana experienced how neoliberal capitalism racialized and reorganized labor in Afghanistan and produced class differences among the occupied, including women: she saw how some women were supported to migrate outward. She attempted to become a more visible and appreciated Afghan mediator for civil-run bodies of the occupation; she tried to be revalued through her work as a female development worker hired to work as an activist in the civil society that was engineered during the occupation. When she found herself on the receiving end as a "beneficiary," she knew she would lose access to the opportunity of moving her family out of Afghanistan. Ahmad, described in his 2017/2018 vocational certificate as an "independently working student" who "eagerly participated in class" and whose "behavior was laudable," was enrolled in a three-month tailoring course offered by an Afghan NGO and funded by the GIZ in Kabul in spring 2021, after which he remained unemployed.

In the military and civil infrastructure that the NATO built in Afghanistan, the "Bundeswehr" (German Armed Forces) were mandated consecutively by the "Deutscher Bundestag" (German Parliament) to support the International Security Assistance Force (ISAF) mission from December 2001 to December 2014, and from 2015 onward also the Resolute Support Mission (RSM) and the work of humanitarian and development actors.[6] The "NATO Civil-Military Co-Operation (CIMIC) Doctrine" (North Atlantic Treaty Organization, 2003) standardized and coordinated the work of armed forces and civil institutions and organizations of member states and NATO allies. The "Bundesregierung" (German Federal Government) discursively rationalized the consolidation of a multilaterally coordinated military, development, and foreign policy through its "willingness to assume leadership responsibility as a framework nation" ("Federal Ministry of Defence," 2016, p. 68). The CIMIC doctrine formalized military operations to build infrastructure required to implement development and foreign policy on the ground. Development and foreign policymakers, including Germany at the forefront, branded the occupation of Afghanistan in public as an Afghan-owned mission ("Government of Germany," 2001, paras. 6–13). About 50 years after the Christian Democratic chancellor Konrad Adenauer declared in front of the German parliament that "Germany, as a result of occupation, the Ruhr Statute, the Marshall Plan and so forth, is more tightly entangled with abroad than ever before," Germany was now working alongside the United States, NATO, and key non-NATO allies, including Pakistan and Qatar in Afghanistan ("Deutscher Bundestag," 1949, p. 23).[7] The CIMIC doctrine built on military theorization and practice that suggested that extracting racialized labor, in this case from Afghans, "to shape the capacity of indigenous actors" is the premise for "an effective counterinsurgency campaign" (Jones, 2008, p. 10).

Mental Health Care and War

The lived experience of deported/coercively returned male, Afghan refugees unravels "imperialist subject-production" (Spivak, 1988, p. 296) in German mental health policies. Specifically, the analytic *German perversions* is used here as a beginning to unravel how development policies relating to mental health care in Afghanistan provided a political arena for Germany to euphemize the violence of neoliberal empire-building. Though the concept of intergenerational trauma can be used to investigate the embodied and social aftermath of exposure to war, political violence, and genocide, it assumes that there is a "post-"phase, which is not the case for deported/coercively returned Afghans. Afghans were placed in neoliberal capitalist relations conditioned by carceral states that reordered racialized labor and affected Afghans different experiences of moving in Germany and the European Union, Afghanistan and on the move. Upon arrival in Afghanistan, German organizations and institutions commodified and selectively governed the deported/ coercively returned male Afghan refugees. Although these men were formally free to move within Afghanistan, they were confined by the ongoing war and the ways in which the occupation manifested in the provinces and cities, with poverty and the stigma related to deportation/coercive return.

I draw here on research that theorizes race, masculinities and governance to investigate how mental health care and war intersected the lived experience of deported/coercively returned male Afghan refugees. (Davis, 2008; Vergès, 2022; Wilson Gilmore, 2017; Shabazz, 2015; Fanon, 2004; Robinson, 2000; Saad-Filho, 2020; Hanieh, 2013; Hall et al., 2002; Khanna, 2003; Wang, 2018). Fanon (2004) argues that in order to maintain domination and the idea that colonialism is the best option at hand, the colonial system "By a kind of perverted logic" uses "the past of the oppressed people, and distorts, disfigures, and destroys it" with tangible consequences in the present (p. 149). Fanon's work as a clinician led him to the political and social analysis of colonial wars and coloniality, and engendered scholarship in humanities and social sciences about embodiment, trauma, political violence, and war in processes of decolonization.[8] Around the same time, in the 1960s, psychological, psychoanalytical, and psychiatric studies, predominantly in US institutions, examined the long-term effects of surviving concentration camps in Nazi Germany on the generation that experienced the Holocaust and their descendants (Niederland, 1968; Rakoff et al., 1966; Sigal, 1971). Continuous warfare led to an increase in veterans who served as combat soldiers in World War II, the Korean War, and the Vietnam War (Liem, 2003; McCormack & Sly, 2013; Rosenheck & Fontana, 1998), and subsequently engendered research on trauma transmission among US veterans to their offspring (Pearrow & Cosgrove, 2009) that further grew with the Persian Gulf war and the wars in Afghanistan and Iraq in North American research institutions. Racial differences in embodied experiences of intergenerational trauma became increasingly integrated in some of these hegemonic bodies of research on indigenous and Black veterans (Coleman, 2016; Holm, 1984).

In the course of the last two decades, research on intergenerational trauma in refugee communities expanded to include first-generation immigrants, refugees, migrants, and their children in North America, Europe, and Australia (Phipps & Degges-White, 2014; Ahmad et al., 2022; Daud et al., 2005; Slewa-Younan et al., 2017). While clinical approaches to intergenerational trauma in refugee communities examine patterns of transmission and symptomatic manifestations of intergenerational trauma within families, these are decontextualized from the entangled structures of violence within which racialized refugees are situated and affected by carceral governance.

Pupavac's (2002) analysis of psychosocial intervention during the Kosovo War (1998–1999) investigates the depoliticized character of the inflationary application of trauma in NGOs while working with refugees. This author argues that in Kosovo, NGOs' "psychosocial intervention as a new mode of external *therapeutic governance*" (p. 490, emphasis in the original) built on the assumption that, for instance, "Kosovo Albanians (the main targets of psychosocial programs) respond to war in the same way as defeated and demoralized U.S. Vietnam veterans" (p. 495). According to Pupavac (2002), the growing coordinated merger between military and humanitarian actors was obvious for refugees, who were in camps that NGOs took over after they were "set up by military contingents of the same nationality" (p. 502).

Critical of the "dominance of 'trauma' in mental health discourses," Behrouzan (2018) suggests a frame of analysis that "can speak to *both* clinical realities and cultural particularities" (p. 137, emphasis in the original). "Anthropological and psychoanalytical listening" in Behrouzan's analysis complicates the individualizing or universalizing uses of the concept of trauma as in the example of "Iranians' generational narratives of past *toromā*" (Behrouzan, 2018, p. 137, emphasis in the original). Behrouzan (2018) pinpoints the spatiotemporal particularity of memory construction on embodied or documented individual and collective experiences of violence. In Afghanistan, affective relations as well as what Behrouzan refers to as "modes of sharing and interpretation" (p. 137) were channeled through the prism of analytical psychology, psychoanalysis, and anthropology in English-, Dari-, and Pashto-speaking places and resources funded by occupying donor states. In other words, governments gathered information about what Afghans thought, felt, hoped, and feared, including those inside and outside of formal prisons, catering to the "War on Drugs," "War on Terror," and "War on Crime" while insisting on caring about the mental health of Afghans.

Missmahl (2018, p. 256), trained as a psychoanalyst at the C.G. Jung Institute in Zurich, came to Kabul, Afghanistan, in 2004 to work for three months at the National Mental Health Hospital. Over four years, Missmahl (2018, p. 259) tailored and modified counseling services for Afghan health care staff and their patients, which led to the founding of the International Psychosocial Support Organization (Ipso) in 2008. Registered in Germany as a company with limited liability and in Afghanistan as a NGO and funded throughout the years by the AA and occasionally by the EU and BMZ, Ipso became a leading institution-building organization in MHPSS in Afghanistan working alongside what was then the Afghan Ministry of Public Health. Afghan health care staff that was trained in the field of psychiatry and psychosocial support by Ipso worked in the MHPSS structure that Ipso created and that was funded by institutions and organizations from occupying donor states (Missmahl et al., 2012). Ipso tailored projects that were implemented across provinces among deportees/coercively returned and Afghans considering migrating to Europe and opened the Psychosocial and Mental Health Center in Kabul (Missmahl, 2018, p. 257).[9]

Based on her impressions in the decade after the invasion in Afghanistan, Missmahl developed "value-based counseling." Her approach builds on the assumption that "Every person, regardless of their symptoms, is at any time able to act" (Missmahl, 2018, p. 257). Afghans are told to unleash their potential to "self-efficacy," and that the solution to their problems lies within themselves while having to navigate systemic unemployment, tensions, and conflict in social and kinship relations and manifestations of war in their living environments (Missmahl, 2018, p. 257). The increasing violence in Afghanistan by 2015, labeled in Europe as a "refugee crisis," turned Ipso into a tool for migration management and prevention and data collection under the pretext to support Afghans to become agents of their own lives following their "return."[10]

"The Mask of Sanity: The German State and Male Afghan Refugees

In his keynote speech at the 2023 Feminist Theory Workshop at Duke University, Ferguson (2023) drew on Toni Cade Bambara's "Language and the Writer" to discuss the continuous importance of the question she posed in the 1980s: "Can the planet be rescued from the psychopath?" and "What are the psychopathic relations that jeopardize the planet in this moment, twenty-plus years into the new century?" Feminist theory offers analytics to study "the culmination of patriarchal pathologies that spew their toxicities across global terrains," and that "make the anti-social the norm of social relations" (Ferguson, 2023, p. 2). Conceptually, scholars have complicated understandings of patriarchy examining historical, social, and spatial constructions of men and masculinities emphasizing that men do not exist outside of "the matrix of the domination they produce" (Shabazz, 2015, p. 9). In recent years, there has been generative research on the interface between affective/emotional politics, discursive and tangible environments, authoritarianism and constructions of masculinity in global perspective (Daggett, 2018; Gökarıksel et al., 2019). Munhazim's (2023) auto-ethnography centers "*murat* world-making" as a transing play with masculinity and femininity and practice of "selfhood" which "was birthed in circles of dancers and sex workers from Jalalabad to Kandahar, Peshawar, Kunduz, Mazar and Kabul, where femininity is both celebrated and very much a zone of danger" (Munhazim, 2023, p. 207). Differences among cis men manifest in political arenas of daily life such as the street (Shabazz, 2015; Amar, 2011), the football arena (Hasso, 2018), or art studios and exhibitions (Musawi Natanzi, 2023), where men encounter men in service of the state or competing with it (Valencia, 2018). In the authoritarian present of the neoliberal capitalist state (Boffo et al., 2019) in Germany, its inherently carceral character is encrypted in the liberal jargon of imperial feminist policy. Racialized, gendered, and people with disabilities are included in institutions under the condition that there is alignment with metanarratives of the state revolving around peace, justice, and security and encompassing the celebration of representation and developmentalism as signifiers of "progress" and civilizational advancement (Puar, 2007). In these structures, the death of some trans and queer refugees becomes more representable than that of others, exposing "the killability of lives that are simultaneously imbued with and stripped of liberal universal rights" (Shakhsari, 2014, p. 95). As such, "the psychopath" is not only embodied in "the figure of the individual," but materializes in structures that "are made to seem rational even as they destroy lives and freedoms" (Ferguson, 2023, pp. 3–4). Since the German government, the GIZ, the BMZ, and the AA have deleted relevant sources online since August 2021, I am referring below to documents circulated to brief policymakers and consultants in Afghanistan on how to adapt to the grammar of migration and labor policies the GIZ tailored on behalf of the BMZ and which makes the fabric of the "mask of sanity."[11]

In cooperation with NGOs, such as Ipso and NGOs founded by Afghans, the GIZ began implementing in 2002 on behalf of the BMZ and in coordination with the AA, infrastructural projects and investing in capacity-building to mobilize the reserve army of labor in Afghanistan. Rostami-Povey (2007) observed in Kabul in the years following the invasion increasing class differences among national elites, foreigners, and Afghan refugees returning from Iran and Pakistan that were exacerbated by incoming foreign contractors and funds. Violence had been intensifying since 2007/2008 as the Taliban and NATO were at war over the occupation. At the time when the RSM began, Daesh (ISIS) had begun to expand in Afghanistan.

Despite the consistently increasing numbers in civilian deaths and the ongoing war[12] in Afghanistan, by 2015 the Federal Office for Migration and Refugees (Bundesamt für Migration und Flüchtlinge (BAMF)) continued to advise precarious Afghan refugees in counseling sessions to "voluntarily" return as they withheld support, and deported Afghan refugees to Afghanistan arguing that they could settle down in "protected zones" (Martin, 2015). Despite what was perceived by European states as a "refugee crisis," the official reasoning of the government of the then chancellor Angela Merkel was that, because of Germany's investments into "economic development" and "reconstruction," Afghans must go back and "reconstruct" the country. Merkel's mantra inflected in daily social encounters Afghan refugees had with white Germans. Asad, for instance, decided to return to Afghanistan, because of the intense precarity he experienced in Germany. Although he had quickly learned the German language and finished his training at the "Volkshochschule," an educational institution that offers classes for student and adult learners without credits, he could not find work as a painter. He says:

> My parents needed me. I just could not live in Germany anymore. Foreigners receive in Germany support. But as an Afghan that was a bit different. After president Ashraf Ghani came and said "send them [the refugees] back," it became very hard for us Afghans in Germany. When I looked for work and asked if they needed workers, people said: "You do not need to work. You are Afghan. You will be sent back anyway."
>
> (P. Musawi Natanzi, Personal interview with Asad, Afghanistan, February 2021)

While Angela Merkel announced during a meeting with president Ashraf Ghani that Germany would increase deportations of Afghan refugees as it continues to invest into the "development" of the country, she also promised to send more

German soldiers to Afghanistan as part of NATO's RSM due to ongoing "terrorist threats" ("Government of Germany," 2015). Germany continued its cooperation with the International Centre for Migration Policy Development (ICMPD) on formalizing labor migration from Afghanistan to Germany – a bureaucratic and diplomatic infrastructure, which by the time the Taliban reached Kabul was still in the early stages of development in Afghanistan. Rather than allowing the refugees to stay, despite acquired language and vocational skills, the Bundesregierung disciplined through punishment for "illegal" trespassing into the EU. While Ahmad and Asad went from Afghanistan to Germany, Majid, another interviewee, began his journey with his brother Masoud in Iran, where they were both born and raised as Afghan refugees. Like Ahmad and Asad, Majid also spoke good German. Although he wanted to enter a pathway that allowed him to later go into higher education, he was sent to a vocational school. In 2018, Masoud died in a car accident in Germany. Majid had to deal with the grief and administrative ramifications after the loss of his brother by himself. "Return" was not an option for Majid, because as an Afghan refugee he could not return to Iran, but would be send to Afghanistan where he had never been before and had no family. Majid's asylum application was rejected, and he was deported in early 2021 to Kabul. In the shelter of an Afghan NGO funded by the GIZ where Majid was allowed to stay for some days, Afghan social workers of the NGO recommended him to do 45 days of "cash-for-work"[13] to make some money, which he urgently needed without any means stranded in a country that the German state claimed to be his "home." At this stage, he had not given up on the dream of going to university to become a software developer. As he calculated, however, a day's labor would never cover his commute costs, rent, study equipment, tuition fees, and costs of living (P. Musawi Natanzi, Personal interview with Majid, Afghanistan, February 2021). Like other male Afghan refugees who were deported or "returned" from Germany or the other EU states, Ahmad, Asad, and Majid, all in their early 20s and of different sectarian and ethnic backgrounds, were supposedly "returning to new opportunities" – the official English title of the BMZ-funded program implemented on behalf of the GIZ. Among the services offered to "target beneficiaries"[14] upon arrival in Afghanistan were next to training and vocational opportunities, job placement services, business start-up advice, and psychosocial support services to back the social "reintegration" of the deported/coercively returned.

The German name of the program, "Prospect home" (Perspektive Heimat), echoes political slogans of the alt-right in Germany, although the GIZ was deeply invested in avoiding such connotations by putting together a communication team to develop a marketing strategy for the program "Migration for Development" (Programm Migration für Entwicklung [PME]). The title PME was meant for internal use only: for "external communication" the involved were told to only use the official title of the program, "Perspektive Heimat." The term "return" was consciously deleted in the official program title to emphasize the focus on "reintegration and prospects on the ground." GIZ-PME worked multilaterally based on agreements among Germany, Afghanistan, the International Organization for Migration (IOM), the Afghan Ministry of Refugees and Repatriations of Afghanistan, and the EU as well as based on bilateral contracts signed between GIZ-PME and Afghan NGOs that implemented the GIZ deliverables. Ipso that had worked in Afghanistan with funds from the AA became involved with the GIZ around 2017. It was tasked with supporting the "social reintegration" of "returnees, IDPs and vulnerable community members," increasing "their level of perceived self-efficacy," and improving "their social skills in individual coaching sessions and in modules-based teaching" ("GIZ," 2021, p. 15). All German-funded NGOs were supposed to set up representatives at the airport to provide information. However, their presence was irregular with some deported/returned not hearing about any services until they learned about them through friends and acquaintances, and others never receiving support because there were not enough resources.

While GIZ-PME in Kabul made suggestions to the headquarters in Eschborn and shared worries and challenges, the responsible parties in Germany merely fulfilled the expectations of their supervisors; their task was to develop content that tells "success stories" of deported/coercively returned Afghan refugees, regardless of how precarious the subjects of these stories were. In the GIZ branding strategy, the "returned" Afghan received through the GIZ's "comprehensive counseling and support" a shot at a "successful new start" (ein erfolgreicher Neustart) in their "country of origin." The GIZ officially avoided mentioning that a deportee could reach out and inquire about psychosocial services, financial starting help, and educational and vocational opportunities.

Conclusion

While Germany ceased deportations shortly before the Taliban reached the outskirts of Kabul on August 15, 2021, other carceral states, in particular Iran, Turkey and Pakistan, prevented refugees from Afghanistan from reaching Europe based on formal and informal agreements with the European Union, and deported alone in the last three years tens of thousands individuals to Afghanistan. This chapter showed that the concept of intergenerational trauma inhabits potentialities that have not been explored yet in the literature. The focus on interpersonal violence and suffering of an individual and their kin disregards the political, economic, and ideological structures that drive intergenerational war and in which the mental and physical suffering and injury of "un/non/subhuman"-ized (Puar, 2017, pp. 28, 29) people is anticipated and commodified and/or treated as without value.

Mental health care became a euphemistic add-on during NATO's occupation. Germany's colonial and fascist historical past of concentrating racialized populations into demarcated geographies in Namibia and during the Holocaust (Olusoga & Erichsen, 2011; Neiman & Younes, 2021) echoes in the neoliberal configuration of the imperial present. Masked in developmentalist narratives the German state suggested that short-term and low paid work and counseling sessions in which the deported/coercively returned would recognize that he is able to "act" at "any time" (Missmahl, 2018, p. 257) – inside of his demarcated area – would set the poor and male Afghan refugee free.

Notes

1 For theorization on the interface between carcerality, neoliberal capitalism, and processes of racialization, see Wilson Gilmore (2017) and Wang (2018).
2 For an ethnographic study of Sweden's deportation of Afghan men, see Khosravi (2016).
3 I refer to semistructured interviews in Kabul in spring 2021 as well as conversations with some of the interlocutors as I accompany them in their search for work. Following the handover of power to the Taliban in Kabul in August 2021, I was in touch with some of the interlocutors as they tried to find pathways toward outward migration from Afghanistan. I also conducted semistructured interviews in spring 2023. The names of all Afghan and non-Afghan interlocutors have been changed.
4 For further information, see Freistaat Bayern (2020).
5 I chose not to provide a detailed account of the pain Farzana suffered since her childhood and her actions.
6 For the archive of all mandates, see "Deutscher Bundestag," 2023.
7 Translation by chapter author.
8 For a postcolonial feminist critique that locates the emergence of psychoanalysis in Europe's history of colonialism and discusses the ways in which during the era of decolonization intellectuals such as Fanon relate to psychoanalysis, see Khanna (2003).
9 The organization continued to operate in Afghanistan following the handover of power to the Taliban. The Psychosocial Support Center is operative. It is unclear what happens to all the data that Ipso has been accumulating over the years as a recipient of AA funds about Afghans.
10 At the same time, Ipso's work expanded to Iraq and Ukraine. Since August 2021, the German Foreign Office refers to its funded projects as contributing to the "humanitarian–development–peace nexus." See German Federal Foreign Office (2023).
11 Ferguson (2023) refers to Hervey Cleckley's "The Mask of Sanity: An Attempt to Clarify Some Issues about the So-Called Psychopathic Personality" from 1941 (p. 3).
12 On September 4, 2009, Colonel Georg Klein, the commander of the German PRT in Kunduz, ordered an airstrike on two oil tanks stolen by Talibs that was executed by a US fighter jet and killed at least 142 Afghans of whom most were civilians. In the aftermath, Germany could not avoid using the term war any longer (Reuters Staff, 2009).
13 "Cash-for-work" was a "low-skill labor" program component that the GIZ required NGO recipients of funds to offer for "returnees, IDPs and vulnerable community members." The "beneficiaries" had tasks such as "cleaning and greening activities of schools, Kindergarten, mosques and public parks" and were given basic equipment.
14 "Target beneficiaries" is a term in the neoliberal development grammar to describe subjects of programming in a site of intervention. "Targets" of PME are returnees and deportees as well as so-called host communities, that is members of the community who have not been on the move, but might consider to do so.

References

Ahmad, M. S., Nawaz, S., Bukhari, Z., Nadeem, M., & Hussain, R. Y. (2022). Traumatic Chain: Korean – American Immigrants' Transgenerational Language and Racial Trauma in Native Speaker. *Frontiers in Psychology*, *13*, 912519. https://doi.org/10.3389/fpsyg.2022.912519

Alimia, S. (2018). Performing the Afghanistan – Pakistan Border Through Refugee ID Cards. *Geopolitics*, *24*(3), 1–35. https://doi.org/10.1080/14650045.2018.1465046

Amar, P. (2011). Middle East Masculinity Studies: Discourses of "Men in Crisis," Industries of Gender in Revolution. *Journal of Middle East Women's Studies*, *7*(3), 36–70. https://doi.org/10.2979/jmiddeastwomstud.7.3.36

Behrouzan, O. (2018). Ruptures and Their Afterlife: A Cultural Critique of Trauma. *Middle East – Topics & Arguments, Bd.*, *11*, 131–144. https://doi.org/10.17192/META.2018.11.7798

Boffo, M., Saad-Filho, A., & Fine, B. (2019). Neoliberal Capitalism: The Authoritarian Turn. *Socialist Register*, *55*, 247–270.

Coleman, J. A. (2016). Racial Differences in Posttraumatic Stress Disorder in Military Personnel: Intergenerational Transmission of Trauma as a Theoretical Lens. *Journal of Aggression, Maltreatment & Trauma*, *25*(6), 561–579. https://doi.org/10.1080/10926771.2016.1157842

Daggett, C. (2018). Petro-masculinity: Fossil Fuels and Authoritarian Desire. *Millennium: Journal of International Studies*, *47*(1), 25–44. https://doi.org/10.1177/0305829818775817

Daud, A., Skoglund, E., & Rydelius, P.-A. (2005). Children in Families of Torture Victims: Transgenerational Transmission of Parents' Traumatic Experiences to Their Children. *International Journal of Social Welfare*, *14*, 23–32.

Davis, A. Y. (2008). A vocabulary for feminist praxis: On war and radical critique. In C. T. Mohanty, R. L. Riley, & M. B. Pratt (Eds.), *Feminism and war: Confronting US imperialism* (pp. 19–26). London: Zed Books.

Deutscher Bundestag. (1949). *Stenographisches Protokoll der 5. Sitzung*, 22–30.

Deutscher Bundestag. (2023). Deutscher Bundestag – ISAF (Afghanistan) – Bisherige Mandate. *Deutscher Bundestag*. Retrieved December 20, 2023, from www.bundestag.de/webarchiv/Ausschuesse/ausschuesse18/a12/auslandseinsaetze/auslandseinsaetze/isaf_bisherige_mandate-247448

European Parliament & Council of the European Union. (2013). Directive 2013/33/EU of the European parliament and of the Council of 26 June 2013 Laying Down Standards for the Reception of Applicants for International Protection (recast). *Official Journal of the European Union*. Retrieved December 29, 2023, from https://eur-lex.europa.eu/legal-content/EN/TXT/PDF/?uri=CELEX:32013L0033

Fanon, F. (2004). *The wretched of the earth*. New York: Grove Press.

Federal Ministry of Defence. (2016). White Paper. On German Security Policy and the Future of the Bundeswehr. *Federal Ministry of Defence*. Retrieved December 20, 2023, from https://issat.dcaf.ch/download/111704/2027268/2016%20White%20Paper.pdf

Ferguson, R. A. (2023). Toni cade bambara, feminist theory, and the super patriarch. *Keynote*. Durham: Duke University, Feminist Theory Workshop.

Freistaat Bayern. (2020). Vollstreckungsplan für den Freistaat Bayern. In der Fassung vom 28. Dezember 2020 [Enforcement plan for the Free State of Bavaria. In the version dated December 28, 2020.] *Bayerisches Staatsministerium der Justiz* [Bavarian State Ministry of Justice]. Retrieved December 20, 2023, from www.justiz.bayern.de/media/pdf/justizvollzug/vollstreckungsplan_2021.pdf

German Corporation for International Cooperation (GIZ). (2021). *Details of IPs services 2-9-2021*. [Unpublished Word-document on file with the author of this chapter].

German Federal Foreign Office. (2023). Federal Foreign Office Support for Peace Mediation, Crisis Prevention, Stabilisation and Post-Conflict Peacebuilding. *German Federal Foreign Office*. Retrieved December 20, 2023, from www.auswaertiges-amt.de/en/aussenpolitik/themen/krisenpraevention/-/231866

Gökarıksel, B., Neubert, C., & Smith, S. (2019). Demographic Fever Dreams: Fragile Masculinity and Population Politics in the Rise of the Global Right. *Signs: Journal of Women in Culture and Society*, *44*(3), 561–587. https://doi.org/10.1086/701154

Government of Germany. (2001). Speech by Herr Joschka Fischer at the Opening of the Special Meeting of the Afghanistan Support Group. *ReliefWeb*. Retrieved December 20, 2023, from, https://reliefweb.int/report/afghanistan/speech-herr-joschka-fischer-opening-special-meeting-afghanistan-support-group

Government of Germany. (2015). Germany will Remain a Partner in Afghanistan. *Government of Germany*. Retrieved December 20, 2023, from www.bundesregierung.de/breg-en/news/germany-will-remain-a-partner-in-afghanistan-438902

Hall, S., Critcher, C., Jefferson, T., Clarke, J., & Roberts, B. (2002). *Policing the crisis: Mugging, the state, and law and order* (Transferred to digital print). London: Macmillan. Retrieved June 10, 2024, from https://sociologytwynham.com/wp-content/uploads/2014/10/policing-the-crisis.pdf

Hanieh, A. (2013). *Lineages of revolt: Issues of contemporary capitalism in the middle east*. Chicago: Haymarket Books.

Hasso, F. S. (2018). Masculine Love and Sensuous Reason: The Affective and Spatial Politics of Egyptian Ultras Football Fans. *Gender, Place & Culture, 25*(10), 1423–1447. https://doi.org/10.1080/0966369X.2018.1531830

Holm, T. (1984). Intergenerational Rapprochement Among American Indians: A Study of Thirty-Five Indian Veterans of the Vietnam War. *Journal of Political & Military Sociology, 12*(1), *Special Issue on Life Course and Generational Politics*, 161–170.

Jones, S. G. (2008). *Counterinsurgency in Afghanistan*. Cambridge: RAND National Defense Research Institute.

Khanna, R. (2003). *Dark continents: Psychoanalysis and colonialism*. Durham: Duke University Press. https://doi.org/10.1215/9780822384588

Khosravi, S. (2016). Deportation as a Way of Life for Young Afghan Men. In R. Furman, D. Epps, & G. Lamphear (Eds.), *Detaining the immigrant other: Global and transnational issues* (First Edition, pp. 169–181). Oxford: Oxford University Press.

Liem, R. (2003). History, Trauma, and Identity: The Legacy of the Korean War for Korean Americans. *Amerasia Journal, 29*(3), 111–130. https://doi.org/10.17953/amer.29.3.k2t76468016pg455

Martin, M. (2015). Merkel Says Afghans Coming to Germany for Better Life Will be Sent Back. *Reuters*. Retrieved December 20, 2023, from www.reuters.com/article/us-europe-migrants-afghanistan-merkel/merkel-says-afghans-coming-to-germany-for-better-life-will-be-sent-back-idUSKBN0TL1D120151202

McCormack, L., & Sly, R. (2013). Distress and Growth: The Subjective "Lived" Experiences of Being the Child of a Vietnam Veteran. *Traumatology, 19*(4), 303–312. https://doi.org/10.1177/1534765613481855

Missmahl, I. (2018). Value-Based Counselling: Reflections on Fourteen Years of Psychosocial Support in Afghanistan. *Intervention, 16 (3)*, 256–260.

Missmahl, I., Kluge, U., Bromand, Z., & Heinz, A. (2012). Teaching Psychiatry and Establishing Psychosocial Services – Lessons from Afghanistan. *European Psychiatry, 27*, S76–S80.

Munhazim, A. Q. (2023). Afghan Muslim Aunties and Their Queer Gifts. *South Asia: Journal of South Asian Studies, 46*(1), 206–217. https://doi.org/10.1080/00856401.2023.2151784

Musawi Natanzi, P. (2023). Visualizing violence: Masculinities and politics of race and death in Afghan/istani visual arts under military occupation. *NC consortium for Middle Eastern studies conference – 'border politics: Bodies, community, and ecology'*. Chapel Hill: University of North Carolina Press.

Neiman, S., & Younes, A.-E. (2021). Anti-semitism, Anti-Racism, and the Holocaust in Germany: A Discussion Between Susan Neiman and Anna-Esther Younes. *Journal of Genocide Research, 23*(3), 420–435. https://doi.org/10.1080/14623528.2021.1911346

Niederland, W. G. (1968). Clinical Observations on the 'Survivor Syndrome'. *The International Journal of Psychoanalysis, 49*(2–3), 313–315.

North Atlantic Treaty Organization. (NATO). (2003). NATO Civil-Military Co-Operation (CIMIC) Doctrine. *NATO*. Retrieved December 20, 2023, from www.nato.int/ims/docu/ajp-9.pdf

Olusoga, D., & Erichsen, C. W. (2011). *The Kaiser's holocaust: Germany's forgotten genocide*. London: Faber and Faber.

Pearrow, M., & Cosgrove, L. (2009). The Aftermath of Combat-Related PTSD: Toward an Understanding of Transgenerational Trauma. *Communication Disorders Quarterly, 30*(2), 77–82. https://doi.org/10.1177/1525740108328227

Phipps, R. M., & Degges-White, S. (2014). A New Look at Transgenerational Trauma Transmission: Second-Generation Latino Immigrant Youth. *Journal of Multicultural Counseling and Development*, *42*(3), 174–187. https://doi.org/10.1002/j.2161-1912.2014.00053.x

Puar, J. K. (2007). *Terrorist assemblages: Homonationalism in queer times*. Durham: Duke University Press.

Puar, J. K. (2017). *The right to maim: Debility, capacity, disability*. Durham: Duke University Press.

Puar, J. K. (2021). Spatial Debilities: Slow Life and Carceral Capitalism in Palestine. *South Atlantic Quarterly*, *120*(2), 393–414. https://doi.org/10.1215/00382876-8916144

Pupavac, V. (2002). Pathologizing Populations and Colonizing Minds: International Psychosocial Programs in Kosovo. *Alternatives*, *27*(4), 489–511. https://doi.org/10.1177/030437540020270040

Rakoff, V. M., Sigal, J. J., & Epstein, N. B. (1966). Children and Families of Concentration Camp Survivors. *Canadas Mental Health*, *14*(4), 24–26.

Reuters Staff. (2009). Guttenberg Spricht von Krieg in Afghanistan [Guttenberg speaks of war in Afghanistan]. *Reuters*. Retrieved December 20, 2023, from www.reuters.com/article/deutschland-afghanistan-bundeswehr-zf-20-idDEBEE5A20IC20091103

Robinson, C. J. (2000). *Black marxism: The making of the black radical tradition*. Chapel Hill: University of North Carolina Press.

Rosenheck, R., & Fontana, A. (1998). Transgenerational Effects of Abusive Violence on the Children of Vietnam Combat Veterans. *Journal of Traumatic Stress*, *11*(4), 731–742. https://doi.org/10.1023/A:1024445416821

Rostami-Povey, E. (2007). Afghan Refugees in Iran, Pakistan, the U.K., and the U.S. and Life after Return: A Comparative Gender Analysis. *Iranian Studies*, *40*(2), 241–261. https://doi.org/10.1080/00210860701269576

Saad-Filho, A. (2020). *Value and crisis: Essays on labour, money and contemporary capitalism*. Chicago: Haymarket Books.

Shabazz, R. (2015). *Spatializing blackness: Architectures of confinement and black masculinity in Chicago*. Champaign: University of Illinois Press.

Shakhsari, S. (2014). Queer death and the politics of rightful killing. In J. Haritaworn, A. Kuntsman, & S. Posocco (Eds.), *Queer necropolitics* (pp. 93–110). London and New York: Routledge.

Sigal, J. J. (1971). Second-Generation Effects of Massive Psychic Trauma. *International Psychiatry Clinics*, *8(1)*, 55–65.

Slewa-Younan, S., Yaser, A., Guajardo, M. G. U., Mannan, H., Smith, C. A., & Mond, J. M. (2017). The Mental Health and Help-Seeking Behaviour of Resettled Afghan Refugees in Australia. *International Journal of Mental Health Systems*, *11*(49), 1–8. https://doi.org/10.1186/s13033-017-0157-z

Spivak, G. C. (1988). Can the subaltern speak? In C. Nelson & L. Grossberg (Eds.), *Marxism and the interpretation of culture* (pp. 271–316). Champaign: University of Illinois Press.

Valencia, S. (2018). *Gore capitalism*. Los Angeles: Semiotext(e).

Vergès, F. (2022). *A feminist theory of violence: A decolonial perspective*. Chicago: Pluto Press.

Wang, J. (2018). *Carceral capitalism*. Semiotext(e) Intervention Series 21. South Pasadena: Semiotext(e).

Wilson Gilmore, R. (2017). In the shadow of the shadow state. In Incite! Women of Color Against Violence (Ed.), *The revolution will not be funded: Beyond the non-profit industrial complex* (pp. 41–52). Durham: Duke University Press. https://doi.org/10.1515/9780822373001-005

Wynter, Sylvia. (2003). 'Unsettling the Coloniality of Being/Power/Truth/Freedom: Towards the Human, After Man, Its Overrepresentation – An Argument.' *CR: The New Centennial Review*, *3*(3), 257–337. https://doi.org/10.1353/ncr.2004.0015

12 History, Trauma, and Identity

The Legacy of the Korean War for Korean Americans

Ramsay Liem

A sense of history does not depend on the depth of generational memory, but identity and consciousness do, because they rest on the linkage of the individual's life history and family history with specific historical moments.
– (Tamara Hareven, "The Search for Generational Memory," 1984, pp. 248–263, 250)

But what about truth? The complexity of this concept also emerged in the debates that took place before and during the life of the Commission resulting in four notions of truth: factual or forensic; personal or narrative truth; social or dialogue truth; and healing and restorative truth ... it also sought to contribute to the process of reconciliation by ensuring that the truth about the past included the validation of the individual subjective experiences of people who had previously been silenced or voiceless.
– (*South African Truth and Reconciliation Commission Final Report*, Vol.1, Chapter 5, 1998, pp. 110–112)

These quotes raise two key points: that the foundations of identity include family history and its intersection with collective history and that personal memories of past social conflict and injustice have a role to play in reconciling that injustice. These are central tenets in an oral history project described in this chapter focusing on Korean American family histories encompassing the pivotal event of the Korean War. My objective is to examine legacies of the Korean War and their implications for identity and community-building, especially for younger Korean Americans who did not experience the conflict personally.[1]

Setting the Stage: History, Memory, and Identity

Just before she began her term of office in the Clinton administration, Secretary of State Madeleine Albright was confronted with the dramatic realization that her life history contained a critical error that went to the very foundations of her identity (Dobbs & Albright, 2000). Rather than the child of a Czech Catholic family, she was the daughter of Jewish parents who converted to Catholicism perhaps as a means to survive the Holocaust. It is suspected that two and possibly three of her grandparents died in concentration camps. We cannot know the full impact this discovery had on Albright nor how completely unexpected it was, but the revelation of this secret evidently touched an existential chord in the public-at-large. For months following this reporting, an outpouring of letters-to-the-editor in the nation's major newspapers revealed numerous similar discoveries – unexpected excavations of family histories – suggesting that Albright was far from unique in her mid-life identity dilemma. The profound psychological impact of a newly discovered family history raises the question whether the most basic sense of who we are – our being-in-the-world – is rooted in "taken-for-granted" pasts. In Erikson's terms, it "draws attention to the meeting between individual life history and the historical movement" (Hareven, 1984, p. 250).

Research on the Holocaust and Japanese American internment also provides insight into how political trauma in the past can carry forward into the present in the psyche and life course not only of those who experienced the trauma directly, but their children and grandchildren, that is, the intergenerational transmission of social trauma. Paradoxically, in both cases silence has been found to be an important carrier of unspeakable pasts – a medium harboring subliminal dread, the object of projected assumptions and expectations, and a source of miscommunication among the generations.

> I hate silence. I hate the screams or are the screams mine? The silence never allowed them to have the right to their own lives and their own deaths . . . they've lived on through others . . . but when what lives on inside others is anger and fear and a sense of impending danger, then it becomes a burden.
>
> (Snider, 1990, p. 320)

Remembering in Order to Move Forward

There are precedents for penetrating silences that shroud painful social conflict and trauma. Public and private ways of remembering the Holocaust abound in order not to forget and to strive to heal (Pfefferkorn, 1985). Pilgrimages to the camps and official testimonies served not only to break Japanese American silence about World War II internment but also to mobilize community action for a successful redress and reparations movement (Hohri, 1988).

A compelling example of silence breaking that fosters not only reclamation of identity and personal healing but also action to achieve social justice is the work of Chilean mental health workers on behalf of survivors of torture during the military dictatorship of Augusto Pinochet (Cienfugos & Monelli, 1983). Their intervention, "Testimonio," combines personal catharsis during a detailed recounting of one's victimization with denunciation of state-sponsored violence through the presentation of these testimonies at international human rights forums. Thus, the process of personal recovery also becomes a weapon in the fight against the repression.

War and Division in the Lives of Korean Americans

The Korean War (1950–1953) and its aftermath are the focus of this Korean American oral history project. The first "hot" war of the Cold War, it was by many accounts (Cumings, 1981; Eckert et al., 1991) a civil conflict exacerbated by the emerging US–Soviet struggle for global hegemony. For the United States, it was the first military encounter on the Asian mainland and the first failure to achieve total victory. For Koreans, this pivotal event occurred just five years after liberation from a brutal Japanese colonial regime. It left a people with 4,000 years of shared history permanently divided into north and south with nearly 10 million people separated from family and relatives and the entire peninsula engulfed in the most virulent of Cold War animosities.

The decimation of the civilian population produced untold numbers of child orphans accounting for South Korea becoming the number one source of international adoptions until 1991. Two million civilians in the north and 1 million in the south died during that conflict along with 1.5 million North Korean and Chinese People's Volunteer Army combatants and 150,000 United Nations forces, 35,000 of whom were from the United States (Halliday & Cumings, 1988). Civilian casualties comprised 70% of total losses as compared to 40% during World War II (Dean, 1999, p. 149).

A cataclysmic event for all Koreans, the ultimate tragedy is that the war is still not over; it remains stalemated in an armistice agreement signed by the United States, China, and North Korea. The Korean peninsula remains divided and the "demilitarized zone" that demarcates the north and south is one of the most heavily fortified borders on the globe (Cumings, 1998).

While scholars have written volumes about the conduct and politics of the Korean War (Cumings, 1990, 1990; Merrill, 1989; Park, 1980), very little can be found about the everyday lives of the Korean people who survived the conflict, let alone its personal and family legacies. The stalemated war and continuing division of the peninsula figure centrally in the contemporary lives of the Korean people in both the north and south (Cumings, 1998).

What is less certain is the impact of the war on Koreans who immigrated to the United States. One estimate is that 50% of Koreans who emigrated to Latin America during the 1960s, many of whom eventually settled in the United States, were originally from the northern part of Korea (Kim, 1981, p. 35). During and following the war, their families migrated from the north to the south where regional and political conflicts with their southern counterparts often limited their economic and social opportunities. Hence, many chose to emigrate, with sizable numbers arriving in the United States after 1965.

These Korean Americans not only lived through the war but chose to leave their native land in part because of entrenched *postwar* tensions that made life in the south untenable. That they made lives in the United States *is itself* a legacy of the unfinished Korean War. How Korean Americans understand the connections between the defining period of the Korean War and their lives in the United States, however, is unknown. The reflections of the people who have participated in this oral history project begin to provide answers to this question suggesting a variety of ways the Korean War has extended its influence across time and place.

Korean Americans Voices

Between 2000 and 2002, I interviewed Koreans living in the Greater Boston and San Francisco Bay areas about their memories of the war, life in Korea after the war, coming to the United States, and life in America. I spoke to about 30 people of all ages, college students, parents and grandparents, some in their 70s and 80s. They included first, 1.5- and 2nd-generation Korean Americans. I know of only two other efforts of this kind, a project growing out of student interviews with parents about their lives during the war directed by Hesung Koh (2000) at the East Rock Institute in Connecticut (R. Liem, Personal communication with Hesung Koh, Boston, MA, 1999), and recent work by Grace Yoo (San Francisco State University) that focuses on older Korean women's memories of mothering during the Korea War.

Interviewing in this project is done with minimal structuring. Participants are asked to recall their personal and family histories to whatever extent possible and in any manner they choose, across four broad periods – before and during the Korean War, the end of the war to emigration to the United States, the early years in the United States, and the recent period. Oral histories are taken in two sessions, the first devoted to verbatim recording of largely spontaneous recollections and the second, to a more interactive process of clarification and inquiry into uncovered areas. Each session takes about two hours.

Because the Korean War is still a flashpoint for intense disagreements and conflict in our community and in the society at large, it takes courage to be among the first to talk about it publicly. However, once agreeing to participate, interviewees tell their stories remarkably freely and with coherence.

Legacies Mediated by Silence

How is the Korean War significant in the lives of Koreans in America, especially younger Korean Americans who know it only through secondary means – schools, literature, the media, private family conversations and artifacts, and even "pregnant silences"? Can a distant "war past" have an important influence on "being" Korean American today?

According to Yael Danieli and others who have studied the intergenerational transmission of political trauma,[2] the inability of some families to speak of the past creates an "audible void" covering over foreboding and anxiety which children sense in their relationships with parents or the family emotional climate. Two interviewees[3] in this project, both in their 30s, spoke in strikingly similar terms.

Kevin Ryu is a second-generation Korean American. His grandfather was a staunch nationalist and labor advocate who was tortured by rightist forces after liberation and eventually killed during the war. Kevin's father has vivid memories of visiting him in jail and experiencing panic when his mother was also incarcerated. Kevin learned of this family past only in his adult years:

> My life seemed a lot like the lives of other kids around me, but there always seemed to be this tension going through my family like an unhappy wind; there were silences which became part of the fabric of our daily lives. The fear and terror of this time period (Korean War) have carried forward into my dad's life. It is visible; if you ever met him, you'd understand what it meant. It's carried forward to my sisters' lives, my life, as a hole, a silence, and in order to move forward into my own life and everything that it means in the present and everything that it can mean in the future, I really feel I have to release the past from this prison of silence.
> (R. Liem, personal interview with Kevin Ryu, Boston, MA, 2001).

Chung Suh came to the United States with her parents in the early 1980s and was "plopped" down in the Midwest. Until recently, she knew little about her family's experience of the war and was startled to learn how raw her mother's exposure to war was – stepping over mutilated bodies, seeing dead babies, fearing retribution for the activities of family members. Her family fled to the United States:

> You know, the fear that she lives in is so imbedded and imprinted in her mind that I can almost hear that fear . . . and one of the things that I had problems with while living in the United States was that I had major insecurity. . . . It's not like I was hungry, it's not like I couldn't function. It's just that I didn't feel secure for some reason. . . . One of the things I learned from my mother was that she had a lot of insecurity herself from the war. Even though she didn't talk about it, I could feel the fear she had so many years ago. What was important to her always was the present, what you need to do to survive in the United States. So she told us to do all the *right* things, just work and study hard, stay away from politics and social things. So I learned, you're supposed to get an education, so you get an education; then you're supposed to get a job, so you get a job; then a house. So finally you finish all those things you're supposed to – then you ask yourself, "now what, now what are you supposed to do with yourself!?"
> (R. Liem, personal interview with Chung Suh, Brookline, MA, 2000)

Both Kevin and Chung were motivated to participate in this oral history project by a desire to fill in the holes in their family histories, for Kevin, to purge the silence of its foreboding, and for Chung, to help distinguish her mother's "shoulds" from her own "wants." From Kevin:

> When I learned these stories, a lot of things just fell right into place, and it was as though a weight had been lifted from me . . . my first reaction I will tell you was not shame or denial. . . . I felt a lot of joy and a real sense of purpose.
> (R. Liem, personal interview with Kevin Ryu, Boston, MA, 2001)

Silence can also operate in different, more complex ways in the lives of war survivors and their children, creating perceived distortions in how children understand parental behavior.

At the age of 16, Ruth Kyungsook Norman fled Pyongyang for the south fearing UN bombing during the war. Following years of refugee status in the south, she met and married a US serviceman with whom she came to the United States in the 1960s:

> The war influenced me for a long time. When my children were growing up, they brought their friends . . . over. I was always hungry during the war, so when they played, I was always trying to give them cookies. I was trying to feed them. I was always trying to give my children everything they needed because I never had anything. When it comes time for their friends to go, I say, "go, have some more, have some more, ok?" My daughter thinks this is because I'm a Korean mother, all Koreans do that. But, looking back at history, I think the reason is because we never had enough food, too many years without. I'm like Americans now. I throw away food even though I should not.
>
> (R. Liem, personal interview with Ruth Kyungsook Norman, Petaluma, CA, 2000)

Ruth Kyungsook Norman is clear that years of deprivation created lasting material insecurities for her and hence her ambivalence years later about wasting food. But this legacy of want also manifests in her parenting style that she believes her daughter misconstrues – that's just the way Korean mothers are. Rather than a person with lived history, Ruth sees herself in her daughter's eyes as a cultural exemplar, an icon of a timeless Korean maternal way of being. The point is not that culture as a framing influence on behavior is irrelevant; rather, that other critical aspects of Ruth's pathway to motherhood and personhood have been inaccessible to her daughter.

Lee Chang-Mo makes a similar observation in speaking of his relationship to his youngest daughter:

> This guy, me, is from the north. Then maybe something happened during the war. . . . I just struggled alone in the south (South Korea). Then I failed, and came over here (United States). Since I had my youngest daughter, I reflected on myself in many ways and then I look back at my behavior and, gee, I'm really a horrible father; I imposed everything on them. The neighbors here in the Korean community think I'm very easygoing, very soft. But inside me, I knew I couldn't do the things I wanted. And then gosh "You (daughters) do those things!" Oh gee, in a sense I'm one of those typical Korean parents who work hard and then didn't accomplish anything, and then turns to their children, "Ok, you guys do it!" Maybe they're gonna go to other Korean families and they realize "Oh gee, my father after all is the standard Korean,

or a little bit worse or a little bit better than standard!" They couldn't know why I am the way I am unless I explained it to them.

(R. Liem, personal interview with Lee Chang-Mo, Cambridge, MA, 2002)

Although these are attributions by parents about how they believe they are seen in the eyes of their children, they convey an estrangement between parent and child in the absence of shared knowledge about the enduring effects of surviving the ravages of war. These excerpts also raise the question just how much of what is culturally stereotyped as "Korean" by the public at large has origins in a hidden past of civil war and years of recovery.

Charles Song further illustrates this point in his thoughts about his father's emotional distance during much of his childhood and early adult years, a quality often attributed to Asian male stoicism. But unlike other younger people I interviewed, Charles spoke often to his grandfather about his life under Japanese colonization and during the Korean War. Charles was a senior in college when we spoke:

> I think one of the reasons Korean fathers seem so emotionally distant is because their own fathers had to keep emotional distance from them during the war. I'm thinking maybe the reason they didn't open up to their children was because they didn't want to get too emotionally attached – because there was this high risk of losing them. That's what happened to my grandfather – he lost a daughter. Besides, there was enough to do just to provide the necessities like food and clothing. So, I think *my* father learned to be distant from his own father.
>
> (R. Liem, personal interview with Charles Song, Berkeley, CA, 2000)

Rather than resort to sweeping cultural stereotypes to make sense of his relationship to his father, Charles uses his knowledge of family history to speculate about the influence severe trauma can have on personality, even across generations. His insight bears a close resemblance to the following observation of a Japanese American woman reflecting on how learning about the internment deepened her understanding of her own behavior:

> From that (life in the internment camps), I learned why it is that I act the way I act. . . . When I was growing up, you always try to act like regular people, regular Americans. . . . I never made any effort to emphasize my difference from anybody else . . . and now I know why; the way *my parents* acted in the camp explains to me why I act the way I do at times.
>
> (Takezawa, 1995, p. 177)

Knowing Is Not Enough

The family silences in which the Korean War past is enveloped create an inexplicable sense of the ominous for some children, but also a barrier to empathy between the generations for others. As a result, parents experience themselves as depersonalized in their children's eyes, cultural types rather than people who have made lives in the face of years of war and recovery in Korea and the United States. This interpersonal divide is just one of the many legacies of the national division of the Korean peninsula still witness to tens of thousands of separated families five decades since the Korean War was paused by an armistice agreement.

Knowing family war histories, however, may not always be sufficient to liberate current generations from inexplicable dread or generational impasses. In fact, knowing can also be immobilizing. When she offered her oral history, Grace Hong described her dilemma as being disempowered by what she *knew* about her family's war history rather than what was hidden. At the time, she was in her early 30s with a background in theology and social policy and strong feminist values:

> I think there is one lesson that my mother learned about herself during the war – that she is dispensable because of her gender and her age. She was in seventh grade when the war broke out. They had to evacuate the town. My mother was the fourth of seven children. The two oldest were girls and, of course, they had to be the first to be evacuated to preserve their virginity. The two sons had to go because they were sons of course, even though one was younger than my mother. And of course the last had to go because she was a baby. My mother had to stay and help my grandmother while she decided if she was too old to evacuate. The decision wasn't up to my mother, which at the time only meant, you know, death. It was okay for her to die, while the other children had to evacuate.
>
> I talked to my mother about this about six years ago. I still remember the expression on her face when she said "it is okay that I die." It was shame and resentment.
>
> My mother was betrayed a second time after she was reunited with her family in the south. All she wanted to do was study but her mother pulled her out of college after one year to marry her off and ease the family's hardships after the war.
>
> I think of these occasions as a mother betraying her daughter. Typically, we say that men oppress women. This may be a part of it, but I think in a very traditional, sexist, patriarchal society like Korea, torn by war and situations that make you just the barest person, my grandmother betrayed my mother.
>
> And I think to this day it is easier for my mother to betray me than my brother or anybody else. She kept telling me "be a normal person." ... I don't know what normal is but it's something she certainly felt that she *could* or *should* have had, but didn't. So, now I must achieve it in my life. But then what happens to *my* desires, *my* dreams. How do I understand this so it doesn't disempower me?
>
> (R. Liem, personal interview with Grace Hong, Boston, MA, 2001)

As if knowing that communication was part of the answer to her question, Grace wrote a song to her mother. She still has not sung it to her.

Mama

"Take me to the place of cherry blossoms and the sea,
Dirt road and a book in your hand.
Perhaps I will meet the woman you were then.

In the line of strong women, you came third, the smartest,
But you gave in to your own mother,
But I felt your anger when you held me.

Oh mama, come hold my hand, see me for what I am
Oh mama, can't you see, the circle must be broken with me, Oh mama, is your fear bigger than your love?

. . .

I gave up trying to change the world,
But I see myself trading my passion for peace.
I want to sprout the seed you implanted in me, secretly, (Though sometimes I wonder if you ever did.)

. . .

Oh mama, I won't give up on you, I'll swim half the world to meet you,
Oh mama, wait for me on your shore."

Yael Danieli speaks of a similar experience in some children of Holocaust survivors who feel the intense need to complete the truncated lives of their parents (Danieli, 1998, p. 5). Grace voices the costs of this desire and is struggling to find a way to fulfill it and yet preserve what is most deeply herself. The song was an effort "to be in solidarity with my mother" – as an ally in overcoming their shared legacy of "being dispensable." Were open engagement with the Korean War past not ostracized in the Korean American community Grace might already have offered her song to her mother.

Time to Break the Silence

The Korean War has been a skeleton in the closet associated with unspeakable pain and a continuing fear of retribution or conflict for those of all political persuasions. We can persist in trying to keep this past buried, or we can look for ways to give it voice to promote greater self-understanding and even healing.

The 50th anniversary of the Korean War two years ago (2000) brought forth unprecedented coverage of the conflict in Korea belying its official moniker as the "forgotten" war. A historic summit meeting between the leaders of North and South Korea two weeks preceding the anniversary also heightened public interest in the war. In early June 2000, the *New York Times*, the *Hartford Courant*, the

Corporation for Public Broadcasting and other print, television, and radio media devoted more attention to the Korean War, national division, and prospects for reconciliation than over the entire previous decade. The Forgotten War emerged in the national consciousness for the first time since the signing of the armistice agreement in 1953. And more than at any other time since Korea was divided, optimism surged in the Korean American community.

Events since then have cast a new pall over the Korean peninsula, and the war a half century ago now looms as a warning of the human disaster that could repeat itself if the drum beat of the new "Evil Axis" mantra is not checked (Wagner, 2002). The urgency to act to prevent a recurrence of war in Korea is self-evident.

> In order to move forward into my own life and everything that it means in the present and can mean in the future, I really feel I have to release the past from this prison of silence and let it come to whatever it may.
> (R. Liem, personal interview with Kevin Ryu, Boston, MA, 2001)

In so doing, we may also discover a common voice with which to also insist that no future generations of Korean Americans should have to wrestle with the legacies of a second Korean War.

Addendum

> "[A]nd there were silences blowing through my family like an unhappy wind."
> (Kevin Ryu, 2005, "Silences," *Still Present Pasts*, para.2)[4]

The "wall of silence" emerged as a central theme among second-generation Korean Americans in my original oral history work. But as I argued in subsequent writing, this conception of silence as psychically and interpersonally mediated within the family fails to acknowledge compounding social and political forces implicating the diasporic community as well as the state in suppressing talk about the war (Liem, 2007). Still riven by civil and international ideological divisions that fueled the Korean War, Korean American emigres abided an "unspoken" pact to erase talk about the fighting to maintain the peace. This community of silence in turn aligned with the US state interests in rendering the brutality of the Korean War as "Forgotten" or sanitized as the heroic rescue of the Korean people from communist dictatorship.

At the urging of elder participants in the oral history project, I organized a collective of Korean and Korean American artists that created a multimedia exhibition embodying memories from my oral history interviews. *Still Present Pasts: Korean Americans and the "Forgotten War"*[5] (SPP) engaged audiences throughout the United States and in South Korea in a community of remembering comprised of visitors often confronting a suppressed past for the first time. The daughter of a war survivor sent me this note after attending the exhibit with her father: "he didn't say a word during our visit but afterwards, over tea, the stories came pouring out."

Memory of Forgotten War[6] (Liem & Liem, 2013), an award winning documentary featuring the lives of four oral history participants, complemented the production of *SPP* and broadened exposure of the enduring legacies of the Korean war. It also softened some of the political divisions within the Korean American community by conveying common longings for relatives lost in North Korea since the hot war. In doing so, it foreshadowed a radical departure from the standard historical timeline situating the war as foreclosed in the distant past. The stories of these four survivors also resonated with younger generations of Korean Americans. Eun-Joung Lee, the daughter of one of the survivors, actually learned of her father's war history while watching the film. Her reaction is video recorded as part of an online archive of Korean War legacies,[7] a follow-up to my original oral history project: "and then I saw the twelve-minute clip and was just overwhelmed by emotion about the story . . . the fact that the family had never really seen it, that he never really talked to us about it" (Liem & Takagi, 2014, para.3).

Radical Departures

Beyond these efforts to counter silencing of Korean War pasts, recent work has cast a critical lens on the dominant paradigm connecting historically catastrophic events to the lives of second and later generations of survivor offspring; the intergenerational transmission of trauma. Kirmayer et al. (2014), for example, note that framing the generational aftermath of war and other forms of violence as "inherited" trauma medicalizes the harm of those ruptures locating it in individual bodies and psyches. In their studies of the aftermath of the violent displacement of native children in boarding schools, they note that focusing on transmitted psychic trauma overlooks pervasive, ongoing group and cultural displacements that undermine the integrity of a people and their collective welfare. This critique harkens back to earlier challenges to the psychologizing of social assaults in and by traditional psychiatric and medical paradigms (Ryan, 1976).

Applied to the Korean War, this critical interrogation of the "intergenerational transmission of trauma" paradigm is trenchant. Rather than solely a civil and Cold War conflict bearing traumatic repercussions in succeeding generations (as rendered in my own early oral history work), the very timeline of the Korean War has been called into question. Rather than a horrific conflagration of the *past*, the war and its reverberations remain present-day imminences. No peace agreement has ever been concluded between the United States and North Korea (two signers of the truce agreement along with China), while threats of renewed fighting continue to escalate reaching nuclear proportions in recent years.

Today, the United States houses over 50 military bases in South Korea, including its largest overseas installation, Camp Humphreys, maintains 28,500 troops in the south, exercises control of combined US–South Korean forces during wartime, oversees the hardened Demilitarized Zone (DMZ), and this past summer launched one of the largest war games on the peninsula in decades, including nuclear capabilities ("WorldBeyondWar," 2023; "United States Force Korea Public Affairs Office," 2023). For its part, current South Korean leadership has reinstated the

National Security Law, a product of earlier crackdowns on any activity in the south deemed sympathetic to the communist north (Seol, 2023). This infamous law is emblematic of the "McCarthyism" entrenched in South Korea after the armistice signing and now reinvigorated by the current South Korean regime.

It is a misnomer to treat the Korean War as a thing of the past. Nonetheless, this is precisely what the dominant US narrative about the war achieves either by erasing it entirely as "forgotten" or by glorifying it as the Cold War rescue of South Korea from the grip of communism. In fact, war in Korea remains an imminent threat.

Informed by this revisionist scholarship, recent contributors have charted new directions in the exploration of past *and* ongoing conditions of war in the lives of newer generations of Korean Americans. In her pathbreaking volume – *Reencounters: On the Korean War and Diasporic Memory Critique* – Crystal Baik (2019) notes that the very language used to describe the emergence of an expanding Korea American community following the 1965 US Immigration Act[8] obfuscates the mark of ongoing war by referencing newcomers as immigrants seeking the promise of the American Dream. In fact, the global diaspora set in motion during and after the Korean War – of tens of thousands of Korean War brides (Yuh, 2002), outcasts under political suspicion in South Korea, others burdened by military dictatorship and a burgeoning, permanent US military encampment – is a pillar of the modern Korean American community. The unended Korea War also perpetuates three quarters of a century of family separations for an estimated 100,000 Korean Americans, persistent Cold War divisions within the community, constant threat of renewed fighting in the homeland, and, of course, unspoken, unreconciled trauma from the hot war passed to children through troubled silences.

Reframed as a "still present past," the Korean War and its continuing assaults have emerged in new scholarship through concepts and methods outside traditional methods of social science research. Second and subsequent generations of Korean Americans self-conscious of their membership in the Korean War diaspora are, themselves, making contributions premised on reconfiguring the war as a present as well as past condition of their lives. One example is Grace Cho's multidisciplinary scholarship wrestling with her family's militarized homeland and its hollowing out of her relationship with her mother. In her award-winning books,[9] she reframes Danieli's "wall of silence" as encounters with "hauntings," gnawing awareness of her mother's troubled past and reconfigurations in the present. Her mother was most likely a sex worker in one of the "camp towns" surrounding the US military bases following the armistice signing and carried suspicion of that troubling moniker to her new home in the United States.

What Cho brings to bear in her quest to understand the many "hauntings" associated with her mother's subsequent behavior and their freighted relationship is a deepening understanding of the Korean War afforded by her generation of scholars implicating US empire-building in Korea's modern fate and testifying to the unfinished business of national liberation. As such, her concept of "hauntings" and quest to honor her mother's life are predicated on a conception of familial relations baked in an unfinished war as well as subject to enduring, traumatic legacies from a distant conflict.

Other recent work, the "Intergenerational Korean American Oral History Project," shares Cho's premise of an *ongoing* Korean War circulating within a diasporic Korean American community (Baik, 2021). It also offers a radical, methodological departure from oral history traditions that prize neutral listening, knowledgeable informants, and the production of archival records for research purposes. A project of Nodutdol for Korean Community Development,[10] this evolving practice is intimately linked to the liberatory and organizing objectives of its parent organization. The project grew out of the desire of Nodutdol's 1.5 and second-generation members to know more about the challenges of the unfinished Korean War ever present in their community and where new alliances could be forged around common purposes.

Nodutdol's oral history work blurs the line between interviewer and interviewee, invites multiple interpretations of narratives, and seeks creative, multimedia methods to engage the wider community in lessons drawn from listening sessions. Interlocutors, Nodutdol members, participate in sharing sessions about themselves prior to meetings with community informants. They center on their own often limited knowledge of the war and their families' ties to the conflict. Then in small groups they participate in listening sessions with older members of the community who have agreed to share their past and present lives as war survivors. Gatherings then evolve into mutual exploration as all parties deepen their curiosity and understanding of the myriad ways the past and present bear the markings of an unfinished war. Baik (2021) refers to this process as "aural" history or engaged listening *and* sharing by all parties to a session rather than a static relation of interlocutor and informant, that is, group dialogue among inquisitor/informants where attentive listening or aurality is the critical medium of exchange.

Rather than seeking *the* central themes in a participant's narrative, the project invites a diversity of learnings in recognition that listening as well as speaking always bear the mark of one's positionality. And multiple discoveries deepen the possibility of solidarity and new organizing objectives and methods.

Sukjong Hong, one of the originators of the project, illustrates the diversity of observations shared by several second-generation participants in a session with a Korean War veteran:

> Someone was attuned to [the elder] speaking about gendered experiences of state violence. Someone else found the history of work and labor really key. And someone else was really interested in the mother-father [aspect] of the story. So, it felt like with multiple listeners – depending on who you are, your own interests – there were multiple highlights and levels of emphasis that could be pulled out of this joint session.
>
> (Baik, 2019, p. 81)

Still an evolving practice and method, the project is wrestling with issues of reporting and archiving. Thus far participants have shared their discoveries through multimedia performances of selected themes largely with Nodutdol members and allies. What this experiment offers more generally is a means of knowledge production grounded in the actual conditions of its query and ongoing actions for change (i.e., aural history as praxis).

Conclusion

In the years since the publication of my research on intergenerational legacies of the Korean War, the lens on the war and its current day repercussions has shifted significantly. The 1.5 and second-generation Korean American scholars and activists, once the object of legacy inquiries, have themselves engaged the vicissitudes of the Korean War informed by an important but limited body of earlier work and now critical contributions of their own. Shadows of unresolved trauma from the original hot war remain to be unearthed within families and across generations. But those traces are no longer the only means through which the 1950 outbreak of scorched earth warring in Korea has shaped the lives of Koreans in America. The new generation of Korean American activist/scholars promises a more comprehensive understanding of the war's "everpresence" through the very act of seeking to overcome it.

Notes

1. A version of this chapter was originally published as Liem, R. (2003). History, Trauma, and Identity: The Legacy of the Korean War for Korean Americans, *Amerasia Journal*, *29*(3), 111–130. https://doi.org/10.17953/amer.29.3.k2t76468016pg455. The Addendum briefly updates the author's and others' related work since this publication.
2. For further details, see Danieli, Y. (1998). Introduction: History and Conceptual Foundations. In Danieli, Yael (Ed.), *International Handbook of Multigenerational Legacies of Trauma* (pp. 1–20). New York: Plenum Press; Shoshan, T. (1989). Mourning and Longing from Generation to Generation, *American Journal of Psychotherapy, 43*(2), 193–207.
3. All interviewee names are pseudonyms.
4. Kevin Ryu. (2005). Silences, *Still Present Pasts*. Retrieved November 15, 2023, from www.stillpresentpasts.org/silences.html.
5. Still Present Pasts. (n.d.) Retrieved November 15, 2023, from www.stillpresentpasts.org.
6. For further information, see Agov (2021) and MuFilms (n.d).
7. Legacies of the Korean War. (n.d.) Retrieved November 15, 2023, from https://legaciesofthekoreanwar.org.
8. See also Cadava (2015).
9. Cho, G. (2008). *Haunting the Diaspora: Shame, Secrecy and the Forgotten War*. Minneapolis: University of Minneapolis Press. Cho, G. (2021). *Tastes Like War: A Memoir*. New York: The Feminist Press.
10. Nodutdol for Korean Community Development. (n.d.). Retrieved November 15, 2023 from www.nodutdol.org.

References

Agov, A. (2021). Memory of Forgotten War. *Pacific Affairs*, *87*(4), 919–921.
Baik, C. (2019). *Reencounters: On the Korean War and Diasporic Memory*. Philadelphia: Temple University Press.
Baik, C. (2021). Intergenerational Korean American Oral History Project. *Journal of American History*, *108*(1), 125–129. https://doi.org/10.1093/jahist/jaab069

Cadava, G. (October 3, 2015). How Should Historians Remember the 1965 Immigration and Nationality Act? *Organization of American Historians*. Retrieved from www.oah.org/tah/august-2/how-should-historians-remember-the-1965-immigration-and-nationality-act/

Cho, G. (2008). *Haunting the Diaspora: Shame, Secrecy and the Forgotten War*. Minneapolis: University of Minneapolis Press.

Cho, G. (2021). *Tastes Like War: A Memoir*. New York: The Feminist Press.

Cienfugos, A.J., & Monelli, C. (1983). The Testimony of Political Repression as a Therapeutic Instrument. *American Journal of Orthopsychiatry*, 53, 43–51. https://doi.org/10.1111/j.1939-0025.1983.tb03348.x

Cumings, B. (1981). *The Origins of the Korean War: Liberation and the Emergence of Separate Regimes, 1945–1947*. Princeton: Princeton University Press.

Cumings, B. (1990). *The Origins of the Korean War, Vol. II: The Roaring of the Cataract, 1947–1950*. Princeton: Princeton University Press.

Cumings, B. (1998). *Korea's Place in the Sun: A Modern History*. New York: W.W. Norton.

Danieli, Y. (1998). Introduction: History and Conceptual Foundations. In Danieli, Yael (Ed.), *International Handbook of Multigenerational Legacies of Trauma* (pp. 1–20). New York: Plenum Press.

Dean, H. (1999). *The Korean War: 1945–1953*. San Francisco: China Books and Periodicals.

Dobbs, M., & Albright, M. (2000). *A Twentieth Century Odyssey*. New York: Henry Holt.

Eckert, C., Lee, K.B., Lew, Y., Robinson, M., & Wagner, E. (Eds.) (1991). *Korea Old and New: A History*. Cambridge: Harvard University Press.

Halliday, J., & Cumings, B. (1988). *Korea: The Unknown War*. New York: Pantheon Books.

Hareven, T. (1984). The Search for Generational Memory. In Dunaway, D., & Baum, W. (Eds.), *Oral History: An Interdisciplinary Anthology* (pp. 241–256). Nashville: American Association for State and Local History.

Hohri, W. (1988). *Repairing America: An Account of the Movement for Japanese American Redress*. Pullman: Washington State University Press.

Kim, I. (1981). *New Urban Immigrants: The Korean Community in New York*. Princeton: Princeton University Press.

Kirmayer, L., Gone, J., & Moses, J. (2014). Rethinking Historical Trauma. *Transcultural Psychology*, 51(3), (2014), 299–319. https://doi.org/10.1177/1363461514536358

Legacies of the Korean War. (n.d.). Retrieved November 15, 2023, from https://legaciesofthekoreanwar.org

Liem, D.B., & Liem, R. (2013). *Memory of Forgotten War* [Film]. Berkeley: Mu Films; Channing & Popai Liem Education Foundation.

Liem, D.B., & Takagi, JT. (2014). Interview with Eun-Young Lee. *Legacies of the Korean War*. Retrieved from https://legaciesofthekoreanwar.org/story/eun-joung-lee/

Liem, R. (2007). Silencing Historical Trauma: The Politics and Psychology of Memory and Voice. *Peace and Conflict: Journal of Peace Psychology*, 13(2), 153–174. https://doi.org/10.1080/10781910701271200

Merrill, J. (1989). *Korea: The Peninsular Origins of the War*. Newark: The Delaware Press.

MuFilms. (n.d.). Retrieved November 15, 2023, from www.mufilms.org/films/memory-of-forgotten-war/

Nodutdol for Korean Community Development. (n.d.). Retrieved November 15, 2023 from www.nodutdol.org

Park, C.Y. (1980). *Political Opposition in Korea, 1945–1960*. Seoul: Seoul National University Press.

Pfefferkorn, E. (1985). *Commemorative Observances for Days of Remembrance*. Washington: United States Holocaust Memorial Council.

Ryan, W. (1976). *Blaming the Victim*. New York: Vintage Books.

Seol, K. (January 26, 2023). Conservative Government is Cracking Down on Militant Labor Unions. *Jacobin*. Retrieved from https://jacobin.com/2023/01/south-korea-conservative-government-labor-unions-cracking-down-national-security

Shoshan, T. (1989). Mourning and Longing from Generation to Generation, *American Journal of Psychotherapy*, *43*(2), 193–207.
Snider, F. (1990). Holocaust Trauma and Imagery: The Systemic Transmission into the Second Generation. In Mirkin, Marsha P. (Ed.), *The Social and Political Contexts of Family Therapy* (pp. 307–330). Boston: Allyn & Bacon.
South African Truth and Reconciliation Commission Final Report, Volume 1. (October 29, 1998). *South African Truth and Reconciliation Commission*. Pretoria. Retrieved from www.justice.gov.za/trc/report/finalreport/Volume%201.pdf
Still Present Pasts. (n.d.) Retrieved November 15, 2023, from www.stillpresentpasts.org.
Takezawa, Y. (1995). *Breaking the Silence: Redress and Japanese American Ethnicity*. Ithaca and London: Cornell University Press.
United States Force Korea Public Affairs Office. (August 14, 2023). *The Republic of Korea and United States announce exercise Ulchi Freedom Shield 23*. Retrieved from www.navy.mil/Press-Office/Press-Releases/display-pressreleases/Article/3491680/the-republic-of-korea-and-united-states-announce-exercise-ulchi-freedom-shield/
Wagner, A. (2002). Bush Labels North Korea, Iran, Iraq an "Axis" of Evil." *Arms Control Today*, *32*(2), 25–25.
WorldBeyondWar (WBW). (2023). *USA's Military Empire: A Visual Database*. Charlottesville. Retrieved from https://worldbeyondwar.org/no-bases/
Yuh, J.Y. (2002). *Beyond the Shadow of Camptowns: Korean Military Brides in America*. New York: New York University Press.

13 The Psychological Well-Being of Children in North Korean Defector Families

The Impact of Intergenerational Trauma

Sang Hui Chu

Who Are North Korean Defectors?

North Korean defectors (NKDs) refer to individuals who fled North Korea and settled in South Korea. As of December 2023, 34,078 NKDs entered South Korea (Korea Ministry of Unification, 2023). Despite sharing the same language and historical–cultural background, North Korea and South Korea have followed different political systems, cultural practices, and economic development trajectories for the past 70 years. This has led to distinctive variations in language, cultural norms, and historical narratives between the two Koreas. Thus, NKDs face significant and additional challenges living in South Korea due to the differences stemming from the unique paths these two societies have taken. In what follows, the historical context that has given rise to the emergence of NKDs is explained.

After experiencing the violent conflict of the Korean War (1950–1953), the Korean Peninsula was divided into two countries under different ideologies and systems, namely, democracy in South Korea and communism in North Korea. The latter has maintained a closed communist economic system and continues to strictly monitor and control its citizens. During the Cold War years, South Korea and North Korea competed against each other based on their reciprocal perception as age-old enemies, thus living without any human or material exchange. In fact, up until 1998, 947 NKDs in total had crossed the heavily guarded border to South Korea, facing formidable obstacles, such as political persecution and other exceptional circumstances. However, in the late 1990s and throughout the 2000s, the number of NKDs increased dramatically ("Korea Ministry of Unification," 2023).

During the 1990s, while South Korea achieved significant social and economic development, North Korea faced a severe economic crisis with the collapse of the economic cooperation system among socialist alliance countries caused by the dissolution of the Soviet Union. The death of North Korean leader Kim Il-sung in 1994 and devastating floods, consecutively in 1995 and 1996, added to the precarity of the state crisis. Consequently, the efficacy of the central food distribution system deteriorated, leading to a surge in malnutrition and disease-induced mortality. According to the Korea National Statistical Office (2010), between 1994 and 2003, the estimated population loss was around 610,000 people, including an excess mortality of 482,000 individuals and an estimated loss of 128,000 births. Obtaining

DOI: 10.4324/9781003385820-14

Table 13.1 The Number of North Korean Defectors Entering South Korea Annually ("Korea Ministry of Unification," 2023)

Year Gender	~1998	~2001	2002	2003	2004	2005	2006	2007	2008	2009	2010	2011	2012	2013	2014	2015	2016	2017	2018	2019	2020	2021	2022	2023	Total (N)
Men	831	1396	510	474	626	424	515	573	608	662	591	795	404	369	305	251	302	188	168	202	72	40	35	32	9,542
Women	116	594	632	811	1,272	960	1,513	1,981	2,195	2,252	1,811	1,911	1,098	1,145	1,092	1,024	1,116	939	969	845	157	23	32	164	24,536
Total	947	1,990	1,142	1,285	1,898	1,384	2,028	2,554	2,803	2,914	2,402	2,706	1,502	1,514	1,397	1,275	1,418	1,127	1,137	1,047	229	63	67	196	34,078
Women's ratio (%)	12.2	29.8	55.3	63.1	67.0	69.4	74.6	77.6	78.3	77.3	75.4	70.6	73.1	75.6	78.2	80.3	78.7	83.3	85.2	80.7	68.6	36.5	47.8	83.7	72.0

Note: * Ministry of Unification.

precise data regarding the exact number of casualties due to food shortages during this period, commonly referred to as the "Arduous March (1995–1997)" in North Korea, poses significant challenges. Nonetheless, the US Foreign Relations Committee estimated that the death toll during this period ranged from a conservative estimate of 1 million to a potentially staggering 3 million individuals (Kim, 1998).

Kim Jong-il, who succeeded Kim Il-sung's regime, actively pursued external economic opening and sought to attract foreign investment to mitigate economic hardships. During this economic reform process, private property rights were partially acknowledged, which later added to the weakening of social control mechanisms. During this period, a notable increase in interregional population mobility occurred, driven by the pursuit of scarce food resources, primarily in border regions. In turn, this migration scheme gave rise to a substantial expansion in the floating population, comprising individuals who temporarily or permanently sought refuge in China intending to acquire sustenance before eventually returning to North Korea (Kim, 1998). North Koreans initially sought to escape the famine and poverty in North Korea and thus crossed the border into China. Subsequently, however, as undocumented immigrants, they faced the challenges of an uncertain legal status, along with the constant threat of arrest and expatriation by Chinese authorities. Due to the persisting economic hardships and lack of resources, many North Koreans were unable to establish stable living conditions in China.

On the other hand, the Constitution of the Republic of Korea designates the North Korean region as part of its territory and recognizes its residents as Korean citizens. According to the Law on the Settlement and Support of North Korean Defectors, the South Korean government started to provide NKDs with a certain level of financial support to help their settlement. This, in turn, has accelerated systematic attempts by NKDS to escape to China and from there to sojourn to South Korea via third transit countries such as Laos, Cambodia, or Thailand. As the number of North Korean escapees to South Korea via a third country increased since the late 1990s, North Korean defector brokers[1] in assisting their escape has grown exponentially, requiring significant financial costs to be paid to enter South Korea (Song, 2012).

Since 2000, the number of NKDs seeking asylum in South Korea has continued to rise. This increase can be attributed to two main factors: first, individuals who fled North Korea during the "Arduous March" period and remained in China have increasingly received assistance from brokers to enter South Korea; second, North Korean residents exposed to South Korean content, such as dramas and music, have developed positive perceptions of South Korea and have sought a better life. (Chung, 2009; Jung, 2016). However, since Kim Jong-un succeeded in power in 2012, the number of NKDs significantly decreased. The setback in attempted escapes is connected to several factors, including heightened control by the North Korean government (such as increased border security personnel in the border areas, the expanded use of CCTV cameras and visible iron fencing, and more road checkpoints), the intensified crackdown efforts by Chinese authorities, and harsher consequences and sanctions for defectors (internment in political prison camps) and their families. Additionally, the recent introduction of electronic passports and facial recognition technology within China has exacerbated these difficulties and has led to an increase in defection costs.

Why Are the Majority of North Korean Defectors Women?

Current statistics show that women make up about 72% of NKDs entering South Korea, with the majority of them coming from the border regions between North Korea and China ("Korea Ministry of Unification," 2023). With only 12% up until 1998, the proportion of female NKDs among those entering South Korea was initially low. However, starting in 2002, a consistent and notable increase in the representation of female defectors became evident, surpassing the proportion of male defectors. In 2018, the ratio of female defectors, as demonstrated in Table 13.1, accounted for a substantial 85% of the total NKD population who entered South Korea.

The increase in female defectors is inextricably related to North Korea's unique political climate and unstable socioeconomic situation. North Korea has a unique social governance system referred to as Confucian-style socialism, where the leader is the "parental leader," and the people are governed by a patriarchal logic in domestic relationships. These characteristics demonstrate the particularity of North Korea alongside the universal traits of socialism. The prevailing societal preference for sons over daughters remains deeply entrenched, resulting in restricted educational and occupational opportunities for women. The consequences of such biases are reflected in the limited avenues available to women to pursue education and engage in meaningful professional pursuits within North Korean society. The representation of women in high-ranking positions within the Workers' Party of Korea stands at a mere 5%, while their presence in central government bureaucratic roles is only 10% ("National Unification Education Institute," 2023, pp. 255–256). These figures highlight a clear indication of the pronounced gender inequality that persists within the political and socioeconomic domains of North Korea.

A key reason for the higher proportion of female defectors among those entering South Korea is the shift in domestic economic strategies, where the previous reliance on the food distribution system has transitioned toward self-sustaining economic activities, primarily led by women. Since the 1990s, it has become evident that the centralized and planned management system is no longer functional in North Korea. This shift prompted residents to rely on emerging markets for their livelihoods. After the economic crisis, except for a small number of professional women and those working in state-owned enterprises, almost 70% are reported to be engaged in informal businesses called "Jangmadang," translating to "marketplace" in Korean (Jung, 2009).

In the context of North Korean society, characterized by strong patriarchal values, the prevailing understanding suggests that the role of food procurement has traditionally been assigned to women. This allocation of responsibility can be attributed to the perception that women who are not actively affiliated with formal employment are better positioned to engage in long-term domestic caretaking. Consequently, the rising participation of women in economic endeavors facilitated women's mobility between regions and migration to China's border areas, thereby promoting exposure to external societal culture and resources, including elements of the capitalist economy.

As women participate in simple barter to large-scale commercial activities, they naturally encounter the outside world. For North Korean women, this exposure facilitated the ability to leave the country for both economic and social reasons. According to the 2023 Settlement Survey on Defector Motives, the majority of female defectors from North Korea cited their primary motive as the desire to escape the surveillance and the control imposed by the North Korean regime, accounting for 36.4% of the respondents. This was followed by the scarcity of food (34.3%) and the desire to improve their economic situation by earning more money (27.7%). Additionally, notable motivations included seeking a better living environment for their family (18.3%), feeling personally threatened (13.4%), and joining family members who had already defected (12.5%) ("Korea Hana Foundation," 2023). In interpreting driving forces for defection among women, these findings highlight the significance of familial considerations alongside the economic and political factors. Comparing the defector motives of men, it becomes apparent that the primary motivations are of political nature, and they express dissatisfaction with the surveillance and control of the North Korean regime, combined with personal threats, comprising 66.4% of their responses ("Korea Hana Foundation," 2023).

Many women who escape North Korea typically enter South Korea through third countries such as China, Vietnam, Cambodia, Thailand, or Russia. During this process, they spend an average duration of over two years residing in either China or other third countries (Lee et al., 2011). It is noteworthy that when passing through China, in particular, these women face significant exposure to various risks, including forced marriages with local residents or "Chosum-jok,"[2] human trafficking, prostitution, and sexual violence. China is one of the regions with severely imbalanced gender ratios due to the legacy of China's one-child policy, and, in rural areas, the gap is wider. Female NKDs often end up marrying and giving birth in China because of human trafficking. According to Moon et al. (2000), a significant number of female NKDs had already entered into marriages and had children prior to their defection. However, upon their escape, they frequently enter into new marriages in China. The living conditions for these NKD women residing in China are marked by insecurity and fear, as they face the constant threat of arrest and forced repatriation by Chinese authorities. Some women also endure captivity under the control of Chinese or North Korean individuals, involving the inhumane experience of being bought and sold. Even after their settlement in China, these women encounter challenges in achieving economic independence, obtaining legal protection, acquiring proficiency in the Chinese language, and adapting to their new surroundings. Through interviews with NKD women in China, Kim and Noh (2003) discovered a shared sense of identity as "Chosun (Korean) women from an unlivable country" (p. 11). Their lives in China are characterized by the absence of financial autonomy, constant vulnerability to social threats, and an overarching sense of uncertainty

In light of the aforementioned, the growing demand among female NKDs to seek social and economic support in South Korea has led to the emergence of specialized brokers who facilitate their journey. Women who have entered South Korea through specialized brokers play a pivotal role in facilitating the immigration of their family members remaining in China to South Korea or aiding their family members in North Korea to enter South Korea with the assistance of brokers.

The Life of NKD Women after Migration

According to a recent study,[3] a higher proportion of women than men stay in neighboring countries (87.3% versus 74.4%), with longer average stay durations (4.0 years versus 1.4 years), and with a higher rate of repatriation (24.9% versus 17.4%). The differential experiences of North Korean women compared to men staying in China can be attributed primarily to the prevalent practice of marriage due to human trafficking in rural areas. While certain marriages may offer stability, a substantial number of North Korean women have encountered distressing circumstances both mentally and physically, encompassing instances of physical abuse, unwanted pregnancies, confinement, and surveillance. The very process of defection itself, coupled with the pervasive fear of forced repatriation, exposes these women to grave human rights violations, such as labor exploitation, unlawful detention, human trafficking, and sexual assault. Therefore, these traumatic experiences have promoted diverse health complications and long-term repercussions for the successful settlement and integration of North Korean women into South Korean society. Notably, studies conducted among North Korean women residing in Hanawon,[4] a settlement support facility for defectors, have yielded noteworthy findings. Among those who endured human rights violations, particularly forced repatriation, elevated levels of depression, anxiety, interpersonal sensitivity, and hostility have been observed. Even after completing social adaptation education, these women continue to exhibit persistent hostility, highlighting the lasting impact of their traumatic experiences (Lee, 2011; Kim et al., 2014). Despite achieving a certain degree of economic stability, many defected women continue to grapple with significant mental health issues. Reports indicate a higher prevalence of post-traumatic stress disorder (PTSD), depression, and heightened levels of stress (Lee, 2011; Kim et al., 2014; Lee et al., 2018). These mental health challenges further impede their successful integration into South Korean society and hinder their active participation in economic endeavors.

North Korean women who resettle in South Korea often invite their children or spouses from North Korea or China or establish new relationships to rebuild their families. Among female NKDs, the highest percentage (45.2%) are married to spouses from South Korea, followed by 29.1% married to spouses from China, and 25.3% married to spouses from North Korea. In contrast, many male defectors (83.5%) are married to spouses from North Korea ("Korea Hana Foundation," 2022). It is worth noting that as the duration of residence in South Korea increases, the proportion of Chinese spouses decreases, while the proportion of South Korean spouses increases. This suggests that some female defectors who have resided in

China for an extended period after defection have married Chinese spouses, but later separated from them and entered into marriages (de facto or formal) with South Korean–born men (Han & Lee, 2014; Kim, 2018; "Korea Hana Foundation," 2022, p. 39). However, it is not uncommon for them to end up in single-parent households due to divorce or separation, with the responsibility of raising children predominantly falling on women. Among female NKDs, 46.2% have school-aged children (Lee et al., 2021; "Korea Hana Foundation," 2022, p. 82), and the average household size, including themselves (defected women), was 2.3 persons as of 2022 ("Korea Hana Foundation," 2022, p. 89). These statistics allow us to infer the characteristics of defector households. It is evident that there is a notable presence of single-parent households with children, with a significant portion of these households being headed by single mothers. Therefore, North Korean women who settle in South Korea play a crucial role as key figures in reestablishing the family unit, and are responsible for raising and assisting their children in adapting to South Korean society.

As of 2022, a considerable proportion of female NKDs (approximately 53.3%) reported not having a spouse ("Korea Hana Foundation," 2022, p. 90). Notably, a substantial percentage of women (66.2%) assumed the role of household heads, surpassing the proportion of female household heads in South Korea (32.7%) reported by the Korea National Statistical Office in 2020.

The notion of the head of the household typically pertains to the person responsible for sustaining the family's livelihood. Thus, it can be inferred that NKD women often find themselves in situations where they must shoulder the responsibilities of both household chores and financial matters for their families. This demanding environment makes it challenging for them to provide emotional care for their children and cope with the competitive educational environment in South Korea. Even if they have a spouse, a significant number of women (55.7%) experienced domestic violence at the hands of their spouses (Cho et al., 2019). In terms of types of violence, emotional violence accounted for the highest percentage at 29.7%, followed by minor physical violence at 17.6%, economic violence at 16.2%, sexual violence at 9.5%, and severe physical violence at 4.1%. Economic problems (28.5%) and issues related to children (19.2%) emerged as the primary underlying causes of violence. Clearly, in addition to grappling with the complexities of housekeeping, childcare, livelihoods, and adapting to South Korean society, many NKD women also face the distressing reality of domestic violence.

In sum, NKD women face various difficulties as immigrants, women, and North Koreans after migration. They struggle with financial difficulties, domestic violence, and the burden of caring for family members.

Children of NKDs

As Table 13.2 illustrates, the proportion of female NKDs in South Korea has been rising, leading to an increase in the number of school-age children born in North Korea or China. The NKD children can be categorized into three cohort groups based on their place of birth: (1) North Korea (defector youth from North Korea),

Table 13.2 Current Statistics on North Korean Defector Students by School Type ("Korea Educational Development Institute Education Support Center for North Korean Refugee Youth," 2023)

School type / Birth of place	Elementary School	Middle School	High School	Other Schools*	Total (N/%)
Born in North Korea	72 (17.1)	149 (29.0)	258 (37.7)	33 (21.9)	512 (28.9)
Born in third country (China, etc.)	349 (82.9)	364 (71.0)	426 (62.3)	118 (78.1)	1,257 (71.1)
Total (N/%)	421 (100)	513 (100)	684 (100)	151 (100)	1,769 (100)

Notes: * Alternative schools, technical high schools, etc. This data does not include preschool children.

(2) a third country (children born in a third country), and (3) South Korea (children born in South Korea). Despite criticisms regarding the classification of NKD children based on their birthplace (Kim, 2022), this categorization is employed here as these groups receive varying legal support from different government agencies. As of April 2023, there were a total of 1,769 NKD children attending school, with 512 (28.9%) of whom were born in North Korea and 1,257 (71.1%) born in third countries such as China ("Korea Educational Development Institute Education Support Center for North Korean Refugee Youth," 2023). However, this number does not include the children who were born in South Korea and teenagers who are currently not attending school.

Defector youth from North Korea are those who migrated with their families or alone from North Korea. The majority of defector youth from North Korea have experienced famine, hardship, death, or separation of family members in North Korea, as well as fear and anxiety during the process of defection and their stay in third countries. Children who were left behind by defecting parents, who later reunited with them, or who joined their parents in China, often struggle with attachment issues because they have been unable to form stable relationships with their parents since early childhood. Children who have experienced separation anxiety and psychological fear are emotionally vulnerable, often displaying aggressive or violent behavior in response to minor stimuli in their daily lives (Kim & Lee, 2016; Hameed et al., 2018). Due to their direct exposure to challenging past traumatic experiences, these children may exhibit symptoms of PTSD (Park et al., 2019).

Children born in a third country are those who were born either as a result of their mothers being subjected to forced human trafficking after defecting or through voluntary marriages with third-country men. Those born in a third country face a range of challenges stemming from the repeated experiences of family dissolution and reconstitution during the migration process. Typically, these children have experienced a series of migrations, either accompanying their NKD mothers or joining their mothers in South Korea who arrived earlier. Children who escaped with their mothers may have been directly exposed to similar traumatic events as those who migrated from North Korea, experiencing fear and anxiety during the process of crossing borders, while most children who entered South Korea at their mothers' invitation have experienced prolonged separation from their parents before reunification, often leading to an increased likelihood of being raised in an unstable caregiving environment. The involuntary nature of "chain migrations" contributes to a renewed sense of identity crisis among children born in a third country. Their non-Korean native language poses challenges in terms of communication and school life in South Korea. According to a qualitative study that examined the meaning of life experiences pre- and post-migration into South Korea for children born in a third country, the fundamental meaning of their life experiences was summarized as "a life without care, enduring it alone" (Jeong & Park, 2016, p. 233). Their experiences in third countries were characterized by "the time of sadness and pain without their mothers" (Jeong & Park, 2016, p. 232). Despite opposition from their third-country families, they came to Korea looking for their mothers. However, their postmigration experiences in South Korea were described as "experiencing confusion and conflict in the changed environment with their changed mothers" (Jeong & Park, 2016, p. 238).

Additionally, defector youth from North Korea and children born in a third country come from diverse backgrounds, which can result in insufficient foundational academic skills and they subsequently struggle to achieve academic success in South Korean education systems. The age and educational disparities between these children and their South Korean counterparts can lead to conflict in senior–junior relationships[5] commonly determined by the grades according to their age and contribute to lower self-esteem within educational environments. These unique characteristics further complicate peer relationships, augment feelings of alienation, and diminish self-esteem.

The final group comprises children born in South Korea, and there is emerging evidence that these children may encounter greater hardships compared to those who directly come from North Korea or a third country (Kim et al., 2016). Growing up within South Korean society, these children acquire the values and norms prevalent in their surroundings, while their parents continue to adhere to the cultural norms and values of North Korean society. This disparity in values frequently occludes parent–child communication with the parents and children struggling to bridge the gap between their respective cultural perspectives. Furthermore, when parents remain socioeconomically vulnerable, their difficulties negatively affect the children, although research specifically focusing on this cohort remains scarce. In the case of children born in South Korea, adapting to new society is no longer a countable factor and their exposure to traumatic events such as witnessing death or separation from family members is of lesser prevalence. However, depending on the relationship with the main caregiver and the parenting environment, this cohort may have similar difficulties as the defector youth from North Korea and the children born in a third country. This is especially relevant in terms of social discrimination as children born in South Korea are classified as "multicultural," which, as a derogatory expression, is often used in South Korean society as it specifically designates "NKD's children." The research report evaluating the vulnerability of adolescents in NKD families emphasizes the prevalence of single-parent households and educational neglect, along with the pronounced vulnerability of their parents (Kim et al., 2016). Despite these challenging factors, government support for children born in South Korea remains largely absent and thus they are at risk of being overlooked due to this policy gap. The report underscored the need to strengthen the role of the private sector in supporting children born in South Korea, and to develop separate educational support addressing financial and socio-emotional aspects (Kim et al., 2016).

More concerning, however, is that most research on the mental health of NKD children has been conducted without a consideration of their unique migration experiences. According to a literature review study on the mental health of NKD children or adolescents from all places of birth, no significant differences in reactions to externalizing problems, such as school-related issues and delinquent behaviors, were indicated as compared to that of the South Korean children and adolescents (Lee et al., 2019). However, the internalization problems, such as depression and anxiety symptoms, were significantly higher among NKD adolescents compared to both South Korean adolescents and other multicultural household adolescents residing in South Korea. Particularly concerning is the suicide risk, as the NKD adolescents showed a four times higher risk of suicide propensity compared to South Korean adolescents. As reactions to internalizing problems may be less discernible to mothers or teachers, the long-term vulnerabilities they pose need higher awareness among respective communities.

In summary, NKD children, depending on their place of birth, may have different levels of direct exposure to trauma. However, a common denominator is their experience of unstable family dynamics and dissolution of relationships. To elucidate the mechanisms through which parental trauma indirectly affects children's mental health in NKD families, it is crucial to consider migration experiences based on place of birth, the parental perception of mental health, help-seeking behavior, and utilization of health care services. These factors should be considered concurrently.

Parenting Behavior as a Potential Mechanism of Intergenerational Transmission of Trauma

The intergenerational transmission of trauma among Holocaust survivors has been explained through various models, such as psychological dynamics, sociocultural models, family systems models, and biological models (Isobel et al., 2019). More recently, research has focused on understanding intergenerational transmission of trauma among refugees and asylum seekers scrutinizing their unique traumatic experiences and pre-and post-migration stressors. There is a growing evidence on the significance of family systems, relationships, and functioning in the indirect transmission of parental trauma to offspring who have not directly experienced trauma themselves (Flanagan et al., 2020; Sangalang & Vang, 2017; Dalgaard & Montgomery, 2017; Thoruo & Montgomery, 2017).

According to Sangalang et al. (2017), maternal traumatic stress is indirectly linked to children's mental health outcomes through parent–child relationships, parenting, and family functioning. For instance, the experience of Southeast Asian refugees evidences that the mother's PTSD symptoms are related to their children's susceptibility to depressive symptoms, antisocial behavior, delinquent behavior, and school-related issues via the mediation of family functioning such as parent–child communication, parent–child conflict, family cohesion, parental warmth, and parental involvement (Sangalang et al., 2017). Importantly, the impact of parental trauma on family functioning and children's well-being varies depending on the children's nationality, their experiences with sociocultural environments, and language acquisition during their developmental years (Sangalang et al., 2017). Therefore, it is plausible to assume that the influence of parental trauma on the mental health of NKD children would also vary depending on the children's unique experiences by birthplace. Additionally, Kelstrup and Carlsson (2022) address parenting and family functioning as potential risk or protective factors in the intergenerational transmission of trauma.

Arguably, trauma can have a profound impact on parenting. Traumatic experiences during defection from North Korea and the accumulated stress during social adaptation in South Korea contribute to heightened levels of parenting stress among NKD families. This increased stress leads to elevated levels of parental aggression and the adoption of negative parenting attitudes, adversely impacting the growth and development of their children (Abidin & Wilfong, 1989; Kim & Park, 2009). Particularly, negative experiences encountered during the defection process have been found to weaken family functioning, induce cultural adaptation stress in an unfamiliar society, and reduce parental self-efficacy, ultimately influencing the occurrence of child abuse (Ryu & Yang, 2021). Lee et al. (2020) highlighted the concerns about present parenting environments in NKD families. The concern is primarily attributed to instances of domestic violence from husbands, emotional disorders experienced by mothers, language and communication barriers, as well as financial difficulties within these families (Lee et al., 2020). In particular, NKD mothers, who are accustomed to a culture where harsh discipline of children is permissible, stated that, instead of verbal correction, they often resorted to physical punishment when their children misbehaved. Furthermore, NKD mothers testified that the emotional foundation for strong physical reactions, even for minor mistakes of the children, was the manifestation of frustration with their husbands, that is, women inclined to project the anger of dislike toward their husband inept behavior onto their children (Park et al., 2011).

After arriving in South Korea, NKD mothers face the difficult task of reunifying with their children who were left behind in China or North Korea. However, after reunification, the mother–child dyad is often challenged by the accepting the altered facets of each other's lives that have evolved during their period of separation. These mothers often work long hours to support their families, which leaves them with limited time to spend with their children. Meanwhile, their children, grappling with the stress of adapting to a new environment, may exhibit challenging behaviors. Children may appear to be seeking compensation for the time they spent apart from their mothers or rebelling out of fear of rejection stemming from separation. Consequently, NKD mothers, facing increased childcare burdens along with their unattended mental health issues, experience negative emotions such as depression, irritability, and anger; these reactions are the catalyst of violent parenting behaviors in response to their children's challenging behaviors, and thus further complicate the already strained parent–child relationship (Baik et al., 2021).

Furthermore, NKDs have a propensity to exhibit authoritarian, controlling, and strict parenting styles, reflecting the authoritative and oppressive parenting culture prevalent in North Korean society (Lee et al., 2010). This influence persists in South Korea, especially among those who have had a short period between defection and arrival, or who have independently established their households upon arrival (Hong & Kim, 2013).

Nevertheless, NKD mothers, driven by a desire for their children's well-being and better futures, have testified to enduring the hardships of unhappy marriages in third countries and choosing to migrate to South Korea. These mothers find profound meaning in the presence of their children, and dedicate themselves to navigating the challenges of single parenthood, while actively working to restore previous mother–child relationships (Kim, 2015a). In the context of NKD mothers, recent research has shown that high levels of psychological hardness, coupled with having four or more supporters, are strongly associated with reduced parenting stress. Moreover, parenting efficacy was identified as the primary factor influencing parent–child relationships, followed by parenting stress (Lee & Jeon, 2021; 2022).

In general, the significance of socioeconomic status, specifically household monthly income, is widely acknowledged as a crucial determinant in child-rearing (Taraban & Shaw, 2018). Upon initial arrival in South Korea, NKDs are typically categorized as recipients of basic livelihood support, while provided essential assistance from the government and simultaneously preparing for employment. Nevertheless, despite government support systems, for women assuming the sole responsibility of raising children without the aid of a spouse or extended family, economic self-sufficiency becomes challenging. The employment-related challenges faced by NKD women predominantly revolve around the demands of childcare and health concerns (Lee et al., 2020). Additionally, they experience a considerable burden due to the substantial financial costs associated with child-rearing, which contrasts with their previous experiences in North Korea. Many NKD women express feelings of anxiety arising from their limited understanding of their children's school life, which impedes their ability to provide adequate support (Jo et al., 2013; Kim & Yang, 2015). Recently, stable economic engagement and harmonious family life for NKD women have been recognized as crucial tasks for enhancing settlement and acculturation within South Korean society. Consequently, efforts have been made to address the adaptation issues of female defectors by prioritizing work-life balance (Wang, 2022) and family-integrated educational support policies (Kim et al., 2016).

On the other hand, the experiences of NKD women in raising children within South Korean society can be understood through distinct stages of adaptation (Hong et al., 2010). They undergo an initial "entry phase" characterized by immersing into South Korean society, while grappling with physical and psychological trauma.

They then encounter the "confrontation phase," wherein they confront the limits of adaptation, including negative experiences such as relative poverty and cultural dissonance. Despite societal biases and feelings of isolation, female NKDs exhibit resilience and persevere through the "struggle phase," actively advocating for their children's well-being. Eventually, they enter the "readjustment phase," wherein they recalibrate their life perspectives and navigate the complexities of parenting. In the context of NKD women, the act of child-rearing can provide opportunities for "posttraumatic growth," defined as a positive psychological change experienced because of the struggle with highly challenging life circumstances. Therefore, there is a need for further comprehensive research that reevaluates the experience of parenting among NKDs, considering their inherent strengths such as resilience and adaptability.

Conclusion

Drawing definitive conclusions regarding the intergenerational transmission of trauma among NKD remains challenging. Specifically, with children born in North Korea or in third countries, a heightened susceptibility to direct exposure to trauma complicates whether the youth's mental health issues can be attributed to the multiple traumas experienced by their parents. Moreover, the scarcity of information on the mental health and behavioral outcomes of South Korean–born children of NKDs, who are frequently classified as multicultural families and discriminated against within South Korean society, represents a crucial limitation to research on the intergenerational transmission of trauma. In turn, this information gap continues to impede and restrict comprehensive inquiry into the interplay between trauma exposure of parents and its impact on subsequent generations.

Recently, a significant decline in the entering population of NKDs has occurred ("Korea Ministry of Unification," 2023), necessitating a paradigm shift in policies that support this group from a focus on the initial settlement to a more inclusive approach aimed at establishing stable and fulfilling lives. Specifically, there is a pressing need for policies that foster the growth and well-being of NKDs' children, enabling them to develop into healthy and integrated members of South Korean society. To enhance this policy transition, further research on the intergenerational transmission of trauma is essential, providing empirical evidence to inform and guide sectoral policy development. Furthermore, it is recommended that studies focusing on positive outcomes, including resilience and post-traumatic growth among NKDs, be conducted to elucidate the impact of positive coping mechanisms on the mental well-being of their offspring. Such research endeavors may enhance a more integrated understanding of intricate dynamics before, during, and after defection and support the formulation of evidence-based policies for NKDs.

Notes

1 North Korean defectors have three key options for defection: motivation, money, and brokers. ("BBC News Korea," 2023) Since the mid-2000s, there has been rapid growth

in the number of North Korean defectors entering South Korea through North Korean defector brokers (Lee, 2015). Many of these brokers are former NKDs who have reentered China or are connected with local Chinese brokers to facilitate the entry of NKDs into South Korea. These brokers operate clandestine networks and have established diversified routes for defection, creating a system that helps NKDs cross from China to Southeast Asia and then to South Korea (Kim, 2015b). Brokers typically charged around $15,000 per defector before COVID-19 pandemics (Kim, 2021). Apart from the bribes to North Korean border guards and fees paid to Chinese collaborators, brokers keep approximately 10% as profit (Kim, 2020). Many brokers see themselves as protectors of human rights, as they help NKDs who face the risk of forced repatriation. However, many NKDs experience various human rights abuses during defection, despite paying fees to brokers. In particular, brokers have developed a post-payment business model, where the costs paid to brokers are equivalent to the resettlement support funds that NKDs are guaranteed to receive upon completion of the mandatory training program from the South Korean government. There are mixed perspectives on brokers, as some argue that they exploit the unstable situation of NKDs for profit, while most NKDs see brokers as essential guides on their journey to freedom (Kim, 2015b).

2 "Chosun-jok" refers to the descendants of immigrants from the Korean Peninsula who predominantly reside in China, mainly in the northeastern regions such as Liaoning, Jilin, and Heilongjiang provinces. The immigration took place in the late 19th and early 20th centuries due to economic hardships and political instability on the Korean Peninsula. The nationality of "Chosun-jok" is of Chinese.

3 This study is part of a nationally funded five-year project "Development of complex post-traumatic stress disorder (C-PTSD) measure based on biomarkers and identification of social factors affecting recovery from C-PTSD in North Korean defectors (PI: Sang Hui Chu, 2019–2024)" supported by the National Research Foundation (NRF) of Korea (2019R1I1A2A01058746). This chapter was also supported by this grant (2019R1I1A2A01058746).

4 Hanawon is a South Korean government resettlement facility that all NKDs must complete before integrating into society. Funded by Korea's Ministry of Unification, Hanawon aims to prepare defectors for future careers by training them for social adaptation in South Korea. After undergoing interrogations by the National Intelligence Service (NIS), defectors attend Hanawon. During their 12-week residency, defectors receive education on essential life skills, including ATM usage, public transportation, workplace etiquette, and mobile phone usage. NKDs also undergo physical examinations and counseling sessions and learn about democracy, human rights, and capitalism. Hanawon organizes group outings to familiarize defectors with local amenities of banks, grocery stores, and the use of public transportation and offers classes in various occupations, such as sewing, cooking, nursing care, and skin care ("BBC News Korea," 2023). Upon completing the program, NKDs receive resettlement support, including 10 million Korean Won (approximately US$8,000) for single-person households housing arrangements, and South Korean citizenship. Additional financial aid is available for NKDs, along with housing and education subsidies ("Korea Ministry of Unification," 2024). For further details, see Kim (2023).

5 In South Korea, influenced by the longstanding Confucian culture, there is a tendency to emphasize social hierarchy based on age. This is also evident in schools, where a cultural norm of senior–junior relationships is established through assigned grades according to age. However, among NKDs, there is often a significant educational gap, resulting in their enrollment in lower grades compared to their South Korean peers. While they are expected to receive senior treatment based on age, the discomfort arises from being in lower grades due to their academic background. An older NKD with lower academic qualifications may find it challenging to tolerate being dismissed or ignored by younger South Korean peers. This situation could potentially lead to confrontation due to the frustration of not being able to tolerate such disregard.

References

Abidin, R. R., & Wilfong, E. (1989). Parenting stress and its relationship to child health care. *Children's Health Care*, *18*(2), 114–116. https://doi.org/10.1207/s15326888chc1802_9

Baik, J., Yoon, Y. J., Gibson, P., Lo, N., Nam, H. E., Im, Y. J., & Lee, H. Y. (2021). Mothering and mothered during defection and resettlement: Experiences of North Korean refugee women and their children. *Children and Youth Services Review*, *130*, 106242.

BBC News Korea. (July 11, 2023). *What is Hanawon, a facility that all North Korean defectors must go through?* Retreived January 28, 2024, from www.bbc.com/korean/news-66152972

Cho, S. H., Sung, J. H., & Shin, E. J. (2019). Domestic violence and it's effects on North Korean female defectors' mental health. *Journal Local History Culture*, *22*(1), 251–278. https://doi.org/10.23013/LOCALH.2019.22.1.009

Chung, Y. C. (2009). Society in disarray: Crime, corruption and deepening cognitive Dissonance in North Korea. *Global Asia*, *4*(2), 26–32.

Dalgaard, N. T., & Montgomery, E. (2017). The transgenerational transmission of refugee trauma: Family functioning and children's psychosocial adjustment. *International Journal of Migration, Health and Social Care*, *13*(3), 289–301.

Flanagan, N., Travers, A., Vallières, F., Hansen, M., Halpin, R., Sheaf, G., Rottmann, N., Johnsen, A. T. (2020). Crossing borders: A systematic review identifying potential mechanisms of intergenerational trauma transmission in asylum-seeking and refugee families. *European Journal of Psychotraumatology*, *11*(1), 1790283. https://doi.org/10.1080/20008198.2020.1790283

Hameed, S., Sadiq, A., & Din, A. U. (2018). The increased vulnerability of refugee population to mental health disorders. *Kansas Journal of Medicine*, *11*(1), 20–23. https://doi.org/10.17161/kjm.v11i1.8680

Han, S. O., & Lee, G. S. (2014). The meaning and experience of marriage between North Korean female defector and South Korean man. *Journal of Womens Studies*, *24*(2), 197–233. https://doi.org/10.22772/PNUJWS.24.2.201406.197

Hong, N. M., Lee, I. J., Kim, G. E., Park, K. H., & Choi, Y. H. (2010). Study on the experience of defecting North Korea women in South Korea: Grounded theory. *Korean Journal of Social Welfare Studies*, *41*(1), 307–343. https://doi.org/10.16999/KASWS.2010.41.1.307

Hong, N. R., & Kim, H. J. (2013). The child-rearing attitudes and social support of North Korean immigrant mothers and Korean low-income mothers with young children. *Journal of Future Early Childhood Education*, *20*(4), 217–236. https://repo.kicce.re.kr/handle/2019.oak/5132

Isobel, S., Goodyear, M., Furness, T., & Foster, K. (2019). Preventing intergenerational trauma transmission: A critical interpretive synthesis. *Journal of Clinical Nursing*, *28*(7–8), 1100–1113. https://doi.org/10.1111/jocn.14735

Jeong, J. Y., & Park, J.R. (2016). A phenomenological study on before and after immigration experiences of North Korean defectors' children born in the third countries into South Korea. *Journal of Youth Welfare*, *18*(4), 219–250. https://doi.org/10.19034/KAYW.2016.18.4.10

Jo, H. Y., Kim, M. K., & Lee, M. O. (2013). Realities and difficulties of English education for young children of North Korean refugee mothers. *Journal of Korean Child Care and Education*, *9*(5), 201–228. https://doi.org/10.14698/JKCCE.2013.9.5.201

Jung, D. J. (2016). Survey analysis of the effects of North Koreans' exposure to South Korean culture on their attitudes toward unification. *Journal of Peace and Unification Studies*, *8*(2), 111–148. https://doi.org/10.35369/JPUS.8.2.201612.111

Jung, E. I. (2009). A study on the organic developmental process of markets in North Korea: focusing on the march of hardship in 1990s. *The Korean Journal of Unification Affairs*, *21*(2), 157–200.

Kelstrup, L., & Carlsson, J. (2022). Trauma-affected refugees and their non-exposed children: A review of risk and protective factors for trauma transmission. *Psychiatry Research, 314*, 114604. https://doi.org/10.1016/j.psychres.2022.114604

Kim, C. H., Shin, H. S., & Lee, E. J. (2016). *A Study on the Relative Vulnerability of Youths with a Background of Defection from North Korea*. Seoul: Korea Peace Institute.

Kim, H. (2015a). A qualitative study on the exploration of connected possibilities from the limited life of second generation North Korean refugees born in a third country: From North Korean parent's perspective. *Gender and Culture, 8*(1), 161–200.

Kim, H. J., & Lee, S. Y. (2016). North Korean refugee children's separation experiences and level of attachment. *Korean Journal of Child Studies, 37*(1), 17–36. https://doi.org/10.5723/kjcs.2016.37.1.17

Kim, J. W. (2022). A critical review of the categorization of 'North Korean defector youths'. *Korean Journal of Reunification Education, 19*(1), 161–189.

Kim, J. Y., Ryu, W. J., & Kim, J. M. (2014). A study on daily life stress and depression – moderating effect of traumatic event. *Korean Journal of Family Social Work, 46*(46), 85–107. https://doi.org/10.16975/kjfsw.2014..46.004

Kim, K. J. (2015b). *East-Asia Refugee Network and the Role of Non-State Actors: Focusing on Missionaries and North Korean Brokers* [Master's thesis, Seoul National University]. dCollection@snu. https://hdl.handle.net/10371/134202

Kim, M. S. (2020.04.06). *Selling Kimch, Doing Manual Labor . . . North Korean Brokers Facing a Slump in Business*. Chosunilbo. www.chosun.com/site/data/html_dir/2020/04/06/2020040603263.html

Kim, M. Y., & Park, D. Y. (2009). Parenting stress, depression and verbal abuse of infant's mothers. *J Korean Acad Child Health Nurs, 15*(4), 375. https://doi.org/10.4094/jkachn.2009.15.4.375

Kim, P. (1998). The impact of North Korea's food shortage on social integration. *International Journal of Korean Unification Studies, 7*(1), 133–162.

Kim, S. K. (2018). Representation of North Korean women defectors' image in the South Korean marriage market. *The Women's Studies, 2*, 232–259. https://doi.org/10.33949/TWS.2018.97.2.008

Kim, S. K. (2023). *A Study on the Improvement of Settlement Support Systems for North Korean Defectors with a Focus on Citizen Participation Activation*. Seoul: National Institute for Unification Education.

Kim, S. N., & Yang, O. K. (2015). Qualitative study on the experiences of child care and education among North Korean refugee mothers. *Social Work Practice & Research, 12*(1), 5–37. https://doi.org/10.36431/JPE.11.4.12

Kim, T., & Noh, C. Y. (2003). North Korean female defectors' voices: Hermeneutical phenomenological analysis of the lived experiences in China. *Journal of the Korean Home Economics Association, 41*(8), 1–17.

Kim, Y. (September 10, 2021). North Korean brokers changing professions due to COVID-19 face a network crisis, impacting North Korean defectors. *VOA*. Retreived Januaey 28, 2024, from www.voakorea.com/a/6220383.html

Korea Educational Development Institute Education Support Center for North Korean Refugee Youth. (2023). *Statistics on North Korean Defector Students*. Retrieved January 23, 2024, from www.hub4u.or.kr/usr/portal/board/146/commonBbsDetail.do?p_pageno=1&p_listscale=10&p_bbs_id=146&p_srch_type=p_srch_pst_title_cntnt&p_pst_id=8326&p_srch_text=

Korea Hana Foundation. (2022). *Social Integration Survey of North Korean Refugees in South Korea*. Retrieved January 23, 2024, from www.koreahana.or.kr/home/kor/promotionData/information/researchData/index.do?menuPos=136&ptSignature=9X4DehSmer8YLPvPCbYgoPURxJ2AjIrFojf5JENBKjOiZQSnb%2FUUuWJSVLbWAI6x9vzQF2RuvWKmwt575I2HIYhvaQE65vIisXDIMyQHPrQ%3D&idx=&act=&searchKeyword=&pageIndex=1

Korea Hana Foundation. (2023). *Settlement Survey of North Korean Refugees in South Korea*. Retrieved January 23, 2024, from www.koreahana.or.kr/home/kor/promotionData/information/researchData/index.do?ptSignature=QnrvtOekxiPklgsn74dfsYRAqgXaIX2EzU5d7cx8ePM%3D&menuPos=136

Korea Ministry of Unification. (2023). *North Korean Refugees Entry Status*. Retrieved January 23, 2024, from https://unikorea.go.kr/unikorea/business/NKDefectorsPolicy/status/lately/

Korea Ministry of Unification. (January 8, 2024). *Highlighting Ministry of Unification Policies in 2024*. Retreived January 23, 2024, from https://unikorea.go.kr/unikorea/news/release/?boardId=bbs_0000000000000004&mode=view&cntId=55323&category=&pageIdx=2

Korea National Statistical Office. (2010). *North Korea's Key Statistical Indicators*. Retrieved June 31, 2023, from https://kosis.kr/bukhan/nsoPblictn/selectNkStatsIdct.do?menuId=M_03

Korea National Statistical Office. (2020). *Korean Women's Lives Based on Statistics*. Retrieved June 30, 2023, from https://kostat.go.kr/board.es?mid=a10301060100&bid=10820&tag=&act=view&list_no=384858&ref_bid=218,219,220,10820,11815,11895,11816,208

Lee, E-S., Lee, Y., & Park, S. (2019). Mental health problems of North Korean refugee youths in South Korea: Literature review of empirical studies. *Journal of the Korean Association of Social Psychiatry, 24*(2), 37–47.

Lee, H. I. (October 5, 2015). *Research on Measures to Provide Judicial Assistance to North Korean Defectors*. Goyang-si: Judicial Policy Research Institute.

Lee, H. J. (2011). The structural abuses of human rights and coping methods that women defectors from North Korea: Focusing on relationships with the opposite sex in emigrant experience. *Peace Studies, 19*(2), 367–404.

Lee, I.-S., & Jeon, J.-H. (2021). Influence of parenting efficacy, parenting stress, and acculturation stress on parent-child relations among North Korean refugee mothers. *Child Health Nursing Research, 27*(2), 171–180.

Lee, I.-S., & Jeon, J.-H. (2022). Influence of hardness, mother-child interactions, and social support on parenting stress among North Korean refugee mothers: A cross-sectional study. *Child Health Nursing Research, 28*(4), 269–279.

Lee, I. S., Park, H. R., Park, H. J., & Park, Y. H. (2010). Relationships between Parenting Behavior, Parenting Efficacy, Adaptation Stress and Post Traumatic Stress Disorder among Mothers who Defected from North Korean. *Journal of Korean Academy of Child Health Nursing, 16*(4), 360–368. https://doi.org/10.4094/jkachn.2010.16.4.360

Lee, K. E., An, J. H., & Kim, D. E. (2018). Clinical characteristics of post-traumatic stress disorder among North Korean defectors. *Anxiety and Mood, 14*(2), 80–87. https://doi.org/10.24986/anxmod.2018.14.2.80

Lee, Y. J., Kim, M. J., & Kim, H. S. (2020). *A Study on the Status of Child Care and Support Plan of Poor Single-Parent Families of North Korean Refugees*. Seoul: Korea Institute of Child Care and Education.

Lee, Y. J., Park, C. H., & Kim, M. J. (2021). *A Study on Support for Early Children of North Korean Defector Families for Reducing the Social Gap*. Seoul: Korea Institute of Child Care and Education.

Lee, Y. S., Ku, H. W., & Han, I. Y. (2011). Systematic reviews of North Korean refugees: Women's distinguishable experience. *The Korean Journal of Unification Affairs, 23*(2), 147–194.

Moon, S. J., Kim, J. H., & Lee, M. K. (2000). A study on the motive of escape from the North Korea and the life situation of female fugitives in China: Based on the interview with North Korean female refugees in Yenben Province. *Journal of the Korean Home Economics Association, 38*(5), 137–152.

National Unification Education Institute. (2023). *Understanding North Korea*. Retrieved August 2, 2023, from www.unikorea.go.kr/books/understand/understand/

Park, H.-J., Kim, Y.-S., & Park, H.-R. (2011). Grounded theory approach to transition process of parenting experience among mothers defecting from North Korean. *Journal of Korean Academy of Child Health Nursing, 17*, 48–57.

Park, J., Catani, C., Hermenau, K., & Elbert, T. (2019). Exposure to family and organized violence and associated mental health in North Korean refugee youth compared to South Korean youth. *Conflict and Health, 13*, 1–12. https://doi.org/10.1186/s13031-019-0230-0

Ryu, W., & Yang, H. (2021). A qualitative case study on influencing factors of parents' child abuse of North Korean refugees in South Korea. *Healthcare, 9*(1), 49. https://doi.org/10.3390/healthcare9010049

Sangalang, C. C., Jager, J., & Harachi, T. W. (2017). Effects of maternal traumatic distress on family functioning and child mental health: An examination of Southeast Asian refugee families in the US. *Social Science & Medicine, 184*, 178–186. https://doi.org/10.1016/j.socscimed.2017.04.032

Sangalang, C. C., & Vang, C. (2017). Intergenerational trauma in refugee families: A systematic review. *Journal of Immigrant and Minority Health, 19*(3), 745–754. https://doi.org/10.1007/s10903-016-0499-7

Song, I. H. (2012). A study on the validity of the contract signed between North Korean defector and broker. *Human Rights and Justice, 423*, 43–59. https://doi.org/10.22999/HRAJ..423.201202.003

Taraban, L., & Shaw, D. S. (2018). Parenting in context: Revisiting Belsky's classic process of parenting model in early childhood. *Developmental Review, 48*, 55–81. https://doi.org/10.1016/j.dr.2018.03.006

Thoruo, N., & Mongomery, E. (2017). The transgenerational transmission of refugee trauma: family functioning and children's psychosocial adjustment. *International Journal of Migration, Health, Social Care, 13*(3), 289–301. https://doi.org/10.1108/IJMHSC-06-2016-0024

Wang, Y. S. (2022). *A Study on the Work-Family Balance of Women Migrants in Korean Society: Focusing on Female North Korean Defectors*. [Doctoral dissertation, Seoul National University]. Seoul National University, Graduate School of International Studies (GSIS), South Korea. Retrieved October 3, 2023, from www.riss.kr/link?id=T16164271

14 Learning Refugee Trauma and Politics through Community Arts Organizing

Phi Hong Su

Introduction

Forty years after his death in 1969, the ghost of Communist leader, Ho Chi Minh, continued to haunt Little Saigon, CA, the capital of the Vietnamese in exile (Brody, 1987). In 2009, anti-communists demonstrated against an exhibit, "F.O.B. II: Art Speaks," organized by the Vietnamese American Arts and Letters Association (VAALA). Protesters rallied against a photograph of a woman sitting next to a bust of Ho and wearing the red flag of the Socialist Republic of Vietnam as a tank top. According to one of the exhibit co-curators, Tram Le,[1] the woman's tank top suggests that the flag is "very commercialized in a communist country." The artwork was a diptych, meant to be viewed alongside a second photo of a Vietnamese man in a Western setting "holding an empty bird cage that's open . . . He's free" (P. H. Su, Personal interview with Tram Le, Ontario, CA, December 27, 2011). Yet, an editorial in the *Los Angeles Times* focused only on the photo that featured the red flag and bust (Tran, 2009). Opening with a reminder that the last public display of this flag "ignited 53 days of angry street protests" (Tran, 2009, para.2), the article sparked demonstrations against VAALA. The city of Santa Ana claimed VAALA lacked proper event permits, and the organization subsequently shuttered its exhibit.

Protesters framed VAALA organizers as children who were behaving insubordinately, and moved swiftly to discipline them. Protesters trained their ire on three daughters of refugees: the two curators of the exhibit, Lan Duong and Tram Le, and VAALA's Executive Director, Ysa Lê. As Lan described, the protesters claimed, "we needed to apologize to our elders because they're the ones who taught us and reared us and bought us to the 'shores of freedom' – that's the quote" (P. H. Su, Personal interview with Lan Duong, Los Angeles, CA, October 23, 2011). Vietnamese-language outlets condemned the women in infantilizing and sexually violent language.

The ordeal that "F.O.B. II" organizers faced raises key questions of whether and how community arts organizing can allow for prohibited conversations. To explore how organizers continue their work after backlash, I began to volunteer with VAALA in summer 2010. I served on the organizing committee for VAALA's 2011 Vietnamese International Film Festival (ViFF). After the festival, I interviewed 20 core organizers (henceforth, ViFFers).

DOI: 10.4324/9781003385820-15

In an earlier version of this chapter, I argued that the children of refugees in this study learn about Cold War politics outside of the family setting through treating Vietnamese ethnic nationhood as a militarized imagined family.[2] Vietnamese ethnonational identity is framed as a *family* because it prescribes social roles to members in a hierarchical fashion (Seol & Skrentny, 2009). It is *imagined* because it eschews connections with all of the potential members of said community (Anderson, 2016). Finally, the Vietnamese imagined family is *militarized* because war created the conditions for the mass migration of Vietnamese (as well as Cubans, Poles, and many more) to the United States (Eckstein, 2009; Erdmans, 1998). The central figure in this militarized imagined family is the refugee soldier,[3] reflecting the masculinist enterprise of nationalism (Nagel, 1998). The war he fought continues to be refracted through "silences, emerging as fragmented knowledges of the war and denied access to family history" (Baik, 2020, pp. 69–70).

This chapter explores how Vietnameseness is imbued with militarism, patriarchy, debt, and discipline, and it marshals these threads to explore how generational trauma can be a tool for teaching and learning an ethnonational identity. The chapter focuses on how the children of refugees learn through silences. As Cho (2008) observes, "It is precisely within the gap in conscious knowledge about one's family history that secrets turn into phantoms" (p. 11). Beyond silences and gaps, the children of refugees also learn through fragments, which Kwan (2020) defines as "snippets of information about suffering that lack contextualization" (p. 30).

I am interested in how children of refugees imperfectly fill in the gaps, seeking to reassemble the experiences they imagine their parents' generation to have had. I will show that as my interlocutors reconstruct the wartime experiences and exodus of their parents' generation, they deepen their understanding of what it means to be Vietnamese. In line with Cho (2008) and others who have offered related analyses, I affirm that "it is not enough to say that the diaspora is transgenerationally haunted by the unspoken traumas of war; it is constituted by that haunting" (p. 12).

What follow is a story of generations and trauma, but not strictly a story of generational trauma – not if the term implies transmission directly through the family or from one migratory generation to the next. To be sure, observers have noted that at "the center of Vietnamese America is a clash, a conflict between generations" (Collet & Selden, 2003, p. 200), the younger of whom do not concern themselves much with homeland politics. Yet younger Vietnamese Americans also protested against "F.O.B. II" (Duong & Pelaud, 2012, p. 249). And among ViFFers, the 1.5 and 2nd generations spanned decades, such that some 1.5-generation ViFFers had been born during the war, and others in the 1980s and 1990s. Hence, a generational framing misses the importance of the imagined family in passing on not just political beliefs, but core identities.

Participant-Observation in Little Saigon

My foray into participant-observation with ViFF began with biweekly meetings, rides, and meals with organizers. I received permission from the VAALA

Executive Director, Ysa, to volunteer starting in summer 2010. Ysa was no stranger to the involvement of academics in VAALA: the Board of Directors then included four professors. ViFF planning began in the autumn, with roughly a dozen ViFFers attending each meeting. Women frequently outnumbered men at these meetings.[4] ViFFers ranged in age from 19 to mid-50s, and included largely 1.5- and 2nd-generation participants. Those with previous experience organizing in Little Saigon tended to be in their 30s and 40s, while younger ViFFers tended to be in our 20s.

Many ViFFers were the children of refugees who had either escaped Vietnam by boat or resettled with their families through Humanitarian Operation, which allowed former reeducation camp prisoners to move to the United States. Approximately 120,000 refugees were processed at Camp Pendleton in southern California during the first wave of arrival (Võ, 2008; Võ & Danico, 2004).[5] Despite racial resentment, refugees began to buy homes, open businesses, and revitalize the local economy (Nguyen, 2017; Võ, 2008). They did so in a Cold War context bolstered by Republican politicians, in a national context that would see Vietnamese American communities similarly develop and protest against communism in Texas, Massachusetts, and northern California (Aguilar-San Juan, 2009; Bloemraad, 2006; Brettell & Reed-Danahay, 2011). These protests, in general, and the "F.O.B. II" controversy, in particular, set the stage for deliberation around a documentary that was critical of first-generation anti-communists.

As part of the ViFF organizing committee, I participated in discussions of *Enforcing the Silence* (*ETS*) (Nguyen, 2011), which retraced the murder of a Vietnamese American community organizer, Lam Duong, ostensibly for his leftist leanings. Shortly after his execution on a San Francisco street in broad daylight, a Vietnamese American anti-communist organization published a letter claiming responsibility. Decades later, many Vietnamese Americans still do not know about the violence committed by and against coethnics who were perceived to be communist (Le, 2009).

Despite the screening committee's unanimous decision to show the film, the larger organizing committee voted weeks later to overturn this decision. We engaged in what some described as self-censorship, which others framed as respecting our elders and the traumas (we assumed) they carried. After the film festival concluded, I interviewed ViFFers about, among other things, the decision to reject *ETS* from the film festival.

Teaching and Learning Refugee Trauma and Politics in a Community Setting

Like other Cold War refugees and immigrants to the United States, young Vietnamese Americans participating in ViFF would come to learn that certain images, references, and ideologies were unacceptable. Young ViFFers like me discerned these lessons even though few of us had ever spoken with our parents about the war. Instead, we learned these lessons through strangely charged conversations about artistic freedom or wanting to visit Vietnam. We learned through subconsciously mirroring others' frowns as they discussed their fears of backlash. We came to interpret these lessons as a reminder of the suffering of our elders.

The clearest example of ViFFers learning and teaching refugee trauma and politics in a community setting followed from discussions of *ETS*. Plied with Vietnamese food, a dozen ViFFers sat cheerfully around Ysa's dining room one afternoon to discuss films under consideration. These included romantic comedies, films addressing themes of youth and labor, and shorts showing slices of everyday life. We laughed ourselves red in the face as we discussed a film that was so unintentionally sidesplitting, we considered offering it as a midnight cult screening.

The discussion of *ETS*, however, marked an end to the hilarity that preceded. Lan, one of the "F.O.B. II" organizers, shared that the screening committee voted unanimously to include *ETS* in the festival and, because of that, "[w]e need to prepare for protest, prepare for backlash because of the subject matter" (P.H. Su, Ethnographic observations, Fountain Valley, CA, February 27, 2011). As we devise ways to offset protest, Ysa probed whether screening this film will be worth potential backlash, given the fallout of "F.O.B. II": "Is it worth it? Yes" (P.H Su, Ethnographic observations, Fountain Valley, CA, February 27, 2011).

Initially, Lan's and Ysa's willingness to confront backlash communicated to younger ViFFers that some stances are worth defending. As the targets of protesters' rage during "F.O.B. II," Lan and Ysa did not shy from controversy. After all, their exhibit aimed to tackle questions of art, censorship, and politics following other instances of protest (Bui, 2018). Soon, the glimpses into their personal histories would signal to younger ViFFers that Ysa and Lan know intimately the costs of mounting such a defense. For now, the organizing team confidently invokes our charge to provide a platform for Vietnamese diasporic storytelling. Nick, a second-generation college student is in his early 20s who is relatively new to ViFF, pulled up the mission statement of the arts organization, read it verbatim, and noted that on that basis alone, he supported showing *ETS*. Yet despite Nick's point and the resolution of the older, more experienced ViFFers to defend artistic expression, the faces that were just laughing uncontrollably minutes ago have turned grave.

When we met at the VAALA studio the following week to discuss how to screen *ETS*, the conversation veered into whether to do so at all. As the conversation shifted, Adrienne, a second-generation ViFFer, defended the documentary as "acknowledging that [the murder] did happen," and as inviting people to "share space with other 2nd-generation filmmakers about addressing a disconnect in our community" (P.H. Su, Ethnographic observations, Santa Ana, CA, March 6, 2011). As Adrienne would later recount in an interview, this conversation paralleled her feelings of helplessness witnessing the fallout over "F.O.B. II" (P.H. Su, Personal interview with Adrienne (pseudonym), Diamond Bar, CA, May 28, 2011). She gleaned the scale and depth of anti-communist resentment through watching her fellow organizers shouted down in their own community space. Long T. Bui, one of the artists whose work was targeted during "F.O.B. II," likewise experienced being "put in [his] place" as a child of the community, despite being an adult at the time of the exhibit (Bui, 2018, p. 99). These examples highlight the kinship frames imposed by protesters and, to some extent, internalized by organizers and artists.

Through arts organizing, young ViFFers came to perceive anti-communism as deeply informed by trauma. One example comes from Nick, who initially supported screening *ETS*. As with other young ViFFers, Nick did not learn about refugee politics at home, but in community spaces. Nick's parents did not talk to him about their refugee passages or about protests in Little Saigon. Months after ViFF concluded, Nick sat with me and discussed anti-communist protest with ambivalence. He asserted the importance of freedom of speech, yet equated symbols of Vietnamese communism with "put[ting] up like a cross and burn[ing] it in the middle of a park" (P.H. Su, Personal interview with Nick (pseudonym), Fullerton, CA, September 4, 2011). Nick's desire to show respect to refugees shows how anti-communism as a discourse travels, is taught, and remobilized by young, 1.5- and 2nd-generation ViFFers.

Although the initial conversations around *ETS* seemingly affirmed our resolution to screen the film, the circulation of affect in the room foreshadowed lingering uncertainty. This presence or haunting "draws us affectively . . . into the structure of a feeling of a reality we come to experience, not as cold knowledge, but as transformative recognition" (Gordon, 2008, p. 8). The recognition was of the plight and subsequent resentment of militant anti-communists we imagined could be protesting us. These imaginations drew inspiration from what we saw in films, read in books, and heard in passing. They did not limit themselves to the factual versus the fictional. Indeed, as Gordon (2008) observes, the boundary between story versus fact, literature versus social science is an unstable one (p. 25). My interlocutors and I drew from cultural productions and hearsay to reconstruct the sources of refugee trauma. We did so in a community setting where younger, 1.5- and 2nd-generation ViFFers learned largely from older 1.5-generation ViFFers.

Filling in Narrative Silences and Fragments

Younger ViFFers came to understand that although art allows for some prohibited conversations, these run up against limits when art "would hurt [our parents' generation]." They learned this about "our parents' generation" in the absence of talking to their parents. Indeed, "parents' refusal to talk about their life experiences [meant that] their *past* acted on [their children's] *present*" (emphasis in the original, Cho, 2008, p. 11).[6]

Even as younger, American-born or American-raised ViFFers extol the open-mindedness of their cohort, their reactions to *ETS* illustrate how refugee identities persist over time (Lupu & Peisakhin, 2017). Instead of acquiring their parents' political attitudes directly, young ViFFers note silences in their families around topics of trauma and learn through such silences. In a community setting, ViFFers also learn through hints and insinuations about the protests to which our coorganizers had been subjected. We had fragmented understandings of events, histories, and people. Writing of his grandfather, for example, Viet Thanh Nguyen (2006) notes, "I know this man only by his title, 'my father's father.' I would never be expected to call him by his name even if I had known him" (p. 34). Recognizing that we knew so little about the experiences of our parents' generation, 1.5- and

2nd-generation ViFFers grappled with how our actions as artists and organizers could cause harm.

ViFFers eventually came to see the ethnic nation as a militarized imagined family through reconstructing the trauma of the first generation. By March, we had been discussing *ETS* for weeks, but most ViFFers had not seen the film. We therefore met at Ysa's home to view it together. *ETS* functions in part as a biopic into Lam Duong's life and community organizing, and includes interviews with colleagues and friends who knew him, as well as the FBI agent who investigated his murder. Speaking of the Vietnamese organization that claimed to have carried out the murder, the FBI agent casually states that these people murdered before in Vietnam and likely did so again on American soil.

On the one hand, some older ViFFers' rejected the FBI agent's comments and, in doing so, critiqued American empire, racism, and militarism. These ViFFers expressed dismay with the filmmakers' use of an image of South Vietnamese Brigadier General executing a disguised Viet Cong officer. The filmmaker contrasts this scene with the FBI agent's assertion that Vietnamese had murdered before. Older ViFFers criticized this comment for its racist inability to see South Vietnamese soldiers fighting for their country as legitimate in the way that American soldiers committing violence in a foreign country presumably are.

Older ViFFers also grasped the masculinist – and emasculated – narrative of militarized refugee nationhood. As Tram Le, one of the "F.O.B. II" organizers, explained:

South Vietnamese men felt – feel to this day . . . [that they're] the losers, right? So I think they're always constantly fighting that powerlessness. . . . So that's a huge problem, why I understand why they still protest, why they still dress up in military garb and still, you know, want to reclaim that.
(P. H. Su, Personal interview with Tram Le, Ontario, CA, December 27, 2011)

As Um (2012) writes, "the struggle against forgetting is not only a way of filling a personal voice but also an important political act. What is individual and personal is also collective and national" (p. 843). By staging returns to the war (Bui, 2018), Vietnamese Americans recognize that "[o]ne does not become recognizably human until one acts in one's history" (Nguyên-Vo, 2005, p. 159).

On the other hand, younger ViFFers did not critique militarism at all. Instead, they objected to the unflattering portrayal of Vietnamese former military, who served under compulsions we could not claim to know. Younger ViFFers bristled at the film's treatment of The Front, the organization that claimed responsibility for Lam Duong's murder. In the 1980s, Vietnamese Americans died following The Front back to Vietnam in a secret effort to overthrow the Communist regime (Nguyen, 2017). The film calls this organization "a joke," which one ViFFer considers "ignorant or insensitive to the struggles of our coethnics" (P.H. Su, Ethnographic observations, Fountain Valley, CA, March 6, 2011). According to May, a 1.5-generation ViFFer, "the FBI agent's comment implicates not just anticommunists [who commit violence] . . . but all Vietnamese soldiers" (P.H. Su, Ethnographic observations, Fountain Valley, CA, March 6, 2011). Adds another ViFFer, "These are our fathers, our uncles," conjuring the horrors our male relatives must not only have witnessed, but possibly committed (P.H. Su, Ethnographic observations, Fountain Valley, CA, March 6, 2011).

As they speak of and imagine their coethnics as an extended family, younger ViFFers filled in the gaps, classifying certain scenarios as being "[in]considerate of [our elders'] feelings" (P.H. Su, Personal Interview, Lynn (pseudonym), Garden Grove, CA, August 20, 2011). Lynn, a young ViFFer who was hesitant about screening *ETS*, later recalled her displeasure with the film's discussion of former officers of South Vietnam: "I [would] feel guilty for supporting to show that movie [because it's like] supporting calling all these soldiers murderers" (P.H. Su, Personal Interview, Lynn (pseudonym), Garden Grove, CA, August 20, 2011). Lynn's reading of the political context sat alongside gaps in her knowledge of her own family:

> The thing is my parents never talked to me about the war or whatever so I never knew how – [never] understood why we were here [in the United States]. . . . [And] in high school we learned about the Vietnam War and I never really quite understood it because my dad never really talked about it and never brought it up.
> (P.H. Su, Personal Interview, Lynn (pseudonym),
> Garden Grove, CA, August 20, 2011)

Despite her own indifference to the red flag and reference to Ho Chi Minh, Lynn felt that she could not support art that seemed to "disrespect people's feelings" (P.H. Su, Personal Interview, Lynn (pseudonym), Garden Grove, CA, August 20, 2011).

Although ViFFers tended to sweepingly mention "our parents' generation," Tram's insight above zooms in on which of our imagined parents ViFFers instinctively saw as the victims of war. ViFFers perceive the war as a violent struggle involving male politicians, soldiers, and prisoners of war, producing a crisis of masculinity. The way to recuperate South Vietnamese national pride and to honor the imagined family, then, is to "acknowledge that this refugee soldier is the bearer of much of empire's brutality and the instrumentalization of a modern racial governmentality" (Nguyen, 2012, p. 81). Tram recognized that Vietnamese men had suffered as the losers in their homeland and newcomers seen as in need of tutorial in their host country.

Younger ViFFers – I included – paid more attention to the refugee soldier slighted by racial empire than to the daughterly figures with whom we organized and had come to know over months of meetings and meals. We learned through hearing fragments of their public thrashing that we needed to pay heed to the suffering of our fathers, uncles, brothers. ViFFers thus inferred from the intensity of previous protests that we were potentially courting fierce backlash.

ViFFers feared jeopardizing the militarized imagined family by sharing stories that we saw as diminishing the trauma of the first generation. ViFFers who rejected the film each had different reasons for doing so, but at least some recoiled at what they saw as the filmmakers' "airing out our dirty laundry" (P.H. Su, Ethnographic observations, Santa Ana, CA, March 6, 2011), sullying the image of the male refugee soldier. One younger, second-generation ViFFer read the filmmaker as intentionally "downplaying all that trauma . . . and kind of taking away their feelings" – even though she described her own parents as not "want[ing] anything to do with politics at all" (P.H. Su, Personal interview with Patricia (pseudonym), Westwood, CA, August 31, 2011).

These negotiations highlight the fraught political landscape of community arts in Little Saigon, where organizers envision the default audience to be a militarized imagined family headed by a male refugee soldier. Given the retaliation against VAALA members two years prior, ViFFers had very legitimate reasons to fear more controversy, and it is not my intention to downplay those concerns. I have focused on how younger ViFFers, then in our 20s, came to recognize the magnitude of those fears and to learn about them in a community setting as our older, more experienced coorganizers shared with us their experiences of navigating political minefields.

But we only received snippets from our older coorganizers, and we could only know in a limited way how they experienced backlash in their bodies, in the tension they felt being in Little Saigon. So we pieced together the silences and fragments of our coorganizers' experience of being publicly vilified. We stitched together a version of what unspeakable traumas might have so imprinted our parents' generation that they could not tolerate forms of artistic expression. Assembling these narratives from silences and fragments, we "bec[a]me *members* of that group via the formation of collective memory" (emphasis in the original, Kwan, 2020, p. 32).

Learning Vietnamese American History through Controversy

VAALA's history of controversy cast a shadow over deliberations in ViFF, but not in the way we might expect. Both curators of "F.O.B. II" as well as the VAALA Executive Director continued to organize after facing backlash. They provided "much of the hidden labor that supports community events" (Bui, 2018, p. 99) and vigorously defended cultural producers, the most visible of whom were men, including Bui and Brian Doan. Protests did not break the women's resolve to organize or steer them away from topics of potential ire.

Instead, the history of protest informed VAALA's organizational culture by alerting younger ViFFers to the hurt of the refugee generation. Younger ViFFers rarely dwelled on the violence that "F.O.B. II" organizers faced, decried as unfilial daughters. Instead, we focused on protesters' wrath as a warning to honor the male soldiers whose sacrifices granted us the gift of freedom. In turn, their role as the head of the militarized imagined family demanded our filial piety.

The quest to honor "our parents' generation" is fraught precisely because the narrative gaps around topics of war and loss means that "infractions are typically identified as such only *after the fact*" (emphasis in the original, Ninh, 2011, p. 43). My coorganizers readily recalled times when they had anticipated protest that ultimately did not materialize. When the Los Angeles Asian Pacific Film Festival screened *ETS* on the anniversary of the fall of Saigon, no reprisal followed. Nguyễn-võ Thu-hương and I also did not meet with censure when we screened *ETS* through the UCLA Center for Southeast Asian Studies in 2013.[7] Such inconsistencies mean that "obedience [is] less a question of walking a line than of picking one's way through a field of land mines" (Ninh, 2011, p. 43). This ambiguity works as a form of power that has organizers anticipating and negotiating potential disputes even in the absence of protesters. Organizing with VAALA exposed young ViFFers to "discursive technologies traditionally under the purview of female authorities: the round of gossip, the cautionary tale" (Ninh, 2011, p. 129) that made visible to us the minefield of Little Saigon politics.

Younger ViFFers transformed these cautionary tales into lessons about the pain of the first generation and our need to repay such debts of freedom through filiality. This struck me when, in a course on ethnographic methods at UCLA, I found myself defending the screening decision to my classmates, who had followed along with my fieldnotes all semester. Like some young ViFFers initially expressed, some of my classmates found it "extreme . . . that anyone would protest a picture of a woman wearing a t-shirt" (Bui, 2018, p. 103), or reject a film that bared an important history of coethnic violence. However well-intentioned, my classmates'

> seemingly rational observation that such passion . . . is out of proportion . . . [reveals] 'an underlying assumption that an appropriate emotional response to . . . violence exists, and that the burden lies on the racialized subject to produce that appropriate response legibly, unambiguously, and immediately.
> (Sianne Ngai as cited in Nguyen, 2012, p. 62)

And so it was that I found myself defending the very decision I had voted against.

The result of the decision-making process was not one of intergenerational censorship – after all, we were mostly 1.5- and 2nd-generation organizers across age cohorts. Instead, it was about how anti-communist discourses entwine themselves with the gift of freedom, filial obligation, and the militarized imagined family. Months after ViFF concluded, organizers continued conversations in person and over email about how to best deal with issues of representation, history, and politics in the future. More than a decade on, ViFF's sponsorship from various Vietnamese outlets and businesses is a testament to their ability to navigate occasional spats.

Conclusion

This study has traced how, in the absence of family narratives of trauma, children of refugees learn about histories of war through arts organizing in a community setting. They realize the severity of refugee politics through hearing about fervent protests, including against older coorganizers, and strategizing how to navigate future controversies. Community backlash becomes part of the political education process. Rather than simply being a form of censorship, protests and ensuing discussions convey to young Vietnamese Americans the importance of an issue to older members of the ethnic nation whose experiences we could never fully know.

I have argued that 1.5- and 2nd-generation ViFFers understand the ethnic nation as an imagined family that is inextricably tied to militarism and masculinity. Although younger Vietnamese Americans may veer from their parents' political identities, their implicit understanding of the ethnic nation as a militarized imagined family suggests that they must continue to negotiate politics within a cultural community that invokes debt against and exacts gendered discipline on its members.

The children of refugees learned about the militarized imagined family through silences and fragments. Such silences prevail in many families, "perpetuating both the immediate and the mediated trauma, and contributing to the generational disconnect" (Um, 2012, p. 842). Indeed, trauma can be defined by this "alienation from a family and cultural history" (Kwan, 2020, p. 29). Building on the work of scholars concerned with empire, militarism, Asian American Studies, and critical refugee studies, I have similarly detailed how silences and fragments can be instructive.

Importantly, learning about the traumas of previous generations does not need to be pathological. Nguyên-Vo (2005) powerfully underscores this, and is worth quoting at length:

> The mode of expression in the Vietnamese American community is mournful of loss and evocative of trauma. It is a world of survivors. Is it then melancholia that afflicts Vietnamese American politics?
>
> My answer is no. An approach premised purely on universalist categories of psychoanalytic pathology misses how a response might be historically and contextually formed. Rather than seeing reiterations of Vietnamese immigrant history in war commemorations, in anti-communist demonstrations and local politics as symptoms of melancholic returns because of failed mourning for catastrophic loss, I submit that these are now acts of anamnesis against historical and ongoing erasure of Vietnamese distinct presence by forced forgetting. We must remember because forgetting deprives us of our humanist agency in relation to our history.
>
> (Nguyên-Vo, 2005, pp. 168–169)

Although my time with ViFF and conversations with ViFFers often conjured trauma and war, I have tried to move beyond "damage-centered research, one of the major activities [of which] is to document pain or loss in an individual, community or tribe" (Tuck, 2009, p. 412). To be sure, many Vietnamese Americans experienced pain and loss, including some of older ViFFers who themselves had escaped by boat or the "F.O.B. II" curators who were verbally and physically accosted in public spaces. Yet I emphasized how young ViFFers interpreted this trauma as producing anti-communism. This politics acts as "the vehicle for sustaining an identity and community in the present and serves as a pedagogical tool for the younger generations of Vietnamese Americans" (Dang, 2005, p. 69).

The ViFFers who shared space with me affirm that refugee trauma and politics are not necessarily transmitted through generations in a strictly familial (parent-to-child) or migratory (1st to 2nd) sense. Instead, trauma can be learned and taught outside of the family and can be transmitted within a migratory generation. ViFFers drew on silences within the family to stitch together the traumas that were often unspoken. We also reinjected the fragments we learned in community spaces to make sense of where traumas might reside in our own family and national histories.

Questions of political learning and socialization in a community setting have taken on renewed importance in the political climate following 2020. In the lead-up to the election, young, progressive Vietnamese Americans worked to bring their political convictions from community organizing back into the family setting (Do, 2020). This study of ViFF offers lessons for negotiating politics that individuals learn outside of the family but that intimately resonate with the family, whether biological or imagined.

Notes

1. With their permission, I have identified the two curators of "F.O.B II" and the Executive Director of VAALA, all of whom have appeared by name in publications on the "F.O.B. II" controversy. I have kept the identities of all remaining ViFFers confidential by using pseudonyms and withholding key details about them.
2. A version of this chapter was originally published as Su, P.H. (2021). The Militarized Imagined Family: How Children of Refugees Negotiate Cold War Politics in Community Arts Organizing, *Amerasia Journal*, 47(2), 253–66. https://doi.org/10.1080/00447471.2022.2028533
3. Although semantically similar, my usage differs from the refugee soldier figure, "the purported 'new friend' of freedom and democracy [who is ostensibly treated] as a worthy subject of state recognition and citizenship" (Vang, 2012, p. 686). I am interested in how Vietnamese Americans, rather than the state, construct the image of the refugee soldier who must be revered.
4. During my fieldwork, participants identified as cis men or cis women.
5. For an overview of waves of Vietnamese arrival, see Le, L.K. and Su, P.H. (2018).
6. Cho is citing Ramsay Liem's oral history project, *Still Present Pasts*.
7. Please note that in some publications, her name appears as Thu-Huong Nguyên-Vo.

References

Aguilar-San Juan, K. (2009). *Little Saigons: Staying Vietnamese in America*. Minneapolis and London: University of Minnesota Press.

Anderson, B. (2016). *Imagined Communities*. London: Verso Books.

Baik, C. M. H. (2020). *Reencounters: On the Korean War and Diasporic Memory Critique*. Philadelphia: Temple University Press.

Bloemraad, I. (2006). *Becoming a Citizen: Incorporating Immigrants and Refugees in the United States and Canada*. Berkeley University of California Press.

Brettell, C., & Reed-Danahay, D. (2011). *Civic Engagements: The Citizenship Practices of Indian and Vietnamese Immigrants*. Redwood City: Stanford University Press.

Brody, J. (January 11, 1987). Little Saigon: Vietnamese enclave succeeds the American way. *The Orange County Register*. Retrieved November 5, 2023, from www.ocregister.com/archive/

Bui, L. T. (2018). *Returns of War: South Vietnam and the Price of Refugee Memory*. New York: New York University Press.

Cho, G. M. (2008). *Haunting the Korean Diaspora: Shame, Secrecy, and the Forgotten War*. Minneapolis: University of Minnesota Press.

Collet, C., & Selden, N. (2003). Separate Ways . . . Worlds Apart? The "Generation Gap" in Vietnamese America as Seen Through *The San Jose Mercury News* Poll. *Amerasia Journal*, 29(1), 199–217. https://doi.org/10.17953/amer.29.1.60433200t7277112

Dang, T. V. (2005). The Cultural Work of Anticommunism in the San Diego Vietnamese American Community. *Amerasia Journal*, 31(2), 65–86. https://doi.org/10.17953/amer.31.2.t80283284556j378

Do, A. (November 2, 2020). Young Vietnamese American Progressives Lead a Generational Split with Conservative Elders. *Los Angeles Times*. Retrieved November 15, 2023, from www.latimes.com/california/story/2020-11-02/vietnamese-american-progressive-movement-backs-biden-campaign

Duong, L., & Pelaud, I. T. (2012). Vietnamese American Art and Community Politics: An Engaged Feminist Perspective. *Journal of Asian American Studies*, 15(3), 241–269. https://doi.org/10.1353/jaas.2012.0034

Eckstein, S. E. (2009). *The Immigrant Divide: How Cuban Americans Changed the US and Their Homeland*. London and New York: Routledge.

Erdmans, M. P. (1998). *Opposite Poles: Immigrants and Ethnics in Polish Chicago, 1976–1990*. University Park: The Pennsylvania State University Press.

Gordon, A. (2008). *Ghostly Matters; Haunting and the Sociological Imagination*. Minneapolis: University of Minnesota Press.

Kwan, Y. Y. (2020). Time-Image Episodes and the Construction of Transgenerational Trauma. *Journal of Asian American Studies*, 23(1), 29–59. https://doi.org/10.1353/jaas.2020.0001

Le, C. N. (2009). Better Dead than Red: Anti-Communist Politics among Vietnamese Americans. In Ieva Zake (Ed.), *Anti-Communist Minorities in the U.S.* (pp. 189–209). New York: Palgrave MacMillan.

Le, L. K., & Su, P. H. (2018). Party Identification and the Immigrant Cohort Hypothesis: The Case of Vietnamese Americans. *Politics, Groups, and Identities*, 6(4), 743–763. https://doi.org/10.1080/21565503.2017.1289849

Lupu, N., & Peisakhin, L. (2017). The Legacy of Political Violence across Generations. *American Journal of Political Science*, 61(4), 836–851. https://doi.org/10.1111/ajps.12327

Nagel, J. (1998). Masculinity and Nationalism: Gender and Sexuality in the Making of Nations. *Ethnic and Racial Studies*, 21(2), 242–269. https://doi.org/10.1080/014198798330007

Nguyen, M. T. (2012). *The Gift of Freedom: War, Debt, and Other Refugee Passages*. Durham: Duke University Press.

Nguyen, P. T. (2017). *Becoming Refugee American: The Politics of Rescue in Little Saigon*. Urbana, Springfield, and Chicago: University of Illinois Press.

Nguyen, T. (Director). (2011). *Enforcing the Silence* [Film]. Birjinder Films.

Nguyen, V. T. (2006). Speak of the Dead, Speak of Viet Nam: The Ethics and Aesthetics of Minority Discourse. *CR: The New Centennial Review*, 6(2), 7–37. https://doi.org/10.1353/ncr.2007.0007

Nguyên-Vo, T.H. (2005). Forking Paths: How Shall We Mourn the Dead?. *Amerasia Journal*, 31(2), 157–175. https://doi.org/10.17953/amer.31.2.g232251372h12k78

Ninh, E. K. (2011). *Ingratitude: The Debt-Bound Daughter in Asian American Literature*. New York: New York University Press.

Seol, D. H., & Skrentny, J. D. (2009). Ethnic Return Migration and Hierarchical Nationhood. *Ethnicities*, 9(2), 147–174.

Tran, M. T. (January 10, 2009). Vietnamese Art Exhibit Puts Politics on Sisplay. *Los Angeles Times*. Retrieved September 2, 2023, from www.latimes.com/archives/la-xpm-2009-jan-10-me-vietarts10-story.html.

Tuck, E. (2009). Suspending Damage: A Letter to Communities. *Harvard Educational Review, 79*(3), 409–428.

Um, K. (2012). Exiled Memory: History, Identity, and Remembering in Southeast Asia and Southeast Asian Diaspora. *Position: East Asia Cultures Critique, 20*(3), 831–850. https://doi.org/10.1215/10679847-1593564

Vang, M. (2012). The Refugee Soldier: A Critique of Recognition and Citizenship in the Hmong Veterans' Naturalization Act of 1997. *Positions East Asia Cultures Critique, 20*(3), 685–712. https://doi.org/10.1215/10679847–1593501

Võ, L. T. (2008). Constructing a Vietnamese American Community: Economic and Political Transformation in Little Saigon, Orange County. *Amerasia Journal, 34*(3), 84–109. https://doi.org/10.17953/amer.34.3.8234012rmn866108

Võ, L. T., & Danico, M. Y. (2004). The Formation of Post-Suburban Communities: Koreatown and Little Saigon, Orange County. *International Journal of Sociology and Social Policy, 24*(7/8), 15–45. https://doi.org/10.1108/01443330410791000

15 The Unheard and Unseen Perspectives on Intergenerational Trauma

Nora Parr, Wendy Sims-Schouten, Jenny Phillimore, Heather Flowe, Sarah Rockowitz, Laura Stevens, Tamirace Fakhoury, and Rana Dajani

Introduction

This chapter presents five vignettes of hitherto unheard and unseen experiences of inter/transgenerational trauma in refugee communities. These vignettes present experiences and realities that are largely invisible within existing approaches. They collectively demonstrate the need to expand temporal frameworks of analysis to access the continuums of harm that many refugees live within. These continuums, the vignettes show, span not only generations but also political, national, and social boundaries. Broadening our understanding of the temporalities of intergenerational trauma, we argue, is essential to grasp its meaning, and how experiences of trauma intersect with the long-term consequences of living in and with harm. The vignettes illustrate how diverse methods for temporal exploration can reveal hitherto unaccounted for harms, including how structures of inequality perpetuate harm for refugees beyond their arrival in host location (where temporalities of harm are usually understood to stop); how harms can echo and change across a 100-year timescale in long-term refugee communities; how epigenetics can reframe trauma beyond the individual and community scale and on the level of human genetics. Looking at experiences of refugees in the UK, Jordan, Palestine, and Eritrea/Sudan, we make connections with previously siloed disciplines, expanding the scope of intergenerational trauma research, and indeed the very boundaries of what is understood as intergenerational trauma.

These cases extend the existing limits of work on inter/transgenerational trauma. The field was created to understand the specific experience of trauma across familial generations and shared group trauma (Pearrow & Cosgrove, 2009; George, 2015). This foundational work established that chronic and acute trauma can be long-lasting and be transferred from one generation to another. However, understandings that undergird the definitions this early work set out – from the scope, geography, and temporality of "generation" and the adopted definition of trauma from the field of trauma studies, as some examples – need now to be challenged and elaborated. Many of the approaches and definitions of intergenerational trauma work stem from the centrality of PTSD in trauma research, where trauma is understood as a reaction to a singular event. Scholars have shown that PTSD-informed mental health evaluation is insufficient for capturing the types,

DOI: 10.4324/9781003385820-16

kinds, and magnitudes of non-Western (or non-normative) experiences of harm (Hammoudeh et al., 2013), and demonstrated that existing methods of description fail to adequately assess diverse conditions (Giacaman & Husseini, 2002). Moreover, work on trauma beyond mental health tends to reproduce the temporal limitations encapsulated by the PTSD framework; the idea that trauma happens in a particular space and time, often a space and time that is "other" to the EuroAmerican and that is discrete from the space and time of the everyday.[1] This concept pervades research from all angles, as we outline below.

Historically, studies on trauma and refugees assumed that trauma "ended" when refugees arrived at a host location. Research on sexual- and gender-based violence (SGBV) now acknowledges that there is a continuum of violence and associated trauma which travels with refugees beyond conflict, well into their journey, and continues in refugee camps (Krause, 2015). However, just what this means, and what the traumas of this continuum look like, has received less attention. While some studies address how this continuum extends into refuge where hostile immigration and asylum regimes, destitution, discrimination, and racism generate additional traumas (Hourani et al., 2021), additional research is needed on the full scope of this host-site trauma perpetuation to understand what can be done at a micro- and macro-scale. Exploring the continuum of trauma beyond specific sites requires a socioecological perspective, which shows how existing approaches ignore the real and lasting impacts of oppression, marginalization, racism, and related postmigrant/refugee experiences. Early work suggests a look at the social and structural bias in contexts that profess to help refugees in new host contexts can provide a broader framework that accounts for the continued legacies of trauma.

Work on child migration has a different set of assumptions and limitations. Here, the idea is that trauma (as a largely singular event) is passed on through epigenetic inheritance, parental mental health/history, family structure, attachment quality, and additional stress and life events. Research focusing on PTSD in refugees has shown that this type of intergenerational trauma is associated with harsh parenting styles, leading to adverse effects on children's mental health. Thus, inter/transgenerational trauma is understood as a singularity that ripples. Research from these findings suggested the need for child mental health programs that consider parental and caregiver-related parenting behaviors that pass traumas along to children along this path (Sangalang & Vang, 2017). While the focus on familial factors and stressors in passing down trauma between generations provides opportunities for treatment and support, its methodologies – looking at the known experiences of trauma survivors and documenting behavior toward their children – limits the temporal frameworks for intergenerational harm. The work requires in-depth oral testimony from multiple living generations. The framework also continues a narrative that pathologizes certain groups, in this case migrants and refugees, and ignores wider societal factors and structures that can maintain or exacerbate the trauma, such as marginalization, discrimination, and disadvantage that these communities often inherit in their "host" locations/locations of displacement. In focusing on trauma as a singular event and understanding inter/transgenerational trauma as simply the passing on of an experience, wider social mechanisms that perpetuate trauma are left unacknowledged.

Expanding thinking about trauma into a "before," a socio-ecological approach draws on cognitive psychology theory to understand how perception of trauma affects not only its experience but also the harms that can happen "after." This demands a blurring of the event-based temporal model and puts focus onto the larger social systems that trauma takes places within. Work outlined in this chapter shows how metacognition, or the psychological perception of PTSD symptoms, can precondition or otherwise determine both personal and communal responses to traumatic events. New work on trauma from this socio-ecological perspective suggests that programs can adopt a long-term perspective in addressing the perception of harm and change the reaction to harm when it happens. Rather than a start and an end that create ripples, this new approach asks the field to widen its temporal perspective to understand trauma and our responses to it in socio-ecological terms.

Literary interpretations have traditionally shared the limited view of trauma as a time-specific phenomenon that rippled across history (Craps et al., 2016). Focus was directed to the ways and mechanisms through which the ripples affected future generations. However, work from postcolonial theorists has challenged this framework, and argued that colonialism itself has caused long-time harm that has gone unacknowledged in existing paradigms (Visser, 2015). While limits were acknowledged, there remains little work that defines or outlines the parameters of alternative understandings of trauma. Further, literary approaches have largely failed to take advantage of the historical possibility in texts preserved across generations. Understanding the meaning of intergenerational trauma beyond a single text, or representations of a single event/phenomena, might then be carried out in readings from across time in a refugee community. Using a larger pool of literary sources allows for a tracing of meaning, changes, consistencies, and understanding the relationship between time and trauma in a much broader frame.

Epigenetics widens the scope of trauma research and refugees even further. It is rare that scholars focus on the impact of trauma on the creation of mechanisms – biological and sociological – that have helped individuals and societies endure. This re-focus requires a temporal shift in research perspective and toward evolutionary history. On an evolutionary scale, there is no such thing as a singular event; trauma happens on a continuum. The tools, strategies, and approaches traditionally employed and deployed fail to function when one looks at trauma as a continuum, because the whole framework is different. Smeeth et al. (2021) discuss a new conceptual model for epigenetic mechanisms in psychological resilience which understands epigenome formation to be the result of exposure to a complex environment of harm and protection in the life history of the individual. This angle of exploration is nascent, and much has yet to be done from an epigenetic point of view to understand the impact of trauma on communities and humans.

New approaches make different traumas visible. This chapter collectively broadens current perspectives and shows that trauma across generations must be explored through a multitude of temporal perspectives.

Intergenerational/Transgenerational Trauma through a Socio-Ecological Lens: Learning from Historic Examples of (Child) Migration

This vignette focuses on how certain events – such as "perceived" discrimination, marginalization, or racism – can be triggers of trauma, leading to "certain" (pathological) reactions and "bad" behaviors. We see this happen, for example, when displaced families/children, unaccompanied minors, and ethnic minority children are positioned within a lower social class/hierarchy and stigmatized as less important than other children/families (Kootstra, 2016). The status of "refugee" or "asylum seeker" is frequently treated as synonymous with the stereotype of delinquency and placed within a "classed/racialized hierarchy" that stigmatizes individuals as less important than others (McLaughlin, 2018; Hopkins & Hill, 2010). To address this, we need to focus on the lasting impact and legacy of the oppressive and dominating (white) society's sociopathy, classism, and eugenics (Sims-Schouten & Gilbert, 2022).

Such a shift means moving away from framing cases of inter/transgenerational trauma through deficit models of health, and instead providing a framework for making sense of meaningful and deeply embedded histories of segregation, stigma, and political violence. This vignette looks at inter/transgenerational trauma through a socio-ecological lens, while incorporating culture and social ecological aspects of trauma and resilience as well as acknowledging the crucial role of community and culture in making sense of lived experiences, including a focus on health resources and experiences. The socio-ecological framework proposes a multidimensional definition of trauma and related interventions, centered on intrapersonal, interpersonal, organizational, environmental, and public policy factors (Harvey, 1996; Kilanowski, 2017). At the core of the model is the person–community relationship and "ecological fit" within individually varied recovery contexts. The role of social structures of inequality, marginalization, disadvantage, and discrimination at the root of trauma can be vividly extracted through the critical discussion and analysis of several historical and contemporary examples of (child) migration. We will share a story of a former Windrush child, from the generation of people arriving in the UK from Caribbean countries between 1948 and 1973. This story originates from an academic at a British University and a former Windrush child[2] who reflects on her time in North England after arriving there from the Caribbean in the late 1950s:

> It was a complicated place in terms of race. A teenager called Sheila lived up the road from us and used to look after me as a babysitter. Her white British family were fairly open and Sheila became quite close to my mum and dad. But in that very English way, things could quickly close down. If their families were visiting, they wouldn't let it be known that they were friends with us or anybody in our house. Situations could turn, and suddenly a racist comment like "jungle bunny" or "blackie" or "wog" or "sambo" would be made . . . It left its mark. In these Brexit times, I'm very alive to overhearing bits of racist commentary, to people not quite looking you in the

eye and slightly avoiding touching you. These behaviors echo through the generations.

(as cited in Brinkhurst-Cuff, 2019, p. 85)

Inter/transgenerational trauma linked to racism and oppression are well documented. For example, there are multiple studies on post-traumatic slave syndrome (PTSS), the passing on of psychological and emotional trauma from slavery (DeGruy, 2005; George, 2015; Leigh & Davis, 2017). Yet, by referring to this as a syndrome, there is the danger that cases of transgenerational/intergenerational trauma are framed through deficit models of health, instead of providing a framework for making sense of meaningful and deeply embedded histories of segregation, stigma, and political violence. Taking a socio-ecological viewpoint, we argue that there is a need to incorporate longer term experiences of migrants and refugees, beyond their pre-refugee trauma, including experiences in relation to racism, marginalization, and the stigma of being a refugee. In this light, we further argue that there is also a need to critically analyze and revisit the notion of a "syndrome," such as in relation to intergenerational trauma linked to slavery. In this vein, some have argued that the so-called syndrome is merely symptomatic of the oppressive and dominating white society's sociopathy and psychopathy (St Vil et al., 2019). For example, talking about the United States, Wilson (1996, p. 91) states that, "The society is sick," stressing that African Americans are simply stomaching the sickness of their long-term oppressors. Definitions of "normal" and "abnormal," rooted in eugenics, are established and implemented by the dominant culture, and when the dominant culture happens to be an oppressive and unwelcoming one, conceptions of normal and abnormal can become misleading, diminishing society's role in their functioning.

The poor assessment of refugees' and migrants' lived experiences of trauma and stress can obfuscate deep political dimensions, occluding opportunities for observing multidimensional factors (intrapersonal, interpersonal, organizational, environmental, and public policy). This has the danger of ultimately biasing the search for empirical "truth." Viewing stressors and traumas that become biologically and socially embodied and transmitted between generations in light of those culturally mediated factors and processes provides opportunities for holistic support and treatment that moves beyond just familial factors (St Vil et al., 2019). This involves viewing the role of a history of traumatic events as either the triggering factor that generates discrimination experiences that undermine well-being (mediated relation) or sensitizes (moderates) individuals' perceptions and appraisals of discrimination (Matheson et al., 2019).

Such experiences and the issues we have raised here demonstrate a need for trauma-informed programs and practices for refugees that take account of their multidimensional lived experiences and incorporate policies of cultural safety, which also involves understanding the nature of the links between the traumatic experiences and discrimination among members of socially marginalized groups, including the specificities associated with each of the groups. Viewing responses and resilience of refugees and displaced individuals in relation to potentially traumatic events at the levels of individual, family/peers, society, and culture (including pre- and post-migration experiences) allows for the formulation of a broad range of causal factors and adaptive responses to environmental change in the formulation of distress (Wells et al., 2018).

The Continuum of Violence Faced by Forced Migrant SGBV Survivors: The Need to Support Women's Recovery to Reduce Intergenerational Trauma

While structural violence and the issue of closed temporalities are closely connected, the following vignette shows how trauma resulting from forced migration is intensified by structural violence. The example is taken from the SEREDA project,[3] which examines the nature and effects of violence experienced from conflict through to refuge. This violence has been invisible in the literature because approaches have assumed that trauma ends once a refugee has resettled. The gap in research, in action, and in understanding of the refugee experience directly undermines the psychological well-being of forced migrant sexual- and gender-based violence (SGBV) survivors and undermines their ability to protect and nurture their children, removing all hope for the mother and child. We illustrate this with the story of Haben:

> Haben's home was Eritrea until the day she is raped and impregnated by a family friend. Unable to tell anyone but her husband, because of the shame she will bring to her family, her journey of many years commences when they escape to Sudan. Pursued by the rapist, Haben leaves the baby with her husband and travels with smugglers to Turkey, where alone and unprotected she is forced to work in a brothel. Once again seeking safety she joins a dinghy heading to Greece; it sinks, she is rescued as others drown. She hides in the forest where local boys rape her and name her "Black" until she is helped by tourists to move on through Europe. Upon reaching France she is raped for days by a "mafia man" and exchanges sex for money which she eventually uses to pay for passage to Canada. Haben does not know that the freezer lorry she shares with several other forced migrants cannot possibly be travelling to Canada. She arrives, frozen and "nearly dead" in the UK where she claims asylum.
>
> ... In refuge in the UK, Haben is not safe. She has no proof of her experiences – what proof could she possibly have? In lengthy asylum interviews she is asked hundreds of questions over many hours about the most intimate aspects of the violence she has repeatedly encountered. The interpreter is a male from her community; she fears the truth might reach her parents. She cries and they laugh. She is placed in mix-gender housing with her small children where there are no locks on bathroom doors and where sexual harassment is routine. Five years after arrival she has received no decision and has little to do but think back over her experiences which makes her feel pain

everywhere in her body. She has lost hope for any existence beyond survival, although she hopes her children will have a better life.

(SEREDA project archives)

With nearly 100 million people forced from their homes, and half of these female, Haben's story of a continuum of sexual- and gender-based violence (SGBV), multiple and compounded traumas, and the absence of any safe place was commonplace in the stories we heard from survivors participating in the SEREDA project. From immigration panels to NGOs, most of the focus on the trauma experienced by forced migrant SGBV survivors is around violence experienced in conflict or camps. SEREDA's person-centered approach means that experiences of individuals from the commencement of SGBV to the present day are recorded. This allows an understanding of effect of violence on women's health and well-being, and on their ability to build a new life once in refuge. It also allows us to see how structural violence plays a key role in embedding existing trauma and introducing new harms, increasing the likelihood of intergenerational trauma.

Humanitarian and asylum systems frequently re-traumatize and generate new trauma. Constant repetition of harrowing experiences and the culture of disbelief that treats survivors as immigration criminals rather than victims, enforced poverty and destitution, unsafe housing, and years of uncertainty undermine mental and physical health in which women are not permitted to work or study (Phillimore & Cheung, 2021); all eventually take a toll on the woman. Throughout these lengthy journeys and after arrival in imagined refuge in Western countries, there is scant protection and almost no services able to address the complex and compound traumas associated with years of violence (Pertek & Phillimore, 2022). While the remit of humanitarian agencies is to deal with SGBV in developmental or conflict settings, and the refugee sector provides food and shelter in camps, forced migrant victims of SGBV on the move have nowhere to go for help because they fall through the gaps. Once in refuge, SGBV survivors are treated as a problem and not a priority, and Western counseling models are not equipped to deal with the combination of past and current structurally sanctioned trauma with which women present. Women and their children are placed in accommodation profoundly unsuited to both, undermining the possibility for women to be the good parents they want to be and to give their children the best possible life.

Often after years of waiting for a decision on their asylum case, the vast majority of SGBV survivors will remain in the country of refuge. Many women win their asylum cases on appeal and then, having been kept outside of society and subject to multiple forms of structural violence in addition to a continuum of SGBV, they are expected to integrate into society where integration "refers to the process of settlement, interaction with the host society, and social change that follows immigration" (Penninx & Garcés-Mascareñas, 2016, p. 11). Our work on the SEREDA project showed that gaining "leave to remain"[4] and finally being able to look forward and engage in education or work offered is for some respondents a route toward recovery. However, for many, the cumulative effect of years of SGBV and multiple forms of structural violence undermine any possibility of hope for the future. In these situations, they stop striving for a good life and instead focus on doing their best for their children. Yet the everyday and slow structural violence which is the reality for all asylum seekers (Phillimore et al., 2022) means they cannot do their best. They try to hide their desperate unhappiness and hopelessness from their children and note that social workers are only interested in the ways that their psychological challenges impact negatively on their parenting. Rather than providing the security, necessities, and social and psychological support needed, social workers do not question that asylum-seeking women are treated differently than are British citizens. They problematize the parent and not the structure which, through pursuing policies intended to create a hostile environment, erodes all hope. Hungry and dirty children are viewed as the fault of the parent who must endure multiple interventions from the state, none of which improve their lives or place them in safe homes. And, if things do not improve, their children will be taken away and their only reason to "keep going" removed.

Clearly, a priority is to protect women like Haben so they do not have to leave their home to escape SGBV and provide safe passage for those who must leave. In the absence of these measures, there is a need for a far more flexible approach to SGBV service provision for forced migrants on the move and in refuge which address the needs of the whole person. Services must be available beyond camps to ensure women can be helped on routes and in hotspots. Furthermore, there is a need for emergency psychological aid as well as post-rape prophylaxis and treatment of wounds and infections. When forced migrants eventually stop their migration pathway (and particularly in refuge), they must first be assured of safety by being housed in single gender accommodation when unaccompanied. Second, they must be treated as victims of SGBV, subject to gender- and trauma-sensitive interviewing to avoid retraumatization, a trend commonly identified by clinicians working with asylum seekers (Schock et al., 2015). Protection mechanisms need to be explained and accompanied by appropriate mental and physical health care, and SGBV must be treated as persecution and therefore as ground for granting refugee or resettlement status. Survivors must be protected from further perpetration and NGOs funded to provide the specialist services needed to enable women to recover and move on with their lives. Finally, if intergenerational trauma is to be avoided, parents need to be enabled to recover from their trauma and not subjected to forms of structural violence that enforce poverty and hopelessness. Likewise, social systems should focus on the well-being of parents as well as children to enable the whole family to live a decent life without fear of return or family separation. While the current emphasis in social work is on implementation of immigration controls, Fell (2013) showed that through partnership working with specialist NGOs, social workers can play a transformative role for asylum seeking adults.

Haben's experience is not unique. Hers is also trauma that extends past her personal experience. Haben is a mother, and many others have become mothers amidst traumatic experiences of SGBV. Beyond meeting immediate needs, women like Haben, their children, husbands, and family will have to find a way to make sense of, account for, and digest the terrible things that happened. What we can learn from Haben and the SEREDA project is that we must broaden our temporal frame and look at where vulnerable refugees land in host societies. Haben's story amplifies and expands the findings of our first case, to show not only how structures in host societies can perpetuate stigma and harm but also how they create gaps in protection strategies that repeat traumas. It is only when we take these structures into account that action can be taken.

Use of Positive Metacognitive Beliefs as a Primary Prevention for Post-Traumatic Stress Disorder within Refugee Communities

Where many social structures disadvantage or even perpetuate harm for refugees, opening our temporal understanding of harm to the "before" of a traumatic event/context offers opportunity for insight. This vignette looks at why the way that communities discuss and perceive traumatic events (metacognition) can be critical to later experiences of post-traumatic stress disorder (PTSD). In other words, that better understanding the communal meaning of harm can help to forestall some of its violent reverberations.

In our work, we study how people's everyday thinking processes affect their responses to traumatic events, and how we can improve these processes to build resilience. Specifically, our work focuses on metacognition and metamemory. Metacognition is broadly defined as thoughts about one's own thoughts. It involves the monitoring, control, and appraisal (i.e., the interpretation) of one's own thoughts. Functioning as an internal guide, metacognition allows people to recognize their own thoughts, helping to act. Common examples of metacognition include awareness that you have forgotten the name of the person you recently met or realizing that you need to refocus your attention because your mind has been wandering as you have been reading this paragraph. Metacognition plays a role in all aspects of our lives; therefore, perhaps unsurprisingly, it has been implicated in the development of psychological disorders.

When individuals are recovering from a traumatic event, metacognition can either be a help or a hindrance. For instance, believing that worrying is helpful (i.e., "worrying helps me cope"; "I must worry in order to be prepared"), or believing that holding negative beliefs about thoughts is dangerous (e.g., "my worrying is dangerous for me; when I start worrying I cannot stop") are examples of maladaptive metacognition that can negatively influence a person's appraisal style and ability to cope (Wells & Cartwright-Hatton, 2004). Metamemory is a type of metacognition that refers to the processes whereby people can examine the content of their memories, both prospectively and retrospectively, and make judgments about them. Thus, metamemory does not refer to memory itself, but rather to judgements and assessments that we make about our own memories. For instance, although evidence for the experience of disorganized memory in PTSD is inconsistent (due in part to difficulties in operationally defining and measuring these types of memories), simply believing or perceiving one's memory to be disorganized is associated with PTSD (e.g., Bennett & Wells, 2010; Segovia et al., 2015).

The metacognitive model (Wells, 2000; Wells & Sembi, 2004) proposes that metacognition plays an integral role in the development of PTSD. According to this model, immediately after a traumatic event, symptoms, including memory intrusions, increased arousal (e.g., heart racing, sweating, rapid breathing) and startle responses emerge. The model suggests that these symptoms are a sign that an individual is attempting to emotionally process the trauma and adjust in a way that promotes future coping. These symptoms are all normal responses that stem from an in-built reflexive adaptation process. The goal of the reflexive adaptive process is to develop new procedures (i.e., metacognitions) for controlling cognition and to develop plans for dealing with any future threats. For most people, this process continues uninterrupted, and symptoms tend to naturally subside. However, for some people, these symptoms persist and can lead to PTSD.

According to the metacognitive model, psychological disorders are caused by an extended pattern of thinking that is known as cognitive attentional syndrome (CAS). The CAS consists of three processes: (1) worry and rumination, (2) threat monitoring, and (3) (poor) coping strategies. The CAS maintains symptoms and prevents cognition from returning to the normal and threat-free mode of processing. The CAS is driven by both positive and negative metacognitive beliefs. Positive metacognitive beliefs are those beliefs that are inaccurately perceived to have positive effect on coping, such as worrying about possible future threats (e.g., "If I worry bad things will not happen"), rumination (e.g., "I must go over the event to make sense of it"), and dwelling on memory and filling in any memory gaps (e.g., "I must have a complete memory to feel normal"). Negative metacognitive beliefs concern the uncontrollability and negative evaluation of thoughts (e.g., "my worrying is uncontrollable"). These types of beliefs, alongside the persistent use of maladaptive thought control strategies, represent an attempt to regulate emotion. However, instead existing understandings of metacognition serve to maintain a sense of threat and lead to persistence in PTSD symptoms according to the metacognitive model.

Experimental research has shown that it is possible to prevent the onset of PTSD by training people to adopt healthy metacognitive beliefs in advance of trauma exposure (Hett et al., 2022). However, to our knowledge no research exists investigating the metacognitive model in refugee communities and the protective measures that might foster resilience. Given the expanse of trauma that refugee communities experience, preventive and protective interventions are a vital area of research that may decrease the prevalence of PTSD across generations.

"It Was Like an Earthquake": Reading Transgenerational Aftershocks through Palestinian Literature

Some of the limits to research of inter/transgenerational trauma and refugee communities are simply the response to the natural limits of memory and the impracticability of coherent research across more than two or three generations. However, trauma contexts within many refugee communities span several (or more) generations. A literary historical approach to intergenerational trauma opens the question: How do we understand the relationship between one harm and another when there is no comparable data, and the vagaries of memory have shifted meaning? This vignette looks at Palestinian fiction and the Arabic newspaper archive to show how literature can add a longitudinal understanding of trauma and begin trace the shifting meanings of harm across a very longue durée.

We begin with a look at the representation of an earthquake that rocked the Palestinian city of Nablus in 1927. The earthquake is documented in diaries, newspapers, and government reports of the era, but in later writing, reference to the quake vanishes, as if it never happened. What the "nakba" (catastrophe) of the earthquake meant at the time, the ways it was understood, and the cultural significance it held were utterly eclipsed by what came to be known as *the* Nakba [al-Nakba] of 1948. It was in 1948 that "Nakba," a term in Arabic that means "catastrophe," was coined to define and describe the displacement of Palestinians from their homes and villages, the death of nearly 20,000 individuals, the destruction of homes and communities, that followed the British withdrawal from Palestine and the advance of Zionist militias in 1948. This event – how it was talked about and represented – for generations occluded the narrative of the earthquake. That is until the Second Intifada.

During the Second Intifada, in 2002, the city of Nablus endured a massive Israeli military invasion. The entrance of tanks into the Old City caused damage to buildings that had remained standing – but only just – after the quake. The experience of the invasion was described as an earthquake. This drew on a language of damage from the quake of 1927, but also on the very large body of discourse that described and interpreted *the* Nakba as an ongoing Palestinian trauma, and not just a single event in 1948. As a "process" and not an event, Nakba – the destruction of the Palestinian people – could be read into a great many methods of oppression and erasure (as is plainly visible in the cataclysmic war on Gaza, whose number of dead and level of destruction has, as of June 2024, far surpassed the initial destruction of 1948). This language of catastrophe as process emerged long after the earthquake, but ultimately meant that the earthquake became visible as a Palestinian trauma. In other words, a new trauma in 1948 made the earthquake invisible, but a new way of understanding trauma in the intervening years brought it back into community consciousness.

Three sections below briefly outline (1) the events and reaction to the quake of 1927 at the time of its occurrence, (2) the disappearance from cultural and literary record in the decades after, and (3) show how language was remobilized within the rhetoric of trauma formed by the Nakba. This challenges the typically linear approach to intergenerational trauma, where trauma is traced forward in time and across generations. The story of the earthquake in the broader story of Palestinian trauma shows that in contexts of multiple, overlapping and ongoing harm, understanding the meaning of any one occurrence requires a long lens.

The Earthquake of 1927

In 1927, a powerful earthquake hit several Palestinian cities, towns, and villages, but brought devastation on the city of Nablus. An estimated 50–150 died, hundreds more were injured, even more homes rendered unstable (Abujidi, 2014). In the city, with a population of 17,000 (Mills, 1933), more than 600 homes were demolished.

Nablus had experienced, as one newspaper put it, "death in the blink of an eye" (*Filistin*, Front Page, Friday July 15, 1927). The experience of harm, however, was exacerbated by the context of the event, coming as it did during a time of political uncertainty.

Under the Ottoman Empire, which had governed Palestine since the early 1500s, aid and repairs could be appealed for by letter to the governor, and then to the Sultan himself. However, less than a decade before the earthquake, the Ottoman rule had been supplanted by the British Mandate, and Palestinian communities had reason to worry that they would not receive adequate support, as preferential treatment around infrastructure and access to government funds had for some time been given to new waves of Jewish communities arriving in Palestine from Europe (Morris, 2009). Therefore, while the quake "frightened people from their homes," sent them "out into the streets," so that people abandoned even "sound houses" for fear of aftershocks (*Filistin*, Front Page, Friday July 15, 1927), there was a heightened sense of unease because individuals did not know where they might turn to for help. Headlines called the quake a "Palestinian Nakba" (*Filistin*, Front Page, Friday July 15, 1927).

In the days and weeks that followed, Palestinian newspapers worked tirelessly to document the damage, and carefully watched Mandate government reconstruction and aid efforts across Palestinian locales and new Jewish-only settlements. In a response, heightening the rhetoric of inequality and sense that Palestinians had to fend for themselves, papers also opened donation centers, announcing the largest contributors, and urging the rest of the Arab world to aid their contemporaries. Adding to the experience of destruction, then, was a sense of government betrayal. It was the betrayal that was remembered, at least initially.

Tragedy Silences Tragedy

Twelve years after the earthquake, when the British Mandate withdrew from Palestine, Zionist forces seized the opportunity and took control of most of the coastal territory of Palestine, the mountainous north, and desert in the south. Nablus would fall under Jordanian control. As author and poet Fadwa Tuqan recalled, "Thousands of refugees, moving eastward in their flight, [and] arrived in Nablus" (Tuqan, 1990, p. 23). The city would eventually host three large refugee camps, which utterly transformed its urban fabric (Abujidi, 2014, p. 95). Almost 20 years later, Palestinian critics would lament that the Nakba left the story of Palestine "in the bottomless pit" (Shunnār, 1965), and it was into this that memory of the earthquake seemed to have been cast. The earthquake did, however, survive anecdotally. As Tuqan noted in her 1990 autobiography: "Like all our people Mother dated events by relating them to outstanding occurrences. She would say: 'That happened the year of the big snow-storm, or the year of the grasshoppers, or the year of the earthquake" (p. 14). If the earthquake was still clocked as an important event locally, it – for a very long time – remained absent from any larger or more meaningful grappling with the significance of an extended experience of harm and displacement.

This absence is preserved as "silence" in the literary record. Beyond the immediate documentation in later published diaries, and recollections of the quake published in newspapers, the only references one comes across are to the same "time marker" as Tuqan noted above,[5] or a sense of foreboding, foretelling the catastrophe and greater displacement that would come.[6] Though the quake and its aftermath attracted attention from Palestinians across what was then Mandate Palestine, its memory would be kept as a faint gesture and as very local knowledge until 2002.

A Third Tragedy and Shift in the Language of Trauma

In 2002, Israeli forces invaded the city of Nablus and laid siege to the city for 18 days (Giacaman & Husseini, 2002), causing an estimated US$114 million (Ibid) in damages to homes and public buildings ("World Bank," 2013). The devastation was described as "an earthquake." Public rhetoric leaned heavily on descriptions of the earthquake of 1927 and framed the 2002 invasion in language that saw both in a continuum of violence and betrayal.

In a book on the invasion *Earthquake in April*, one NGO captured public sentiment and the link made between the 2002 and 1927 events. The editors wrote that the "Earthquake this time was not like before from the guts of the earth, but rather falling from the highest sky, where Israeli warplanes screamed over the old city" (Amiry & Hadid, 2002, p 12.). This shift suddenly made the earthquake of 1927 "speakable" in a national imaginary. As the introduction to *Earthquake in April* illustrates: "Most events [In Nablus] are referred to as 'before' or 'after' the earthquake. But from now on, this will cease to be the case" (Amiry & Hadid, 2002, p. ii). And indeed, from 2002, reference to the earthquake was more frequent, and it would explicitly make links between the destruction of the city in 1927, and the duty of Palestinians to rebuild amidst the ongoing destruction of Palestine by military occupation.

The earthquake, its destruction of homes and livelihoods, is today discussed as part of an ongoing Palestinian catastrophe. Uncertainty around aid and reconstruction – a direct result of British control and ambivalence about Palestinian sovereignty – can be clearly linked to larger and ongoing colonial processes. Culturally speaking, the earlier trauma became visible when the temporal framework widened to see the "befores." At the same time, the past trauma might be said to have given Nablus residents a language to describe what they had endured. Talking about the past became a way of cataloging the harms of the present.

Tracing catastrophe and its expression across generations through literature allows for the mapping of a complex web of inter-reference. A past trauma once silenced and overshadowed by a larger "more important" trauma, is claimed as a trauma for individuals, for a city, and a national community. As a collective trauma, its language is also then mobilized as a way of telling and a method of expression for yet another layer of experienced harm. This reading of the earthquake across nearly a century of trauma shows that understanding buried traumas from generations ago can help illuminate and understand the experiences of the present. This presents an intricate framework across which trauma is communicated and taken on and suggests a matrix of traumatic experience that is neither predictable nor closed. The events in Gaza to which we have been witness during 2023–2024 compound the urgency for a matrix and vocabulary of trauma that can account for its occlusion, and its articulation across time and community.

Epigenetics of Trauma across Generations among Refugee Communities

Another unseen perspective of intergenerational trauma is epigenetics. A relatively new field of science, epigenetics studies the interplay between the environment and genetics. The manifestation of this process is the organism phenotype. Epigenetics is the molecular process through which social–environmental factors impact not only biology and physiology but also behavioral outcomes of organisms. Epigenetics has been studied extensively in mammals but less so in humans, especially when dealing with human behavior.

The study of the epigenetic effects of war, trauma, and displacement on refugees and similar vulnerable communities is still in its early stages. An important reason for paucity of research in this area is the lack of intimate knowledge of the history and culture of communities, as well as access to these communities essential for trust-building and maintaining dignity in the conduct of scientific studies. Scientists have been able to overcome many of these challenges by engaging the local community in novel ways and being mindful of local mindsets and mechanisms of belonging.

Epigenetics can redefine our approach and understanding of existing tools of research around intergenerational trauma. For example, resilience is defined as the capacity of an individual to overcome adversity. Until recently, however, resilience was considered a stable trait and only recently has the concept been considered a dynamic and flexible process comprising multiple factors, including genetic variation and socio-environmental factors, which allows an individual to maintain good psychological health despite major adversity (Smeeth et al., 2021). This extends the time frame of resilience, but does not quite imagine resilience at the genetic level or think about the effect of resilience on the genome. Weaver et al (2004) has shown so far that there is a disparity in sensitivity to the environment that can be explained by genetic variation (Weaver et al., 2004). But this tells us only that the phenotypes that result from resilience are a complex process.

Including local scientists who are intimately knowledgeable about the history and culture can uncover different phenomena that were not visible to the outside observer. This creates new meanings and posits new questions, thereby enriching science and science inquiry. The impact of inclusion extends beyond improvements in basic science and has implications for policy, ensuring that policies are informed by local knowledge to benefit the community. One example is *We Love Reading*,[7] a local refugee-developed intervention that focuses on changing mindsets through reading to create changemakers. This program is a product of not only local expertise, experience, and knowledge, but is based on scientific evidence created by teams of local and international scientists from multiple disciplines, collaborating to provide evidence beyond behavior to biological and epigenetic. This approach looks at people beyond brain, "under the skin," if you will, beyond time and across generations. Those working with *We Love Reading* have raised the question of resilience and trauma, and ask if it is possible that the impact of trauma can be viewed through a positive lens (not in the Western sense of celebrating a redemptive trauma) but because the refugee scientists we work with see that things cannot get worse. These scientists are the victims of the trauma and are searching for a positive way out and insist on proceeding (Dajani, 2022, p. 363). However, as with all science, when one proposes novel approaches, it does not find traction but slowly gains attention. Hence, this review by Smeeth et al. (2021) was published despite the paucity of evidence on the impact of trauma on epigenetics of the psychology of resilience.

It is well documented that trauma and socio-environmental factors have an epigenetic signature; however, what is not well-known is if that epigenetic signature can be transferred across generations. Multigenerational epigenetic studies are typically possible only in plants or animal models. We propose that DNA marks may have evolved in humans as an adaptation to increasingly complex stressors that are not experienced in most plants or animal models. This adaptive signaling may augment or refine the normal developmental pathways that are informed by long-term environmental signaling and largely implemented through transcription factor-mediated gene regulation (Ptashne, 2013). The difficulty is in dissecting social transfer versus biological transfer of the impact. Without intimate knowledge of history and events, one ethically cannot construe such an experiment. Therefore, including local scientists and creating conversations and dialogues with local people is essential to find the natural experiments that human behavior has created to be able to ask these questions. This approach is relatively recent and calls for local ownership for success.

The field of social and behavioral epigenetics is at a transition. We now have a lot of data on different sociocultural/psychosocial exposures and epigenetic variation. Many epigenetic signatures are weak or non-existent. These negative results make sense because we do not expect every experience in our lives to leave an epigenetic signature. However, some might see those negative results as an indication that epigenetics is not the way to go. Another issue is that we are only assaying a fraction of the CpG sites in the human genome (850,000 sites versus 28 mill CpG sites in the human genome). It is unknown how many unassayed sites influence gene expression, and this will remain unknown until we look further and until sequencing the epigenome becomes more affordable.

In terms of future research, there are several studies on the importance of a match, or mismatch, between the prenatal and postnatal environments (Serpeloni et al., 2017). For instance, a preliminary study by Tobi et al. (2018) is focusing on natural selection acting on DNA methylation. Likewise, research addressing epigenetic age and the implications of accelerated aging is being conducted (McGill et al., 2022). Other research addresses how epigenetic clocks do not predict birth outcomes and cautions against a move to epigenetic determinism (Ryan et al., 2022). An anthropological context is particularly useful for investigating the transmission of adaptive responses to psychosocial stressors across generations and the idea that psychosocial exposures, like racial discrimination, can become biologically embedded (Gravlee, 2009; Non et al., 2019; Thayer & Kuzawa, 2011; Thayer & Kuzawa, 2015). Finally, epigenetic modifications have been proposed as a mechanism by which prenatal exposures could reprogram the genome of the developing fetus and lead to intergenerational impacts of maternal stress (Thayer & Kuzawa, 2011; Mulligan et al., 2014; Thayer & Kuzawa, 2015).

Conclusion

This chapter aimed to provide manifold perspectives on inter/transgenerational trauma by addressing cardinal questions: How does inter/transgenerational trauma among displaced individuals and refugee communities manifest itself across time and place? What multilayered policy and humanitarian aid legacies perpetuate and amplify intergenerational trauma? How, and to what extent, accumulated policy, aid, and humanitarian practices have shaped the lasting impact of intergenerational trauma and postmigrant/refugee experiences? How can novel research perspectives help in overcoming key structural failures and misperceptions regarding the way we have been studying and looking at intergenerational suffering and trauma?

The chapter unlocked new research perspectives with a view to transcending "structural failures" and dominant views that have shaped how we deal with intergenerational trauma. Building on rich array of examples and perspectives, the chapter has broader insights to convey. First, looking at trauma as a continuum of temporal legacies, histories, and accumulated struggles that span several contexts and political geographies is key to recognizing how trauma is transmitted across generations. The entryway for research provided in these vignettes is also key for unpacking some of the assumptions that the field of intergenerational trauma work has carried with it, and now needs to let go of and expand. In particular, the field's embedded notions of safety and trauma that split experience between refuge/trauma (where the refuge is safe and the place of trauma has been left behind) and trauma/normal (where the "normal" of a daily space is understood to be safe and separate from the experience of trauma). Beyond breaking open these foundational notions, these vignettes challenge established concepts linking time and trauma, as in the notion of ripples, which assumes a singular point of origin and ignores the complex, intersecting, and ongoing factors in the experience of trauma across time. Ultimately, we have much to gain from studying intergenerational trauma through research perspectives that bring various disciplines and methodologies as well as regional and historical contexts together. As illustrated in this chapter, building bridges across epistemological siloes is essential: it allows for longer (literature) and broader (epigenetics) scope for the meaning of "intergenerational," and complicates assumed definitions of "trauma," and indeed of inheritance Third, it is paramount that public policy models grappling with intergenerational trauma embrace dynamic approaches that look at trauma as a multidimensional and multilayered phenomenon that is nestled within overlapping realities, temporalities, biographies, and journeys. To that end, integrating refugees' experiences and everyday narratives of communal and collective remembering is central to informing the development of critical policy models.

Notes

1. See Cowan et al. (2016).
2. Windrush was the name of a ship that traveled from the Caribbean to the UK in 1948 carrying over 1,000 passengers who had been invited to come to live and work in the UK following World War II. The men and women who came on the ship were not documented upon their arrival, so that many would later be deported, including their children a generation later. This practice of poor documentation upon arrival in the UK lead to tens of thousands of wrongful deportation cases and other violations of rights.
3. Sexual- and gender-based violence in the refugee crisis: from displacement to arrival (SEREDA) is a project based at the University of Birmingham and funded by the Wellcome Trust, Volkswagen Stiftung and Riksbankens Jubileumsfond through the Europe and Global Challenges Initiative. For further information, see SEREDA Project. (n.d.). Retrieved November 29, 2023, from www.birmingham.ac.uk/research/superdiversity-institute/sereda/index.aspx
4. "Leave to remain" is the UK government term for residency status.
5. This can be seen in particular in the works of Nablus native Sahar Khalifeh (2012, 2020, 2021), who does mention the earthquake in three of her novels. In her 2012 and 2020 works, the reference to the quake is to date an event, or mark it as in the very distant past. The later work directly discusses the quake in relation to the Second Intifada and its meaning shifts.
6. See, for example, Jabra Ibrahim Jabra's *The First Well*.
7. We Love Reading. (n.d.). Retrieved November 29, 2023, from https://welovereading.org/

References

Abujidi, N. (2014). *Urbicide in Palestine: Spaces of Oppression and Resilience*. Abingdon: Routledge.
Amiry, S., & Hadid, M. (2002). *Earthquake in April*. Ramallah, Palestine: RIWAQ, Center for Architectural Conservation.
Bennett, H., & Wells, A. (2010). Metacognition, memory disorganization and rumination in posttraumatic stress symptoms. *Journal of Anxiety Disorders*, 24(3), 318–325. https://doi.org/10.1016/j.janxdis.2010.01.004.
Brinkhurst-Cuff, C. (Ed.) (2019). *Mother Country. Real stories of Windrush Children*. London: Headline Publishing Group.
Cowan, C. S. M., Callaghan, B. L., Kan, J. M., & Richardson, R. (2016). The lasting impact of early-life adversity on individuals and their descendants: Potential mechanisms and hope for intervention. *Genes, Brain, and Behavior*, 15(1), 155–168. https://doi.org/10.1111/GBB.12263.
Craps, S., Cheyette, B., Gibbs, A., Andermahr, S., & Allwork, L. (2016). Decolonizing Trauma Studies Round-Table Discussion. In Sonya Andermahr (Ed.), *Decolonizing Trauma Studies: Trauma and Postcolonialism* (pp. 189–207). Basel: MDPI.
Dajani, R. (2022). Exploring the epigenetics of resilience. *Nature Genetics*, 54(4), 363–363. https://doi.org/10.1038/s41588-022-01050-x
DeGruy, J.A. (2005). *Post Traumatic Slave Syndrome: America's Legacy of Enduring Injury and Healing*. Milwaukie: Uptone Press.
Fell, B. (2013). Social Work Practice, Asylum Seekers and Refugees. In Davies Martin (Ed.), *The Blackwell Companion to Social Work* (pp. 299–308). Hoboken: Wiley Blackwell.
Filistin (Friday, July 15–22, 1927). Jaffa: Issa El-Issa.
George, C. (2015). Do you have Post-Traumatic Slave Syndrome? *Ebony*, 70(11), 67–70.

Giacaman, R., & Husseini, A. (May 16, 2002). Life and health during the Israeli invasion of the West Bank: The town of Nablus. *Reliefweb*. Retrieved December 30, 2023, from https://reliefweb.int/report/israel/life-and-health-during-israeli-invasion-west-bank-town-nablus.

Gravlee, C. C. (2009). How race becomes biology: Embodiment of social inequality. *American Journal of Physical Anthropology, 139*(1), 47–57. https://doi.org/10.1002/ajpa.20983.

Hammoudeh, W. H., Hogan, D., & Giacaman, R. (2013). Quality of life, human insecurity, and distress among Palestinians in the Gaza Strip before and after the winter 2008–2009 Israeli war. *Quality of Life Research, 22*(9), 2371–2379. https://doi.org/10.1007/s11136-013-0386-9.

Harvey, M. R. (1996). An ecological view of psychological trauma and trauma recovery. *Journal of Traumatic Stress, 9*(1), 3–23.

Hett, D., Takarangi, M. K. T., & Flowe, H. D. (2022). The effects of computerised metacognitive cognitive bias modification training on the development of adaptive metacognitive beliefs and post-traumatic stress disorder symptoms. *Journal of Behavior Therapy and Experimental Psychiatry, 75*, 101 76. https://doi.org/10.1016/j.jbtep.2021.101716

Hopkins, P., & Hill, M. (2010). The needs and strengths of unaccompanied asylum-seeking children and young people in Scotland. *Child & Family Social Work, 15*(4), 399–408. https://doi.org/10.1111/j.1365-2206.2010.00687.

Hourani, J., Block, K., Phillimore, J., Bradby, H., Ozcurumez, S., Goodson, L., & Vaughan, C. (2021). Structural and symbolic violence exacerbates the risks and consequences of sexual and gender-based violence for forced migrant women. *Frontiers in Human Dynamics, 3*, 1–13. https://doi.org/10.3389/fhumd.2021.769611.

Jabra, J. I. (2012). *The First Well: A Bethlehem Boyhood*. (Issa Boulatta, Trans). London: Hesperus.

Khalifeh, S. (2012). *Of Noble Origins*. (Aida A. Bamia, Trans.). Cairo: American University in Cairo Press.

Khalifeh, S. (2020). *Passage to the Plaza*. (Sawad Hussein, Trans.) Kolkata: Seagull Books.

Khalifeh, S. (2021). *My First and Only Love a Novel*. (Aida A. Bamia, Trans.). New York: The American University in Cairo Press.

Kilanowski, J. F. (2017). Breadth of the socio-ecological model. *Journal of Agromedicine, 22*(4), 295–297. https://doi.org/10.1080/1059924X.2017.1358971.

Kootstra, A. (2016). Deserving and undeserving welfare claimants in Britain and the Netherlands: Examining the role of ethnicity and migration status using a vignette experiment. *European Sociological Review, 32*(3), 325–338. https://doi.org/10.1093/esr/jcw010.

Krause, U. (2015). A continuum of violence? Linking sexual and gender-based violence during conflict flight and encampment. *Refugee Survey Quarterly, 34*(4), 1–19. https://doi.org/10.1093/rsq/hdv014

Leigh, K. T, & Davis, M. D. (2017). US public education: The ivy tower of historical trauma. *Journal of Philosophy & History of Education, 67*, 21–35.

Matheson, K., Foster, M. D., Bombay, A., McQuaid, R. J., & Anisman, H. (2019). Traumatic experiences, perceived discrimination, and psychological distress among members of various socially marginalized groups. *Frontiers in Psychology, 10*, 416. https://doi.org/10.3389/fpsyg.2019.00416.

McGill, M. G., Pokhvisneva, I., Clappison, A. S., McEwen, L. M., Beijers, R., Tollenaar, M. S., Pham, H., Kee, M. Z. L., Garg, E., de Mendonça Filho, E. J., Karnani, N., Silveira, P. P., Kobor, M. S., de Weerth, C., Meaney, M. J., & O'Donnell, K. J. (2022). Maternal prenatal anxiety and the fetal origins of epigenetic aging. *Biological Psychiatry Journal, 91*(3), 303–312. https://doi.org/10.1016/j.biopsych.2021.07.025.

McLaughlin, C. (2018). 'They don't look like children': Child asylum-seekers, the dubs amendment and the politics of childhood. *Journal of Ethnic and Migration Studies, 44*(11), 1757–1773. https://doi.org/10.1080/1369183X.2017.1417027.

Mills, E. (1933). *Census of Palestine 1931: Palestine*. Alexandria: Whitehead Morris Limited.

Morris, B. (2009). *1948: A History of the First Arab-Israeli War*. New Haven: Yale University Press.

Mulligan, C. J., Rodney, N. C., & Hughes, D. A. (2014). The effect of maternal stress on newborn birth outcome and methylation profiles. *American Journal of Physical Anthropology, 153*, 191–191.

Non, A. L., León-Pérez, G., Glass, H., Kelly, E., & Garrison, N. A. (2019). Stress across generations: A qualitative study of stress, coping, and caregiving among Mexican immigrant mothers. *Ethnicity & Health, 24*(4), 378–394. https://doi.org/10.1080/13557858.2017.1346184.

Pearrow, M., & Cosgrove, L. (2009). The aftermath of combat-related PTSD: Toward an understanding of transgenerational trauma. *Communication Disorders Quarterly, 30*(2), 77–82. https://doi.org/10.1177/1525740108328227.

Penninx, R., & Garcés-Mascareñas, B. (2016). The Concept of Integration as an Analytical Tool and as a Policy Concept. In B. Garcés-Mascareñas, & R. Penninx (Eds.), *Integration Processes and Policies in Europe: Contexts, Levels and Actors* (pp. 11–29). London: Springer International Publishing. https://doi.org/10.1007/978-3-319-21674-4_2.

Pertek, S., & Phillimore, J. (2022). *"Nobody Helped Me." Forced Migration and Sexual and Gender-Based Violence: Findings from the SEREDA Project*. Birmingham: University of Birmingham. Retrieved November 29, 2023, from www.birmingham.ac.uk/documents/college-social-sciences/social-policy/iris/2022/sereda-international-report.pdf.

Phillimore, J., & Cheung, S. Y. (2021). The violence of uncertainty: Empirical evidence on how asylum waiting time undermines refugee health. *Social Science & Medicine, 282*, 114154. https://doi.org/10.1016/j.socscimed.2021.114154

Phillimore, J., Pertek, S., Akyuz, S., Darkal, H., Hourani, J., McKnight, P., Ozcurumez, S., & Taal, S. (2022). "We are forgotten": Forced migration, sexual and gender-based violence, and coronavirus disease-2019. *Violence Against Women, 28*(9), 2204–2230. https://doi.org/10.1177/10778012211030943.

Ptashne, M. (2013). Faddish stuff: Epigenetics and the inheritance of acquired characteristics. *The FASEB Journal, 27*(1), 1–2. https://doi.org/https://doi.org/10.1096/fj.13-0101ufm.

Ryan, C. P., Rege, R. J., Lee, N. R., Carba, D. B., Kobor. M. S., MacIsaac, J. L., Lin, D. S., Atashzay, P., & Kuzawa, C.W. (2022). Maternal epigenetic clocks measured during pregnancy do not predict gestational age at delivery or offspring birth outcomes: A replication study in metropolitan Cebu, Philippines. *Clinical Epigenetics, 14*(1), 78. https://doi.org/10.1186/s13148-022-01296-6

Sangalang, C. C., & Vang, C. (2017). Intergenerational trauma in refugee families: A systematic review. *Journal of Immigrant and Minority Health, 19*(3), 745–754. https://doi.org/10.1007/s10903-016-0499-7.

Schock, K., Rosner, R., & Knaevelsrud, C. (2015). Impact of asylum interviews on the mental health of traumatized asylum seekers. *European Journal of Psychotraumatology, 6*, 1–9. https://doi.org/10.3402/ejpt.v6.26286.

Segovia, D. A., Strange, D., & Takarangi, M. K. (2015). Trauma memories on trial: Is cross-examination a safeguard against distorted analogue traumatic memories? *Memory, 25*(1), 1–12. https://doi.org/10.1080/09658211.2015.1126608.

SEREDA Project. (n.d.). Retrieved November 29, 2023, from www.birmingham.ac.uk/research/superdiversity-institute/sereda/index.aspx

Serpeloni, F., Radtke, K., de Assis, S. G., Henning, F., Nätt, D., & Elbert, T. (2017). Grandmaternal stress during pregnancy and DNA methylation of the third generation: An epigenome-wide association study. *Translational Psychiatry, 7*(8), e1202. https://doi.org/10.1038/tp.2017.153.

Shunnār, A. (1965). Introduction. *al-Ufuq al-Jadīd, 4*(1), 1–3.

Sims-Schouten, W., & Gilbert, P. (2022). Revisiting 'resillience' in light of racism, 'othering' and and resistance. *Race & Class, 64*(1), 84–94. https://doi.org/10.1177/03063968221093882.

Smeeth, D., Beck, S., Karam, E. G., & Pluess, M. (2021). The role of epigenetics in psychological resilience. *The Lancet Psychiatry*, *8*(7), 620–629. https://doi.org/10.1016/S2215-0366(20)30515-0.

St Vil, N. M., St Vil, C., & Fairfax, C. N. (2019). Posttraumatic slave syndrome, the patriarchal nuclear family structure, and African American male-female relationships. *Social Work*, *64*(2), 139–146. https://doi.org/10.1093/sw/swz002.

Thayer, Z. M., & Kuzawa, C. W. (2011). Biological memories of past environments: Epigenetic pathways to health disparities. *Epigenetics*, *6*(7), 798–803. https://doi.org/10.4161/epi.6.7.16222.

Thayer, Z. M., & Kuzawa, C. W. (2015). Ethnic discrimination predicts poor self-rated health and cortisol in pregnancy: Insights from New Zealand. *Social Science & Medicine*, *128*, 36–42. https://doi.org/10.1016/j.socscimed.2015.01.003.

Tobi, E. W., van den Heuvel, J., Zwaan, B. J., Lumey, L. H., Heijmans, B. T., & Uller, T. (2018). Selective survival of embryos can explain DNA methylation signatures of adverse prenatal environments. *Cell Reports*, *25*(10), 2660–2667.e2664. https://doi.org/10.1016/j.celrep.2018.11.023.

Tuqan, F. (1990). *A Mountainous Journey: An Autobiography*. (Olive E. Kenny, & Naomi Shihab Nye, Trans). St. Paul: Graywolf Press.

Visser, I. (2015). Decolonizing trauma theory: Retrospect and prospects. *Humanities*, *4*(2), 250–265.

We Love Reading. (n.d.). Retrieved November 29, 2023, from https://welovereading.org/

Weaver, T., Maurer, J., & Hayashizaki, Y. (2004). Sharing genomes: An integrated approach to funding managing and distributing genomic clone resources. *Nature Reviews Genetics*, *11*, 861–866. https://doi.org/10.1038/nrg1474.

Wells, A. (2000). *Emotional Disorders and Metacognition: Innovative Cognitive Therapy*. Chichester: Wiley.

Wells, A., & Cartwright-Hatton, S. (2004). A short-form of the metacognitions questionnaire: Properties of the MCQ-30. *Behaviour Research and Therapy*, *42*, 385–396. https://doi.org/10.1016/S0005-7967(03)00147-5.

Wells, A., & Sembi, S. (2004). Metacognitive therapy for PTSD: A preliminary investigation of a new brief treatment. *Journal of Behavior Therapy and Experimental Psychiatry*, *35*(4), 307–318. https://doi.org/10.1016/j.jbtep.2004.07.001.

Wells, R., Lawsin, C., Hunt, C., Said Youssef, O., Abujado, F., & Steel, Z. (2018). An ecological model of adaptation to displacement: Individual, cultural and community factors affecting psychosocial adjustment among Syrian refugees in Jordan. *Global Mental Health (Cambridge, England)*, *5*, e42. https://doi.org/10.1017/gmh.2018.30.

Wilson, C. A. (1996). *Racism: From Slavery to Advanced Capitalism*. Thousand Oak: Sage Publications.

World Bank. (2013). Twenty-seven months – intifada, closures, and Palestinian economic crisis: An assessment. *World Bank*. Retrieved from http://hdl.handle.net/10986/14614

Index

Note: Page numbers in *italic* indicate a figure and page numbers in **bold** indicate a table on the corresponding page.

affiliation 65–67
Afghan refugees 184–188, 191–194; mental health care and war 188–191
Africa/African diaspora 98–99; challenges inherent in literature 99–101; legacy of slavery and its stressors 110–113; PTSD future pathways 117–119; resilience to trauma and stressors 113–115; root causes of unrest 101–110; testing intergenerational cases 115–117
aftershocks, transgenerational 255–259
anxiety: existential 26–29; resources 92–93
Armenian diaspora 11–19
arts 233–234, 241–243; controversy 240–241; filling in narrative silences and fragments 237–240; participant-observation 234–235; teaching and learning refugee trauma and politics 235–237
attitudes toward the government 92
avoidance 91–92

beliefs 254–255
Bosnian Americans 160–164, 178–180; experiences of 164–178; integrating collective trauma 173–178; PTSD 164–168; silencing the past 168–170; trauma and identity construction 171–173
burden, intergenerational 71–72; background 72–75; ending the silence 77–79; pathology of recognition 75–77; residual trauma and postgenerations 79–81

Call Me Zebra (Oloomi) 26–29
Canada, and forced migrant SGBV survivors 251–254; *see also* literary space

carceral systems 184–188, 191–194; mental health care and war 188–191
cascading displacement 54–56, 60
Central America 84–85, 87–88, 92
child/children 1–7; Afghan refugees 187–189; Africa and African diaspora 100–101, 104–109, 116–117; Armenian diaspora 15–16; Bosnian Americans 162–165, 167–171, 173–175, 177–179; community arts organizing 233–237, 241–243; Holocaust survivors 53–57, 60–67; Holodomor survivors 72–80; Korean Americans 199–202, 204–207, 209–210; Nicaraguan Americans 86–93; North Korean defector families 215–227; Palestinian refugees 43–48; refugee literary space 24–28, 32–34; resilience to trauma 113–115; socio-ecological lens 249–251; Somali refugees 126, 128–133, 135, 137–138
choice 53–54, 67–68; cascading displacement 54–55; chosen memory frames 60–65; mnemonic choice 65–67; mnemonic macroframes 56–58; "refugees" in their own country 58–60
Cockroach (Hage) 29–32
community: Armenian diaspora 11–19; Bosnian American 162–163; refugee 254–255, 259–261; teaching and learning 235–237
community arts organizing 233–234, 241–243; controversy 240–241; filling in narrative silences and fragments 237–240; participant-observation 234–235; teaching and learning refugee trauma and politics 235–237

conflict 1–2, 24, 27, 252; Africa and African diaspora 105–108; Bosnian Americans 169–170; Korean Americans 199–201, 207–211; North Korean defector families 223; Palestinian refugees 45–46; Somali refugees 127, 133–137
continuum of violence 251–25
coping strategies: Palestinian refugees 46–47

Daughters of Smoke and Fire (Homa) 32–35
decolonizing 32–35
defectors *see* North Korean defectors (NKDs)
deportation 184–188, 191–194; mental health care and war 188–191; Siberian deportees 60–65
developmentally based trauma framework (DBTF) 124–127, 133–138; implicated mechanisms in ITT literature 127–129; theorizing marginalization 130–133, **131**
diaspora 98–99; Armenian 11–19; challenges inherent in literature 99–101; Eritrean 146–156; legacy of slavery and its stressors 110–113; PTSD future pathways 117–119; resilience to trauma and stressors 113–115; root causes of unrest 101–110; testing intergenerational cases 115–117; Ukrainian 73, 81
displacement 2, 24–28, 31–35, 53–60, 63–65, 110–111, 209, 256–259

earthquake of 1927 (Palestine) 256–258
ecology *see* socio-ecological lens
epigenetics 259–261
Eritrean independence struggle 146–149, 155–156; and homeland 152–154; politicization of collective trauma 149–152; second diaspora generation 154–155
existential anxiety 26–29

forced migrant SGBV survivors 251–254
fragments, narrative 237–240

genocide 2–3, 11–19, 32–33, 55–56, 71–80, 163–166
Germany 62–64, 71–73, 151, 155, 184–188, 191–194; mental health care and war 188–191

government, attitudes toward 92
Gulag 55–58, 62, 68

Hage, Rawi 29–32
healing 25–27, 35–36, 173–175, 199–200
health care 184–185; and carceral systems 185–188; and the German state 191–194; and war 188–191
historical background/context: Armenian pilgrimage 12; child migration 249–251; Holocaust survivors 54–55; Holodomor survivor literature 72–75; Korean Americans 199–200; Palestinian refugees 41–43, *41–42*
history 199–200, 208–212; breaking silence 207–208; knowing is not enough 205–207; Korean American voices 202; legacies mediated by silence 202–205; war and division 201–202
Holocaust 53–54, 67–68; cascading displacement 54–55; chosen memory frames 60–65; mnemonic choice 65–67; mnemonic macroframes 56–58; "refugees" in their own country 58–60
Holodomor survivors 71–72; background 72–75; ending the silence 77–79; pathology of recognition 75–77; residual trauma and postgenerations 79–81
Holodomor: Silenced Voices of the Starved Children 77–79
Homa, Ava 32–35
homeland 45–47, 92, 99, 147, 161, 210; Armenian diaspora 11–19; Eritrea 150–155

identity: construction of 171–173; ethnic 34, 54, 156, 174, 179, 234, 242; Holocaust survivors 65–67; Korean Americans 199–212
immigrants/migrants 29–31, 189; Africa and African diaspora 113, 118–119; Bosnian Americans 163–164, 167–168, 171–173; forced migrant SGBV survivors 251–254; Holodomor survivors 71–74; Nicaragua 86–88; Somali refugees 126–127; *see also* migration/immigration
independence, Eritrean 146–149, 155–156; and homeland 152–154; politicization of collective trauma 149–152; second diaspora generation 154–155
intergenerational trauma/transgenerational trauma: Armenian diaspora 11–19;

Index

Bosnian Americans 160–180; Eritrean 146–156; Holodomor survivors 71–81; Nicaraguan American families 84–93; North Korean defector families 215–227; Palestinian refugees 40–48; refugees in Africa and African diaspora 98–119; refugee literary spaces 24–36; Somali refugees 124–138; unheard and unseen perspectives 246–262
Iranian refugees see *Call Me Zebra* (Oloomi); Oloomi, Azareen Van Der Vliet

Jewish returnees 53–54, 67–68; cascading displacement 54–55; chosen memory frames 60–65; mnemonic choice 65–67; mnemonic macroframes 56–58; "refugees" in their own country 58–60

Korean Americans 199–200, 208–212; breaking silence 207–208; knowing is not enough 205–207; legacies mediated by silence 202–205; voices 202; war and division 201–202
Kurds 17; *see also Daughters of Smoke and Fire* (Homa); Homa, Ava

Lebanese see *Cockroach* (Hage); Hage, Rawi
legacy 17–19, 76–79, 146–147, 174–177; of the Korean War 199–212; of martyrs 149–152; of slavery 110–113
literary space 24–26, 36; *Call Me Zebra* 26–29; *Cockroach* 29–32; *Daughters of Smoke and Fire* 32–35
literature 71–72; background 72–75; challenges 99–101; ending the silence 77–79; ITT 127–129; pathology of recognition 75–77; reading transgenerational aftershocks through 255–259; residual trauma and postgenerations 79–81
Little Saigon 234–235
lost homeland 11–19; *see also* homeland

marginalization 124–127, 133–138; implicated mechanisms in ITT literature 127–129; theorizing 130–133, **131**
martyrs 146–147, 149–153, 155–156
mass migration 86–87; *see also* migration/immigration
mass violence 3, 40
memory 53–54, 67–68, 199–200; cascading displacement 54–55; chosen 60–65; collective 13, 25–30, 42–44, 54–56; mnemonic choice 65–67; mnemonic macroframes 56–58; postmemory 13, 24, 71, 147, 150–156, 174–175, 179
mental health 1–2, 30, 246–247; Afghan refugees 184–185; Africa and African diaspora 105–108; Bosnian Americans 160–166; and carceral systems 185–188; and the German state 191–194; North Korean defector families 220, 224–227; Palestinian refugees 43–46, *45*; Somali refugees 126–129, 132–138; and war 188–191
migration/immigration 1–2, 57–58; Afghan refugees 191–193; Africa and African diaspora 105, 118–119; Bosnian Americans 160–164; forced migrant SGBV survivors 251–254; Nicaraguan American families 84–89; North Korean defectors 217–224; socio-ecological lens 249–251; Somali refugees 126–130, 133–138
mnemonic choice 65–67
mnemonic macroframes 56–58

Nakba see Palestinian literature; Palestinian refugees
narrative silences and fragments 237–240
NATO 184–188, 191–194; mental health care and war 188–191
Nicaraguan American families 84–93
North Korean defectors (NKDs) 215–220, **216**; children of 221–224, **222**; life of women after migration 220–221; parenting behavior 224–227

Oloomi, Azareen Van Der Vliet 25–29
organizing *see* community arts organizing

Palestinian literature 255–259
Palestinian refugees 40–48
parenting behavior 224–227
participant-observation 234–235
past, the 32–35; past/present dynamics 26–29; silencing 168–170
pathology of recognition 71–72, 74–77, 89
pilgrimage, Armenian 11–19
Poland 53–54, 67–68; cascading displacement 54–55; chosen memory frames 60–65; mnemonic choice 65–67; mnemonic macroframes 56–58; "refugees" in their own country 58–60

politics 233–234, 241–243; Africa 101–110; Central America 84–85; controversy 240–241; filling in narrative silences and fragments 237–240; participant-observation 234–235; politicization of collective trauma 149–152; teaching and learning refugee trauma and 235–237
postgeneration *see* second generation/postgeneration
post traumatic stress disorder (PTSD) 1–3, 246–248; Africa and African diaspora 99–100, 104–110, 113–115; Bosnian American 160–168, 178; future pathways in refugee settlements 117–119; Nicaraguan American families 88–90; North Korean defector families 220–222; and positive metacognitive beliefs 254–255; Somali refugees 129–130
psychological 1–2, 31–34, 248–255; Africa and African diaspora 99–100, 104–109, 112, 115–117; Bosnian Americans 160–162, 168–169; Eritrean independence struggle 149–150, 153; Palestinian refugees 42–48; Somali refugees 127–129; well-being of children 215–227, **216, 222**

recognition 71–72; background 72–75; ending the silence 77–79; pathology of 71–72, 74–77, 89; residual trauma and postgenerations 79–81
recovery 116, 176, 200, 205–206, 249, 251–254
refugee/s: Afghan 184–194; African 98–119; and community arts organizing 233–243; epigenetics of trauma 259–261; Holocaust survivors 53–68; literary space 24–36; Nicaragua 87–88; Palestinian 40–48; PTSD 117–119, 254–255; Somali 124–138
resettlement 1–3, 93; Africa and African diaspora 102–103, 109; Bosnian Americans 160–166, 177–178; and marginalization 125–127; Somali refugees 124–130, 133–138; trauma 88–89
residual trauma 79–81
resilience 25, 35, 248–250, 254–255, 259–260; Africa and African diaspora 113–115, 118; Bosnian Americans 173–176; Nicaraguan American families 84–93; North Korean defectors 227
returnees 53–54, 67–68; cascading displacement 54–55; chosen memory frames 60–65; mnemonic choice 65–67; mnemonic macroframes 56–58; "refugees" in their own country 58–60
root causes of political unrest 101–110

Sandinista Revolution 85–86, 91–93
second generation/postgeneration 1–2, 33, 43, 89; Africa and African diaspora 101, 107, 114; Bosnian Americans 160–180; community arts organizing 236, 240; Eritrean independence struggle 150–151, 153–156; Holodomor survivors 71–81; Korean Americans 202, 208, 211–212
settlements, refugee 106, 117–119
sexual- and gender-based violence (SGBV) 247, 251–254
Siberians 53–54, 67–68; cascading displacement 54–55; chosen memory frames 60–65; mnemonic choice 65–67; mnemonic macroframes 56–58; "refugees" in their own country 58–60
silence 25–27, 30, 32–33, 35–36, 71–72, 237–240; background 72–75; Bosnian Americans 168–170; ending the silence 77–79; Korean Americans 202–205, 207–208; pathology of recognition 75–77; residual trauma and postgenerations 79–81; tragedy silences tragedy 257–258
Silent Memories, Traumatic Lives 75–77
slavery 110–113
socio-ecological lens 249–251
Somali refugees 124–127, 133–138; implicated mechanisms in ITT literature 127–129; theorizing marginalization 130–133, **131**
stressors: of legacy of slavery 110–113; and resilience 113–115
survivor/survival 1–4, 11–15, 18–19, 24–26; Afghan refugees 187–189; Africa and African diaspora 100–104; Bosnian Americans 162–164, 168–169, 173–176; Eritrean independence struggle 148–151, 155; forced migrant SGBV survivors 251–254; Holocaust survivors 53–68; Holodomor survivors 71–81; Korean Americans 208–211; Nicaraguan American families 84–93; Palestinian refugees 43–46

transgenerational trauma *see* intergenerational trauma/ transgenerational trauma
transmission: Eritrean 146–156; Nicaraguan American families 84–93; Palestinian refugees 40–48; parenting behavior as potential mechanism 224–227; Somali refugees 124–138
trauma: collective 30, 0, 43, 46–47, 54, 149–152, 154–155, 173–179; and community arts organizing 233–243; cultural 7, 27; cumulative 48, 124, 130, **131**; current knowledge of 102–110; developmentally based trauma framework 124–138; epigenetics of 259–261; and identity construction 171–173; immigrant/refugee 87–88; Korean Americans 199–212; language of 258–259; mechanism of transmission 90–91; resettlement 88–89; residual 79–81; resilience to 113–115; testing intergenerational cases of 115–117; *see also* intergenerational trauma/ transgenerational trauma
traumatization 31, 252–253; Africa and African diaspora 105–106, 118–119; Bosnian Americans 166–168; Eritrean independence struggle 152–154; implicated mechanisms in ITT literature 127–129; Nicaraguan American families 89–91; Somali refugees 124–127, 133–138; theorizing marginalization 130–133, **131**

Ukraine: background 72–75; diaspora 73, 81; ending the silence 77–79; Holodomor survivors 71–72; pathology of recognition 75–77; refugees 7, 62; residual trauma and postgenerations 79–81
UNHCR 1, 34, 98, 102–103, 133, 185
United States: Armenian diaspora 12–14; Bosnian Americans 160–180; Korean Americans 199–212; Nicaraguan American families 84–93; Somali refugees 133–135; Vietnamese Americans 240–241
USSR 53–54, 67–68; cascading displacement 54–55; chosen memory frames 60–65; mnemonic choice 65–67; mnemonic macroframes 56–58; "refugees" in their own country 58–60

veterans 53–54, 67–68; cascading displacement 54–55; chosen memory frames 60–65; mnemonic choice 65–67; mnemonic macroframes 56–58; "refugees" in their own country 58–60
Vietnamese American history 240–241
violence, continuum of 251–254

war 184–185; and carceral systems 185–188; and the German state 191–194; Korean War 199–212; and mental health care 188–191; wartime refugees 60–65; well-being 215–220, **216**; children of 221–224, **222**; life of women after migration 220–221; parenting behavior 224–227
women: forced migrant SGBV survivors 251–254; North Korean defectors 218–221

9781032473789